AF622365

INDIA

History, Religion, Vision and Contribution to the World

Volume II

Alexander P. Varghese

ATLANTIC

PUBLISHERS & DISTRIBUTORS (P) LTD

Published by
ATLANTIC
PUBLISHERS & DISTRIBUTORS (P) LTD
B-2, Vishal Enclave, Opp. Rajouri Garden,
New Delhi-110027
Phones : +91-11-25413460, 25429987, 25466842

Sales Office
7/22, Ansari Road, Darya Ganj,
New Delhi-110002
Phones : +91-11-23273880, 23275880, 23280451
Fax : +91-11-23285873
web : www.atlanticbooks.com
e-mail : info@atlanticbooks.com

Branch Office
5, Nallathambi Street, Wallajah Road,
Chennai-600002
Phones : +91-44-64611085, 32413319
e-mail : chennai@atlanticbooks.com

Copyright © Atlantic Publishers and Distributors (P) Ltd., 2008

ISBN 978-81-269-0903-2 (Vol. I)
ISBN 978-81-269-0904-9 (Vol. II)
ISBN 978-81-269-0905-6 (Set)

All rights reserved. No part of this publication may be reproduced, stored in a retrieval system, transmitted or utilized in any form or by any means, electronic, mechanical, photocopying, recording or otherwise, without the prior permission of the copyright owner. Application for such permission should be addressed to the publisher.

Printed in India
at Nice Printing Press, Delhi

Preface

When I was a boy of nine, my parents, along with all children, embraced a religious denomination, different from that of the rest of the members of our extended family tree. This incident naturally incurred the wrath of our friends and relatives that culminated in imposing on our family isolation, a sort of ostracism. Ever since, it was an amusing pastime for many elders in our neighbourhood to confront me with puzzling or mischievous questions on religions, in a playful way, that inevitably led me, an ignoramus on religions, to concede defeat. Repeated defeats at their hands not only wounded my self-esteem but also emboldened me to take it up as a challenge to learn more on religions, preferably to equip myself to counter the arguments of opponents, which developed, in the course of time, into a fascination. Thenceforth, I utilised every opportunity that came across me – sermons, speeches, books, magazines, pamphlets, dialogues, discourses and so on – to enrich my knowledge on religions. But the more I learnt, the more I succumbed to temptations in the form of scruples and scepticism. Resultantly, I had the feeling of an evolutionary transformation from theism to materialism slowly taking roots in me. But I never ventured to forsake my yearning for learning on religions. Concerted efforts to acquire more knowledge, coupled with the growth in maturity in consonance with age, exerted a tremendous impact on me – a full-scale retraction from a sceptic to a monotheist. In the latter half of my thirties, I was fully relieved from scepticism that made my faith in God more deep-rooted and unshakeable. One wise man once said, 'One who is not a socialist before twenty-five and one who is a socialist after twenty-five, both are fools.' These circumstances provided me with the requisite inspiration to put pen to paper aimed at sharing my knowledge on religions with those who aspire for it.

This book is basically an academic endeavour to enlighten students, teachers, religious preachers, educationists, libraries and all English-knowing people, who aspire to enrich their knowledge on one's own or others' religion or both. Eleven world religions, according to UN statistics, are dealt with in the book with emphasis on major religions like Hinduism, Christianity and Islam having adherents crossing 4.2 billion, around two-thirds of today's world population. Two among these eleven religions, Confucianism and Shintoism do not deserve to be treated as world religions in the strict sense of the term, as the former is a socio-ethical system and the latter being a primitive animism, strictly restricted to the Japanese citizens.

The manner of presentation of each religion is matter-of-fact, historical and authentic, supported by authoritative contextual references supplied then and there. Clarity, the hallmark of presentation, is maintained by elucidating matters in comprehensible language and wherever possible, with the help of illustrative charts, pro formas, specially devised formats and statements. Religion, being a sentimental issue for its adherents everywhere, particular care has been taken to avoid ugly insinuations or satire or similar other adverse comments likely to wound the sentiments of the readers. Here, the author wishes to clarify that the attempt in this book is only to factually introduce the religion within the ambit of its theoretical framework and not to present a critique of any religion on any count.

Besides religions, more than thirty philosophies representing various shades of thought, classified into five broad categories, introduced in the book are:

(i) Saddarsanas (Six Visions)

These philosophies, inspired by the *Vedas* (the basic scripture of Hinduism), are independent in approach and arguments, but not fully isolated from each other. Some ideas are seen common to all systems.

(ii) Sramana Philosophies (Sramanas mean Strivers)

These propositions, independent of the Vedas, emerged in the sixth century B.C. that repudiated the conventional value system in Hinduism. The proponents of these systems were generally empiricists appealing to experience and observation as source of knowledge. These systems dominated the Indian philosophy for several centuries.

(iii) Modern Philosophies in Hinduism

Many of these philosophies emanated from the movements for revival of Hinduism initiated by reformist organisations like 'The Hindu Free Thought Union', 'The Hindu Tract Society', 'The Brahma Samaj', 'The Arya Samaj', 'The Theosophical Society' and so on. The struggle for Indian independence provided them with a fertile ground for their growth.

(iv) The Upanishadic Philosophies

These independent thoughts mainly contained secret or esoteric doctrines of a philosophical character that revolve around two main conceptions, the Absolute and the individual Self – the *Brahman* and the *Atman*. In few modern Upanishads, materialist ideas and rational approaches are seen.

(v) The Philosophies of Religions

Each religion has its own exclusive philosophy as basis of its faith and practices propounded either by its founder or by successors, e.g.: Zoroaster, Confucius, Buddha etc.

It is hoped that the book will prove a lasting valuable source for both the students and teachers of History, Philosophy and Religion.

Lastly, I take this opportunity to thank all those persons who have directly or indirectly helped me in bringing out this book. Any suggestions from the readers of the book for the enhancement of its value will by gratefully acknowledged.

Alexander P. Varghese

Contents

PART SIX: **JUDAISM (ISRAEL)**

PART SEVEN: **OTHER WORLD RELIGIONS**

PART EIGHT: **HINDUISM VS CHRISTIANITY (ACCORD & DISCORD)**

Annexures

PART FIVE

CHRISTIANITY

Historical Personage and Datable Events

The Christian conception of salvation is worlds apart from that of the mysteries. Unlike mystery religions with their myths linked with the myths of nature, Christianity was founded in a historical personage connected with datable events. A Christian was to be a pure person who did not cling to his possessions, not self-seeking, truthful and brave, relying not on his own strength in the moral struggle but on God's grace. They loved one another, helped the sick and infirm, the disabled, the marginalised and the poor with the power of love.

To sum up, the remarkable growth and expansion of the Church in the first century owed much to the political, social and cultural situations. But, the main reason for its success was that it provided the best answers to the questions of the tortured soul by inculcating worship of one God, creator of all. By its preaching of Jesus, the divine Saviour, risen and to come again, brought assurance of liberation from sin, eternal resurrection and a motive to lead a life of faith, holiness, self-control, love and brotherhood.

The rituals of Holy Eucharist and baptism gave the Church a sense of oneness in Christ. The traditional Catholic view of the organisation of the Church is that Jesus himself organised it by appointing the Apostles and giving them authority to assume control of the Church after his death. An objection generally raised against this view is that if Jesus put the twelve apostles in charge, why some of them completely disappeared from subsequent history? Many historians prefer the view that the primitive Church slowly organised itself and shaped its system of authority in response to the situations that developed in various localities. Gradually it evolved and settled on a three-tier structure – bishop, priest and deacon – as the most conducive to its mission. Those who favour this theory cite Paul in this respect. According to Paul, Spirit is the one who organizes the community that means love is the unifying and organizing element. Paul lists the various ministries in his Epistle to the Corinthians. "God has given the first place to the Apostles, the second to prophets, the third to teachers, after them miracles and after them the gift of healing, helpers, good leaders, those with many languages." Here Paul does not limit apostleship to the original twelve. According to him, "an apostle is one who had specially been commissioned to preach by the risen Jesus, as a witness to the resurrection, authorized to found and lead churches. But, he is to exercise his authority in fellowship with all other members of the community." (2 Cor. 10:13-16; 13:10; 1 Cor. 11:34; Th. 3:4)

Paul's system of charismatic leadership worked all right as long as the Church lived in immediate expectation of the end of the world and the Second Coming of Jesus. But, two things necessitated a change, firstly the expectation of the End faded as awareness grew that the Church was destined to continue in history for a longer period, secondly the Apostles passed away one by one. The Church was faced with the problem of how to stay in touch with its origins and preserve its unity and continuity. There was a real danger of conflicting interpretations of the meaning of Christ's life and resurrection. For instance, a group called Gnostics put forth an interpretation of Jesus that could subvert the basic doctrines of the Church. According to them, Christ was not a true man, but a particle of divinity that had merely assumed a human costume. Marcion, one of their leaders, rejected the Old Testament as the work of an evil, inferior demigod and professed belief only in Paul's writings. To meet the challenge, a solution was gradually devised, a specially commissioned ministry was established, an authoritative list of apostolic writings was issued and a rule of faith or creed was drawn up.

Elders and deacons as had apparently prevailed in some churches placed the specially commissioned ministry on a system of governance. In this system, it was not the Spirit who conferred office as envisaged by Paul, but conferred by formal appointment presuming that the appointee was endowed with the gift of the Spirit. The recipient was ordained by laying on of hands. In the Pastoral Epistles, we see Timothy and Titus appointed as elders with right to choose reliable men to succeed them and those in turn would choose their successors. The Epistle of Peter also refers to such a system in operation, with presbyters and elders engaged in an orderly ministry with no outward distinction between clergy and laity, the whole church being royal priesthood.

In a letter written in around 96 AD by the Roman Church to the Church in Corinth the First Epistle of Clement, at the time of a schism in Corinth, the Presbyterian system was asserted. Similarly, *Didache* (a Syrian catechetical manual dating the end of the first century), instructs the congregation to elect bishops and deacons, if prophets and teachers were in short supply. The term 'bishop' was a secular Greek expression, 'episcopos' meaning supervisor or overseer. The usage of this term in the early Church was synonymous with the word 'elder' or 'presbyter'. Gradually, one presbyter became powerful and concentrated the various ministries in his hands. To distinguish him from other presbyters, who were his subordinates, he was called 'bishop'. In the letters of Ignatius, Bishop of Antioch (eventually martyred) he enunciated a system wherein the Bishop is the focal point of the congregation, who alone had the right to lead public worship and administer sacraments. Thus 'monarchical episcopate' came into being practically everywhere, around the middle of the second century. Four factors contributed for the triumph of this system.

First, the need for one presbyter to represent Christ at the Eucharist.

Second, the need for a competent person to carry on correspondence with other churches.

Third, the need for one person to represent a Church at general gatherings.

Fourth, the need for one person as the focal point of unity and an authoritative spokesman of doctrine, especially in view of the Gnostic heresy.

The authority of this monarchical bishop as a guarantor of the oral tradition was that he stood as the legitimate successor in a line reaching back to the Apostles. The presumption was that his teaching would be in conformity with his predecessors. In around 185 AD, this concept was given a classic form by Irenaeus to justify the pre-eminent status of Rome.

The next measure taken up by the Church was to guarantee the bonafides of its tradition and also to protect its identity with the Church of the Apostles. With this end in view, the Church decided to recognise a limited number of writings as 'Scripture'. The canon of the New Testament was to contain authentic tradition about Jesus. Their writings were to be set apart as sacred, it meant that the Church would forever be subject to them as an absolute norm of its faith and life. Judgment about the authenticity of the canonical writings was based on the understanding that the tradition of the Church in this matter was trustworthy in general, although there could be flaws in details. The scholars had difference of opinion among them. The first thing to be verified was about apostolic authorship. St. John's Gospel was not readily accepted at first. After Irenaeus gave sufficient proof of its authorship only, it was accepted. The same thing occurred with St. Paul's Epistle to the Hebrews, which the writers in the Western Church refused to quote for nearly two hundred years. The canon was virtually complete by the early decades of the second century, but it was finalized in the West at the close of the fourth century and later in the East.

To uphold its authority and to safeguard orthodoxy, the Church felt that the formulation of a creed was essential. The sample of a creed was available in the writings of Irenaeus. It asserted the Church's faith in one God, the Father and Creator of all things; the incarnation of God in Christ Jesus; and in the Holy Spirit through whom the prophets were inspired to foretell the events of salvation through Jesus Christ.

Thus, the Church erected a durable structure of authority, a framework that enabled it to meet all possible challenges and threats through an authoritative creed, through a Canon of Scripture and through Bishops claiming succession of Apostles.

The relationship between individual churches remained unsettled. The missionaries and their converts kept their churches in touch with each other. Their relations remained personal and often informal. The translation of these contacts into institutional and organisational was a gradual process. The bishops used to meet at the local level to discuss common problems and solutions. This provided a useful forum to start with inter-church relationships. Gradually certain churches assumed authority over other churches. They acquired so-called metropolitan status that elevated them over the churches of a province. Political factors were mainly responsible for such distinctions. The political preponderance of a town inevitably acquired ecclesiastical preponderance as well. The Bishop of the capital of a Roman province was granted superiority over the bishops of that province. The Churches of Rome, Alexandria and Antioch acquired suprametropolitan status. The fourth canon of the Council of Nicaea officially sanctioned this principle and recognized the primacy of Rome, Alexandria and Antioch.

Rome enjoyed some attributes over and above political preponderance, that raised it above all other churches. First, it could claim special status as the See of the Apostles Peter and Paul, the pre-eminent example of apostolic succession. Second, as the capital of the Empire, the Churchmen elsewhere were desirous of having the support of the Bishop of Rome. Third, the Church in Rome was wealthy and noted for its munificent charity and influence due to its willingness to liberally assist other churches all over the world.

Above all, the local church had a head in the Bishop and the Provincial Church had a head in the metropolitan. It is only logical that the norm applied at the local and provincial level is extended to the universal level to provide structural compactness and a centre of unity and leadership for the whole church in the World. No church other than the Church of Rome could put forth a valid claim to fill this leadership. Thus, a monarchical episcopate with the Bishop of Rome (Pope) at its helm, a natural and unanimous choice, became established by the end of the third century.

In the eleventh century, we find the authority of Pope developing into one of the main bones of contention, leading to the emergence of several orthodox churches independent of papal control. Later in the 15th and 16th centuries we see the emergence of churches questioning not only the authority of Pope but also the entire episcopal system, through Protestantism.

In the foregoing pages, we saw the Church spreading across the Roman Empire in the first three centuries and presenting itself as an institution with a clearly defined system of authority. In the course of this growth, the Church had to face twin adversities, one from outside the Church and the other from within the Church, the mighty Roman Empire on one side and heretical teachings on the other side.

Persecution

Octavian Augustus Caesar was the Emperor of Rome (27 BC – 14 AD) when Jesus was born. His period was one of prosperity and security under a republican constitution. After Augustus up to 323 there were 34 Emperors and two Civil wars. The Empire was tolerant in principle towards all religions. But, when it realized that the aim of Christianity was total triumph over all other religions, the Empire became hostile towards Christianity. The mood of the general populace was also anti-Christian. The Emperor preferred to move along public opinion. The Christians were treated as atheists and moral monsters because of their refusal to join in pagan worship.

The secrecy surrounding the Christian services, their absolute rejection of the gods worshipped by Rome, their view that the Emperor need be obeyed only so long as it is in harmony with the will of the true God revealed to the Church etc. aggravated the hostilities. The result was a series of persecution and horrifying torture. Though there was calmness during the period of a few Emperors, when homicide maniacs and sadists occupied the throne, brutalities, atrocities and murder became common entertainments arranged in public for the people to enjoy and reached its zenith in the third century. The chronology appended will give a vivid picture.

Even in the midst of these persecutions, the Church spread abundantly, proving the words of Tertullian 'the blood of martyrs is the seed of Christians'.

Two byproducts of the persecution were that:

Christianity, till then latent or hidden in the different corners of the Roman Empire, has come out to the open,

No.	Name of Emperor	Period	Incident
1.	Tiberius Claudius Nero	14-37 AD	Crucifixion of Jesus.
2.	Caligula	37-41 AD	Assassinated.
3.	Claudius Tiberius	41-54	Wife Agrippina, mother of Nero poisoned him, to pave the way for her son Nero.
4.	Nero	54-68	Martyrdom of Peter and Paul. Murdered his mother, two wives and children and Britanicus, the rightful heir apparent and many popular leaders. The Christians were charged with the burning of Rome and persecuted.
5.	Civil war for 18 months (Galba, Otho and Vittellius)	69 AD	
6.	Vespasian	70-79	Destruction of Jerusalem city and Temple, 70 AD.
7.	Titus (Havius Vespasianus)	79-80	Nothing noteworthy.
8.	Domitian (Titus Havius Domitian)	80-96	Wholesale murder of citizens. Last among Caesars (St. John exiled).
9.	Nerva	96-97	(Only 16 months)
10.	Trejan	97-117	Suppressed Christians as politically dangerous. No extreme steps.
11.	Hadrian	117-138	Martyrdom of Ignatius. Good government.
12.	Pius (Antonius)	138-161	Martyrdom of Polycarpus. Peace in Europe.
13.	Marcus Orillius	161-180	A stoic philosopher. Martyrdom of Justin. Persecuted Christians harshly for their hostility towards other religionists.
14.	Commodus	180-192	Peace.

(Contd.)

No.	Name of Emperor	Period	Incident
15.	Pertinax	192-197	Peace.
16.	Septimius Severus	197-211	Edicts issued to Governors to persecute Christians. Roman citizens banned from accepting Christianity. African martyrs.
17.	Karakalla	211-217	No persecution.
18.	Marcinus	217-218	No persecution.
19.	Elgabalus	218-222	No persecution.
20.	Alexander Severus	222-235	No persecution.
21.	Maximinus	235-237	No persecution.
22.	Gordion	237-244	No persecution.
23.	Philippus	244-248	No persecution.
24.	Dishius	249-251	His reign lasted only for a few years. A harsh persecutor, Pope Fabian suffered heroically and died. Bishop Cyprian of Carthage, Pope Sixtus II and Deacon Lawrence were victims. A large number of Christians apostatized.
25.	Galus	251-252	No persecution.
26.	Emilianus	253	No persecution.
27.	Valerian and Galinus	253-260	Persecution again.
28.	Galinus	260-268	No trouble.
29.	Claudius II (Gothicus)	268-270	An excellent prince and a good General.
30.	Orillian	270-275	No trouble.

(Contd.)

No.	Name of Emperor	Period	Incident
31.	Tacitus	275-276	No trouble.
32.	Orillius Proabs	276-282	No trouble.
33.	Querus	282-284	No trouble.
34.	Diocletian	284-305	In 303, Porphyry, a pagan intelligentsia published a book *Against the Christians* which attacked the Scriptures, Eucharist and ridiculed the Christian works of mercy. This was the prelude to the attacks by Diocletian. At a public pagan sacrifice, the Pagan priest claimed that the presence of Christians invalidated the sacrifice and thus endangered the state. This triggered the repression. Diocletian ordered destruction of Christian places of worship, burnt the scriptures, forbade the assembly of Christians and denied the protection of the laws. A second decree singled out bishops, priests and deacons for special attention. The Christians had their eyes and tongues gouged out, their feet sawed off, they died at the stake or in a red-hot chair. Some were thrown to the wild beasts, others were starved to death or thrown into dungeons. It was mainly in the East that the blood flowed. Under his successor Galerius also, the atrocities continued but the Civil War broke out.
35.		305-323	Civil War.
36.	Constantine	323-361	New Era begins.

became world-famous, grown in purity of faith, acquired moral courage in witnessing Christ and ultimately transformed into a powerful religion of authority even surpassing the might of the Roman Empire.

The Church obtained invaluable assets through a series of books and literature dealing with Christian faith and life known as 'Apologies'. The aim of these books was to defend the historical verity of the Christian religion in opposition to the rationalist and mythical theories, thereby removing the misconceptions of Emperors, judges and the people at large about Christianity. The authors of these books include Martyr Justin, Origen, Tertullian, Philix, Athangores, Clement of Alexandria and several others.

Emperor Constantine and New Era

The era of persecutions ended not with a whimper, but with a bang when the Emperor Constantine himself went over to the side of the Christians. Constantine, the son of the co-Emperor Constantius Chlorus, was hailed as Emperor by his troops on the death of his father in 306 AD. But his rival Maxentius, who managed to secure Rome as his stronghold, foiled this. Lactantius, a Christian writer says that on the eve of Constantine's battle against Maxentius, he had a vision of Christ who told him to ornament the shields of his soldiers with the Saviour's monogram – in Greek letters *Chi* and *Rho*. Eusebius in his writings *Life of Constantine* says that the whole army of Constantine saw a luminous cross in the sky with the message 'in this conquer'. Constantine won the battle, became the Emperor in 323 and ruled the Empire without any challenge to his supreme authority till 361. Constantine attributed his victory to the help of the Christian God. Anyhow, the probability of Constantine having some religious experience to turn to the God of the Christians cannot be ruled out. A full-fledged conversion of Constantine to Christianity did not occur immediately, he was not baptized till his final illness. Some historians argue that he underwent baptism on his deathbed.

At first, Constantine attempted to correct paganism of which he was the Supreme Pontiff. But he was careful not to antagonise the aristocracy of Rome and pagan masses. But, his true feelings were gradually revealed through his actions mentioned below:

Imposed restrictions on pagan practices.

The Christian symbols were publicly displayed.

A cross emblazoned with the monogram of Christ was attached to the standards of the Army.

Coins were issued picturing himself with a helmet stamped with the Christian monogram.

Identified the interests of the State with those of Christianity.

Intervened in Church affairs and used the power of the State to end the Donatist schism in Africa.

When Arianism threatened the unity of the Church, he took the initiative to convene the General Council of Nicaea, which he personally attended.

Generously lavished donations to the Church.

Erected numerous magnificent basilicas, including one over the supposed tomb of St. Peter in Rome and another over the tomb of Christ in Jerusalem.

Surrendered the Emperor's Lateran Palace in Rome for a residence for the Bishop of Rome. (It remained the papal residence till 1308. Five out of the 21 General Councils of the Church were held at Lateran.)

In 324, he moved the capital of the Empire to Bizantium, renamed after him as Constantinople and erected numerous churches there including two great ones dedicated to Peace and the Holy Apostles.

Bestowed the Christian clergy with many important privileges including exemption from forced labour and military service.

Invested the judicial decisions of the Bishop with civil authority.

Modified the Roman laws in accordance with the Christian values.

Sunday was made a day of rest.

Sexual offences like adultery, concubinage, prostitution etc. were dealt with strictly.

Adopted a more humane attitude towards slaves, children, orphans and widows.[2]

Emperor Constantine's Decree of Milan in 313 AD is the Charter of Freedom of the Christian Church in the Roman Empire. The Christians regained the properties confiscated by the Government, the losses of the Church were compensated and Christianity became a religion recognized by the Government entitling its members to enjoy all the rights and privileges of Roman citizens.

Thus, under Constantine, the Church was firmly set on the road to union with the State. This alliance with the State brought about profound changes in the thought and life of the Church. Along with its advantages, it entailed serious disadvantages that were visibly reflected in the subsequent centuries:

Widening of the gap between the clergy and the laity.

The freedom of the Church was exploited for political purposes.

Motivations for mass conversions became social conformity, rather than faith.

Degeneration of the clergy.

Persecution of dissenters became a threat to the unity of the State.

To sum up, the Church drifted away from its position of spiritual and moral authority to a parallel monarchy engaged in intrigues, politics, rivalries and even wars. The Eastern Schism, the papal Schism, wide acceptance for the Reformation Movement, Dechristianisation Movement during French Revolution etc. are pointers to the loss of spiritual elan in the Church. The Church would never be the same again – for better or for worse – Constantine era is certainly one of the greatest turning points in the history of the Church as well as the world.

Threats of Heresies

In the early stages of the growth of the Church, several schools of thought projected different doctrines, contrary or deviating from the basic doctrines of faith of the Church. Some of them died out on condemnation by local synods. A few of them snowballed into movements spreading to different places, threatening the unity of the Church. Most of them emanated from the Church in the East. The first eight Ecumenical Councils were held in the East to deal with, among other things, these heresies. After condemnation by the General Councils, most of them gradually disappeared. But, the heresies of Monophysitism and Nestorianism continue to exist even today as dissident Churches in some parts of the world. The Church survived the threats and maintained the Rule of Faith (Creed) approved by the General Council of Nicaea in 325 AD, with slight modification later, till today.

A brief description of the main heresies is given below:

Gnosticism. The word 'Gnosticism' is derived from the word 'Gnosis' meaning knowledge. Marcion, a rich shipping magnate of his days, was the champion of this theory. Gnosticism extracted an esoteric meaning out of the Christian scripture and Gospel history and set a higher value for knowledge than faith. They denied the possibility of the 'Word' becoming flesh. According to them, Jesus is not God, but only a particle of divinity. Though this theory found easy acceptance among the intelligentsia and educated class in general, this heresy died out on condemnation by the Church.

Arianism. Arius (280 – 336 AD), a presbyter of Alexandria was the founder of this heresy. He denied the consubstantiality of the Son with the Father in the Trinity. According to him, Jesus was a composite intermediary Being – the Word made flesh – neither true God, nor true Man. Therefore, Christ was not the mediator who unites God and Man in his person. This doctrine hovered in the Church for a long time between acceptance and rejection. It found wide acceptance in the East. On condemnation by the General Council of Nicaea, this heresy withered away.

Donatists. Donatus, the Bishop of Carthage was the proponent of this heresy. His theory was that no one, who was not of divine election, is entitled to be a member of Christ's body. He brought forth this theory to thwart the attempt of Emperor Constantine to thrust a bishop on the Church at Carthage. The Saracens later annihilated a community established by Donatus in the 7th century.

Appolliniarism. The proponent of this heresy was Appolliniarsus, the Bishop of Lavodicaea in Syria. He unduly reduced the humanity of Jesus as a sequel to the theory of Arius denying the divinity of Jesus. The General Council of Constantinople in 381 AD affirmed the integrity of Christ's humanity more directly and condemned Appolliniarsus. Thereupon, this heresy gradually disappeared.

Montanism. Montanus, a Phrygian is the founder of this heresy. He insisted on the permanency of the spiritual gifts vouchsafed to the primitive Church and the restoration of the severe discipline then prevailed. Montanus claimed himself a prophet filled with the Holy Spirit and proclaimed the imminent end of the world. The Church rejected Montanism and the Montanists were declared non-Christians. This heresy gradually disappeared.

Monophysitism (Eutychianism). A monk named Eutychus, in the 5th century AD, maintained that on being united to the divine nature, the human nature of Jesus became absorbed in the divine nature, so that there remained only one 'nature' in Jesus. Consequently, Christ's humanity was not consubstantial with ours. This theory was condemned by a Synod in 448 AD. At the instigation of Dioscoros, the Patriarch of Alexandria another Synod convoked in 449 AD with the permission of the Emperor set aside the decision of the Synod of 448 AD. The General Council of Chalcedon in 451 AD declared the Synod in 449 AD 'a robber Synod' and condemned Eutychus and Nestorius and their heresies by one stroke.

Nestorianism. According to Christian faith, Christ is God and Man. The extremists in the Antiochian School conceived the distinction in the two natures in Christ as of two persons. Nestorius, a priest belonging to the Antiochean School, later became the Patriarch of Constantinople. The Nestorian theory of two persons in Christ met with strong opposition. A crisis arose when Anastasius, a pawn of Nestorius, publicly denied to Mary the title 'Mother of God' (*Theotokos*). According to this proposition, Mary is only the mother of Christ (*Kristotokos*), to whom the person of the 'Word of God' united himself. Though this union was sublime and unique in the order of Grace to the extent of constituting between the two a unique figure (*prosopon*) – the word of God dwelling in Christ as in a temple – it was nevertheless but an accidental union between two persons. Accordingly, it was not the 'Word of God' but Christ, who died on the cross. The General Council of Ephesus in 431 AD condemned and deposed Nestorius.

- 'Patripassianism' according to which the Father himself and not the Son Incarnate would have undergone the sufferings on the cross.
- 'Double Sonship' of Christ, one eternal and the other temporal, attributed to diodorus of Tarsus.
- 'Macedonianism' which denied the divinity of the Holy Spirit.
- 'Pelagianism' which reduced the supernatural to the natural order of things.
- 'Monothelitism' which held that there was only one will, the divine in Christ.
- 'Adoptionism' which claimed that Christ was not the son of God by nature but only by adoption.
- 'Iconoclasm' which held that the use of images was idolatry and so on.

FOOTNOTES

1. Thomas Bokenkotter, *A Concise History of the Catholic Church*, pp. 24-25.
2. *Ibid.*, p. 39.

Life, Faith and Worship

27

The period from Constantine to Pope Leo the Great (440-461) was one of remarkable importance in Church history. Many basic features fixed during this period continued for the next one thousand five hundred years without many modifications.

The Mass was standardized and ritualized.

The belief in Christ, God and man, was affirmed and clarified.

Practices fundamental to discipline and life were incorporated in the canon law.

Clergy became a sacred caste submitted to celibacy.

Monasticism spread across Christendom.

Basic principles of social and personal ethics achieved a permanent form.

The Holy Eucharist

The *Mass* (as it was called from the 5th century onwards), the breaking of bread, was originally celebrated in the afternoon followed with a regular meal of ritual character. The mass has now become a separate rite celebrated on Sunday morning with a service of reading and preaching and the common meal was separated from it. On some occasions, a reading of the prophets and the memoirs of the Apostles, as well as a homily by the President preceded the mass. Earlier, there were no special holy places or temples for the celebrations. Usually it was celebrated in a spacious room in one of the members' home. The main focus of the rite was the praying and worshipping community itself. But, when the number of participants grew, spacious buildings have come up. Massive and ornate altars decorated with marbles and gems replaced the tables. Churches, splendid,

INTRODUCTION AND JUDAIC BACKGROUND

Christianity, population-wise top among the world religions of today, always claimed as its founder Jesus of Nazareth, the dynamic Jewish preacher and healer born around the beginning of the first century AD. In the growth and development of this religion in the last twenty centuries, a series of splits and divisions occurred resulting in the birth of innumerable denominations, each one claiming itself as true Christian Church with unadulterated Christian faith and practices. The only unanimity we find among them is the acceptance of Jesus Christ as their founder. This religion began in Jerusalem as a small group of disciples who shared faith in the resurrection of their master and Lord Jesus. Even in the first century AD it rapidly spread to countless cities in the Roman Empire. Their adamant opposition to the Roman religion, morals and culture invited the wrath of the State and ignited the savage fury of the Romans that took the form of inhuman torture and persecution. But, the spiritual acumen and zeal of the new converts were only magnified by the repressive measures unleashed by the State and the Roman religion and the growth of the Church remained unaffected.

Judaic Background

Judaism, one of the oldest religions in the world, is founded on the first five books of the Old Testament of the Bible known as *Torah* (law). Based on the prophecies of the Prophets in the Old Testament, a concept of Messianism (the expectation of a Messiah – A Redeemer, at any point of time in one form or another) influenced the Jewish thinking throughout the ages. In the fullness of time, the promised Messiah was born in a stable.

This day in the city of David,
A Saviour has been born for you
The Lord Christ Himself. (LK. 2:11)

This is the sign by which you are to know Him;
You will find a child in swaddling clothes,
Lying in a manger. (LK. 2:12)

The Jews failed to identify their Saviour. How can their Messiah take birth in a stable as the son of a carpenter? What is the sign? They asked. Had He, who is Omnipotence had come with thunderbolts, there would have been no sign. When He said 'I am the Son of God', it was impersonation.

Again, when He said 'I am the way, I am the Truth, I am the Life', their confusion confounded. They found in him a messianic pretender. According to the priests and the Pharisees, a blasphemer was not entitled to live. The Jews, God's own chosen people, plotted to eliminate Him to save their religion. Two charges were levelled against Him – claims of Kingship and exhortation to establish a Kingdom, treason and subversiveness, deserving capital punishment according to the law of the Romans. The Jews conspired with the Romans, the complicity in crucifixion of both are equal. Jesus was a Jew in birth, a Jew in life and a Jew in His death. All His disciples and early followers were Jews. But, vested interests neither change, nor repent. Bishop Fulton Sheen put it in the following words:

> "He was wrapped in swaddling bands in His birthplace, He was again laid in swaddling clothes in His tomb-clothes symbolic of the limitations imposed on His Divinity when He took a Human form."[1]

But, the life of the founder of Christianity, having begun with the cross, ends with the empty tomb and victory. Now, the followers of 'blasphemer' comprise 33 per cent of the World population. Judaism was the prelude to Christianity.

The Church came into being

The image of the Church in the first and second centuries of the Christian Era was clearly revealed in the strict observance of two important rituals, the Eucharist and the Baptism. The Eucharist was celebrated, in strict obedience to the command of Jesus Christ at the Last Supper over bread and wine, in the firm conviction that their Risen Lord was present in the bread and wine. A treasure of meaning was attached to this ritual. It was a sharing of his body and blood; it was a re-presentation of Christ's sacrifice that marked the beginning of a new covenant between God and man. The second ritual was baptism, an initiation ceremony, a cleansing with water symbolizing conversion to Christ and opening of the door to the Christian community. These rituals provided the Church with a sense of supernatural oneness in Christ, even in the absence of any organizational structure. By the end of the second century, the Church emerged as a well-defined organization based on its scripture, its creed and a hierarchical set up consisting of bishop, priest and deacon.

The fight against adversities strengthened the unity of the Church and exalted the position and influence of the Bishop of Rome. In the early period of the fourth century, the Church won a decisive victory over paganism when it drew to its side the Roman Emperor Constantine himself who showered it with many privileges and favours.

From then onwards, the fortunes of the Church were intimately interlinked with the State. When the Western Empire fell apart consequent on the onslaught of the Barbarians, the Christian Church alone survived without total disruption.

Later, under the able leadership of Popes like Gregory the Great (who converted the Barbarians to Christianity) the foundations of a new Christian civilization were laid in the Western World – Christendom.

Even from the days of its inception throughout history, the Church had to confront a series of tribulations and challenges:

Persecution by the Romans
Mystery religions
Heresies like Arianism, Montanism, Gnosticism, Monophysitism, Nestorianism etc.
Birth of Islam and invasion of Europe and North Africa by Muslims
Confrontation with European monarchs
The Crusades
Decline of papal monarchy
The Eastern Schism and Orthodox Churches
Aristotelian Influences
Renaissance in Europe
New Schools of thought and internal strife

Jansenism, Gallicanism and Febronianism
Degeneration of the Curia, papal schism and Conciliarism
Reformation led by Martin Luther, Calvin, Swingli and others
Issue of divorce and second marriage of Henry VIII of England
The French Revolution and Napoleon
Social Catholicism
Threats of Communism, Nazism, Fascism and so on.

Juxtaposed to the above factors, several favourable factors enabled the Church to survive and grow as the foremost religion in the world. They are:

More centralized structure of Church government under the papacy given shape to by Popes like Leo the Great, Hildebrand (Gregory VII), Innocent III and others
Support and favours from Emperors like Constantine and Charlemagne
Shaping of an orthodox theology and spirituality by teachers like Ambrose, Augustine, Jerome, Thomas Aquinas etc.
Spread of monasticism
Colonial expansion by Spain and Portugal and the Padroado
Counter Reformation initiated by the General Council of Trent and continued by the General Councils of Vatican I and Vatican II.
Defeat of Napoleon
Success of the Allies in World Wars
Emergence of democratic systems of Government in Europe
Fall of Communism in Russia and East Europe

FOOTNOTE

1. Bishop Fulton J. Sheen, *Life of Christ*, p. 15.

25 Jesus

The early life of Jesus is clouded in obscurity. The only sources available about his life are the four gospels in the New Testament of the *Bible*. The gospels of Mark and John bypass the birth of Jesus altogether. The gospels of Mathew and Luke refer to the birth of Jesus but the clues given by them do not reconcile. According to Mathew, Jesus was born during the reign of Herod who passed away in the year 4 BC. Luke dates it as the period when Quirinius was the legate of Syria, which according to historians were from 6 to 9 AD. Historians still differ on the year of birth of Jesus but a majority of them put it as 4 BC.

These two evangelists also differ on the genealogy of Jesus. It is clear that the intention of all the evangelists was not to present a historical or biographical account of Jesus and therefore we do not have details of his physical features and appearances, personal habits, his psychological development and the influences that shaped his personality. But, we need not be skeptical. All the evangelists unanimously introduce Jesus as son of David and Son of God, the long awaited Redeemer (Messiah) to bring salvation to both the Jews and the Gentiles. More than a century of critical analysis of the New Testament has not disproved the belief of Christians that their scriptures are based on the words and deeds of a unique historical personage. All the authors of the four gospels are again unanimous in their description that at his baptism, the Spirit descended on him from heaven to establish that Jesus is the messenger of God.

Mark is the first to cast a gospel on the basis of the oral traditions. It appeared before the fall of Jerusalem in 70 AD.

Some ten years later, Mathew and Luke produced their works relying on Mark, the Quelle (a collection of the words of Jesus) and the materials these evangelists collected on their own. John's work appeared at the turn of the century. It differed from the other three in its portrait of Jesus. The intentions of all these evangelists were the same, to project Jesus as the promised Messiah.

The Public Life of Jesus

The public life of Jesus begins with his baptism at the Jordan. The message conveyed by Jesus is simple, "The Kingdom of God is at hand, repent." John, the only herald of Jesus proclaimed this in advance. Some scholars argued that this announcement of Jesus about the incursion of God into history as purely something to happen in future, at the end of the world. But, now all scholars agree that this reference in Jesus' teaching was meant both for the present and for the future. Some of his parables like the one about the prodigal son who was welcomed with love by his father emphasise the point that God with abundant generosity and fantastic goodness was extending mercy to the sinners. When he ate and drank with publicans and harlots, his message was clear; salvation is now offered to all, a gift in no way dependent on one's merits or righteousness.

Jesus never made a radical break with the *Torah*. He recognised it as the sacred law and authentic voice of God, but he did not hesitate to modify it, e.g. prohibition of divorce. The main thing he insisted in his teachings was complete submission to the Will of God. He summed up all his teachings in his command to love, God first and then to all human beings including enemies. The commandment of love that existed in Judaism was expanded and radicalized by Jesus by removing all restrictions. He emphasized the motive for love; we were to love others out of gratitude for God's love for us.

God's Kingdom inaugurated by Jesus found its expression in prayer. He was always a constant example of prayerfulness. As a pious Jew, he observed the three daily liturgical prayers and took part in the worship in synagogues and temple. At the same time, he challenged the tradition and customs. He warned the people against routine and formalism in public prayer. He spent whole nights in prayer and encouraged secret prayer. Moreover, he gave them a unique prayer, the Lord's Prayer that expresses the fulfilment of Christian life.

The Kingdom of God unfolded by Jesus meant a transformation radically changing the order of values. One who aspires to follow Jesus must free him from attachments, whether to the family or property or business. He warned them of the special danger of riches. When he sent out messengers to spread the good news, he wanted them to go as poor men. In short, every follower of Jesus was to deny himself, for the Kingdom of God could not be brought without suffering. Affliction and suffering were to be seen in a totally different perspective. Not that they were desirable in themselves, but for one who accepted the Kingdom of God, sufferings could not prevent him from enjoying the love of God and might be of help in this regard, whereas riches, abundance of friends, comforts, luxuries etc. were evils hindering one from seeking the Kingdom of God.

In the house of Simon the Pharisee, his encounter with a harlot provided an occasion to Jesus to establish his authority to forgive sins. When the woman lavished signs of her love upon him, he accepted it and consoled her with the words "Your sins are forgiven." Miracles and exorcisms played a very important part in the ministry of Jesus. It may not be in conformity with 'modern ideas' but parallels to Gospel miracles can be found in contemporary pagan and rabbinic literature as well as in the Old Testament; storms quelled, change of water into wine, demons expelled and so on. In short, Jesus did exercise extraordinary powers of healing which projected him as one victorious over all the forces that degrade man.

Jesus not only preached the good news of the Kingdom of God, but also gathered his disciples into a fellowship. They often took their meals together celebrating their covenant with God, always anticipating the glorious banquet to come in the Kingdom of heaven. He called his disciples 'the light of the world', 'the city of God' and 'the salt of the earth'. They were a family united by common devotion to God far more intensely than the relationships of flesh and blood. The members of Jesus' Kingdom always experienced an intimate relationship with God whom they loved to address as 'Father'. Jesus taught them to live sincerely as God's children. Always he spoke in terms of extreme urgency about the need to repent so as to accelerate and facilitate the incursion of God into history.

The authority of Jesus soon became a prime issue among the Jews. Instead of appealing to traditional forms of authority, Jesus invoked his own religious experiences and exhorted his audience to do the same. To establish the primacy of 'love' over 'law', he even attacked Jewish traditions like the observance of Sabbath and spoke about the temple slightingly. To sum up, his performance was a tremendous challenge to the establishment that could not be left unanswered. He had a premonition of his approaching end. Therefore, he gathered his faithful for one last meal together, probably the night before the Jewish Passover, offered them bread and wine, his body and blood which would be sacrificed to establish the new covenant between God and the humanity. The taking of bread and wine, offering of thanks, the breaking of the bread, the sharing of food and drink – all these were well-known and regular Jewish practices. But, Jesus gave an entirely new significance to this ritual when he commanded them to repeat this practice as a memorial of his passion, a pledge of his continuing presence with them and of his coming again.

According to the Gospels, the same night, Jesus was arrested at the instigation of both Roman and Jewish officials, produced before the Sanhedrin for grand jury proceedings and found guilty. The Jewish authorities found Jesus as a messianic pretender and his teachings of God's Kingdom as necessitating a political revolution likely to provoke a brutal repression by the Romans resulting in the ruin of the whole Jewish nation. The Sanhedrin also had religious reasons warranting the death of Jesus: his claim to unique authority was blasphemy, his criticism of the Jewish law and words against the temple were sacrilege.

According to the gospels, Pilate, on investigation, found the charge untenable. After interrogation of Jesus, Pilate resolved to release him. But, the Jewish leaders threatened Pilate of dire consequences. They forced him to have Jesus executed. The narration of the event in the gospel lead us to conclude that Jews alone were responsible for the crucifixion. But, the modern historians are skeptical. They argue that the authors of the gospel aggravated the responsibility of the Jews in the death of Jesus and minimized Roman participation. Their intent would have been to allay any suspicion of the Romans that the Christian Church might be subversive by clearing the name of their founder of any such implication. So they transferred the chief responsibility for the death of Jesus to the Jews. Some scholars even go up to the extent of exonerating completely the Jewish authorities and attribute the whole affair to a political conflict between the Romans and the Jews. Some other scholars do not subscribe to this view. They argue that some Jewish leaders, especially the priests, had strong antipathy towards Jesus and they would have had a role in the death of Jesus. In any case, all should have ended at Calvary. But something strange occurred, an experience that convinced the followers of Jesus that he was still alive. It became a turning point in their outlook.

Resurrection

What happened on the morning of the First Easter is described differently in the Gospels, the Acts of the Apostles and the writings of St. Paul. They do not agree on as to where and to whom Jesus first appeared. For example, according to St. Paul, Jesus appeared first to Peter. Joachim Jeremiah offers the probable sequence of events.

"Mary Magdalene went alone at dawn on Easter day to the tomb to mourn there for Jesus. From a distance, she could see that the stone sealing the tomb had been rolled back. Concluding immediately that someone had broken into steal the body, she ran to give alarm to Peter. He in turn raced to the tomb and found the linen burial clothes lying about and the tomb indeed empty. He rushed back to the disciples. Then the decisive event occurred. The risen Lord appeared to Peter."[1]

The Resurrection of Jesus was the climax of the several paradoxes in his life that began from his birth from an earthly mother and a heavenly father. All along His life we find several paradoxes; Lazarus again rising from the dead, feeding five thousand people with five pieces of bread, journey to Calvary, crucifixion and death and so on confirming what he said earlier "I am the Resurrection and the Life; he that believeth in me, although he be dead, shall live" (Jn: 11:25). St. Paul summed up the message "And, if Christ be not risen again, then is our preaching vain and your faith is also vain." (1 Cor: 15:14)

This was the dawn of a new history.

FOOTNOTE

1. Thomas Bokenkotter, *A Concise History of the Catholic Church*, p. 15.

The Catholic Church

26

The literal meaning of the word Catholic is 'Whole'. It originally referred to complete doctrinal integrity. Today, this word has come to mean the totality of the Christian communities in communion with the Church of Rome. Christian communities like the 'Orthodox' and Anglicans also use this term to denote them as the carriers of the 'Whole' Christian faith.

The Catholic Church is the oldest institution in the modern world. For nearly thousand years it presided over the total life of Christendom. It animated the laws, institutions, customs, literature, art, architecture, scripture, philosophy, theology and above all a creed. Its Popes established their supreme authority over the whole of Christendom, including the monarchs. Though shaken by crisis after crisis, the most notable being the French Revolution in 1789, the Church managed to keep its ranks together with its faith unchanged. All Christian denominations trace their origin in the Catholic Church. It is the mother or grandmother of all denominations claiming Christian heritage and patrimony. In the early centuries, Christianity spread all over the Roman Empire and later to all other continents under the aegis of the Catholic Church. In the modern world also, after a series of heresies, schisms and blasphemies, this Church enjoys the representation of Christianity and authority of Christian voice. No study on Christianity can be unbiased and comprehensive unless it starts from the Catholic Church. Hence, this study also starts with Catholic Church that can throw light on the origin of many other Christian Churches.

The Church Spreads

The resurrection of Jesus was the starting point of Christian faith. The disciples first gave voice to this faith in various formulae. In the first epistle of St. Paul to Corinthians he says, "Christ died for our sins in accordance with the scriptures...he was buried and, in accordance with the scriptures rose on the third day."

The beginning of the Church is considered to be only with the Pentecostal explosion of the Spirit, the event which occurred on the Jewish feast of Pentecost when the first believers were filled with the Holy Spirit who confirmed them in their faith and ignited a zeal in them to witness publicly and urge others to believe, repent and be baptized. Twelve men chosen by Jesus, later known as apostles led this small community of believers at Jerusalem. Their leader was Peter (Cephas in Greek). He is the first to see risen Jesus, the first to preach the sermon and the first to work a miracle. The first apostles were all Jews and so were their early converts. For a time, the Church remained completely Jewish, a sect within Israel who believed in the resurrection of Jesus and regarded him as the promised Messiah who was to come again to establish the reign of God. They were faithful in their daily prayer in the temple. The Sadducees among the Jews wanted to suppress them. But, they were unable to do it because public opinion favoured and admired the Christians for their fervent piety and fidelity to Jewish custom.

The spread of the Church outside Jerusalem was a gradual process. The disciples carried their message to the communities of Jews along the Mediterranean coast. In the early stages, they confined their evangelisation efforts among the Jews in conformity with the words of Jesus that he had come to preach only to 'the lost sheep of Israel'. After the death of Stephen, their deacon, there was widespread persecution and his followers went elsewhere and preached the gospel wherever they travelled.

This growth of the Church had a momentous turning point in Antioch. There, they preached the gospel and baptized the Gentiles. Those baptized were not required to be circumcised under the Jewish law. This annoyed the traditional-minded Jews. A great controversy ensued which shook the very roots of the evangelisation efforts, whether the Church should remain a Jewish affair or stretch out to the outside world encompassing the whole humanity. Paul understands the Gospel as liberation from the law was not an academic theory but one at the very heart of his conversion experience. When he heard the arguments of the traditionalists to circumcise the Gentiles, he insisted "What makes a man righteous is not obedience to the Law, but faith in Jesus Christ...if the law can justify us, there is no point in the death...when Christ freed us, he meant us to remain free. Stand firm, therefore, and do not submit again to the yoke of slavery."

But, gradually the conflict became shrill and bitter and the unity of the Church was strained, particularly in Antioch. A resolution of the issue without delay was necessitated. A council was held at Jerusalem in 49 AD (or 48?). This is known in history as the Synod of the Apostles, the first of its kind and the forerunner of General Councils in the Church – the assembly of the fathers of the Church for collective decision on important matters concerning church. After a long and stormy session, it was resolved that circumcision would not be required for the Gentiles. To pacify the traditionalists, a compromise was arrived at insisting on observance of some Jewish laws. But this did not clear up all dissensions. In the long run, the Church shed its exclusively Jewish character and became a church of entire humanity and Paul's understanding of the Gospel was officially accepted by the Church as its own. This landmark decision of the Church paved the way for an incessant flow of Gentiles to the Church not only in Antioch, but also in all corners of the Roman Empire.

Now, Paul set his eyes on Spain, the oldest Roman province, and a centre of Roman civilization. But before he could set sail to Spain, he had to return to Jerusalem to deliver the collections he mobilized for the poor from amongst his churches and for fostering the unity of the Church there. He was obsessed with two themes, the unity of the Church and the worldwide spread of the Gospel. 'One Lord, one faith, one baptism' was the way he put it. When in Jerusalem, James and other elders advised him to show his reverence to the Law through a ceremonial purification in the Temple. There, the Jews who identified him raised a hue and cry against him as a traitor. A tussle followed. The Roman tribune rescued and imprisoned him.

As he was so hungry to spread the gospel, he appealed to Emperor Nero and was sent to Rome and detained there for two years under house arrest. He was charge-sheeted as the ringleader of a revolutionary cult which might undermine the social order of the day, tried and executed probably in 64 AD. When he died, his dream of a Church as wide as humanity was on its way to realization, mainly due to his vision and organizing skill.

There were many other missionaries, but we know little about them, including Peter. Unanimous Christian tradition testifies Peter's death in Rome under Nero. Similarly, second century legend is there to fill up the lacunae in our knowledge about others which tells St. Thomas evangelized the Parthians, (the possibility of his coming to India from Parthia cannot be ruled out), St. Andrew the Scythians, St. Bartholomew went up to India and to southern Arabia, Philip died at Hierapolis in Phrygia. Anyhow, we can rightly conclude that the travelling missionaries successfully performed their mission that by the end of the first century, Christianity was well established in that part of the world.

Reasons for the Rapid Growth of the Church

First, after four centuries of expansion, the Roman Empire encircled the Mediterranean Sea stretching from Euphrates River in Syria to the Thames in Britain, from the Rhine and the Danube to the sands of Sahara. This vast medley of people of many races and languages were bound together with a marvellous system of roads and sea-routes. This greatly facilitated the work of the missionaries, who could travel the length and breadth of the Empire with comparative ease.

Second, the Romans promoted a common culture derived from Hellenism. This enabled the missionaries to preach in Greek in almost all major cities and be understood by the people.

Third, the world was largely at peace during the period of Emperor Octavian Augustus who defeated Antony and

Cleopatra and won supreme command over the Empire. He fashioned a new system with astute vision – the principate – outwardly preserving republican forms but concentrating power in the Emperor. The new constitution enabled him to rule unchallenged for forty years. The Empire with a stable government kept the Barbarians at bay and provided the nation with peace and security. The atmosphere of security for travellers helped the missionaries, to a very large extent to travel extensively.

Fourth, increasing prosperity brought forth a series of opportunities for enjoyment – theatres, stadia, amphitheatre, baths etc. The rapid social change unsettled many minds. The successors of Augustus were a strange lot. Bizarre incidents and crimes darkened their personal lives. Tiberius, under whom Christ was crucified, was a competent soldier but later on he became dejected and depressed and retired to Capre, where he spent the rest of his life. Caligula, a megalomaniac was assassinated. Claudius, weak in body and will, was dominated by his wife Agrippina, who later poisoned him to make room for her son Nero. Nero murdered not only his mother Agrippina but also his two wives and children and all the outstanding leaders in Rome, unleashed a reign of terror and finally committed suicide. The political climate became most depressing. These led to a spiritual unrest of extraordinary dimensions. The Christian Church alone could fill the vacuum.

Fifth, the efforts of the Jewish Christians among their fellow Jews met with hostility and rejection. In 55 AD, a formal anathema of the converted Jews was incorporated in the Synagogue liturgy. The attitude of the Gentiles at the time of destruction of Jerusalem and the temple in 70 AD by the Romans was pessimistic, attributing the incident as punishment of God. The Church was gradually focusing its attention towards the Gentiles, when the scope for attracting the Jews was doomed.

Sixth, the life of the Christians was the greatest attraction. The depth of their faith and a life oriented in strict conformity with what they preached crowned all the efforts of the missionaries. We do not find in world history any movement comparable to the enthusiasm and dynamic growth of Christianity in those days.

Mystery Religions

But, it is wrong to assume that the Christian Church had no rivals in this period. Much more powerful as a rival were the mystery religions that sprang up numerously and spread up rapidly in those days. They were syncrestic kinds of faith, a fusion of Hellenic and oriental thoughts. They were called mysteries, as their central rites were kept secret, except from the initiates. Though they had differences among them, some characteristics were common: a sublime view of the godhead, a profound sense of cleavage between spirit and flesh and yearning for a redeemer who would deliver the devotees from all guilt and confer on them eternal life. Some similarities in the rites of both mysteries and the Christian church, washings, anointing, sacred meals etc. led the people to think that Christianity is one among the mystery religions. Some of the important mystery religions, which came into prominence in that period, were:

The Dionesian and Orphic mysteries of Thrace
The Eleusianian from Eleusis near Athens
The religion of the Great Mother Cybele in Asia Minor
The Persian religion of Mithra
The Egyptian cult of Isis and Osiris.[1]

The most prominent among them were Mithra and Mother Cybele. Mithraism was the most prominent rival of Christianity. Mithra was a Persian sun god who had slain the cosmic bull, whose blood was treated as the source of life. His images always show him fighting – for right against wrong – an appealing image for soldiers. It was the soldiers of Alexander the Great who spread this religion around the Mediterranean. This cult promised immortality to the initiates.

Attis is the deity of Mother Cybele. They had frenzied dancing and in the ecstasy, some of their men castrate themselves, imitating their deity. They smear blood over themselves and at times drink it.

public and imposing built in 'Church architecture' have become common.

Faith, Discipline and Practices

Influenced by the Constantinian Revolution, millions of pagans entered the Church and some of their customs automatically crept into the liturgy. The use of the kiss as a sign of reverence, genuflection, devotion to relics, use of candles and incense and other ceremonial features were derived from the imperial courts. The Christians began facing the East while praying which made it necessary for the priest to lead the prayers with his back to the congregation. Belief in the presence of Jesus in the form of bread and wine animated the faithful, but there was no official formulation of the doctrine of 'Transubstantiation', which happened only later. For a long time, the celebrant was having considerable freedom to improvise the liturgy. Even the wording of the canon was left to his discretion. When heresy increased and the Church organization became more centralized, some amount of conformity was imposed. The liturgies of particular linguistic areas were standardized. Five liturgies came into prominence, three in the East, the *West Syrian of Antioch*, *the Coptic of Alexandria* and *the Bizantine of Constantinople* and two in the West, *the Romano-African* which stemmed from Rome and North Africa and *Gallican* covering Western Europe till 9th century still surviving in Milan (Italy).

The formation of the liturgical calendar began with special significance to Sunday as the day of Resurrection of Jesus. By the beginning of the second century, Easter was celebrated very early, but the dates were calculated differently in the Church of the East and the West. In Rome, it was observed on the Sunday after the Jewish Passover. In Asia, it was observed on the Sunday following the 14th day of the Jewish month of Nisan, the beginning of the Passover. Pope Victor persuaded the Asians to conform to Western usage, but failed. But, finally, Roman custom was accepted everywhere. Pentecost and Epiphany were also added to the calendar, the latter on 6th January, coinciding with Pagan New Year. December 25th was fixed for Christmas from 4th century coinciding with the pagan festival celebrating the birthday of Sun.

Although Eucharist and baptism were accorded special significance, other rites were also instituted as sacraments, though seven sacraments were officially listed only in the Middle Ages.

No other sacrament has undergone as much change as the sacrament of penance. The early Christians were reluctant to entertain the idea that a person once converted to Christ could sin and be forgiven again. According to most of them, a second remission of sin was unthinkable. So, the Church gradually developed a system for handling the problem of a sinner in its midst. Excommunication of notorious troublemakers, arbitration for settling disputes among members etc. seem to have been in vogue in the early Church. With these practices as the cue, the Church developed a system by which one guilty of grave sin could be pardoned after undergoing penance. He was then publicly excommunicated by the Bishop and relegated to a reserved section at the rear. Cyprian says he could no longer receive communion and was obligated to lead a life of utmost austerity, wearing coarse garments, hair cropped, abstaining from sexual relations and other pleasures. In this state of humiliation, he might have to remain for years. Thus, penance was always public; it was never administered more than once to the same person. Even after absolution, he had to live like a monk. Rather than subjecting himself to the rigours of penance, the sinner deferred it until his deathbed or even postponed baptism till late in life. Thus, the earlier system failed. In the Middle Ages, the Celtic monks devised a new system which was private and extended to all sins and frequent confession.

In the realm of faith, we have seen the General Council of Nicaea condemning Arianism and upholding the divinity of Jesus as the fundamental doctrine of faith. But, peace was not to be had so easily. Constantius, the son of Constantine, who ascended to power favoured the Arians and tried to crush the Nicaeans. Unity was restored in the Church at the General Council of Constantinople in 381 AD, which reaffirmed the Nicene faith and endorsed the consubstantiality of the Spirit, thus giving the doctrine of Trinity its definitive form 'the Son is generated, but the Spirit proceeds'.

Clergy – A Sacred Caste

The ministry of the Church developed a high degree of organization. In 250 AD Pope Fabian divided Rome into seven regions with a deacon in charge of each region. Eusebius, the Church historian gives us the list of ministers in the Church of Rome as forty-six presbyters, seven deacons and seven subdeacons, forty-two acolytes and fifty-two readers, exorcists and doorkeepers. The deacon for a long time exercised important role, next to the bishop, in the Church. Elected by the community, he was charged with administering communion to the faithful, alms to the poor, leading the prayer, in short, the right hand man of the bishop. His control of finance helped him to wield influence in the community and thereby becoming bishop, bypassing priesthood. But, as the Church spread to the countryside multiplying the number of churches called parishes, the Presbyter assumed functions monopolised by the bishop, presiding at the Eucharist, preaching, absolving the penitent etc. Gradually, the office of deacon became a step leading to the priesthood.

At first, the clergy were not differentiated from the laity. They married, raised families and pursued some trade or profession to earn their livelihood. But, when the practice of paying them for clerical work became common, they withdrew from secular pursuits. By the fourth century, such withdrawal has become obligatory.

In the early stages, the Christian presbyter avoided resemblance to pagan or Jewish priests and even refused to be called a priest. He saw his primary function as the ministry of the Word and the ritualistic features were kept in a low key. His main task was preaching. Gradually, the image of the presbyter assumed a sacred character. A clear indication of this is visible in the requirement of celibacy and virginity; which was adopted mainly on the ground that sexual intercourse was incompatible with the sacred character of clerical duties. The

Popes from Siricius (399 AD) onwards enforced clerical celibacy in their decretals.

Monasticism

Even from the early days of Christianity, men and women practised some form of asceticism by renouncing marriage and leading a life of seclusion from the world, while living with their families. Later, these ascetics, in order to achieve complete seclusion from world, left their families and went to wilderness and deserts. Monasticism was gradually germinating. St. Antony of Egypt is the pioneer. He sold his properties, gave the proceeds to the poor and took up an abode on the East bank of Nile and led a life of complete solitude. Many others gathered around him thereby forming a large number of monks in the deserts south of Alexandria, many of them living in communities. Pachomius, another Egyptian shaped it into an organization in 290 AD integrating work, study of scripture and prayer in the normal schedule. Thus, full-fledged monasticism originated in the Church.

Dualism, a philosophy that saw the world as evil, a place of exile and the body as a prison of the soul, found widespread acceptance among the people. The mystery religions and Neo-Platonism were dualistic. The general Christian attitude in the early period was also hostile to sex. Monasticism involved continence and renunciation of sex. Therefore, it found wide acceptance and spread to many parts of the world. The Church also encouraged the movement. Later on, men and women in large numbers came forward to establish religious congregations encouraging monastic life. In the course of time, monasteries produced scores of men of learning who could convincingly defend the Church in the realm of knowledge; philosophy, theology, history, dogma, education, scripture and so on whereby today monasticism has become a strong supporting arm of the Church.[1]

Military Service

Up to the period of Constantine, the general thinking of Christians was against becoming soldiers. As many Christians were serving in the Roman legion, this idea failed to get wide acceptance. Athanasius taught that it was lawful and even meritorious to kill enemies in times of war. St. Augustine formulated a theory of 'Just war'. Thomas Acquinas supported the Augustinian theory and it still remains the standard approach of the Church towards military service.

FOOTNOTE

1. Thomas Bokenkotter, *A Concise History of the Catholic Church*, pp. 93-94.

Victory Over Paganism and Growth

28

Growth of the Church

At the beginning of the fourth century, Christianity was only a religion of a minority in the Roman Empire. North Africa alone has become largely Christian in 300 AD. The progress of growth in the fourth century was so dramatic that by the time Emperor Theodosius declared Christianity as the official religion of the Roman Empire in 380 AD, it has become a religion of the majority.

Emperor Julian who took office in 360 AD was opposed to the Christian religion and he challenged its dominance. According to him, the Roman religion of the gods was not a mere religion but the marrow of the Romanitas and the source of Roman morality whereas Christianity was the recurrence of the age-old barbarism, a silly religion, the teachings of which were weak, impractical and subversive. In order to reverse the trend, he revoked the privileges granted to the Christian priests and made all efforts to revitalize the pagan religion by developing its theology on Neo-Platonic lines. His anti-Christian ideas failed to withstand the vital and simple message of Christianity. Julian's death, after being struck by a Persian arrow in the Mesopotamian desert in 363 saved Christianity from all the threats unleashed by him. Jovian, a General famous for his Christian faith, succeeded Julian. He restored the lost official status and privileges of the Church. But his reign was short (363-364). Another Christian Valentinian who succeeded Jovian was fully engaged in wars against Franks and Saxons in which the Goths slaughtered two-thirds of the Roman army including Valens in 378 at Hadrianople.

While the Empire was gradually weakening, the Church gained popular support and official standing. One of the most potential reasons for this popular appeal of the Church was its magnificent system of charity. In this period, the Church turned towards opening charity institutions like old age homes, hospitals, orphanages etc. When the State has become unable to cope with the burden of distress of the people due to frequent wars, the Church came to the rescue of the State. The bishop was given public judicial authority in all matters relating to social welfare. The bishop was supposed to eat with the poor, which he often did. Bishop Ambrose wanted no gold utensils on the altars when the people were suffering. Pope Gregory the Great felt personally guilty when a poor man was found dead due to starvation. The bishop has become the champion of the oppressed and gradually the most important figure in the city, although they were dressed in an aura of prestige and pomp.

Emperors Gratian and Theodosius who finally accepted Christianity as the basis of the social order in the Empire duly recognized the influence of the Church over the masses. The epoch-making decree promulgated in 380 AD by Theodosius amply testifies his intent. It reads "we desire that all peoples who fall beneath the sway of our imperial clemency should profess the faith which we believe has been communicated by the Apostle Peter to the Romans and maintained in its traditional form to the present day".[1] Theodosius declared Paganism illegal, outlawed their rites and practices and abolished pagan priesthood. He exempted the Catholic clergy from trial except in ecclesiastical courts. The pagan calendar was revised on the lines of the Church. Christmas and Easter were declared legal holidays, private or public secular activities were banned on Sundays. Various forms of heresies were proscribed. The Emperor personally witnessed his respect for the authority of the Church when he, after ordering a horrible massacre of the citizens of Thessalonica, accepted the rebuke of Bishop Ambrose and did public penance at the door of the Cathedral in Milan. This single act of Emperor Theodosius declared to the world the authority of the Church over the State and laid the foundations of papal monarchy over medieval Christendom.

What really contributed to this triumph of the Church? The well-knit organizational structure of the Church extending from the wall of Hadrian to the Euphrates River, the refuge for the oppressed provided by the Church and its activities as the champion of social justice have contributed in a very large measure to the Church's exalted position. One of the great historians of that period commented: "In its high ethical appeal, its banishment of the blood and sacrifice from worship and adherence to a God at once transcendent and active in the universe, Christianity presented in a coherent form ideas to which the pagan world was groping."

In the fifth century, the Roman Empire started its decline and eventually fell in 476 AD due to the frequent invasions by Goths, an uncivilized sect. Visigoths, an important sect among the Goths were already Christians but followers of the heresy of Arius. They accepted Christianity through the efforts of Ulfilas, one of the main leaders of Visigoths who was made Bishop in 341 AD and deputed to convert the Visigoths. He made a Gothic translation of the New Testament. Later many tribes known as Visigoths, Austrogoths, Lombards, Vandals etc. left Arianism and joined the Catholic Church during the last decade of the sixth century (around 589 AD).

Clovis I, the King of the Franks conquered the Romans in 486 and made Rome his capital. He married Clotilda, a Christian in 493 AD. He believed that his success in the war against the Germans at Cologne in 496 AD was due to the assistance of the God of Clotilda, and therefore, got baptized by St. Remi at Reims along with his three thousand soldiers. He overthrew the Visigoths and made Paris his capital. The conversion of the powerful Franks was a landmark in the history of the growth of Christianity in Europe.

There was Christianity in England even before the period of Emperor Constantine. In the sixth century, the Anglo-Saxons occupied many parts of England. This weakened the power and influence of the then Christians who were Celtic in racial origin. But in due course, the Anglo-Saxons also embraced Christianity due to the efforts of Pope Gregory the Great who sent some Roman monks under the leadership of Augustine to evangelize them. The queen of the Kingdom of Kent was a Christian and through her efforts, the King and the people of Kent accepted Christianity. Later, the Anglo-Saxon Kingdoms of Northumbria (it ceased to exist in 827) and Mercia also became Christian. By 651 AD, England has become a Christian country. The Pope appointed Augustine as the Archbishop (Metropolitan) of Canterbury. Thence onwards, the head of the Church of England was designated 'Archbishop of Canterbury'.

Ireland became a Christian country through the evangelisation efforts of St. Patrick, known as the 'Apostle of Ireland'. Patrick, born in 389(?) in Wales, spent six years as slave in Ireland in his young days, therefrom he went to France, joined a monastery and returned to Ireland as a missionary bishop in 432. Due to his strenuous efforts, by 461 AD, Ireland was completely Christianized. It is said that there was scattered presence of Christianity in Ireland even before the period of Patrick.

It is not clear as to when Christianity entered Scotland. A monk named Ninian is said to have done evangelisation work in Scotland in the fourth century. But St. Columba (521-597), an Irish monk, who established several monasteries in Ireland, was instrumental in the spread of Christianity in Scotland. He established a monastery at Ayona, which was famous in the Christian world of those days for sending missionary monks to many parts of Europe including Italy and Germany in the sixth and seventh centuries.

In Germany, though a group of pagans were Christianised by Bishop Ulfilas in the early decades of the 7th century, the majority of the pagans there remained ignorant of Christianity. The evangelisation of Germany took place in the 8th century through the efforts of an Englishman named Alboniface (also named Winifrid). Boniface (680-755) born in Davenshire in England, after some learning and training in a monastery went to Phrygia Island (Present Holland) to evangelise the land of his forefathers. Pope Gregory II, who was impressed by the zeal and intelligence of Boniface, consecrated him as bishop and deputed him to Germany for missionary work. He established several monasteries and convents in Germany. In 733, Pope Gregory III appointed him the Archbishop of Mainz. He evangelized not only Germany but also contributed in large measures to Christianise many other countries in Europe. In 754, he again went to Phrygia to continue his mission, but there the pagans assassinated him in 755. The Church in Germany will ever remember the services of Boniface as an evangelist, leader and administrator.

Christianity spread to Denmark, Norway, Sweden, Bulgaria and Russia in the 9th, 10th and 11th centuries (800-1073). In the first three centuries, a monk named Ansgar laid the foundations of evangelisation, but it gathered momentum during the days of Norwegian King Olaf (995-1030), who strove to propagate Christianity by fire and sword that led to a rebellion. The King had to flee to Russia, later came back to recapture the throne but was defeated and slain. He was canonised in 1162 and is patron saint of Norway. In the Slavic countries of Bulgaria, Moravia and Bohemia, Koorilos and Methodius, two monks of the Greek Church, carried out the evangelisation work. In Poland, the Church spread from Bohemia. Koorilos translated Bible into the Slav language. Vladimir I, the King of Russia, after study of several religions, finally embraced Christianity (Greek Church) and compelled his subjects to accept Christianity.

In short, by the year 1000 AD, almost the entire Europe, except Lithwania, Baltic coasts and a part of Spain came under the flag of Christ. These countries later accepted Christianity in the 13th and 14th centuries.

Advent of Mohammedanism

Before concluding the progress of growth of Christianity in Europe, it is relevant to point out how the Church got out of a danger of extinction. Mohammedanism, which sprouted and spread in the seventh century in Arabia spread to Europe in the 8th century. The Saracens conquered and occupied Spain, the first province of the Roman Empire and threatened to swallow many other countries in Europe. But the King of Franks Charles Martel (688-741), also known as Charles the Hammer, the grandfather of Charlemagne, defeated the Saracens at Tours in 732 and drove them to a corner of Spain, paving the way for the Christianisation of Europe. Spain terminated this Saracen occupation in 929.

FOOTNOTE

1. Thomas Bokenkotter, *A Concise History of the Catholic Church*, p. 57.

Establishment of Primacy of Papacy

29

T. Jalland says that until the fourth quarter of the fourth century, the Church was hardly accustomed to "speak in the language of Jurisdiction whether papal or otherwise and that in consequence the crucial question which See possessed its plenitude did not arise. But, it is clear that the Church was moving in the direction of providing herself with the machinery for corporate action as an ecumenical society on an equal footing with an ecumenical State."[1] We see the bishops of Rome putting forth their role as the chief shepherds of the flock of Christ. Pope Damasus (366-384) formally claimed at a Council in 382 the possession of primacy over all other Churches by virtue of the Lord's promise to St. Peter. Pope Siricius (384-399) went a step further and claimed the right to hear appeals. In his letters, later known as *Decretals*, he clearly claimed the right to take decisions with universal application on both doctrinal and disciplinary matters. These claims did not meet with acceptance from all sides, especially in the East. There was ambiguity in the West as well. Many of the successive popes did their little bit to supplement the idea of papal primacy, but tangible results were achieved by the genius and statesmanship of a few popes like Leo the Great, Gregory the Great, Hildebrand (Gregory VII) and Innocent III. In this chapter, we are making an attempt to peep into their periods.

Leo the Great (440-461)

The period of Pope Leo I is one of the momentous turning points in the history of papacy. When the world was cracking at the Seams, Leo, one of the greatest ecclesiastical statesmen, stood forth as a Pope of commanding genius and character who successfully asserted the supremacy and authority of papacy.

According to him, "Peter was 'the rock' on which the Lord built his Church; his successors, the popes were merely his temporary and mystical personifications. By virtue of his office, the Pope had the plenitude of power over the universal Church. He was its supreme ruler, its supreme teacher and its supreme judge. All other bishops only shared in his responsibility for the whole Church."[2]

Leo took charge of the papal office at a crucial time when the mighty Roman Empire was gradually cracking up. Aetius, the last effective Roman General in the West won some notable victories by using the Barbarians against the Barbarians, defeating the Visigoths with the help of Huns and defeating the Huns with the help of Visigoths. But, the Emperor Valentinian III murdered Aetius by cutting down him with his own sword. After a few months, the guards of Aetius revenged his death by assassinating Valentinian. In the absence of secular leadership, it was Leo who took charge of the fate of the City. He personally went to Mantua to meet, Attila, the leader of the Huns and dissuaded him from attacking Rome. Again it was Leo who met Gaiseric, the conqueror at the Gates of the City to insist on peace.

Tome of Leo

Leo's most memorable act of authority was in settling a doctrinal crisis in the Church on the relation of the divine to the human in Christ. Flavian, the Patriarch of Constantinople, found Eutychus, a monk who propagated the heresy, guilty and relieved him of his office. But, Eutychus was only a pawn in the hands of Dioscoros, the Patriarch of Alexandria who was on the lookout of an opportune occasion to embarrass his rival Flavian. Dioscoros succeeded in turning the tables against Flavian and levelled charges of heresy against Flavian himself and persuaded the Emperor to call a Council to settle the issue.

Actually, the issue was a longstanding controversy between two schools of theology in the East, the Alexandrian and Antiochean. Antioch's theological authority, Theodore of Mopsuestia insisted on the full and genuine manhood of Christ, opening them to the charge that the union was only moral rather than essential. On the other hand, the Alexandrians, through Cyril of Alexandria, an outstanding theologian, emphasized the unity of manhood and divinity. This theory was criticized by the opponents as one submerging the humanity in the divinity of Christ. Nestorius, the Patriarch of Constantinople (predecessor of Flavian) a partisan of the Anitochene school could not reconcile with the expression 'Mother of God' (*Theotokos* in Greek) while referring to Christ's mother. The Council of Ephesus in 431 AD endorsed the Alexandrian theology, condemned Nestorius as a heretic, exiled him to Egypt and accepted the use of the word *Theotokos*. But, this decision failed to bring about peace. A few bishops under the leadership of John of Antioch refused to accept the decrees of Ephesus. A compromise arranged in 433 also failed to settle the issue. Dioscoros, the supporter of Eutychus and opponent of Flavian wanted a definite triumph for the Alexandrian theology. He insisted on another Council to give a final verdict.

The Emperor convened another Council at Ephesus in 449 AD and appointed Dioscoros to preside over the Council. Backed by an army of monks and favoured by the Emperor, Dioscoros was equipped to get things done on his choice. He heard the confession of Eutychus, condemned Flavian and passed sentence of deposition against him. Those bishops who were reluctant to sign were forced to do so by soldiers, amidst violence and disorder. After four days, Flavian passed away, allegedly due to manhandling. Dioscoros won the game.

Even when the struggle between Dioscoros and Flavian originally started, Pope Leo studied the matter in detail and decided in favour of Flavian. He sent a letter to Flavian known as 'Tome of Leo', a masterpiece in dogmatic theology. When Leo knew about the happenings in Ephesus, he was outraged and called the Council of 449 a 'Latrocinium' (Synod of Robbers) and urged Emperor Theodosius to convene another Council. But, the Emperor did not oblige as he treated the question as already settled. But the Emperor's sister, Pulcheria, who was married to Marcion, the successor of Theodosius, exerted her influence to change the policy of Theodosius and a fresh Council was convened. But, on second thought, Leo was not in favour of another Council, as he feared risks to papal primacy if a Council was held. Moreover, as the *Tome of Leo* was accepted widely throughout the Church, another Council would be superfluous and irrelevant, he felt. But Marcion overruled Leo's contention.

In obedience to the Emperor, the Council was held in 451 at Chalcedon in which more than five hundred bishops attended. The papal legates presided. At the insistence of the Legates, Dioscoros was seated among the accused. When evidences of the unseemly and violent methods adopted by Dioscoros in the Council of 449 piled up, the followers of Dioscoros deserted him. The papal Legates declared the sentence of deposition of Dioscoros, which reads "Leo through us and the present Holy Synod together with St. Peter...deprives him of his episcopal office and of all sacerdotal dignity." When the Tome of Leo was read, the bishops cried out "This is the faith of the Fathers and of the Apostles. This we all believe. Peter has spoken through Leo: thus Cyril taught: Leo and Cyril teach the same; anathema to him who teaches otherwise."

The matter ought to have ended there. But, the imperial commissioners wanted to plug all loopholes and make a foolproof definition that would secure the unity of the Empire. Perhaps they would have feared that a ratification of *Leo's Tome* alone would have ascribed too much importance to papal authority. Whatever it is, at their insistence, a formulary was prepared and accepted by the Council unanimously as follows:

"One and the same Christ, Son, Lord, the only Begotten, made known in two natures (which exist) without confusion, without change, without division, without separation; the difference of the natures having been in no wise taken away by reason of the union, but rather the properties of each being preserved, and (both) concurring into one person (*prosopon*) and one *hypostasis* – not parted or divided into two persons (*prosopa*) but one and the same son and Only Begotten, the divine Logos, the Lord Jesus Christ."

Leo had won a great victory. But it failed to bring forth unity. Two schisms occurred later. The Nestorians rejected the

Chalcedonian formula on the ground that it confused the relations of the divine persons in the Trinity. The Monophysites denied that Christ's humanity was consubstantial with ours. The Byzantines for a long time interpreted Chalcedon in a pro-monophysite sense, mainly for other reasons, likely to be political.

Leo's apprehensions about using Chalcedon to set up Constantinople as rival to Rome were proved prophetic. Despite protests of the papal legates, the Council passed Canon 28. It states:

"Following in all things the decision of the holy Fathers and acknowledging the canon, which has just been read, of the One hundred and Fifty Bishops beloved-of-God (who assembled in the Imperial city of Constantinople, which is New Rome, in the time of the Emperor Theodosius of happy memory), we also do enact and decree the same things concerning the privileges of the most holy Church of Constantinople, which is New Rome. For the Fathers rightly granted privileges to the throne of Old Rome, because it was the imperial city. And the one hundred and fifty most religious bishops, actuated by the same consideration, gave equal privileges to the most holy throne of New Rome, justly judging that the city which is honoured with the Sovereignty and the Senate, and enjoys equal privileges with the old imperial Rome, should in ecclesiastical matters also be magnified as she is, and the Thracian Dioceses, the metropolitans only and such bishops also of the dioceses aforesaid as are among the barbarians, should be ordained by the aforesaid most holy throne of the most holy Church of Constantinople; every metropolitan of the aforesaid dioceses, together with the bishops of his province, ordaining his own provincial bishops, as has been declared by the divine canons; but that, as has been above said, the metropolitans of the aforesaid Dioceses should be ordained by the Archbishop of Constantinople, after the proper elections have been held according to custom and have been reported to him."[3]

Pope Leo refused to accept this Canon. The Council of Constantinople had granted (referred to at the beginning of

Canon 28) an honorary precedence to the See of Constantinople above the See of Alexandria. The Council of Chalcedon now raised this status to a position of such magnitude that when supported by the Emperors it might severely threaten the unity of the Church and even endanger Rome's primacy. Moreover, Canon 28 was based on the principle of political accommodation.

Even though things were patched up with Leo accepting a conciliatory letter from the Patriarch of Constantinople who agreed not to officially promulgate Canon 28, the misunderstanding continued and finally played a role in the final schism of the East about which we shall deal later elsewhere in this book.

St. Gregory the Great (590-604)

Consequent on the fall of the Roman Empire, the imperial administration collapsed, the social order disintegrated and chronic insecurity prevailed everywhere. But the Popes were never desperate. They accepted the fact that the Barbarians had come to stay and the obvious option before them was to convert and incorporate the Barbarians in the Christian mainstream. Though it was a strenuous effort spanning centuries, the untiring perseverance of the Church eventually bore fruits. The pre-eminent efforts of the Popes, the labours of many monks and the political prowess of the Franks contributed to achieve the end. Pope Gregory the Great laid its foundations at the end of the sixth century, but its full realization came through only when Charlemagne accepted the crown of the Emperor from Pope Leo III on the Christmas Day in 800 AD.

The death of a major chunk of the Roman soldiers including Emperor Valentine in 378, the establishment of a visigothic Kingdom in Southern Gaul, the conquest of Africa by Vandals, the occupation of the West bank of Rhine and the Northern and central Gaul by the Franks, Burgundians and others foreshadowed the doom of the Empire in the West. The Lombards, a migrating Germanic tribe seized Milan in 568. In 579, they unsuccessfully besieged Rome. It was the final blow to the Roman civilization. Against this backdrop came to the throne of St. Peter, one of its noblest occupants Gregory I, later known as St. Gregory the Great, a man of genius, profound spirituality and untiring energy.

Gregory was born in Italy with all advantages of birth and wealth. After becoming the prefect of the city, the highest post in Rome, he abandoned the world altogether. He founded several monasteries with his own wealth and even his own palatial home was converted into a monastery and there he led a life of asceticism and study. From there he went to Constantinople as papal envoy, spent six years there and returned to his monastery. When the papal office fell vacant, the people clamoured to make him Pope. After initial reluctance, he accepted the post in 590 AD.

It was Gregory who laid the foundations of medieval Christendom. The lasting influence of his four historic achievements will amply testify his greatness.

He made the Popes the *de facto* rulers of Central Italy.

He strengthened the papal primacy over the churches in the West.

He immensely furthered the work of conversion of the Barbarians and initiated the conversion of the Anglo-Saxons.

He left behind some exquisite writings on theology and spirituality that tremendously influenced the shaping of medieval thought in the Church.

Considering the inability of the Eastern Roman Empire to check the Lombards, he took up the responsibility of feeding the people of Rome and mustering of troops. He recognized the rights of the Patriarchies of Jerusalem, Antioch, Alexandria and Constantinople but never hesitated to interfere in the life of his own Church in the West. In accordance with his own dictum "I know of no bishop who is not subject to the Apostolic See when fault is committed" he corresponded frequently with the bishops and monks advising them on administration and discipline. Though the Churches in Gaul and Spain were enjoying practical independence, he familiarized with them by the sheer weight of his spiritual and moral authority and advised them to look to Rome whenever any special guidance is required. He personally commissioned Augustine, a Roman monk, to convert Angles and Saxons and was highly elated by speedy conversion of the King of Kent. Boniface who converted Inner Germany worked in close submission to Rome. Consequently, the whole Western Europe and England were brought into close relationship with Rome.

Shortly before the accession of Gregory to the papal throne, Recared, the visigothic King abjured Arianism and embraced the Catholic Church at a great Synod at Toledo in 589. Through shrewd diplomatic moves, Gregory paved the way for the eventual conversion of the Lombards as well.

A New Civilization

Another important contribution of Gregory was the shaping of a new civilization out of the ruins of the old one – a new political, cultural and social unity of Europe. Next to papacy, a pivotal force in the making of Catholic Europe was the monasticism. Gregory created an atmosphere for his successors to continue the efforts to make papacy and the Church a spiritual force with the help of the monks and Franks.

Unlike the Church in the Eastern Empire, the Western Church was largely an urban religion with little or no influence among the peasants in the countryside. The dissolution of the Roman Empire directly resulted in the breakup of the city-life and the emergence of an agrarian economy and rural society. The monks who located their monasteries in the rural areas were in an advantageous position to shape this civilization. The monastic movement introduced by St. Patrick in the Far West – mainly in Celtic lands – were organized from the very start centred on tribal units. The Church was also organized on monastic units rather than on episcopal units. These monasteries became units of excellence in learning and ecclesiastical life. The Egyptian model of monasticism lacked a system of authority. St. Benedict provided his monasteries with a system of authority. The Benedictine monks brought Christianity to England. (Augustine came from Pope Gregory's Benedictine monastery.) The statesmanship of Pope Gregory made full use of these advantages to stabilize the Barbarians in Christian faith by planting amidst them a solid Church.

The supposed ruler of Rome was the distant exarch at Ravenna, the Vicar of the Eastern Roman Emperor. But, the actual ruler was the Pope, the exarch being only a *de jure* figure, shadowy and ineffective. So, when the Lombards occupied Ravenna in 751 and expelled the exarch, it caused no impact in Rome. The Popes had for long been recognized as the only effective ruler not only of Rome but the whole non-Lombard Italy. As such, it has become the responsibility of the Pope to deal with the Lombards. Though converted to Christianity, the Lombards nurtured the ambition to rule the whole Italy. The Pope was not in a mood to allow it, and therefore, sought the help of the Franks to confront the Lombards. Pepin, the King of the Franks, who was obliged to the Pope for acceding to his request for seizure of the crown from the successors of Clovis I, readily agreed to help. This alliance between the papacy and the Franks was a longstanding one. It strengthened both the papacy and the King and continued during the successors of Pope Gregory and Pepin with mutual benefit. By the year 800 AD the Kingdom of Charles, the son of Pepin stretched from the Atlantic to the Southern Italy, from the Pyrenees to the Elbe, constituting the political unity of the Western Roman Empire. But, the title of Charles was 'King of the Franks and Lombards and Patrician of the Romans' (a title conferred on Pepin and his two sons by Pope Stephen II). This relation culminated in 800 AD (Dec. 25) when Pope Leo III surprisingly crowned Charlemagne as Emperor during the Christmas mass in St. Peters, while the whole assembly roared out 'Hail to Charles the Augustus, crowned of God, the great and peace-bringing Emperor of Rome'. The words 'Crowned of God' and 'Emperor of Rome' are specially noteworthy. Gregory's dream about papacy has become true. The position of the Pope above all monarchs was well established and declared before the whole world.

It was Gregory who sowed the seeds of faith developed in later years on Purgatory (Dialogues 4:39), intercession of saints, transubstantiation, absolution of original sin through baptism etc. Later, Gregory was canonised.

Gregory VII (Hildebrand) (1073-1085)

Charlemagne's Empire in the 9th century was idealistically treated as a continuity of the Roman Empire, but it had several limitations, Roman law, Legions, Senate etc. were conspicuously absent. Truly speaking, it was a shapeless conglomeration with no trade or urban centres. Nevertheless, it was a commonwealth of Christian peoples organized in many States bound together in a common faith and common culture where all Europeans felt they belonged. Therefore, even after its breakdown, the idea of such a framework inspired the emergence of a new order in the 11th century. This unique commonwealth had two heads, the Pope and the Emperor – Church and State. Naturally, one question as to who is the final authority arose and remained unanswered.

During Charlemagne's period, no one dared to challenge his authority and resultantly there was no problem. He was concerned with every thing affecting the government of the Christians including matters involving the life of the Church. In fact, the exercise of authority by Charlemagne was not in consonance with the longstanding theory enunciated by the Popes on the relation of the temporal authority to the spiritual authority. According to the concept put forth by the papacy, the Emperor was merely to protect the temporal welfare of his subjects and their corporate union. This was the message implied in the handing over of the sword to the Emperor by the Pope in the coronation ceremony. Accordingly, Popes after Charlemagne's period tried to assert their supreme authority over Christendom. Pope Stephen IV crowned Charlemagne's son Louis. Louis' son Lothar went over to Rome for coronation in 823. Henceforth, Rome was considered the only right place for imperial coronations.

Succeeding Popes in the ninth century asserted this supremacy of the spiritual over the temporal power. Nicholas I (858-867), while giving the sword to the Emperor at the coronation ceremony, emphasised its symbolic meaning. Pope John VIII (882) advanced the cause of papal supremacy by asserting that the right of the Popes was not only to crown but also to choose the Emperor. It really happened in 875 when he offered the crown to Charles the Bald. Another indication of this supremacy over the temporal order is visible in the change in terminology of the papal residence – the residence at Lateran known as "patriarchate" was changed as "Sacred Palace of the Lateran", presumably in 813.

By the last decade of the 9th century, both the Empire and the papacy began to disintegrate. Louis the pious, the weak son of Charles had four sons. They picked up quarrel among themselves and with their father for their share of the Empire. The Empire was divided among the surviving three members. Under Charles the Fat, the Empire was reunited but it did not last long. The Franks deposed Charles the Fat in 887. The total crumbling of the Empire occurred when Viking and Magyar invaders ran amok resulting in anarchy and the emergence of feudalism all over Europe.

Simultaneously, the papacy also slid into the abyss. It became a victim of political intrigues. The pontificate of John XII (964), who ascended the throne at the age of eighteen, through his eccentric style of functioning reminded the age of Emperor Nero in the first century. Consequent on this disintegration, the question of supremacy faded away. When the Empire was revived, the Emperors were in a better position to exercise both temporal and spiritual supremacy.

The revival of the Empire happened in the German segment of the old Empire under a new dynasty of Henry, the Duke of Saxony. In this area, feudalism had not become so deep-rooted. Henry's son Otto the Great revived the traditions of Charlemagne by seeking the Crown from Pope in 962 at St. Peter's Basilica. Otto was shrewd enough to realize that in his struggle against disorder, the Church is an effective force to be made use of in reviving the Empire. He considered the bishops as the most suitable collaborators in his efforts by reason of their education and lack of children. According to him, one of the chief threats to monarchy in a feudal society was that the families getting control of lands, treating it as their independent domain, thereby creating a rival dynasty to that of the King. If a bishop holds it, on the death of a bishop, the King was free to choose a successor he preferred, stalling the automatic transfer of rights to the son. So, wherever he could, he appointed bishops in charge of dukedoms or counties. His own brother Bruno, Archbishop of Cologne was appointed Duke of Lotharingia.

Otto confirmed the donations (to the Church) of Pepin and Charlemagne and guaranteed the independence of the Papal States. The bishops were appointed in key positions of authority in the State. The claims of supremacy of the papacy over temporal power were either set aside or sank into oblivion. At the same time Otto deposed Pope John XII on charges of treason and nominated a layman in his place. He also decreed that in future no Pope was to be consecrated until he had first taken an oath of allegiance to the Emperor. In the Ottoman Empire, the Popes like the bishops ought to be the nominees of the sovereign. Henry III, the most powerful among the Emperors, chose Popes and bishops, making sure that the candidate was suitable for the office. When Pope Benedict IX was chased by an anti-Pope, who was replaced by John Gratian the arch priest, Henry intervened, deposed all three of them and installed four Popes of his choice successively – Clement II, Damasus II, Leo IX and Victor II (All of them were men of calibre suitable for the post). The old Canon law that insisted on a bishop to be elected by clergy and people was thrown to the winds. The whole transaction was tainted with Simony.

When the deeds of Henry III led the Church to the other extreme through lay investiture, proprietary Church system etc., spiritual energy again began to drain away from the Church. The great monasteries reformed by Cluny, the influential Burgundian monastery, Cardinal Humbert and many others came to the fore to raise the question "How can laymen hold supreme authority over the body that Christ had committed to His apostles and their successors, the bishops?" They were satisfied with nothing less than the total sovereignty of the Pope over the world. But before dreaming anything, it was necessary to liberate the papacy itself from the iron grip of the Emperor. A chance occurred when Henry III died in 1056 leaving behind his six-year-old son Henry IV and the death of Pope Victor II in the succeeding year. The Curia used this opportunity to elect one of their men Stephen IX as Pope who died soon. Then they elected a reform-minded Churchman Nicholas II (1061) making things clear. The epoch-making Decree of 1059 excluded the Emperor and the riotous Roman nobles from any role in the papal elections. Henceforth, only Cardinals were to elect the Popes, although some type of confirmation was allowed to the Emperor. This system modified later making it foolproof and a wholly Church affair that is still in vogue. At the death of Nicholas, the Cardinals elected another reformer Alexander II. But to ascend the throne he had to overcome the combined forces of the Roman Nobles, Lombard bishops and imperial magnates.

But, with the election of Hildebrand (Gregory VII) in 1073, a man with colossal will power to put Humbert's theory into practice and assert papal supremacy ascended the papal throne. His physical qualities were unexceptional, small in stature, weak in voice, moderately learned, temperament of a prophet, vigour of imagination, bright keen eyes and tremendous passion for righteousness. He was committed to an unqualified papal authority. According to him, all souls must obey his definitions of right and wrong, he had unlimited power of excommunication and absolution: God alone could judge him. He claimed right to punish and even to depose disobedient rulers as papacy was to the Empire as the Sun was to the Moon.

Pope's Tussle with Henry IV of Germany

The new Pope in his famous *Dictatus Papae* (1075) showed his view of an unqualified papal authority. On taking charge he found the situation encouraging. The papal elections have become independent. Popes gained authority over all archbishops and bishops and gradually recovered the rights over the papal States. But, problems were also there. The clergy stoutly resisted the papal decrees on clerical marriage and simony. The young Henry IV showed little sympathy towards reforms as he was bent upon keeping royal controls over episcopal nominations. Gregory's relations with Henry IV have become smooth when Henry yielded to the will of the Pope in an episcopal appointment in Milan. It was soon found that his compliance was due to some internal pressure in Germany. He was waiting for an opportunity to show his real intention for subordinating the papacy. The issue that forced a showdown was lay investiture or lay control over episcopal appointments. A decree against lay investiture was passed by Gregory's synod in 1075. But Henry was not in a mood to give up his control over the bishops. So, deliberately Henry defied the decree and invested his own man as archbishop of Milan.

A momentous question has come to the surface. Gregory was not the type to leave things unchallenged. He sent an ultimatum to Henry IV: either respect the decree against investiture or face excommunication and possible deposition. This reached the Emperor when he was in a mood of victory against the Saxons. He summoned a Council of his puppet bishops and pronounced a scathing judgment against Hildebrand.

"Hildebrand, at present not Pope daring to depose the Emperor as if the Kingdom and the Empire were thine and not in God's hands" and cried out "Descend? and relinquish the apostolic chair which thou hast usurped...Descend? Descend? To be damned throughout the ages."[4] Gregory hastily convened a synod of bishops, considered the Decree of the Emperor, decided to excommunicate Henry and declared him deposed.

The papal ban struck Henry. His supporters left him and his enemies used it to denounce him. A Diet at Tribur on October 10th, 1076 gave Henry time till 22nd February 1077 to obtain absolution and invited Pope to preside over the German Council to decide on the worthiness of Henry IV to continue his reign. Henry became desperate, resolved to take a retrograde step and proceeded to meet the Pope at Canossa where the Pope was taking rest on his way to Germany. Garbed in penitential rags, Henry stood barefooted in the snow-filled courtyard of the Castle to seek absolution. At last, the priestly conscience of Gregory prevailed, and absolution was reluctantly granted.

The enemies of Henry were not deterred by the absolution granted by the Pope. They deposed him and elected the Duke of Swabia, Rudolf to succeed Henry. Both parties appealed to Pope for a judgment in this tussle. But Henry did not accept the mediation of Pope. Thereupon, Pope again excommunicated Henry and deposed him. Matters did not end there. Henry's triumph over Rudolf changed the course of events. The public opinion in Germany favoured Henry treating Pope as the aggressor trespassing the limits of his powers in dethroning the Emperor of Western Christendom. Emboldened by the turn of events, Henry deposed Gregory, put an anti-pope in his place, marched to Rome and besieged Gregory who managed to escape to the Castle of Sant Angelo. Robert Guiscard, the Norman ruler of southern Italy came to the rescue of Gregory and drove Henry out. But, in doing so, he reduced Rome to ashes. The Roman populace was infuriated and turned their ire against Gregory who had to seek refuge with Robert in Salerno. There, due to the deep sense of failure and realizing the fact that the anti-pope is ensconced in Rome, Gregory breathed his last on 25th May 1085 uttering the words "I have loved justice and hated inequity: therefore I die in exile."[5]

Gregory passed away, but his ideal remained alive. Though his immediate successor was a non-entity, the ascension of Urban II, Gregory's legate in Germany during the critical years and a Cluniac monk like Gregory, was the right choice to continue the work.

Henry IV, deserted by wife and son and surrounded by enemies, died among the wreckage of his hopes and ambitions, while papacy under Urban moved forward with success after success. When Urban exhorted the knights of Christendom for Crusade against the Muslims, the Lords of Europe rallied around him with enthusiasm, which shows the power exerted by the Popes over the minds and hearts of the people.

Nevertheless, the practice of lay investiture continued in varying degrees in different nations in Europe. A compromise formula was worked out for this thorny issue; the clergy would elect the bishop with a minimal participation of the laity and in the presence of the monarch – therefore with some influence by him. The temporal ruler would invest him with the symbols of his temporal authority and offer homage to him (in Germany this would take place before consecration as laid down in the Concordat at Worms 1122). Thus the Emperor was in a position to exert a lot of influence in the choice of bishops.

The final victory of Hildebrand was due to historical and accidental factors. Henry V, the son of Henry IV died in 1125. He was succeeded by Lothar, a member of the Welf family that supported the papacy in the struggle against Henry IV. Moreover, Lothar needed Church's help to control the German bishops.

Anyhow, Hildebrand's dream materialised. A new papacy, wearing the imperial insignia, including the 'tiara', a conical shaped headdress with a crown surrounding it, emerged. Later, Pope Innocent III changed the number of crowns to two and Pope Boniface VIII raised the number of crowns to three.

Innocent III (1198-1216)

Innocent III was a man small in stature but with enormous talent, one of the finest legal minds of the age and the first Pope to take the title 'Vicar of Christ'. He advanced the claim of papal supremacy by claiming that the temporal power was derived from the Pope. Innocent intervened in the political affairs of the West and made himself the arbiter of its destiny. When there was a contention for the imperial crown between Philip and Otto in Germany, the Pope chose Otto, who in return assured to maintain the independence of the Papal States. This strife resulted in a war between Philip and Otto. Otto fled to England, but returned after eliminating Philip through an assassin. But, once crowned, he reneged on his promises and invaded the papal domain. Innocent resorted to his final weapon of excommunication and deposition and chose a youngster of sixteen to succeed Otto, Frederick II, the ruler of Sicily. To settle the issue, another war was necessitated, the battle of Bouvines between Otto and Frederick in which England supported Otto. Frederick won the battle with the support of France.

King John of England and Magna Carta

The greatest triumph of the spiritual power of Innocent was his victory over King John of England, after a quarrel, which led to a memorable event in world history – the signing of the Magna Carta. The trouble began when King John tried to impose his own nominee as Archbishop of Canterbury. On appeal, the Pope decided against the King and proposed one Stephen Langton, who was duly elected by the clergy. The King did not allow Stephen to enter England. The Pope placed England under interdict. No religious services except baptism and funeral were allowed. This dragged on for nearly six years. The religious life of England came to a halt. Finally Innocent in alliance with King Philip Augustus of France threatened to invade England. It was too much for John to bear, as he was unsure of the support of his own subjects. He yielded abjectly, performed an act of homage and placed England under feudal vassalage to the Pope.

Later, another paradoxical scene in the drama appeared placing the Pope and John together on one side and Archbishop Langton and barons together on the other side. The barons revolted against certain abusive demands of the King and forced him to guarantee their rights. A duel of arms and wits ensued. The King claimed the immunity of a crusader and right to papal intervention. But the barons finally succeeded in forcing the King to sign the Great Charter of Magna Carta at Runnymede on June 15, 1215, which consecrated the principle of Government by law as against arbitrary despotism, a turning point in the history of not only England but the whole world.

John appealed to the Pope and was able to have the charter quashed by Innocent. The Pope, preoccupied with the Ecumenical Council (Lateran IV) was unaware of the ground situation. His finding was that the charter was invalid as it was obtained by force by the barons acting as judges in their own case. He excommunicated the enemies of the King and suspended Langton from office. However, John died suddenly. Most of the nations rallied around the young King Henry. The Archbishop, reconciled with the Pope by visiting Rome, came back as mediator and settled the issue.

Marriage of King Philip of France

Another King who was forced to recognise the superior authority of Pope Innocent was Philip Augustus of France (1180-1223). The King, due to some physical aversion towards his beautiful wife Ingeborg of Denmark, wanted separation on the morrow of their wedding. Despite failure to obtain an annulment, the King openly lived with his mistress and made the life of Ingeborg more miserable. She approached the Pope for justice. But Pope Celestine III dragged on the issue without a decision. Pope Innocent was of a different mould. He resolved that the Kings are also subject to the moral law of the Church. Though he was in need of the friendship of King Philip for political reasons, the stubborn attitude of the King forced the Pope to lay an interdict on France. It was lifted only when Philip accepted Ingeborg as Queen but refused to treat her as his wife. The affair dragged on for many years, but the Pope granted no divorce. Finally, after twenty years, the King accepted Ingeborg as wife and queen.

One of the greatest contributions of Innocent III to the Church was that he enacted laws regulating the life and status of each member of the Church. The decrees were embodied in the Canon law that was the most civilized law of the age influencing medieval civilization. He made substantial contributions to the mass of papal decretals that were eventually incorporated into Gregory IX's collection of *Decretals*, the first to have the force of universal law. He convoked the Fourth Ecumenical Council of Lateran IV in 1215 which was attended by more than 400 bishops, eight hundred abbots and priors and numerous ambassadors from all kingdoms. In consonance with his efforts to raise the standards of both lay and clerical life, the Council made obligatory annual confession of serious sins and annual reception of the Eucharist.

The Council introduced auricular confession (confession before the priests) and made official use of the term 'Transubstantiation' and defined it. Conditions were laid down for valid election of bishops, prescribed qualifications for admission to the clergy, regulated the life of the clergy by insisting on their dress and recreations and reorganized the

Curia. One of Innocent's less glorious titles to fame was that he was the first Pope to use force to suppress religious opinions through the introduction of 'Inquisition'. The Roman Emperors used it to award even death penalty to the heretics. The Pope used force in dealing with the Cathari, an anti-social sect that preached that the material world was the creation and tool of *Satan,* and therefore, prohibited marriage, encouraged suicide etc. and condemned all things materialistic. In 1207, Innocent's legate Peter of Castelnan was brutally murdered at the instigation of a suspected Catharist. This necessitated the adoption of a different tactic. A crusade was proclaimed against these Albigenses, as they were sometimes called, and thousands of them were murdered. Inquisition originated from this crusade. Special tribunals were appointed by the Pope to ferret out heretics. At first, the responsibility was vested with the bishop. Later, delegates were sent out with special powers, independent of the episcopate, to identify heretics and to annihilate them.

The spiritual and temporal powers of the Pope reached its zenith during the period of Innocent III. His period is considered to be the period of supremacy, fame and glory of papacy. Though he reformed the Curia, brought forth orderliness in Church affairs including the selection of bishops and clergy, convened a widely represented General Council and introduced several measures which still exist in the Church, the inquisition remains a black spot in his otherwise glorious image.

Innocent IV and Boniface VIII

Following the footsteps of his predecessors, Innocent IV (1243-59) treated Emperors and Kings as Pope's vassals. Even though he succeeded in his struggle with Emperor Frederick II, he never earned a status equal to Gregory I or Innocent III, as he was a worldly man with no commitment to justice. His lust for power was very much visible in the administration of the Church as well. According to him, the laymen need know only that there is a God who rewards virtues. In all other matters, they should believe whatever the Church believes. And regarding bishops and priests, they need know Apostles' Creed and that the body of Christ is built in the Holy Mass and nothing more than that.

Pope Boniface VIII (1294-1303), who was the embodiment of pride and arrogance, claimed powers which none of his eminent predecessors dared to claim. At the time of his accession, two Kings were asked to hold the stirrup of his horse. When the Yovel festival was celebrated in Rome in 1300 AD, he appeared in public one day with all the vestments of the Pope and on another day with all symbols of royalty, sword, crown and sceptre and shouted 'I am Caesar', 'I am the Emperor' etc. In 1296, Boniface issued a Bull *Clericis Laicos* that anyone who levies tax for Church properties without the authorization of the Holy See shall be excommunicated. This appeared to the Kings as a challenge to their authority and a clarion call for confrontation. Edward I, the King of England, with the concurrence of parliament, defied the Pope's directive. King Philip of France, with the intention of teaching the Pope a lesson, imprisoned papal legate and publicly burnt the papal Bull. Thereon, the Pope summoned a Council of French bishops and issued a warrant to the King to personally appear before the Pope and submit his explanation. The King did not oblige. The defiance of the King provoked the Pope to promulgate a second Bull, a historical document titled *Unam Sanctum* highlighting the prerogatives and sovereignty of the Pope. It was therein emphasized that the temporal and spiritual authority of the Pope far exceeds the authority of anyone in this world, that God alone can judge the Pope, that there is no absolution of sins or salvation outside the Church and that all human creatures are bound to obey the Pope for the sake of salvation. This later became a much-trumpeted teaching of the Church.

The King wanted to bring the Pope before a Council for trial. But the Pope breathed his last in the custody of French soldiers, before facing trial. With the death of Boniface VIII, the claim of sovereignty of papal monarchy also ended. Clement V who succeeded Boniface in 1305 shifted the papal headquarters from Rome to Avignon in France and the papacy remained there till 1378 embracing the Pontificates of seven

Popes, Clement V, John XXII, Benedict XII, Clement VI, Innocent VI, Urban V and Gregory XI who returned to Rome.

FOOTNOTES

1. Thomas Bokenkotter, *A Concise History of the Catholic Church*, p. 78.
2. *Ibid.*, p. 793.
3. *Ibid.*, pp. 84-85.
4. *Ibid.*, p. 106.
5. *Ibid.*, p. 107, Para. 4.

The Orthodox Churches (The Eastern Schism)

30

The Rise of Constantinople

In 324 AD, Constantine, the Roman Emperor, moved the capital of the Empire to Bizantium and renamed it after his name as Constantinople. Constantine erected numerous churches there including two magnificent ones, one dedicated to Peace and the other dedicated to the Holy Apostles. His period was one of tremendous growth of the Christian Church in the Empire and consequently Constantinople has become a centre of Christianity in the East and the Church in the Eastern Empire was known as the Eastern Church. Three liturgies based on different linguistic areas developed in the Eastern Church from the very early days of Christianity, the West Syrian of Antioch (the Antiochean Rite), the Coptic Alexandrian Rite and the Bizantine Rite of Constantinople. The political preponderance of Constantinople as the capital of the Empire inevitably led to ecclesiastical preponderance for the Bishop enjoying a suprametropolitan status patriarchal. The General Council of Constantinople in 381 AD made the Bishop of Constantinople, the ranking prelate in the East with primacy next to that of the Bishop of Rome. The Moslem seizure of the three Patriarchates of Alexandria, Antioch and Jerusalem and their consequent isolation left the Patriarch of Constantinople the sole unquestioned head of the Eastern Christendom.

The relations between the Sees of Rome and Constantinople were marked by occasional friction. Many reasons, political, social, religious and cultural were putting the Sees apart on different occasions. Canon No. 28 of the Council of Chalcedon (451 AD) which granted great jurisdictional power to Constantinople was not acceptable to Rome. The relations were restored when Constantinople abandoned its position. The attempt of the Eastern Emperor to enforce a policy of iconoclasm (the abolition of all religious images) in the 8th century again flared up the conflict with the Popes. When Pope Stephen appealed for military assistance in 753, the Emperor refused it. This led the Pope to approach the Franks for assistance, which ultimately resulted in the imperial coronation of Charlemagne.

In the year 858, Emperor Michael III deposed Ignatius, the Patriarch of Constantinople and appointed one Photius as Patriarch. Pope Nicholas I was horrified by the irregularities in the appointment. Though Pope had some difficulties with the deposed Patriarch Ignatius, he sent legates to Constantinople to enquire into the irregularities. The legates decided in favour of Photius. But, when Photius indicated that he did not accept the supremacy of the Pope, Nicholas refused to recognise him as patriarch. Another incident in the Balkans aggravated the tension between the two Sees. Roman missionary Bishop Formosus collided with Bizantine emissaries on some Bizantine traditions like marriage of clergy and the Lenten fast.

FILIO QUE

A doctrinal difference widened the gulf between the two Sees. In the Nicene Creed formulated by the General Council of Nicaea as modified by the General Council of Constantinople in 381, the wording relating to the Holy spirit was "And in the Holy Spirit, the Lord (to *Kurion*) and Giver of life who proceeds from the Father, who together with the Father and son is worshipped and glorified." A local Council at Toledo in Spain in 589 added the word *FILIO QUE* to the Creed, the Latin word expressing the idea that the Holy Spirit proceeded from both the Father and the Son. This usage already occurred in Spain. From there it spread to Gaul and Germany. Under the Carolingian Empire, a Synod at Aachen (809) requested Pope Leo III to introduce it in the entire Latin Church. The Pope did not agree to this request for fear of imposing a clause added to the traditional text of the Creed. Later, Pope Benedict VIII introduced it in the Creed (1022). The Greeks ignored *FILIO QUE* and denied the right to make any addition to the Creed.

The Westerners argued that the addition of the word *FILIO QUE* was only the refinement of one idea already in the creed. The Easterners who were more sensitive to the Trinitarian terminology viewed that the addition upset the delicate balance of properties in the Trinity. According to them, the Trinity emphasized the omnipresent and all pervasive nature of the Holy Spirit descended through the Son, not from the Son. Another legal issue was also involved in the dispute. Can a local Synod or the Pope alter the decision of a General Council? For them, only an Ecumenical Council can amplify or explain the definition of a previous Council. These arguments for and against the change eventually led to the question of the authority of the Pope – 'Infallibility'. This remained an issue in the Church for centuries. Only the General Council of Vatican I settled the matter by declaring the 'Infallibility of the Pope' on faith and morality in the Dogmatic Constitution.

Side by side, another development took place in the East. Basil, the Macedonian usurped the throne of the Emperor in 867. He removed Photius and restored Ignatius. Hadrian II, the new Pope, seeking reconciliation sent delegates to a Council held at Constantinople in 869. But the climate at the Council was not favourable to the legates. The Council assigned the Church of Bulgaria to Constantinople, overriding the claim of Rome. On the death of Ignatius, Photius was re-appointed. This time, Photius had a change of heart. He wished to have good relations with Rome. Another Council at Constantinople in 879 annulled the decisions of 867 and restored Bulgarian Church to Rome, but it did not materialize, as King Boris of Bulgaria did not agree to go back to Rome. The episode continued till complete reconciliation between the two Sees in 962, when Otto the Saxon revived the Western Empire with pre-eminence of German influence over Rome. This meant the permanent addition of *FILIO QUE* to the Creed, substantial increase of tourists to Jerusalem and a friendly attitude on the part of Moslems. Patriarch Eustathius in 1022 proposed a formula with the backing of Emperor Basil II allowing primacy to Rome and autonomy to Constantinople. The Pope was at first agreeable to the proposal. But the Cluniac monks objected to the parcelling out of the domain of St. Peter and the Pope withdrew his agreement. This estranged the relations between the Pope and the Patriarch.

The Byzantines returned to power in Southern Italy. This gave rise to resistance and revolts. When the people took arms against the Greek oppressors with the help of the Norman knights, the Pope looked on with little regret over the Norman victories, as they were Latin Catholics. But when they began to threaten Pope's own territories, the Pope preferred an alliance with the Byzantines. In 1043, Michael Cerularius has become the Patriarch of Constantinople. He was an arrogant and ambitious civil servant very popular among the people but not well-disposed towards the papacy. When the Pope insisted on Latin usages in Norman occupied territories in Italy, Cerularius ordered the Latin Churches in Constantinople to adopt Greek usages. When the people refused to comply with, he ordered to close them and ordered Leo, the Archbishop of Bulgaria to write to the Bishop of Trani in Southern Italy to denounce the Latin customs like use of unleavened bread in Eucharist. This letter was to be passed on to the Pope. When letter from Cerularius reached Pope, he was in an unfortunate mood and in honourable captivity. His Cardinal Secretary Humbert, perhaps due to his limited knowledge of Greek, translated the letter exaggerating its offensive tone. The Pope was outraged and when he was about to despatch a reply, a courier arrived from Constantinople with conciliatory letters from both the Emperor and the Patriarch. But, regrettably, Cerularius in his letter addressed the Pope as 'Brother' instead of the customary system of addressing as 'Father' and signed it as 'Ecumenical Patriarch'. The Romans misconstrued it as a claim of headship over the whole Church (The Bizantine use of the word *Oikoumene* only meant Empire).

Humbert, who had no love for the Greeks, played the tricks. He decided to send legates, drafted two letters to be carried by the legates, one to the Emperor and the other to the Patriarch. The one to the Patriarch condemned his title 'Ecumenical', took umbrage at his criticism of Latin usages and prayed that the legates would find him repentant. When the two legates, one Humbert himself, on their arrival were offended by the protocol of their reception, thrust the letter in the hands of Cerularius without even a greeting. Cerularius had a very high impression about Pope Leo as a courteous gentleman. He could not believe that such a man, especially in prison, would send such boorish legates or a letter like the one he received. He, therefore, refused to accredit the legates' authority or any dealings with them. The Emperor received them in a dignified manner. Humbert and his colleague strode into the church, laid in the altar a bull excommunicating Cerularius and departed after ceremonially shaking the dust off their feet.

The entire drama was a big humbug. Besides refusing the title of Patriarch to Cerularius, the bull accused the Greeks of purely absurd charges like simony, rebaptising Latins, baptizing women in labour, refusing communion to men who had shaven their beards and finally of omitting a clause in the Creed. To calm down the ire of the populace for showing favour to the Latins, the Emperor was compelled to burn the bull in public. A synod condemned the actions of the legates and anathematized Humbert and his associates. No word was mentioned about papacy, leaving the door open for the Popes to resume negotiations. Pope Leo passed away even before the arrival of the legates in Constantinople. Actually, the legates were doing things without authorisation. But, subsequent Popes followed the Humbert line. Gregory VII was a close friend of Humbert. They believed that Humbert had done the right thing in excommunicating an unrepentant bishop. The successors of Patriarch also did not seek absolution. By continuing to elect and support schismatic bishops, the whole Patriarchate of Constantinople was eventually included in the excommunication. As the Pope was in close alliance with the Normans, the Eastern Emperor found it advantageous to him to be close to Henry IV, the archenemy of Pope. In 1081, Gregory VII excommunicated Alexius, the Eastern Emperor. By the year of Gregory's death, the relations between the Eastern and Western Christendom were very much strained, but with no real schism.

Pope Urban II (1088-1099) was a statesman who was against strife and controversies. He lifted the ban of excommunication against the Emperor and resumed negotiations with the Bizantine Court. Alexius held a synod at Constantinople, found the name of the Pope omitted from the diptychs, the list of bishops and others worthy of the prayers of the faithful. (Throughout the controversy, both Rome and Bizantium were removing the names of their opponents from the diptychs.) Alexius proposed the restoration of the name of Pope if a gesture of reconciliation comes from the Pope. It never came. Things continued as they were.

Crusades Led to Schism

In 1095, Pope Urban called for a crusade at Clermont. One of his motives was to help the beleaguered Eastern Christians and thereby to dissipate the past ill feelings. But, the effects of the crusade were just the opposite. The Emperor and the crusaders seized the city of Antioch. When the Crusaders seized the city of Antioch, the Greek Patriarch was driven into exile and a Latin patriarch was installed in his place. Until this incident, the other Eastern Patriarchs were well disposed towards Rome than Constantinople.

The fourth crusade (1202-1204) resulted in another blunder, sealing a possible future rapport. The Crusaders, directed by Innocent III to the Holy Land, misled by some external forces promising rewards, proceeded to Constantinople, sacked the splendid city, not even sparing the churches. This outrage, which stamped indelibly in Bizantine memory, made the schism between the Latin and Greek Churches complete.

There were two later attempts to heal the wounds and plug the breach, one in the Council of Lyons and the other by Pope Eugenius in 1439 which reached the brink of success but failed when the Greek Church refused to ratify the agreement. After the Vatican Council II, some significant moves were made but still nothing tangible has been achieved. Let us be optimistic.[1]

These separatist churches not in communion with Rome were known as Orthodox churches. The doctrinal differences in the schism were not of a serious nature and therefore surmountable, once the Greeks agree on accepting the supremacy of Pope.

The churches not in communion with Rome, consequent on the schism are listed below:

The Patriarchal Church of Constantinople (the city is now known as Istanbul).
The Patriarchal Church of Alexandria.
The Patriarchal Church of Antioch.
The Patriarchal Church of Jerusalem.
The Church in the Cupros Island (once under Antioch).
The Church on the Sinai Mount (earlier under Jerusalem, later became independent in 1782).
The Russian Orthodox Church (became the fifth patriarchal Church in 1591).
The Church in Greece (Independent from 1850 onwards).
The Church in Bulgaria (Independent from 1870).
The Church in Serbia (Yugoslavia) (Independent from 1879).
The Church in Romania (Independent from 1885).
The Church in Gorgia.[2]

FOOTNOTES

1. Abraham, C.E. (Rev. Dr.), *Summary of Church History* (Mal.), pp. 192-93.
2. Thomas Bokenkotter, *Concise History of the Catholic Church*, pp. 120-26.

The Decline of the Papal Monarchy and Conciliarism

31

Decline of Papacy

As we have seen, Clement V transferred the papal court to Avignon in Southern France. He thought of it only as a temporary residence. But, due to several factors, the stay was prolonged for 73 years under seven Popes. At the accession of John XXII, Clement's successor, the Curia was disorganized, the apostolic treasury was empty and the independence of papacy was compromised due to the intrigues of King Philip. The Avignon Popes strove tirelessly to revitalise their authority and to make its influence felt in every corner of Christendom, but much of their work was undone by forces beyond their control. The Black Death, a fatal disease spread by black rats, decimated the population in Europe. The Freebooters ransacked the monasteries and convents. A dangerous rabble seized the Church property, defied all authority and preached revolution. In their efforts to govern the Church effectively, the Avignon Popes were hard-pressed for money. A series of taxes were levied on the bishops, clergy, abbots etc. This provoked wide criticism and resentment. The tax collectors were hunted down and thrown into dark prisons, mutilated and even strangled by the taxpayers. The Avignon Popes used the money for external pomp and resorted to harsh measures to squeeze money from defaulters. Several bishops, Patriarchs and Abbots were excommunicated for default of payment. With the money thus squeezed, they built massive palaces and decorated them without paying attention to the revival of devotion and spirituality. Escorted by two thousand men-at-arms, Pope Urban V (1362-70) entered Rome in 1367. When discord broke out in Rome, he returned to Avignon for safety. Urban's successor Gregory XI, realizing the damage likely to be caused to the papacy and the Church by the Popes keeping themselves away from Rome, also returned to Rome. But before accomplishing anything worthwhile he passed away on March 27th, 1378. By the time the Cardinals gathered in Rome to elect the next Pope, it was at crossroads. The big question before everyone was 'could the decline be arrested'?

A major factor in the origin of this 'Great Schism' was the part played by the people of Rome. The behaviour of the Romans followed a curious, unpredictable pattern. They are fickle-minded to undo what they themselves have done on the previous day. The absence of papacy resulted in a major loss of revenue from tourism for Rome. The death of Gregory XI shattered the hopes of Romans to revive the papacy in Rome. As French cardinals were in a majority in the Conclave, a Frenchman was likely to be elected and the papacy may again be shifted to Avignon, they feared. Sixteen Cardinals assembled on April 7th, 1378. Some of them were assaulted by bullies in the streets and warned to elect an Italian. The guard of the Conclave is reported to have told them "you risk being torn to pieces if you don't hasten to elect an Italian or a Roman".[1]

The cardinals quickly elected an Italian, the Archbishop of Bari, Bartholomew Prignano who was not one among them. While waiting for Prignano, the mob became impatient and restless and the Cardinals presented before the crowd, one among them duly dressed in papal robes, to pacify them. Prignano, the Vice-Chancellor of the Curia was a well-known person with dependable character. But, once he has become Pope with name Urban VI, there happened a sudden change in his behaviour. Seizing every opportunity, he upbraided the Cardinals for their vices, treachery, simony and luxury. Some historians attribute that the sudden change in his behavioural pattern would have been the result of the mental derangement caused by the unexpected election of him as Pope. Those Cardinals who elected him, who earlier claimed the election as free and unanimous, who paid their respects and submission to the new Pope, found it difficult to bear the ignominy any more. They took a decision to undo what they have originally done.

This decision brought forth a terrible catastrophe to the Church, utter degradation to the papal office and authority and led to a Great Schism. The Cardinals, thirteen in number, enlarged as sixteen by later addition of three Italian cardinals abandoned Rome, took refuge at Fondy and declared the election of Prignano invalid and elected a new Pope in his place, Robert of Geneva, who later took the name Clement VI. Two Popes at a time, something unbelievable happened – A Great Schism. The believing Catholics gazed with dismay and utter despair.

Here, politics played its role. The Holy Roman Emperor, England, the Netherlands, Castille, Hungary, Poland and Portugal stood behind Urban. France, Scotland, Austria and Luxemburg supported Clement, who returned to Avignon. Italy was too confused to be counted on either side. Aragon remained neutral. Urban proclaimed crusade against Clement and England invaded France to break the support to Clement. Both sides appealed to a decision of arms. Urban turned more violent and savage. Suspecting plotting by his own cardinals, he subjected them to inhuman torture, five of them died shortly afterwards, probably thrown overboard from Pope's warship. Urban VI died in 1389. His fourteen Cardinals immediately elected a successor who took the name Boniface IX.

This rupture of Church unity was a terrible trial for all believing Catholics. They were really pained on seeing the papacy made an object of derision. Saints, bishops and intellectuals on both sides offered several alternatives: arbitration, a general Council or resignation of both Popes. The idea of resignation was the one favoured in poll by the students in the University of Paris. Resignation was, at that time, considered the best solution. Hopes were stirred up when the Avignon Pope Clement died in 1394. Each of the candidates likely to succeed him swore an oath that if elected, he would be prepared to resign his office for the sake of unity. The one elected Benedict XIII, a prelate of incredible tenacity and guile, soon showed that he was not in a mood to honour his oath. In disgust, France withdrew officially its obedience to Pope Benedict. The King, Cardinals and Bishops tried in vain to persuade Benedict. They even laid siege to his palace. The indomitable and wily Benedict refused to bend a bit. After five years, France returned to his obedience.

Hopes were again renewed in 1406 with the election of Gregory XII, a pious and austere person, as the Roman Pope. He agreed to resign if his rival, the Avignon Pope, would do the same. At the same time Benedict had to face another move by his clergy to withdraw obedience to him. He realized that he could no longer appear less anxious than his rival for the reunion. Finally, both Popes seemed willing for negotiations to discuss their joint resignations. The venue of their meet was fixed as Savona, west of Genoa near the border of Italy and France. In the meantime, Benedict prepared secretly a military expedition to Rome. He moved upto Porto Venere. Gregory moved from Siena to Lucca. In short, both did not come close to each other. The attempt to bring them around a table miserably failed. The Cardinals on both sides felt that a General Council alone would be the best solution. The idea of a General Council was already there from 1380 onwards. The general consensus evolved was called Conciliarism; the basic principle was that in case of dire necessity a council could be called without the Pope's consent or even against his will and that its decrees would be valid without the Pope's consent. This doctrine of Council's supremacy was revolutionary inasmuch as it contravened the general tradition of papal supremacy over a Council. There was general agreement for the proposal all over Europe as the best solution, though it sacrificed the canon law of papal prerogatives. So, at the behest of cardinals of both allegiances, a mammoth assembly of churchmen including almost all dignitaries gathered at Pisa on March 25th, 1409. They acted out a ceremony of summoning the absent Popes to present themselves. After a pause, the Council declared both Popes as contumacious, schismatically heretics and guilty of scandalizing the Church and therefore deposed. The people reacted with wild joy and burned both Popes in effigy. Thereafter a new Pope was elected, seventy-year-old Cardinal of Milan, Peter Philagiri who took the name Alexander V.

A solution within hand slipped away like a mirage. Confusion confounded. A contention between two claimants has become a triangular contest. The new Pope Alexander did not even reach his See of Rome before dying at Bologna on May 3rd, 1410. His successor, who took the name John XXIII was an odd choice, a moral and spiritual cypher. John entered Rome behind an army on 12th April 1411. The first act he did was to summon a Council to meet at Rome. According to reports, a screech owl settled on John's head at the opening of the Council when he intoned the invocation "Come! Holy Spirit" and he was supposed to have muttered "a strange shape for the Holy Spirit". The Council was suspended due to lack of participants. It was becoming more and more clear that if unity is to be restored, John was not the proper man to do it.

The General Council of Constance (1414 AD)

At this juncture, Sigismund of Luxemburg, recently elected Roman Emperor, a man dedicated to the cause of unity of both the Church and Europe came to the scene. After some arm twisting, he persuaded John to call a universal Council of the Church to be held on 1st November 1414 at Constance, an imperial city chosen for its location and climate.

On Oct. 28th, 1414, a huge crowd of ecclesiastics from all over Europe filled the streets of Constance. According to one Chronicle, five patriarchs, twenty-nine cardinals, thirty-three archbishops, more than five hundred bishops, a hundred abbots, three hundred doctors of sacred sciences and eighteen thousand other clerics were present. John XXIII entered the Constance town on a white horse clad in the vestments of liturgy under a golden canopy followed by his cardinals amidst the hosannas of a jubilant fanfare. In his opening address, the Pope defined the objectives of the Council, unity and reform. Serious work began only after the arrival of Sigismund. The assembly was divided into conservatives and liberals. The liberals agreed that to restore unity, John must be put down and all the three Popes should be persuaded or if necessary forced to resign. John XXIII had deliberately stacked the episcopate with his supporters, thus controlling a large chunk of the votes. To pre-empt the nefarious design of Pope John, the Council changed the traditional voting pattern of 'one vote one bishop' to a system of 'one nation-one vote'. John, realizing that the Council had outmanoeuvred him, declared before the Council that he is willing to abdicate provided the other two Popes do so. John's statement was greeted with jubilation and Sigismund knelt and kissed Pope's feet. On March 20th under cover of night, John escaped from Constance, disguised as a groom, followed by a number of Council dignitaries and found refuge with the Duke of Austria. When the news broke out, the people were outraged and pillaged the papal palace. The Council might have dispersed at that point, but for the presence of Sigismund, who rode through the streets urging the people to remain calm and peaceful. Discussions were resumed. It was first resolved that the exit of Pope John would alter nothing. The fathers were not dissuaded by the conciliatory messages of John. They decided to continue the session till the Schism was fully healed. The Council passed a number of decrees, the most famous among them being *Sacrosancta* of April 6th, 1415 which asserted the superiority of the Council over the Pope, its power being 'directly from Christ and that all persons of whatever rank or dignity, even Popes, are bound to obey it in matters relating to faith and the end of the Schism and the general reformation of the Church of God in head and members...and that any person...even a Pope who contumaciously refuses to obey...be subject to condign penalty'. The humiliation of the papacy in all three of its claimants was indeed shameful. John found himself deserted by his protector and left to the mercy of the Council. He was taken back to Constance, tried by the Council, found guilty of numerous crimes and deposed. Gregory XII of the Roman line had a dignified end. He officially convoked the Council to formalize its legitimacy and then voluntarily resigned. The Avignon Pope Benedict XIII, the last among the trio, resisted the most heroic efforts of even Sigismund, remained adamant on his refusal to resign. The Council tried him in *abstentia* and deposed him. He took refuge in the fortress in Pensacola on the coast of Spain where his end came years later and his last surviving cardinal elected himself Pope.[2]

In the midst of this entire furore over John, another event occurred: John Huss, the Prague Reformer was burned at the stake on July 6th, 1415.

The next question before the Council was whether a new Pope need be elected immediately. Emperor Sigismund was of the opinion that reforms should take precedence to avert the possibility of a new Pope jeopardizing the reforms. Finally, a compromise was arrived at. The decree *Frequens* was passed whereby all future Popes should call regular Councils at stipulated intervals. A new method for electing the Pope was also devised. Six delegates of each nation – altogether thirty – were to participate in the election along with the Cardinals. Accordingly, Oddo Colonna, a prelate honoured by all for piety, wisdom and moderation was elected who assumed the name Martin V. Thus, the Great Schism was over.

The first objective of unity was achieved. The second objective of reform remained. The areas where reforms were necessary were identified:

the degradation of the papacy,

the exorbitant demands of papal tax collectors,

the breakdown of the Church courts,

the absenteeism of bishops,

the ignorance and the immorality of the clergy,

the widespread simony especially that of the Curia,

Excessive dispensations, and

Indulgences.

The abuses were identified, but agreement among various groups on the eradication of the abuses was a problem. As the Council failed to sort out matters, a vague and general decree was passed which limited papal powers, condemned simony and called for regularity in clerical conduct. Other reforms were left to the Pope to be carried out by means of Concordats with individual nations pointing out the German Concordat of 1418 as a model. This strategy later proved thoroughly inadequate.

The liberals were optimistic about the reform of the Church through future Councils. To achieve this, Pope and Council have to work together harmoniously. 'But, if that does not happen, what is the remedy?' The pessimists were asking. History vindicated the foreboding of the pessimists.

Pope Martin V

The new Pope took two years to return to Rome, which was then in a wretched condition. He concentrated his attention on Italian affairs. There he succeeded but he failed to reform the Church that was badly needed. This failure led to the later protestant Reformation. Many historians are of the view that this situation could have been averted, had Martin acted skilfully at the appropriate time. Two reasons are attributed for Martin's failure. First, he wanted to restore papal monarchy within the framework of limited Conciliarism. Second, he never wanted to carry forward the contentious spirit manifested in Constance. That is why he dissolved in 1424 the Council at Pavia-Siena, which he himself convoked in 1423, without accomplishing anything.

The Council of Basel

Eugenius IV, the successor of Martin was opposed to Conciliarism that could turn the absolute papal monarchy to a limited monarchy. He ratified the convocation of the Council at Basel but issued orders to his legate Cesarini in 1432 to dissolve it. Cesarini advised the Pope against dissolution but the Pope was adamant and rejected Cesarini's plea. The Council rejected the papal bull and carried Conciliarism to the point of absolute revolution. It went on with vengeance on the fiscal abuses prevalent in the Curia. The bishops swept away completely the right of the Pope to tax the clergy, to collect the annuals and to promulgate indulgences making the Pope a penniless figurehead depending upon the Council for finance. In 1433, the Pope retracted his acts against the Council and recognized its rights without any reservation.

At this point of time, the Eastern Emperor, besieged by the advancing Turks, was anxious to have Western support, opened negotiations with both the Pope and the Council on the reunion of the Eastern and Western churches. The choice of the venue for discussions became a bone of contention. This divided the Council members into groups opposing each other amidst wild scenes of disorder leading to hand-to-hand fight to seize the rostrum. Even in the Mass, the followers of each group faced each other like an army. It marked the beginning of the end of the Basel Council. Many bishops left in disgust and joined the Pope. Finally the Greeks accepted the Pope's suggestion to hold discussions in an Italian city. Cesarini deserted the Council on June 25, 1439. In defiance, the Bishops at Basel deposed Eugenius and elected their own Pope, Felix V, the last anti-Pope in history.

By this time, Eugenius solemnly concluded the reunion of the Eastern and Western churches on July 5th, 1429. This tremendous achievement was nullified as the Eastern Church refused to ratify the union. Finally the Holy See signed the Concordat at Vienna with Emperor Frederick and German Princes. The Emperor ordered the members of the Basel Council to quit Basel. Felix V resigned in 1449 and the Council was dissolved.

The papacy triumphed over Conciliarism but it failed to re-establish its moral and spiritual leadership over Christendom. In fact, the real victor was the Modern State. Resultantly, in England, France and Spain, national churches sprang up.

FOOTNOTES

1. Thomas Bokenkotter, *A Concise History of the Catholic Church*, p. 166, Para. 2.
2. *Ibid.*, p. 171.

The Reformation Movement

32

The Great Schism was a thing of the past, but its spiritual effects were subsisting. Conciliarism was put down, but papal authority could not recover fully from its disastrous effects, when Christians witnessed three men wearing the papal tiara, anathematizing each other. The papacy was not alone in trouble, the condition of the whole Church gave cause for alarm. Decay and degeneration encroached upon every level of Church life. The Roman curia, the top body in the Church pyramid was the worst affected. "The members were sick because the head was sick" it was said. Simony was at the heart of the entire curial system. The Popes had gained control of nearly two thousand ecclesiastical appointments and the sale of these jobs was a lucrative and necessary source of income of the Popes. These jobs were literally sold to the highest bidder. Even a Cardinal's cap was no exception.

Another practice odious to many was pluralism – the practice of conferring more than one ecclesiastical benefice of office on one person. This was simply a financial expedient – a means to boost the income of the Churchmen. Here also Albrecht of Bendenburg, the Archbishop of Mainz, holding two other bishoprics and a large number of rich Abbeys is a classic example. This practice by its very nature entails absenteeism. Some of these bishops had never seen their dioceses. The result was low morale and multiplication of abuses in the absence of authority to check them. In Germany, the percentage of resident pastors was awfully as little as seven, it was pointed out.

Another obvious fall out was the monopoly over high offices of the Church acquired by the nobility, which they often utilized for personal and worldly purposes. It became quite common for princes to have their younger sons appointed to bishoprics, which secured for them a style of living appropriate to their status.

The lower clergy were in no better shape. There was utter decay at every level; neglect of pastoral residence, accumulation of benefices and worldliness to the brim. The so-called 'mass priests', whose only work was to say daily mass, constituted ten per cent of the population in many cities. Preaching was conspicuously absent. Very often these priests were as ignorant and superstitious as the laity. Concubinage had become the order of the day. Clergy's training was an ignored item in the agenda of the Church.

The conditions differ much from country to country and order to order. In France, the after-effects of the Hundred Years War and the Black Death brought forth anarchy, which undermined monastic discipline beyond recovery. In Germany and Italy, the strife between the Pope and the Emperor and the Great Schism brought monasticism to the low ebb. Many monks obtained permission from Rome to live outside their monasteries. Those who lived within the cloister used their cells as their own personal property. Even very loyal Catholics like Ignatius Loyola and Thomas More were very much annoyed by the sad state of affairs in the Religious orders. Disorganization and decay affected every wing of the Church. To cap it all, there came the sale of indulgences for collecting money for the construction of St. Peter's Basilica in Rome.

Most Catholic leaders were aware of the situation and wanted measures to reform the Church. But the problem was how to achieve it. Many people favoured reform by General Council. Externally, the popes were concerned with papal grandeur. They wanted to make Rome a top centre of Renaissance and devoted their full attention for the artistic beautification of Rome. It is true that imperishable works of arts adorned Vatican, which remain even today. But, morally and spiritually, there was terrible decline everywhere. Papacy was immersed in corruption after the tenth century, especially during the periods of popes Sixtus IV (1484), Innocent VIII and Alexander VI (1503).

They actually bought the tiara and used it mainly for personal and dynastic interests, the college of cardinals was filled with relatives and ineligible candidates. The religious functions were subordinated to unworthy temporal motives. Pope Julius II (1513) made the papal states a leading power in Europe, but the methods adopted to achieve this end were dubious, sacrificing the integrity of the spiritual mission of popes.

Several suggestions were put forward for reform, the main suggestion with wide acceptance was to convoke a General Council. But after the failure of Basel, it was obvious that such a Council could be successful only under the leadership of popes. But, none of the popes in those days took the initiative to convoke a Council mainly because the Council of Constance was haunting the Popes. Even those Popes concerned about reform thought in terms of direct papal action, papal bulls or decrees or works through legates.

Even Pope Pius II, who himself was a conciliarist, tried to eradicate the idea of Council's supremacy over the Pope. He was a Pope sincerely committed to reform and he drew up a bull *Pastor Aeternus* based on the reform programme of Nicholas Cusa, but he died before it could be issued. Pope Leo X (1521) had no idea of the volcano under his feet and little sense of responsibility for the salvation of the souls. And nothing was actually accomplished.

Reform movements of the laity – The oratory of Divine Love which aimed at personal sanctity and good works, the attempts of secular princes to reform the monasteries, reform of the Spanish Church by Ximenes de Cisneros, the Archbishop of Toledo, the intellectual and artistic movement called Humanism which criticized old scholastic assumptions in philosophy and theology and dedicated themselves to reform through education and example – all were bright spots, but they could touch only the tip of the iceberg. A general reform of the Church could have succeeded only if it had reached the top and caught hold of the papacy itself. Unfortunately, this did not happen.

The pioneers of the Protestant Reformation Movement were John Wycliff, John Huss, Martin Luther, Ulrich Swingli, John Calvin, John Knox and several other religious preachers.

John Wycliff (1320-1384)

John Wycliff, known as the morning star of the Reformation Movement, was born in 1320 in Yorkshire in England, studied at Oxford, became Master of Balliol in 1361, professor of Divinity in 1372 and Rector of Lutterworth in 1375. He held strong antipapal views, he was condemned in 1382 as a heretic and his works were burned. His greatest work was the translation of the Bible from Latin vulgate into English. He was struck with paralysis on 29th December 1384 and breathed his last on December 31st that year. His remains were exhumed 31 years after his death and burnt and the ashes were thrown to River Swift, close by the town, as decided by the General Council of Constance in 1415.

When Pope Clement V issued notice to Edward III, the King of England for payment of the due tribute, Wycliff joined the King's side and parliament in refusing payment. Through his speeches and writings, he warned the Pope against ecclesiastical appointments in England, advised the Church leaders to lead simple life leaving aside lust for money and temporal assets. In the latter part of his life (1378-1384), he questioned not only the temporal powers of the Pope but also opposed certain rituals and teachings of the Church. He argued that Christ alone is the head of the Christian Church, intercession of saints is unnecessary, God alone can grant absolution of sins, auricular confession and absolution of sins by priests are absurdities, extreme unction has no scriptural basis, the basis of faith is not the Canon law of popes but the word of God alone and so on. Though he opposed the doctrine of 'transubstantiation' taught by the Church, he never agreed with the views of the subsequent reformists that the Eucharist is only a memorial. His view was that the presence of Christ is there in the consecrated bread and wine but it could be seen only through the eyes of faith. He sent 'poor priests' known as *Lollards* to all parts of England to propagate his reformist teachings.

The Oxford University banned the teachings of Wycliff. Many of his priests and followers were imprisoned. But the seeds of reform sowed by Wycliff lay dormant in England till the latter half of the 16th century.

John Huss (1370-1415)

John Huss, a Bohemian (Bohemia is the earlier name of the present Czechoslovakia) born in 1370, took his Masters Degree from Prague university; accepted priesthood in 1401 and one year later became the Rector of the university. He was very much impressed by the teachings of Wycliff and did much to propagate the views of Wycliff in Bohemia. In his speeches in the Bethlehem Chapel, he earned the support of the general public for his stand favouring the Bohemians in their strife against other sects in the Church. In 1412, he opposed the bull of Pope John XXIII granting indulgence to the people who take part in the war against the King of Naples. He argued that absolution of sins can never be earned by money and the Pope has no authority to subjugate anyone by force. This led to a revolt against the Pope's bull, which was publicly burnt by the people. Thereupon, Pope excommunicated Huss; he went underground and from there he published his book *De Ecclesia.*

In 1414, he was summoned to Rome through Emperor Sigismund for being tried by the Council of Constance. The Council found him guilty but Huss stood steadfastly in his views; therefore condemned, imprisoned, and later burnt at the stake as a heretic. Huss accepted the views of his teacher Wycliff that the word of God is the basis of faith and that the governance of the Church is not in consonance with the teachings of Christ. But he upheld the teachings of the Catholic Church on transubstantiation, intercession of saints and the Mass for the dead against the teachings of his master Wycliff.

Ulrich Swingli (1484-1531)

Ulrich Swingli, born in Switzerland in 1484, supposed to be the Father of the Reformation in his country, was a contemporary of Martin Luther in Germany. After early education at Basel and Vienna, he became a priest in 1519 in Zurich City. He taught that Bible is the basis of the faith and life of Christians and that traditions and teachings of the Church are not of equal importance to the Bible. When Luther was teaching against the Indulgence in Germany, Swingli taught the people of Switzerland against pilgrimages. The people of Zurich hailed and accepted his teachings. Gradually, it spread to the entire Switzerland. In 1522, Swingli severed his relations with the Roman Church and established a reformed Church in his country. He introduced several reforms like removal of the statues and images of Saints from the Church, stoppage of Mass for the dead, destruction of the remains of the saints, permitted marriage for the clergy, simplification of the ceremony of Last Supper, abolition of tithe for baptism and burial of dead bodies, compulsory reading and sermon on gospel as part of service and so on.

He passed away in 1531 at the age of 47. He is remembered in Church history as the first to establish a reformed Church, though confined to Switzerland, inflicting a severe blow to the mighty Catholic Church.

Martin Luther (1483-1546)

Luther was born in 1483 in Eisleben in Germany in a peasant family. After customary schooling in those days, he joined the Erfurt University, had his masters Degree in Arts in 1505 and earned proficiency in Latin, Hebrew and Greek. After a moment of panic during a terrible thunderstorm throwing him to the ground, he joined an Augustinian monastery at Erfurt as a novice. Even from early childhood, his disposition was deeply introspective and melancholy. The monastery he chose was a very strict religious house where he was bound to follow a severe routine of fasting, prayer, silence and study. As he continued with his study of theology, he became a victim of general depression, terrible trial and anguish of spirit with sudden spasms of terror and despair. In his own words, it was a torment so shattering that had it lasted even the tenth part of an hour; his bones would have crumbled into ashes. Day by day, he was becoming more and more conscious of his guilt and sinfulness strengthening the fear that the living God would punish and cast him into the hell at any moment. In extreme situations of agony, he cried out his hatred of God, which exacerbated his feelings of guilt. He wrote "For I hoped I might find peace of conscience with fasts, prayer, vigils with which I miserably afflicted my body, but the more I sweated it out like this, the less peace and tranquility I know." Later in life he interpreted his trials as the consequence of the defective nominalist theology he was trained in.

While intermittently suffering his agonies of spirit, he continued his study of theology and was assigned to lecture on Aristotle at the newly founded University of Wittenberg. In 1509, he began lectures in Erfurt. At this stage he began reading Augustine along with the Bible. This exerted a predominant influence on the later formation of his personal theology. He was again transferred to Wittenberg where he took his doctorate in theology. All along, he was confronting a question as to how one can love a God who punishes sinners, who stood before him as an avenging God as the phrase 'the Justice of God' (Rm.: 1:17) often reminded him.

The crisis was resolved when a kind of mystical illumination occurred which opened the "saving gospel" to him – the true meaning of Paul's phrase "the Justice of God". During the period of studies, he construed these words to mean the justice by which God rightly punishes the sinners. But, now he realized that it meant just the opposite. It is the Justice of God by which He justifies us through faith. When Luther juxtaposed the phrase "the Justice of God" with the phrase that follows in the same verse (Rm.: 1:17) "For the Justice of God is revealed therein, from faith unto faith as it is written. The just man liveth by faith." In other words, it is not through our merits that we are saved but through the unfathomable mercy and boundless generosity of God, who justify us in spite of our sins. Our part in the whole process is not active but only passive. With this doctrine of Justification by faith, he found confidence in the place of despair, that his justification was not his own holiness but the mercy of God, true faith henceforth included firm certainty of his own salvation. Even earlier, Luther arrived at this understanding while working on his commentary on

Psalms (perhaps Psalm 70 or 71). This remained the starting point of a distinctive theology that became the basis of all subsequent Reformation theology. This theology of Luther was something new, original and profoundly biblical. How much it is compatible with the Catholic theology is still a matter of debate. A catholic scholar recently opined that the real paradox of the Reformation was that until the Council of Trent, Martin Luther became one of the few theologians in Germany who uncompromisingly defended the biblical and catholic teaching of man's bondage to sin. Another Catholic scholar wrote a book indicating that Luther and Aquinas were in basic agreement in the matter of the believer possessing certitude of salvation.

According to Luther, 'God's Justice' means God's saving righteousness by which He extends to us in Christ the gracious gift of salvation, wherein human merit plays no role. Thus, there is no free will, the human will is always enslaved in sin. The question then arose was the usefulness of good works. Are good works superfluous, if faith in Christ and His righteousness have already justified us? Luther answers this question "The faith of none is so great that it cannot be or ought to be increased. Thus, for its increase, good works are to be done and bad ones avoided." Luther stresses the divine initiative and action in our works. We are the instruments of God.

This Lutheran theology stirred up controversies, but it was limited among the academicians and the intelligentsia. This had no impact on the public at large. It was only when Luther attacked the Church's system of indulgences, the whole world listened to him as it involved the life of everyone.

The sermons of Luther before 1527 indicate that he was fully aware of the state of affairs in the Church. Like many others, he complained about the avarice, simony and ecclesiastical robbery connected with appointments to high and low offices in the Church. For a man like Luther, a theologian with religious experience and spiritual responses, the Church practices of the day would have been an excruciating trial. The Church in various ways seemed to teach the opposite by putting excessive emphasis on the role of man in the work of salvation. Pope Clement VI sanctioned the view that Christ and the saints had left a treasury of merits that other members of the Church could draw on for the remission of temporal punishment for their sins. One could obtain a share of these merits by means of indulgence usually granted by the Pope in exchange for some good work, often donation of money, though doctrine insisted on the repentance on the part of the recipient. Later, the doctrine of indulgence was extended to the souls in purgatory. In practice, a door was opened to the unscrupulous to present an indulgence as a semi-automatic and easy means of salvation. What actually aroused the wrath of Luther was a particular indulgence for collection of money to rebuild St. Peter's Basilica. It was a deal concocted among the Fugger Banking firm, the Curia and the twenty-two-year-old Archbishop of Mainz who agreed to divide the proceeds. Albert, the Archbishop thereby hoped to pay the huge tax levied on him by the Curia for the dispensation he needed to hold three dioceses, Mainz, Madgeberg and Halberstadt. Johan Tetzel exclaimed to the crowds in sermons "Drop a few coins in the box, you can rescue the souls of your friends or relatives from the flames of purgatory."

Luther heard about the preachings of Tetzel and considered the indulgence as a licence to sin. On October 31, 1517, he sent the ninety-five theses in Latin to his own bishop and to the bishop who licensed Tetzel. (The general impression that Luther pasted the 95 theses on the walls of the Wittenberg Church seems to be a legend.) When the bishops failed to answer his questions, he published the ninety-five theses. He denied the power of the Pope over the souls in purgatory or to control the merits of Christ or saints. His aim was to challenge the interpretations of Tetzel and not to condemn them altogether. He only wanted to put them in the proper perspective and voice his pastoral concern about the spiritual dangers involved in such teachings. Luther feared that the people would believe that a payment of money could very well appease the wrath of God.

At first, Luther spoke as a loyal Catholic. When the controversy over his ideas erupted, he was prepared to submit them for the judgment of the Church. He never considered his theses as a revolutionary manifesto, nor did he treat it as an appeal to the nation. But, the tone and tenor of his arguments had an anti-Roman note with demagogic appeal. For instance, Thesis 50 reads "Christians are to be taught that if the Pope knew the exactions of the indulgence preachers, he would rather that the basilica of St. Peters were burned to ashes rather than built up with the skin, flesh and bones of his sheep." Thesis No. 82 reads "Why does not the Pope empty purgatory for the sake of holy love and the dire need of souls that are there if he redeems an infinite number of souls for the sake of miserable money with which to build a Church."[1]

A tragedy of the affair was that none of the opponents of Luther was prepared to meet him on theological or scriptural grounds. The Archbishop of Mainz was concerned only about the loss of income and not about the theology involved. Tetzel scorned off the invitation for debate. The occasion for a calm debate was furnished only by his fellow Augustinians at their chapter in Heidelberg on April 26, 1518 where Luther won over majority to his views. Pope Leo X, who was preoccupied with Italian affairs, was neither interested in theology nor aware of the seriousness of the affair. He treated it as another monk's squabble and turned a deaf ear to Luther's humble appeal of May 30, 1518. When the Pope was finally made aware of the gravity of the situation, he issued a summons to Luther to appear in Rome to answer the charge of heresy. Prierias, the private theologian of Pope, drafted the official document accompanying the summons. Instead of dealing with the abuses connected with indulgences, the document indulged in abusive tirade against Luther calling him 'a leper and a loathsome fellow, a dog and son of a bitch born to bite and snap at the sky with his doggish mouth' having 'a brain of brass and nose of iron'. But Luther enjoyed the protection of his ruler.

But due to some political factors, Rome was compelled to take a conciliatory stand. Cardinal Cajetan was instructed to meet Luther. It became a fateful meeting. They failed to diffuse the situation as Luther upheld the primacy of faith while Cajetan was upholding sacrament over faith. The dialogue ended in a deadlock. In the night, Luther slipped away. A few months later, he issued an appeal for convening a General Council. But Rome was still preoccupied with other political affairs and hence nothing tangible took place within the next two years. In this interregnum, Luther was involved in great public debate riding the crest of a deep wave of public support and enthusiasm. He hammered out a powerful alternative to the Roman ecclesiastical and sacramental system through sermons, pamphlets and debates that had an enormous appeal to the German populace. He argued that the existing Church was not a divinely founded institution but only a community, the origin of which was purely human and historical. This perspective questioned the divine authority of papacy and hierarchy and the distinction between laity and priesthood. In the debate at Leipzig in July 1519, John Eck, the German theologian cleverly managed to get Luther publicly admitting that he no longer believed in the divine origin of papal primacy or infallibility of General Councils. According to Luther, scripture alone was the supreme and infallible authority in religion, which later became the rallying point of Protestantism. After the report of several commissions of enquiry, Pope issued the bull *Exsurge Demine* on June 15th, 1520 which condemned 41 propositions of Luther as "heretical, scandalous or offensive of pious ears" without identifying the propositions condemned. Eck brought the Bull to Germany and found the populace ready to revolt if any attempt is made to squelch Luther.

Now, Luther made use of the newly invented Printing Press and addressed the whole German nation through three revolutionary manifestos *To the Christian Nobility of the German Nation, On the Babylonian Captivity of the Church* and *On the Freedom of the Christian Man.*

In the first one addressed to the *Nobility*, Luther enumerated the German grievances against the Curia and exhorted to end celibacy, masses for the dead and several other traditional practices. He was aware that reform could not succeed unless and until the powers of Pope were curtailed and therefore advocated limiting the spiritual powers and abolishing the temporal powers of Popes.

In the second manifesto *Babylonian Captivity*, he presented the outline of a church replacing traditional Catholicism by reformist ideas like common priesthood of all believers, rejection of apostolic succession and recognition of only two sacraments, Baptism and Eucharist. According to him, ordination was merely for providing 'order for the assembly'. Its appeal lay in its simplicity compared to the sophisticated and complex catholic system. To substantiate the system he visualized, Luther argued that the Gospel is simple, nothing to do with ritual and pomp differentiating between clergy and laity.

Movement Gathers Momentum

Gradually, the Lutheran thesis was taking shape. The new liturgy reflected his belief in simplicity. He stripped down the Catholic Mass to its bare essentials and made it understandable to the people by translating it into the local language facilitating participation by the whole congregation who were taught to sing new hymns composed by him. The congregation was invited to take in their own hand and receive the species, wine and bread. Sermon was the central feature of the service. In 1520, Luther, along with his students and well-wishers publicly burned Pope's Bull *Exsurge* and the copy of the Canon Law.

Now the Emperor decided to act to root out the heresy. Luther was summoned to the Diet of Worms on April 18th, 1521. But, in the presence of the Emperor and all the dignitaries, Luther refused to recant because "his conscience was held captive to the word of God". This militant posture of Luther was enough to burn Luther as a heretic as was done in the case of John Huss of Bohemia, a century before. But the Emperor Charles V found the Estates reluctant to concur with his views and therefore deferred a decision. By the time Charles took a decision, Luther absconded. The people hid him safely in a castle at Wartburg. There, he achieved one of his monumental achievements – the translation of the Latin Vulgate of the Bible into German. In spite of Charles' ban, the movement gathered momentum and spread like wildfire. The free cities of Germany were the first to opt for the new religion. The electors then followed. Though those who opted one side or other were motivated by different reasons, no one can deny the pre-eminence of the religious factor involved in the choice. But, for a long time, the lines were not sharply drawn. Some felt that everything could be settled once the ecclesiastical abuses were wiped out. Some others considered theological disagreement as the core issue. Yet others thought it as 'free will', 'baptism', 'indulgence' and so on. The Humanists were of opinion that unity could be restored if priests could be allowed to marry. Luther himself maintained that it is about the proper understanding of Christ. Papal primacy was the bone of contention within the Roman Church itself. The Bishops of Germany failed to give proper leadership in explaining matters to the people. Only a General Council could have clarified the position, but the Curia was dead against such a proposition. Lutheranised priests began to marry. New protestant congregations were set up which stood in opposition to the old parishes. Charles V was involved in the political affairs of Spain (1521-1530) and his absence helped the Protestants to consolidate their success. Another factor, which emerged from the Peasants' Revolt in 1524-26, was that political and military factors dominated in the debates. The most determined to defend the Church of Rome was Charles V, perhaps more than the Pope himself. An agreement was reached at Regensburg in 1541 when Catholics and Protestants agreed upon four main conclusions: marriage of the clergy, Real presence of Christ in the Holy Eucharist without defining the manner of transubstantiation, communion in both species and freedom from papal jurisdiction as distinct from papal primacy. But, the Pope did not yield. Political considerations played a part in the decision of the Pope, as he feared imperial power gaining supremacy over papacy. The failure of Charles' attempts sealed the schism, legally recognizing in Germany both Catholic Church and Lutheran Confessions.

Luther's ideas spread to the entire Europe and found a receptive audience everywhere. In fact, a settlement in favour of Protestantism occurred only where the monarch supported the new teachings. The religious polarization led to political divisions and conflicts. The *Schmalkalden League* of the

Protestant princes was formed in 1530 and the *Nuremberg League* of the Catholic princes was formed in 1538. Attempts for reconciliation failed. Finally, an agreement known as *Augsburg Settlement* was reached in 1555, which acknowledged the principle of "*Cujus Regio, Ejus religio*", meaning 'the religion of the ruler is the religion of the people'.

Reform in England

The Reformation in England is a classic example of the decisive influence of the monarch. Henry VIII of England was a staunch supporter of Catholicism. In spite of his schism with the Pope (Clement VII) over his divorce of Queen Catherine and marriage of Anne Bolin, he preferred England to remain Catholic true to the honour 'Defender of Faith' conferred on him by the Pope, for his treatise 'The Defence of the seven Sacraments'. But, under his son Edward VI, Protestantism enjoyed a definite triumph with Parliament's imposition of the *Book of Common Prayer* and *The Forty-two Articles* later reduced to *The Thirty-nine Articles* that form the basis of faith of the Church of England. Queen Mary Tudor (1553-1558) wanted to restore Catholicism but her reign was too short to achieve success. Her successor and stepsister Elizabeth was motivated more by political than by religious considerations. She devised a settlement of moderate Protestantism retaining much of the Catholic past including the episcopal system and blending the Catholic, Lutheran and Calvinist elements. Though the Reformists nicknamed 'Puritans' sought to cleanse the English Church of all they considered superstitious, idolatrous and popish, it retained vestments, sign of the cross, kneeling at communion and formal prayer. Attempts to introduce Presbyterian form of Church government were followed.

Under the Stuart Kings James I (1603-1625) and Charles I (1635-49) the strife between the 'Puritans' and the 'Episcopalians' became bitter. During Charles' reign, the puritans were discouraged and the anti-puritans were encouraged. William Land, the Archbishop of Canterbury undertook an aggressive campaign for the revival of the Catholic tradition. The Puritans were forced to conform to the old traditions under severe penalties. Consequent on this development, thousands of puritans fled to New England in 1630s.

These developments led to the formation of three groups within the Anglican Church, the Low Church party, the Moderate Churchmen's union and the High Church party.

The Low Church party follows the traditions of Thomas Cranner and the Archbishops of Canterbury like Mathew Parker, Edmund Grindel and John Whitegift. They considered John Wycliff as the model reformer, but followed John Calvin in theology. Evangelical teachings and puritanical lifestyle were their essential characteristics; episcopacy and priesthood not essential, ignore traditions and only symbolic value for the sacraments. The Tract Society, The Church Missionary Society, Young Men Christian Association, British Foreign Bible Society, Salvation Army and Methodist Movement developed in the group.

Moderate Churchmen's Union, who held radical views, objected uniformity in worship and theology and left the questions of divorce and birth control to the choice of the individuals.

The High Church Party is known as Anglo-Catholics. They follow Catholic doctrines except papal primacy and infallibility. Episcopacy and Eucharistic sacrifice were acceptable to them.

Presbyterian Church, Congregational Church, Methodist Church etc. emerged in the Church of England from the interaction between the Church of England and Protestantism, based on the teachings of Wycliff, John Knox and Calvin.

John Calvin

John Calvin, known as the architect of international Protestantism, was born at Nayon, France in 1509. In preparation for priesthood, he studied theology in Paris and thereafter turned to law and classical languages. In those days, Lutheran teachings were widespread in the entire Europe. But Calvin has claimed that his conversion to Protestantism was not prompted by Lutheran teachings but by his own experiences. He devoted himself to the task of setting up a new religion and thereby came to the forefront of the protestant movement in France. But, soon he found that espousing Lutheran ideas in a country under a Catholic King – Francis I – were a risk for his life, especially after the *Affair of the Placards* an episode which occurred in 1534 when a few protestant enthusiasts flooded Paris with posters denouncing the Mass were rigourously punished or executed. Calvin, therefore, took refuge in Basel.

In 1536, Calvin published the first edition of his book *Institutes of the Christian Religion*, a lucid handbook of protestant doctrines. Later, he translated his book into French and repeatedly revised and enlarged it. He always maintained that papacy was not based on scripture, but only a tyranny based on empty claims. One day, *en route* his return journey from Italy, Calvin accidentally met Guillaume Feral, the Protestant reformer in Geneva, who invited him to take part in the struggle to transform Geneva, a town with thirteen thousand inhabitants, into a wholly protestant township. He, therefore, undertook the task of creating a 'well ordered and regulated Church' in Geneva. A *Confession of Faith* to be signed by each citizen was accordingly drawn up. When Calvin and his followers demanded the right to enforce their discipline under penalty of excommunication, the Magistrates hesitated to accept the demand. Controversy on the right to use the baptismal font and some other issues were also hotting up among the people, leading to tension and turmoil. Ultimately, the civil authorities banished from the town Calvin, Feral and their followers. At this stage, Calvin went to Strasburg at the invitation of Brucer, an ex-Dominican Lutheran preacher. In the theology subsequently developed by Calvin, the influence exerted by Brucer was clearly visible. Calvin resided in Strasburg from 1538 to 1541. By this time, Calvin's supporters gained ascendancy in Geneva and he returned to Geneva to continue his unfinished mission. There, he presented and got approved by the General Council the blueprint of his project named *Ecclesiastical Ordinances* for the establishment of a reformed Church. In drawing up the ordinances, he relied on the organization of the Church envisaged in the scripture, establishing four offices, pastors, teachers, elders and deacons.

According to Calvin, strict discipline was the key to success and therefore entrusted the task of disciplining the community to a body called the *Consistory* made up of the ministers and the elders. They were charged with the responsibility of closely watching the behaviour of their fellow-citizens.

An unusual feature of medieval town-life was the regulation of the private behaviour of the citizens through legislation. Even trivial offences like laughing during a sermon, singing defamatory songs, dancing, frequenting a fortuneteller etc. were severely dealt with. Prostitution, a notorious feature of pre-Calvin Geneva was stamped out and death penalty was prescribed for adultery and actually imposed in several cases. Jacques Gruet, one of the Libertines who resisted the lifestyle imposed by Calvin was arrested, tortured, convicted and eventually beheaded. Another anti-Trinitarian, Michael Servetus, a physician was burned at the stake for heresy, at the behest of Calvin.[2]

In 1559, Calvin established the Geneva Academy to educate candidates for the ministry. It became a powerful instrument for the spread of Calvinism. His end came in 1564. The whole populace in the city followed his dead body with tears.

Calvin, the supreme genius of protestant theology, completed the groundwork for theological developments within most of the non-Lutheran protestant churches all over the world. He agreed with Luther on the basic principles – scripture alone as the sole source of saving truth, salvation by faith alone, the priesthood of all believers etc. But he disagreed with Luther on some other important points, Lord's supper, the Canon of scripture, predestination, Christology, sacraments etc. He was a vigorous and systematic thinker who maintained logical consistency in expounding his conclusions on Christian doctrines. He systematized his materials around biblical themes to give unity to the scripture without trying to resolve the paradoxes and logical lacunae found there. One of the serious allegations he levelled against the Roman Church was that it domesticated God. According to him, the God projected by the Roman Church was "a God, who could be summoned at clerical command, localised and dismissed by the chemistry of stomach acids". Against this, Calvin presented a hidden God who could only be found in the scripture if we read it with reverence, faith and love. God revealed himself in scripture only through Jesus Christ, who is the sole essence and content of its meaning. He argued that we could recognise the Word of God speaking to us in the scripture only through the interior witness of the Holy Spirit. Scripture testifies the all-embracing sovereignty of God who governs all things by his providence. Calvin always insisted on God's absolute transcendence, incomprehensible essence, unfathomable purpose and inscrutable decrees. According to him "Faith is a firm and sure knowledge of the divine favour towards us founded on the truth of a free promise in Christ and revealed to our minds and sealed on our hearts by the Holy Spirit."

Calvin always stressed that the Church is a divinely willed institution as the means to help the weak and infirm man along the path to salvation. The supreme Church is the invisible one made up of the totality of the elect but there is a visible Church also formed by the gathering of believers. Here, Calvin closely follows Luther. He totally rejected the Roman view that the Church existed only where bishop succeeded bishop, a concept which is too organizational, mechanistic and not concerned with purity of doctrine.

As regards sacraments, he attacked the Roman doctrine that sacraments conferred grace of themselves (*ex opere operate*). He stressed the importance of the faith of the recipient and the role of sacraments as a part of a personal dialogue between the believer and God. For Calvin, there were only two sacraments attested to in the scripture, Baptism and the Eucharist.

In his doctrine of the Eucharist, Calvin followed the theology of his friend Martin Brucer harmonizing the views of both Luther and Swingli, while Luther insisted on the objective real presence of Christ's body in the bread and wine (Consubstantiation) Swingli upheld only a memorial presence. Brucer favoured that the divine gift was given not *in* or *under* the bread and wine, but *with* the bread and wine, Calvin presented it with cogency and clarity. According to him the presence of Christ in the Eucharist was an objectively real presence.

John Knox (1513-1592)

John Knox was born in Giffordgate in Scotland in 1513, studied at Glasgow University, became a priest and went over to the cause of the Reformation early in his career. He learned Calvinism from the lips of his master John Calvin himself at Geneva. He joined a group of rebels, who after assassinating Cardinal Beaton, the primate of Scotland, occupied the castle of St. Andrews. The rebels were taken prisoners and Knox also had to be a slave in a French Galley for nineteen months. After Mary Tudor's death in 1559, Knox and others returned home. The withdrawal of English and French troops by the Treaty of Edinburgh in 1560 and the death of Regent Mary of Guise allowed Knox and his band of reformers to persuade Parliament to favour reformation ideas. *The First Scottish Confession*, a reproduction of Calvinist doctrines was passed by the Parliament in 1560. Till 1647, it remained the confessional standard of the reformers. Queen Mary Stuart who ascended the throne of Scotland wished to undermine Knox's work, but she herself was imprisoned for the murder of her husband. Therefore, Calvinists continued their work under the leadership of Knox. Though Knox died in 1572, Calvinism succeeded completely in Scotland with a Presbyterian system of Church government in accordance with *the Ecclesiastical Ordinance* prepared by John Calvin.

Conclusion

There cannot be two opinions on the necessity of reform in the Church as the abuses and decay in the Church was so widespread at all levels from top to bottom. The Popes who were to take action failed to take the initiative in time. The Church has become a pilotless ship at the time of crises. Martin Luther provided the infrastructure and John Calvin built upon it a new Church called Protestantism. As historian Jedin says "The Protestant Reformation owed its success to the fact that the attempt at reform which sprouted from the soil of the

Church did not come to maturity". The result was a vertical split in Christendom.

On the other side, the principle 'Scripture alone' was not sufficient to maintain a consensus. Consequently, Protestantism had to admit that it was a divided house. In the subsequent centuries it gave birth to innumerable denominations with no uniformity in faith or practice. Actually only three or four types emerged in the beginning, the Lutheran, the sectarians or radicals that would include the Baptists, Quakers, the anti-Trinitarian and rational Pietists and finally the Calvinists. Further branches sprouted from each of them, fighting one against the other presenting before the non-Christian world a dilapidated Christianity.

Only Germany and Scandinavia preferred Lutheranism. Most of the other countries accepted Calvinism or some thing close to it. John Calvin ranks with Luther as one of the giants of the Reformation who provided Protestantism with a theological exposition of faith, systematic, logical and cogent. Calvinism was also not immune to the later shocks. No one today accepts it as a complete system.

The world cannot deny that Calvin's contribution to Christian life and thought has been one of the highest orders. Half of Europe was lost to the Roman obedience and the unity of Christendom has become a thing of the past, a fading memory.

Reformation provided a brighter side for the Catholics. An interior and spiritual renewal occurred within the Catholic Church during the sixteenth century that made it once more a sturdy spiritual household. Luther, Calvin, Swingli and other reformers intensified and ignited the feeling of urgency of reforms, the necessity of which was already prevalent in the Church for some time past. A careful study of Luther makes it clear as daylight that Luther, at the initial stages, never wanted to split the Church. He wished reform within the Church. But his appeal to Pope and other Church leaders fell on deaf ears as a cry in the wilderness, leading him to preside over a split. His dream was accomplished, of course, at the cost of the unity of Christendom.

FOOTNOTES

1. Thomas Bokenkotter, *A Concise History of the Catholic Church*, p. 193, Para. 2.
2. *Ibid.*, p. 204.

The Church Regains Spiritual Elan

33

From the very beginning, the Catholic Church had to confront many crises. It survived Roman persecution, mystery religions, heresies, papal schism and even eastern schism. But the quake caused by Lutheran revolt was the most devastating and the worst crisis ever faced by the Church. Half of the Church in Europe severed obedience to Rome. Many priests and nuns deserted their cloisters. The unity of Christendom became a fading memory. The Church stood dumb founded by the effects of the shake all over Western Christendom.

Even during the pre-Lutheran period, there was uproar from all quarters demanding reform in all branches of the Church. The clergy and the laity initiated some localized efforts. Ximenes de Cisneros in Spain, Oratory of Divine Love, an organization of half laity and half clerical in Italy, another similar organization named *Samaschi* in Venice, Ignatius Loyola and his followers (later known as Society of Jesus) in Paris, Gian Matteo, the bishop of Verona, Capuchins, Franciscans. Theatines (an offspring of the Oratory) under Giana Carafa (later Pope Paul IV) were all pioneers in the reform process in the Church. They all succeeded in their respective localities in giving a new thrust for awakening in the areas of liturgy, preaching, monasticism, social apostolate and other allied branches of Catholic life. The fact that the later General Council held at Trent incorporated verbatim all these items in the legislation of the Council testifies the success of their endeavour. Similar groups soon spread throughout Italy. A small group under Gaspar Contarini, a Venetian took root even in the Roman Curia, the target of very serious allegations.

These were pointers to the realisation of the depth of degeneration and the intensity of the need for reforms. These localized efforts, though successful, did not bring about any tangible result in the Church as a whole.

The General Council of Trent

The problems facing the Church – doctrinal confusion, fiscal abuses, organizational breakdown, widespread ignorance – were of too grand a scale to be tackled at the parochial level. A General Council alone was the remedy. But, the tragedy is that the Church took twenty-eight years after Luther's first cry for reforms, to convene a Council. Several obstacles stood in the way of convoking a Council, viz.: the nightmare of Conciliarism, opposition of anti-reformists in the Curia, the hostility of the German Princes and the political rivalry between France and Spain. Pope Leo X excommunicated Luther in 1521. Popes Adrian VI (1522-23) and Clement VII (1523-34) who succeeded Leo X did not dare to convoke a Council.

Pope Paul III who ascended the throne in 1534 took 11 years to overcome the obstacles and convene a General Council at Trent in Italy in 1545. Within the span of 24 years between 1521 and 1545, the whole Christendom was vertically split into two, the Catholic Church and Protestantism. It took eighteen years for the Council of Trent to complete its work though it was in session only for a little more than three years. The interlude between the second and third sessions was ten years for different reasons, prominent among them being the attempt for a reconciliation between the Catholics and protestants through dialogue and the attitude of Pope Paul IV who ascended the throne in 1555 preferring direct papal action to a Council. The next Pope Pius IV alone succeeded in reassembling the Council in 1562.[1]

The Council first addressed itself to sort out the doctrinal confusion and to set right the breakdown at the organizational level.

On the Lutheran theory of 'justification by faith alone', the Council ruled out men's total corruption by original sin and asserted that justification was not by faith alone, but also by 'hope' and 'charity'. It was also clarified that charity ought to be expressed in good works carried out by the co-operation of the human will with God's grace.

Again, contradicting the Lutheran contention that scripture alone as basis of faith, the Council declared that both scripture and tradition are required to determine the faith of the Church. With regard to other Lutheran arguments, the Council asserted:

The divine validity of seven sacraments.

The hierarchical structure of the Church.

The divine institution of priesthood.

The traditional teaching on transubstantiation.

The sacrificial character of the mass.

The Council reaffirmed the papal supremacy, throwing to the winds the ghost of Constance. While submitting the decrees for the assent of the Pope, by entrusting the pontiff with the task of completing the remaining items of reforms, the papal authority was further emphasized and unambiguously acknowledged. Another major decision of the Council was that it placed the bishops in absolute control over their dioceses. Thus, a new structure of church government, authoritarian and centralized, was shaped with an autocratic Pope at the top with autocratic bishops under him.

The setting up of a commission to reform the mass was another epoch-making decision of the Council. The medieval mass has become a theatrical-type spectacle, the faithful having no sense of participation. As the liturgical books were handwritten ones, local variations and abuses were prevalent. The celebrants indulged in their own eccentricities, simony (priests hawking the mass) and superstitions (celebration with specified number of candles to guarantee desired benefits etc.). The protestants were vehemently opposing these abuses. The Commission finished its work very quickly and the *Missale Romanum* was issued in 1570 whereby the priests were obligated under penalty of mortal sin to adhere to even the minute prescriptions. The allegorical mass was thus replaced by rubrical mass. It was highly effective to secure a uniform religious expression in the whole Church. The question of participation of the laity was left untouched.

Another important decision of the Council was the establishment of seminaries for the training of priests. It was stressed that such training should be fully traditional, paying no heed to the advancement in biblical studies by humanists.

A critical analysis of the Council reveals that it was extremely conservative, narrow-minded and orthodox in its approach, especially on the doctrinal issues. The liberals were not heard. The tradition was re-emphasised sealing any compromise on protestant views. A sharp line of demarcation was drawn between the Catholic and protestant teachings. It seems that the Council was overwhelmed by a feeling that no room for victory should be given to the Protestants and that any concession or compromise with them would be against the claim of divine authority by the Catholic Church. The use of the vernacular in the mass, successfully introduced by the Protestants, was not attempted. Regarding the participation of the laity, the medieval mass remained unchanged. To feel involvement in the mass, the laity were to engage themselves in some extra-liturgical devotions during mass. In the new set up of Church government also no role was assigned to the laity. The changeover to the rubrical mass overthrew the myth of unchangeability of the Catholic mass. Many Catholics found it difficult to agree with the Council on doctrinal issues.[2]

Conservative but Positive Results

Despite criticism, the Council of Trent produced many positive results. The Council acted as a tool to provide clarity, stability and universality to the catholic doctrines. By redefining the key doctrines of the Church, the Council served as a propellant to bring the whole Church into the path of reforms.

By acknowledging the supremacy of papacy, the Popes became sincerely dedicated to proceed with the reforms dictated by Trent to their logical conclusions. Without the dynamic leadership of Popes, reforms would have remained mere aspirations. The steps taken by three subsequent Popes – Pius V, Gregory XIII and Sixtus V – which we will deal later, shows the relentless endeavour on the part of the Popes to set up a high standard of papal morality and to push the reform process throughout the Church. Consequently, all levels and branches of the Church came under the grip of a reform mania.

The Trent Council viewed the reform of the bishops as the key to the reform of the entire Church. Their authority was strengthened with a view to enable them to deal with abuses effectively. The bishops were asked to reside in the dioceses, and not to leave without permission. The medieval abuses like absentee episcopate and dualism were put a stop to. They were entrusted with the responsibility of preaching regularly, visiting parishes, holding annual synods, building seminaries, ordaining as priests only worthy candidates after rigorous scrutiny, overseeing discipline in convents and other religious houses, rooting out concubinage among priests and giving good personal example by their own dress, charity and modesty.

Strict vigil in the selection of candidates for priesthood, intensive training through seminaries, vigorous action against concubinage, plugging loopholes for abuses through the standardization of mass, regular visits to parishes by bishops with authority, annual synods at the diocesan level and the personal example of bishops – all these have, in a very large measure, contributed to reform the clergy and free them from abuses and superstitions.

Though the aspect of participation of laity was overlooked, the reform of the mass had a very positive impact throughout the Church. The message of reform was seen and felt by every member of the Church. Devout Catholic laymen began receiving communion once a week and confessed sins frequently rather than once in a year as practised in the medieval Church. Many bishops and priests began daily celebration of the mass. The Eucharistic piety was extended to many non-liturgical practices like adoration of the host, benediction and forty hours. Tridentine spirituality became sacrament-centred on the Eucharist. This reformed Mass continued without any change till 1960s.

The decree on justification emphasized the importance of charity and encouraged a meditative form of mental prayer. Under the leadership of eminent masters like Ignatius Loyola, Francis de Sales, Vincent De Paul, Scupoli De Berulle and others, a practice of meditation developed and was used by the Church as an instrument to reform the clergy and the laity. The new spirituality produced vigorous men and women whose impact was strong enough to give rise to new schools (Bratorian, Saletian, Carmelite etc.).

The first and greatest among the Reform Popes was Pius V (1566-1572) an ascetic and a man of prayer who transformed Vatican into a monastery. He was previously a renowned Inquisitor. He threw himself into the work of reform with tireless energy, published the *Roman catechism* and the revised *Roman Misal (Missale Romanum)* and cleansed the curial bureaucracy. By heroic determination, he succeeded in all his efforts.

Pius V's successor Gregory XIII (1572-1585) was not an ascetic like his predecessor. His contribution to the world is the revised calendar (1582). With the help of Charles Borromeo, he was committed to reforms and appointed a committee consisting of four reform-minded cardinals to implement Trent's decrees. Gregory's successor, Sixtus V (1585-1590) was highly energetic and a man with big ideas. He unleashed ruthless measures against bandits who infested the Papal States. A report in 1585 shows that there were 'more heads of bandits exposed on the St. Angelo Bridge than the melons in the market'. At the same time, Sixtus was not so severe in crimes against faith. He appointed as cardinals only men of sterling qualities. By the reorganization of the Curia, he gave the Church a centralised and uniform administrative structure that is retained throughout modern history.

The instrument used by the Popes for the Catholic reconquest was Inquisition supported by the congregation of the Index (periodical publication of the list of condemned books). All heresies were suppressed, especially in Italy and Spain. Archbishop Curranza of Toledo was kept in prison for seventeen years on mere suspicion of heresy shows how severely repressive was the Inquisition. Intolerance and repression were not confined to the Catholic Church alone. It was prevalent in Protestantism as well.

Another institution of singular importance in the success of the Catholic reform was the Jesuit order. No single Catholic did more than its founder Ignatius Loyola to offset the devastating effects of Lutheranism. He gathered a small group of men around him in Paris and induced them to take vows of chastity, obedience and poverty, thus creating a force that would help transform the Catholic Church and shape its history in the succeeding four centuries. He was a God-intoxicated soul, a mystic with unique genius for conveying his own love of God. Canisius, a Jesuit known as the second Apostle of Germany, was another multifaceted genius. He published *Catechism* to match various levels of age and education. The new spirituality that embraced the Church produced a sizeable number of saintly men and women like Philip Neri (Oratorians), Teresa of Avila and John of the Cross (Carmelite order), Francis De Sales (Visitation sisters), Vincent De Paul (congregation of the Missions and the sisters of charity), whose works exerted tremendous impact in the revival of the Church.[3]

The Post-Trent Church

The revitalized spirituality of the Post-Trent Church manifested in an imposing theological and intellectual revival associated with the Catholic Universities of Salamanca Rome, Paris and Louvain. The result was a new awakening and renaissance in theology creating interest in Thomas Aquinas (*Summa theologiae*), Robert Bellarmine (*Disputationes du Controversiis Christian Fidei*) and Francis Suarez (Commentary on Aquinas), symptomatic of the renewed spiritual energy in the Church.

Another visible sign of renewed spirituality is the work in overseas by the missionaries. Catholic priests accompanied the explorers who opened up a new era of Europe's relations with the outside world. Prince Henry the Navigator's pioneering explorations in Africa resulted in the establishment of Catholic missions in Africa. Columbus carried missionaries to America and there the missions flourished by the conversion of all of Central and South America. The gospel was brought to the Far East and Franciscan John of Montecorvino was sent to

Peking (China) as Archbishop in 1307. But the hostility of the ruling Ming dynasty and the Black Death in Europe dashed the hopes. In 1498, Vasco de Gama reached India. With the conquest of Goa in 1510, the Portuguese gained control over the Arabian Sea. Significant gains in evangelisation work were achieved through St. Francis Xavier who reached India in 1542. His successors Robert de Nobili and Martyr John De Britto continued the work. The most successful missionary effort in Asia was in Philippines, where eighty per cent of the population is now Catholics. The success of the missionary efforts in the East was facilitated through the Padroado whereby Pope Leo X granted the following rights to the monarch:

To present candidates for ecclesiastical benefices.
To erect and maintain churches, monasteries and institutions.
To maintain the clergy, the bishops, priests, seminarians etc.
To provide all necessary accessories to the above mentioned.
To send clerics abroad for missionary works.

In 1622, the Pope established the Congregation for the Propagation of the faith (*Congregatio de Propaganda Fide*) striking down the royal patronage, which exploited the missionary movement for political purposes.

By 1563 when the Council of Trent ended, Protestantism held sway over half of Europe. This trend was later reversed. The upsurge of a new vitality in the Catholic Church under a regenerated papacy and the enthusiastic Jesuit Order recaptured large blocks of territory. Poland came back to Catholicism. Large parts of Germany, France and Southern Netherlands were restored to communion with Rome. After 1563, the Protestants achieved no significant gains. The Catholic Church made good the losses in Europe by the gains in America, Africa and Asia. The demarcation of territory between the Catholic Church and other Christian denominations was settled for the next three centuries. It may be noted that three most populous countries in Europe excluding France – England, Sweden and Prussia remained Protestant. But the Catholic Church recovered its spiritual élan and became a strong, self-confident and spiritually revitalized organization.[4]

FOOTNOTES

1. Thomas Bokenkotter, *A Concise History of the Catholic Church*, pp. 215-16.
2. *Ibid.*, p. 217, Para. 2.
3. *Ibid.*, p. 221, Para. 2.
4. *Ibid.*, p. 226, last para.

Renaissance and French Revolution

34

The vigour of the Catholic Reformation exhausted by the middle of the seventeenth century. Both the Catholics and the Protestants settled down for an uneasy truce. The seventeenth and eighteenth centuries were a period of advancement in Science and Technology, with far-reaching consequences. This led to three revolutions:

Revolution in thought and perspective of man known as 'the Enlightenment'.

The Industrial Revolution started in England that spread to other European nations.

The French Revolution during the close of the 18th century.

The Enlightenment

Copernicus (1473-1543) published his thesis in Astronomy entitled *Revolutionibis Orbium Celestium* wherein he claimed that the Sun is the centre of the solar system and that the earth and planets circle around the Sun. This work was dedicated to Pope Paul III and accepted by the Church. Copernicus favoured a Sun-centred universe. This theory postulated the fantastic notion that the seemingly static earth was moving around the Sun at a predetermined time-frame.

Galileo (1564-1642) in 1613 published his treatise supporting the Copernican theory of the universe and invented a practical telescope to prove his claim. Copernicus rejected the idea of the earth as the centre of the universe held by the medieval thinkers, based on the observations of Aristotle (384-322 BC) and Ptolemy. Brilliant minds like Kepler, Galileo and Newton supported Copernicus revolutionizing our understanding of the universe on Copernican lines.

Galileo Adamant

The reaction of the Catholic Church to modernity had always been negative. It was often unable to confront the freethinkers on their grounds. A state of siege-mentality became the characteristic of Catholicism and therefore the Church frequently, to meet challenges, resorted to condemnation of new ideas and repression. The new cosmology originated with Copernicus terribly threatened the Church, as it would undermine the doctrinal framework based on the Aristotelian and Ptolemaic astronomy. The Church condemned Galileo, banned the teachings of his ideas and imprisoned him by inquisition on charge of challenging the age-old traditional faith of the Church. Galileo in his letter to Castelli said:

> "The authority of the sacred scripture has as its sole aim to convince men of those truths which are necessary for their salvation.... But that the same God who has endowed us with senses, reason and understanding should not wish us to use them and should desire to impart to us by another means knowledge which we have it in our power to acquire by their use – this is a thing which I do not think I am bound to believe."

The 'Enlightenment' germinated from this cosmology. It is a movement that advocated rationalism – a new approach to life based solely on human reason towards everything including religion, philosophy, theology etc. Immanuel Kant says "have courage to use your own reason – that is the motto of 'Enlightenment'." Rene Descartes (1650), the founder of the movement of critical rationalism applied to philosophy the mathematical method proven effective in Science. The seventeenth century physicists accepted nothing as true until it was established beyond all possible doubts. Descartes' principles of doubting everything was extended to every aspect of Christian tradition and questioned the very idea of tradition itself.

Religious Freedom

Another major source of conflict between the Enlightenment and the Church was the issue of religious freedom. The idea of unity of religion as basis of social order was very strong both in the Catholic and Protestant Churches. Bodin's idea that religious unity was not a necessity to maintain social order was not acceptable to the Church. The individual was not free to worship God as he saw it. Even presumably progressive countries like England in 1660 and France in 1685 revoked the privileges to the individual.

The philosophers of the Enlightenment devoted their energies to fight for religious freedom. Their main argument was that one's religious commitment was of a personal nature because religious truths are not susceptible to objective proof as in the case of scientific truths. Therefore, coercion is evil as it destroys personal choice, the essence of a religious commitment, they argued. Diderot said, "The mind can only acquiesce what it accepts as true. The heart can only love what seems good to it, violence will turn a man into a hypocrite if he is weak and into a martyr if he is strong.... Teaching, persuasion and prayer – these are the only legitimate means of spreading the faith."

The churches had little sympathy for these ideas of religious freedom and autonomy. The Catholic Church, with a high degree of centralisation and efficiency, proved to be more adamant and successful in detecting and suppressing heresy. It was, therefore, looked upon as the bastion of bigotry and intolerance, more than other churches. Closely connected with this issue came the development and material progress of community life. The findings of Isaac Newton created a new confidence in the power of reason and a feeling that the evils of superstition, fanaticism, dogmatism and unreason need be conquered to gain happiness, so far denied to them by vested interests and archaic institutions.

Another bone of contention was the teaching of original sin, the Christian answer to the age-old problem of human evil and wickedness. The enlightened philosophers opposed this contention as repugnant to commonsense and to reason. In their view, man is born naturally good and with powers of reason. These qualities in themselves, if properly used, would assure natural happiness, they contended.

The advocates of the new secular faith questioned many of the sacred tenets of the Christian Church such as nature of man, the source of evil, the rights of individual conscience, purpose of life and the very idea of revelation. The Deists found their way in some sort of Unitarianism and laid stress on the reasonableness of Christianity. They dismissed revelation as superfluous and pleaded for a 'natural' and 'reasonable' religion, one that is simple and sufficient for humans. An orderly universe planned, built, and set in motion was enough to demonstrate the existence of God. The religion evolved by them was basically rational theism, combined with a radical criticism of the Bible. In the name of Enlightenment, Voltaire, a stinging satirist in France, declared war on the Church by his savage attack on its dogmas, ethics, traditions, clergy, the Trinity, the chastity of Virgin Mary, the presence of body and blood of Christ in mass, morality etc. His work *Dictionnaire Philosophique*, an antichristian *Summa*, was burned in Genoa, Netherlands and France. In 1762, the Pope suppressed the Jesuits. This doomed the prospects of a positive relationship with the Enlightenment.

The Abbe de Peres presented at Sorbonne University in Paris a thesis for a degree in theology supposed to be a summary of arguments in defence of the Christian revelation. On scrutiny, it was found that it was actually a comprehensive attack on the dogmas of the Church. When Sorbonne, the highest seat of learning in theology in those days, was found contaminated by the theory of rationalism, a public uproar exploded. Gradually, Enlightenment was growing into an irreconcilable movement against Christianity. Till the eve of the French revolution, it was not sure whether the Church had lost the battle against rationalism. But enthusiasm aroused by the Enlightenment was found confined to a restricted section of the general public only.

Jansenism

Cornelius Jansen, the bishop of Ypres and a professor at Louvain University wrote a book *Augustinius*, published only after his death. He questioned the authority of St. Augustine (354-430), (the African bishop philosopher accepted as the authority of Church's philosophy) in expounding theories on the nature of original sin, human freedom and the nature and efficacy of God's grace. This led to a violent debate in France. A papal commission was appointed at the request of the French bishops. On the basis of the findings of the commission, Pope Innocent X in the Papal Bull *Cum Occasione* in 1653 condemned as heretical five propositions of Jansen. This did not end the affair. The nuns of the Convent of Port Royal under the leadership of Antoine Arnould refused to capitulate.

The Jansenists evolved a pessimistic theology. They held that without the total help of Grace, man remained totally depraved, all his actions were wicked and even his pretended virtues were vices. Grace was available only to those predestined, all others are doomed to eternal punishment due to lack of Grace. The Church favoured the Jesuit theology that human efforts counted for something in the work of salvation. The mathematician and inventor Blaise Pascal in his masterpiece of satire, the *Provincial letters* devastatingly attacked the chief enemy, Jesuits.

Finally, the Jansenists were asked by King Louis XIV and Pope Alexander VII to sign a statement renouncing their errors. After extreme pressure, they agreed for a 'respectful silence' regarding the accuracy of the papal bull. However, Pope Innocent XI seemed to have some inclinations towards the Jansenists. He condemned sixty-five propositions drawn by Jesuit moral authors and appointed De Noailles, a sympathizer of Jansenism, as Archbishop of Paris. In the meantime, Quesnel, successor of Arnauld, published a book *Reflexions Morals* reaffirming all Jansenist tenets.

The next Pope Clement XI was not favourably disposed towards the Jansenists. He launched the bull *Unigenitus* condemning ten propositions of Quesnel. The King drove the nuns out of Port Royal and levelled the convent to ground. The reaction brought about a deep division in the French Church. Nearly sixteen bishops led by Cardinal Archbishop of Paris and a large number of clergy refused to submit. They claimed that a papal bull was infallible only when it had the assent of a General Council of the Church. Later, Cardinal De Noailles retracted in 1728 and the number of dissenters came down substantially by 1760.

Gallicanism

Gallicanism is a movement that agitated the Church in the seventeenth and eighteenth centuries. The word is derived from the Latin name 'ecclesia Gallicana' meaning the 'French Church' but the movement was not confined to France alone. It reflected the general trend among all European governments to subordinate the Church as a department of the State; a tight union of Church and State with the Church as the junior partner. Gallicanism opposed Roman papal centralization and the interference of the Pope in the national churches. It stood for dignity and independence of the bishops and strictly limited authority for Pope over temporal rulers. They held that infallibility is theologically for the whole Church and not personally for the Pope. As such, a General Council should express infallibility and papal decisions claiming infallibility are subject to the assent or ratification by the Council.

In the latter half of the seventeenth century, Louis XIV was the King of France who led France to the pinnacle of European power. He unilaterally extended the traditional royal right of *Regale*, empowering the King to administer and appropriate the revenue of a diocese and also for appointing bishops till the election of a new bishop. Many decisions of the King were in flagrant disregard of the Canon law of the Church. The Pope at that time was Innocent XI (1676-1689) an austere, unworldly and scholarly person who was loved by the people for his piety and generosity. The Pope issued a brief to the King condemning his action and demanding to repeal the right of *Regale*. At first, the King dragged on the issue. When the Pope insisted under threat of excommunication, the King summoned an assembly of the clergy that lasted from Oct. 30th, 1681 to May 9th, 1682. The Assembly formulated the notorious *Four Articles*:

- Denying the authority of the Pope over temporal affairs,
- Reasserting the validity of the decrees of Constance which affirmed the superiority of the General Council over a Pope,

- Making the authority of papal decrees conditional on their acceptance by the Church, and
- Rejecting the separate infallibility of the Pope.

The King ordered to teach these articles in universities and seminaries as official doctrine of the Church. In the eyes of Rome, the Assembly overstepped the limits of its authority by teaching matters that belonged to the General Council. The Church also suspected heresy in teaching matters against the accepted theological stand of the Church. The rift between France and papacy continued till the death of Pope Innocent XI in 1689. After his death, a compromise was worked out, whereby the teaching of *Four Articles* was stopped but Pope yielded to *Regale*. Pope Innocent paved the way for the later acceptance of 'Infallibility of Pope' by the General Council of Vatican I in 1870 establishing eventual victory of papacy over Gallicanism.

Febronianism

Gallicanism appeared in Germany under the name of Febronianism in 1790 through the writings of Nicholas Von Hontheim who wrote under the pseudonym of Febronius. The archbishops of Cologne, Tier, Mainz and Salsburg met at Bad Ems and issued a declaration of episcopal independence from Rome. This declaration was on the lines of Febronius' programme. But, the declaration failed to rally the support of German bishops who preferred Roman yoke to the archbishops' yoke.

On the whole, eighteenth century was one of great challenges for the Church. The 'Enlightenment', Jansenism, Gallicanism and Febronianism encroached upon the traditional rights and prerogatives of the Church. The secular governments also played their part. The rulers of Spain, Austria and France exerted heavy influence in papal elections. They blocked by veto any candidate unfriendly to their interests. The result was election of compromise candidates. Eight Popes ruled from 1700 to 1800 were mediocre personnel, the only exception being Benedict XIV.

The suppression of the Jesuits, the section with absolute loyalty towards papacy, was a great blow to the Church in confronting the freethinkers. France in 1764 banned the Jesuits. Portugal and Spain drove them out. Earlier, in 1715 Pope Clement XI condemned the mission strategy of the Jesuits compromising with pagan rituals and customs in China. Pope Benedict XIV reiterated this in 1742. The enthusiasm of the Jesuits to defend the Church and papacy at any cost landed them in trouble alienating the sympathies of many sections, even the Franciscan and Benedictine orders. In the election of Pope Clement XIV, the promise to suppress the Jesuits was a condition and in 1769 the Pope suppressed the Jesuits. Consequently, the Jesuit General was thrown into prison, nearly six hundred of their religious houses were destroyed, hundreds of schools were closed and over twenty thousand priests and brothers were uprooted.

Thus, due to several factors, the scholastic controversy over the nature of grace, the decline of the papacy's vigour, the suppression of Jesuits, the failure to come to terms with scientific truths and new philosophies, set back in missionary efforts, decadence of religious orders and above all the failure of the Church to keep pace with the fast changing world, there occurred a spiritual and intellectual debility in all spheres of the Church. By the end of the eighteenth century, the intelligentsia in Europe regarded the Church as an anachronism in a world moving towards profound transformation.

The Industrial Revolution

The invention of Ark Wright's spinning frame, Kay's weaving loom, Watt's steam engine, Stephenson's locomotive, Macadam's roads, Brindley's Canals, Telford's bridges etc. led to an Industrial Revolution in England. It spread to all countries in Europe in the nineteenth century leading to economic prosperity and emergence of a capitalist class at the expense of the labour. The oppression and exploitation of the labour prompted Karl Marx to publish his treatise, the famous *Das Capital* visualizing a new social order under the dictatorship of the proletariat. It was put into practice in Russia through another political revolution in 1917, known as the Bolshevik Revolution.

The French Revolution (1789)

The French Revolution was the climax of the 'Enlightenment'. The long despotic rule of the Bourbon Kings in France claiming 'Divine Right' to govern the country, the success of the American War of Independence in 1776, the writings of rationalist writers like Voltaire and Rousseau, the development of Science and technology, Gallicanism and Enlightenment – all these have created in Europe, especially in France, a new awakening among the people. A social order created by the union of the Church and the State that lasted for nearly thousand years seemed destined to continue for a long time more. The new awakening enkindled the hopes of the people for the creation of a new social order based on Enlightenment under a rational and responsible Government. For this, the existing social order has to be dismantled. The revolution in thought and perspective was to be applied to the social and political spheres. This urge for change was not confined to France alone. This awareness was prevalent in almost all areas of Europe. But, France has become the laboratory to test the change due to the peculiar situation prevailing there at that period of time.

In the eighteenth century, despite internal decay, the Catholic and Protestant Churches were outwardly prosperous and powerful and very much an integral part of the old social order. The clergy has become a State within the State with undue privileges and power. The Nobles were a part of the Government. The clergy and the Nobles together, the beneficiaries of the existing social order resisted any change that would be detrimental to their interests. The French Revolution began as a non-violent political experiment to reform the French Government and the creation of a new social order.

Demand for New Social Order

Louis XVI, the King of France (1776-1793) in 1789 summoned a meeting of the States General, the representative body of the people consisting of one thousand two hundred elected members, to discuss some financial crisis of the nation. Once gathered, the six hundred commoners, called the Third

Estate, demanded a new social order based on the political and economic ideals of the 'Enlightenment' – a movement that advocated rationalism, a new approach based on human reason to every aspect of life in the light of the advancement in Science and Technology.

The King and the Nobles naturally resisted the demand for a new social order based on the 'Enlightenment'. Thereupon, the deputies questioned the 'Divine Right' of the King to govern the nation and demanded to share power with people's representatives. The King alienated public opinion by engaging in treacherous plots to suppress the movement with the help of mercenaries. This triggered a non-violent political movement to turn into a widespread and bloody revolution eventually resulting in the formation of a revolutionary army called the National Guards, the establishment of a Republic and the fall of the Bastille. Louis lost his popularity by supporting the Emigrant, his attempts at flight and negotiations with the enemies. He was shut up in the Temple, arraigned before the Convention, condemned to death and guillotined.

As an integral part of the old social order, the overthrow of monarchy was bound to affect the Church that enjoyed a privileged position as the only form of Christian public worship allowed in France. Its nearly hundred thousand clergy which formed the First Estate were enjoying several privileges and rights. The laymen in the National Assembly at first showed no animus towards the Church. They agreed to recognise the Catholic Church as the official form of public worship, even though they, against the wishes of the Catholic Church, accorded civil rights to the Protestants and the Jews. Though the Church was officially in favour of the old order, majority of the clergy in France was in favour of the Revolution and willing to part with their privileges. This divided the clergy into two groups, one supporting the Revolutionist constitution known as the 'Constitutionalists' and the other loyal to the Pope known as 'Non Jurors'. But the leaders of the Revolution blundered into a quarrel with the Church and resultantly the Revolution turned into a movement for 'Dechristianisation', aiming to wipe out Christianity.

The Dechristianisation Movement

The Dechristianisation was bent upon removing all vestiges of Christianity. With this end in view, the Gregorian calendar was replaced by a Republican calendar, a ten-day-week was put in the place of the seven-day-week, all Christian holidays were cancelled, a new 'Cult of Reason' was introduced and the cathedrals and churches were turned into 'Temples of Reason'. Fouche, a bloodthirsty ex-priest took up the leadership of the campaign of Dechristianisation. His inauguration of the campaign itself was by unveiling a bust of Brutus in thc Church of Saint Cyr at Nevers. Wherever he travelled, he turned the churches into temples of Reason and pressurised the priests to marry. He presided over ceremonies that caricatured the Christian liturgy. Many priests and bishops abandoned the ministry, some of them taking wives to prove their break with Orthodox Catholicism. Many constitutional priests went into hiding. By 1794, the Dechristanisers had achieved a large measure of success. In the hysterical blood bath, three bishops and two hundred and twenty priests lost their lives. Another twenty thousand priests put aside their cassocks and many of them married.[1]

Napoleon Bonaparte

In this melee of destruction, turmoil and lawlessness, a Corsican Army Commander named Napoleon Bonaparte by a *coup d'état* came to the forefront as First Consul and later as Emperor of France. Dechristianisation spent its force by 1794 and by a Decree in 1795, free exercise of any religion was allowed resulting in a rush to reopen the churches. When the Church was about to be revived, Napoleon's Italian campaign began in 1796. He occupied Milan and set up a number of Republics in Italy. At first, he spared Rome and by a Treaty at Tolentino recognised the sovereignty of Pope over the Papal States. But in 1797, a Corporal of the Pontifical Guards assassinated a French General. In retaliation, Napoleon sent the French troops to Rome and took Pope Pius VI as prisoner. Fearing that the Austrians might rescue the Pope, the French General Berthier was asked to take the Pope to France. The eighty-one-year Pope could not bear the rigours of the journey. On the way, he expired at Valence. The Conclave for the election of a new Pope held at Venice under the protection of the Emperor of Austria elected a Benedictine Bishop named Chiaramonti who assumed the title Pius VII, a man with right combination of qualities to meet the crisis in the Church.

Napoleon unleashed a series of wars against adjoining nations causing terror among the entire people of Europe. In 1802, an agreement between Pope and Napoleon was signed at Notre Dame Cathedral with pomp and fitting celebrations. This ended the schism between the constitutional and non-juring clergy and the Church was recognised as 'the religion of the great majority of the Frenchmen'. The chief points of the Concordat were five:

All bishops, both constitutional and non-juring, were to hand over their resignation to the Pope.

The First Consul had the right to name the bishops and the Pope had the right to institute them canonically.

The Church would not seek to recover its alienated property.

The clergy would derive their income through salaries paid by the State.

The practice of the Catholic religion would be subject to whatever police regulations required for public order.[2]

Napoleon was an adventurous Army Commander and a shrewd and ambitious politician. The last Article in the Concordat was the one that he had in mind to control the Church. He gained it. In Goethe's phrase, he liked to think himself as the rightful heir of all that was "reasonable, legitimate and European in the revolutionary movement". Napoleon's code did embody the essential elements of the Revolutionary programme, the right of the individual to choose his profession, the supremacy of the Lay State and tolerance for all religions.

The relations between papacy and Napoleon soon became strained. Napoleon induced the Pope to attend to his coronation as Emperor to show to the world that the papacy that condemned the Revolution has bestowed its blessings for the

Empire, but the Pope refused. When Napoleon wanted the Papal States to join in a blockade against England, the Pope did not concede to his request. Pius VII also refused to institute any bishop for France. Consequently in 1814, many dioceses in France were headless. When the Emperor seized the Papal States in retaliation, the Pope excommunicated Napoleon. To seek revenge, he arrested the Pope in 1808 and kept him a prisoner for long six years in France. The Pope stood steadfast on his principles, leading the life of a monk in humiliating captivity, spending time in reading and prayer.

Though Napoleon won many wars, he was defeated in the war against Russia in 1814. When he found his enemies encircling him, he made a virtue of necessity and released Pope from captivity. The Pope returned to Rome for a tumultuous welcome. In 1815, Wellington defeated Napoleon at Waterloo. He abdicated the throne and was exiled (or retired) to St. Helena and died there in 1821.

The effect of the Revolution was very much beneficial to the Church, though it suffered severe damage. The heroic stand of Pope Pius VII enhanced the papal image. The churches were reopened. The revolution shattered the ancient monarchies and freed the Church from servitude to Gallican monarchs who placed their stooges on the throne of St. Peter. In the subsequent years, the clergy became ultramontane (a term used to emphasize the authority and leadership of Pope) looking to Rome for leadership. The overseas missions were revived under Roman command. The Church came back to its true spiritual mission. The old order of Popes ended. The Rule of Bourbon dynasty was restored. The common people who never abandoned the Church came back to faith. The alliance between the Church and the State, continued from the period of Constantine, was coming to an end. The Revolution was in fact a blessing in disguise; all sufferings being the price paid to rescue the Church from its enemies.

The Church in the Aftermath of French Revolution

After the disappearance of Napoleon, in the nineteenth century, we see the emergence of a new era in Church history witnessing a full-scale revival, a spiritual and intellectual renaissance making the Church a vital and vibrant institution and a dynamic force in the modern world. Several factors facilitated this transformation.

The French revolution miserably failed to achieve its aims. The autocratic monarch Louis XVI was executed. In the place of the King, the French people obtained as ruler a despotic Emperor in Napoleon who impoverished the nation with incessant wars.

The Bourbons came back. Movements like Jansenism and Gallicanism, the offshoots of the 'Enlightenment' generated some hue and cry but faded away as a cry in wilderness. A new social order based on the Enlightenment remained a dream of a few people.

The 'Cult of Reason' was the imagination of a few eccentrics. The sponsors of the 'Cult' failed to present an alternative to Christianity. Some hysterical destruction was the sole result. Dechristianisation never percolated to the grass-roots level of the Church. It disappeared like a mirage.

The heroic and principled stand of Pope Pius VII against the mighty Emperor Napoleon exalted the position and image of papacy, re-emphasizing the leadership and authority of Pope – a strengthening of Ultramontanism. The humiliating end of Napoleon was a lesson to other monarchs, who thereafter never attempted to subjugate the Church and papacy. The Fascist ruler Benito Mussolini in Italy, the Nazi leader Adolf Hitler in Germany and the Communist leader Joseph Stalin in the Union of Soviet Socialist Republics in the twentieth century desired to subjugate or even to annihilate the Church but refrained from open confrontation to lead their aspirations to logical conclusions. They preferred to confine themselves to duel of words and some action within their own territories in the form of persecution and hostile rules and regulations.

The re-establishment of the Society of Jesus in 1814 followed by the establishment of new religious orders such as Marianists, Marists, Christian Brothers, Sisters of Charity, Sisters of Laureto, Paulists, Salesians, Society of the Divine

Word and White Fathers provided the key to the renewal of the Church by engaging in a variety of social and pastoral ministries, education and missionary work. To crown all these efforts, the Society of Foreign Missions was also revived in 1815.

These do not mean that the Church survived the Revolution unscathed. A feeling of anti-clericalism, civil marriages, civil divorce and secular educational system existed as scars on the body of the Church as remnants of the Revolution. On the political side, an urge to end absolute monarchy came to the fore all over Europe. Some advocated limited monarchy, the majority demanded people's representative governments. All these movements earned a certain amount of success, visible in the change of the political spectrum of the countries in Europe by the end of the twentieth century. The reforms introduced by Napoleon, known as "the Napoleanic Code" became the blue print for all reforms in the social and economic fronts in France in the post-Napoleanic era.

Intellectual Liberalism

As a result of scientific developments, the Enlightenment, the French Revolution and the changes in the political sphere, a new awakening took shape in the realm of thought in the Church. Many brilliant thinkers and writers within the Church demanded the Church to abandon its siege-mentality and to come out to the open for a more positive relation with the liberal secular culture. 'Liberalism' is the term used for the movement favouring change and establishment of a new order. In the political sphere, they demanded constitutional or representative governments in the place of monarchies, religious tolerance, the separation of Church and State, freedom of press and freedom of education. Later, the liberals wanted to apply the ideas of liberalism to the faith of the Catholic Church. They called it intellectual liberalism. The liberals joined the Nationalists demanding liberation for 'oppressed' and 'enslaved' people. With the advance of industrialisation, 'economic liberalism' also came to the fore, practically hostile to trade unions. Because of their opposition, trade unions were recognized in England only in 1871 and peaceful strikes were allowed only in 1906. Lamennais, the champion of Ultramontanism (emphasis on the authority and leadership of Pope) advocated political liberties as a way of freeing the Church from political allies. In England and Germany, a group of Catholics, supposed to be intellectual liberals, desired that the Catholic faith be examined and presented in the light of modern philosophy, scientific advances and new method of historical studies. Some German scholars sought the renewal of the Catholic theology. They looked upon the Church and Church doctrine not as static and unchanging but as dynamic, alive and developing like the human body. In England, Lord John Acton and John Henry Newman (a leader of the Oxford Movement aimed at Renewal of Anglicanism who later embraced the Catholic Church and became a Cardinal) shared the demand for a new approach to catholic theology that emphasized Catholic tradition and openness to new avenues of thought. A section of Catholics opposed political liberalism as they feared a recurrence of anarchy and chaos similar to the French Revolution. Liberalism succeeded in Belgium and South America to bring in representative governments replacing autocrats. Pope Gregory XVI (1831-46) in his encyclical *Mirari Vos* (1832) condemned the ideas of liberalism. On condemnation by the Pope, Lamennais, a staunch supporter of political liberalism, deserted the movement, but the liberal Catholics did not abandon the idea. Montalembert took over the leadership of the movement. They adopted a pragmatic stance and sought to avoid a confrontation with the papacy on theoretical grounds. Montalembert organized a catholic political party to secure liberty for the Church in education. Frederic Ozanam, a devout liberal Catholic founded the Society of St. Vincent De Paul to aid the poor.

Pope Pius IX (1846-1878)

Pope Pius IX ascended the throne of St. Peter in 1846 and adorned the throne for long 32 years, the longest period of a Pope in papal history. He was reputed to be something of a liberal and his election caused jubilation for the liberals and alarm for the opponents of liberalism. In the beginning, the

Pope lived up to the reputation. He issued general amnesty to the prisoners, gave the laymen a share in the government of the papal States, subject to veto by Pope, included a form of *Habeas Corpus* in the constitution and abolished political press censorship. Liberals all over Europe hailed these reforms with enthusiasm. In fact, he was not in favour of liberal ideas or freedom of religion within the Church. The steps taken by him as regards papal States were only due to political compulsions.

A mishap occurred which altered the situation altogether. Pope's parliament declared war against Austria to bring the papal States into alliance with the Italian movement for liberation and unification of Italy – *risorgimento*. The Pope was opposed to a war against Catholic Austria. He, therefore, vetoed the decision of the parliament though he was very much sympathetic towards the cause of Italian unity. It was an unpopular decision resulting in fury to run wild in the streets of Rome. An assassin stabbed Pope's Prime Minister. A mob in frenzy surrounded the papal palace making the Pope a virtual prisoner. Pius IX in the guise of an ordinary priest escaped and found lodging in a second class hotel. Guiseppe Garibaldi, the leader of the liberation movement entered Rome and set up a democratic republic. Giuseppe Mazzini inaugurated a new religion of humanity and progress. But the French and the Pope chased out these unorganized democrats on 12th April, 1850. The Pope with the bitter experience of liberalism resolved to show no more leniency towards the liberals.

The worst was in store. The liberals in the meantime took over the northern Italian State of Piedmont. Camillo Cavour, the Prime Minister enacted a number of laws against the Church, abolished most of the religious orders and stripped the Church of control over education. His aim was to seize the papal States leaving to the Pope the city of Rome alone. He engineered a series of uprisings to move the army under the pretext of maintaining law and order. The Pope attempted to resist the military action but failed. A settlement offered by Cavour was not acceptable to the Pope, though it contained several conditions similar to the one accepted seventy years later by the Church in the Lateran Treaty.

The Pope·decided on a policy of intransigence, spared no efforts to recapture the papal territories and declared war on the secular liberal concept.

Syllabus of Errors

The *Syllabus of Errors* was the final and emphatic 'No' by the Pope to the liberals and the liberal Catholics. But, before recounting that chapter, another aspect of the liberal Catholic movement – their quest for more intellectual freedom in the Church – has to be examined. Intellectual freedom became an important issue in the debate between the liberals and the conservatives in the Church. Germany being the only country in the world with theological schools located in secular universities, the Catholic community there kept themselves in touch with scientific developments and therefore strongly felt the need for the Church to face realistically the problems raised by the modern culture. The issue of intellectual freedom was vigorously debated among English Catholics under the leadership of Lord Acton. He earned the support of Henry Newman who occupied the centre stage of the Church of England in the eighteen thirties and forties. Newman never fully subscribed to Acton's view but he was sympathetic towards the basic view of liberalism that faith must reconcile with modern culture as far as possible. The *Syllabus of Errors* of Pius IX appeared on December 8, 1864 accompanied by an encyclical *Quanta Cura*. The syllabus listed eighty errors including rationalism, naturalism, and socialism that would subject the family to the State and liberal capitalism that had no motive other than material gain. Condemnation of the freedom of religion, progress and liberalism were included in Error No. 77 that read "It is no longer expedient that the Catholic religion should be treated as the only religion of the State, all other worships whatsoever being excluded." Error No. 80 reads "The Roman Pontiff can and ought to reconcile and harmonise himself with progress, with liberalism and with modern civilization."

This resulted in a public commotion unparalleled in the history of the Church. Gregory XVI issued *Mirari Vos* when the sentiments of the majority in Europe were conservative and reactionary, but *Syllabus* struck against the mainstream of public opinion. Even the average Catholic was shocked to hear the Pope condemning progress and modern civilization. Moreover, the formulations in the *Syllabus* were ambiguous providing much scope for misinterpretation. The word 'civilization' actually meant a system to weaken or overthrow the Church. But, the people took it as war declared by Pope against modern world. On this occasion, a French bishop Felix Dupanloup came to the rescue of the Church by publishing a commentary of the *Syllabus,* explaining the context in which the particular phraseology was used in each Error. The liberal Catholic movement was not completely wiped out by the *Syllabus* but it was checked. But due to the interpretation of Dupanloup, they could not be stamped as heretics. The sponsors of Liberalism became more prudent enough not to invite the wrath of the Pope with its own consequences. The liberal Archbishop of Paris. Darboy issued an appeal to the Pope "you have just...condemned the principal errors of our time. Now, turn your eyes towards its honourable and good features and give them your support...for it is your duty to...reconcile liberty with authority."

The proclamation of the dogma of Immaculate Conception on December 8, 1854 was a distinct triumph for the Ultramontanes as the whole affair was dramaticised to declare the authority of the Pope.

Ultramontanism

In the 19th century, the authority and influence of papacy were enhanced considerably. Many factors favoured the development of this ultramontanism. Political conservatives considered papacy as a bulwark against liberal and revolutionary ideas. The heroic stand of Pius VII against Napoleon considerably enhanced the prestige of papacy. Clergy who lost their properties and privileges due to the Revolution found Pope alone as their protector from the interference by the Lay State in their affairs. Priests who suffered persecution for loyalty to Pope came out openly in favour of strengthening papacy. According to the Concordat of 1801, the Bishops were asked to submit their resignation to the Pope demonstrating the authority of Pope over the episcopate. The same Concordat allowed unlimited authority for the bishops over the priests leading the priests to see the Pope alone as the safeguard against the arbitrariness of the bishops.

A new feature developed in modern Catholicism on account of this neo-Ultramontanism is a 'personal devotion to Pope'. This enthusiasm for things Roman and the Pope got out of the track developing idolatry to the papacy. One bishop has gone to the extent of claiming that God was incarnate in the Pope. The extremists in this neo-montanism attributed infallibility to every statement of the Pope.

This ultramontane movement had no strong opposition except from the German theologians and the French bishops led by Doellinger, the leader of the German intellectuals and Bishop Maret, a theologian of repute in the Episcopal bench and Darboy, the Archbishop of Paris.

Vatican Council I

In 1867, Pope Pius IX announced his intention to call a General Council. The general impression was that the Council would be for ratifying the hostile stand of the Church towards rationalism. But, the Pope wanted the Council to discuss two issues: (1) The relation between faith and reason, and (2) the question of primacy (governing authority) and the teaching on the infallibility of the Pope.

The Council passed two constitutions: (1) *Dei Filius* which spoke of the ultimate authority of God's revelation and taught that nature and reason are subordinate to grace and faith, and (2) *Pastor Aeternus* which taught that when the Pope speaks *ex cathedra* (literally meaning 'from the chair' of Peter) that is, speaking in his office of Chief Shepherd of the Church and as the successor of St. Peter, he is granted by the Holy Spirit the gift of infallible truth when he formally defines a doctrine concerning faith and morals. This does not, in fact mean that whatever the 'Pope says is infallible, although non-Catholics in general and many Catholics misunderstood this to mean that even the ordinary teaching of a Pope is true and infallible.

In 1870, the Vatican Council I came to an abrupt end due to the outbreak of the Franco Prussian War. Emboldened by the acts of the Council, Pius IX continued his policy of intransigence towards modern secular liberal culture clearly showing that he was not prepared to adapt the Church to the profound social and political transformations taking place around him. At the time of his death in 1878, the Church was left virtually in a state of war with the rest of the society.

The real success of Pope Pius IX was in the realm of interior renewal of the Church. He deserves the credit for the exemplary leadership he gave for deepening its piety and spirituality. He revitalized the old religious orders. The Jesuits, the Dominicans, the Franciscans, Saint Sulpice, Brothers of the Christian Schools, the Passionists, the Redemptorists, the Benedictines, the Cistercians, the Trappists and Carthusians – all filled their monasteries with vigour and new recruits.

Recently, Pope John Paul II initiated steps for the canonization of Pius IX that gave rise to some hue and cry in the different corners of the Church.

Pope Leo XIII (1878 to 1903)

Pope Leo XIII, the successor of Pope Pius IX was not a liberal, but a diplomat who realized that the only way to prevent the Catholic Church from appearing as a foreign element in the modern world was to arrive at conciliation with the modern world and learning. He took a series of steps in this direction during his papacy spanning twenty-five years.

In order to promote the Church in England, John Henry Newman, who was previously suspected as a dangerous liberal, was made a Cardinal.

Instead of denouncing the errors of democracy, he always behaved as a friend of democracy and constitutional governments. He supported the French Republic.

He opened up the Vatican archives to researchers and encouraged Catholics to pursue studies to blend Catholic theology with biblical criticism.

In 1879, he declared the theology of St. Thomas Aquinas to be the standard for judging all Catholic theology and philosophy.

Reconciliation with Modern World

Pope Leo in his encyclical *Rerum Novarum* (1891) demanded Justice and better living conditions for workers and exhorted Catholics to take active role in providing constructive solutions for the problems of injustice brought about by the Industrial Revolution. This encyclical is the first in the line of social justice. To commemorate the 40th Anniversary of *Rerum Novarum*, Pope Pius XI issued the encyclical *Quadragessimo Anna* (1931) highlighting the development of a social philosophy initiated by Pope Leo. Pope John XXIII celebrated the 70th Anniversary of *Rerum Novarum* by issuing the encyclical *Mater et magistra* (1961) which emphasized the developments in social thoughts after the days of Leo. In another encyclical *Pacem in Terris* Pope John XXIII outlined the conditions for peace among nations. Pope Paul VI in his encyclical *Populorum Progressio* focused the problems of underdeveloped countries and urged wealthier countries to discharge their responsibilities to alleviate poverty. Pope Leo initiated the necessity of the Church to devote its attention to social justice.

Pope Leo established the Indian catholic hierarchy in 1886 through the promulgation of the Bull *Humane Salutes* creating six archdioceses (Agra, Bombay, Calcutta, Madras, Pondichery and Verapoly) and ten dioceses (Allahabad, Cochin, Coimbatore, Hyderabad, Krishnagar, Mysore, Pune, Quilon, Tiruchchirappally and Visakhapatnam). In 1887 Pope established the Vicariates of Trichur and Kottayam for the Syro Malabar faithful.

In 1888 in his encyclical *Libertas,* Pope Leo pointed out that it was a vain calumny to accuse the Church of looking at most modern political systems unfavourably and rejecting all the discoveries of contemporary genius, thereby beginning the reconciliation of the Church with the modern world.

In 1893, the Pope promulgated the encyclical *Providentissimus Deus* affirming the complete inerrancy of the Bible, defending it from rationalistic interpretations.

In 1899, Pope Leo condemned a heresy called *Americanism* that viewed human virtues more valuable than supernatural virtues like humility and charity.[3]

Pope Leo XIII succeeded in pursuing a careful path of reconciling the Catholic Church with the modern world and dealing with its challenges with more creativity and pragmatism. Thus, he led the Church boldly out of confusion for renewal in the twentieth century. He proved himself a diplomat to the core. His *Rerum Novarum* summarized the best catholic thought on social problems, focused on the main themes and laid down the lines the Catholics should follow henceforth. All subsequent teachings of Popes on social justice found *Rerum Novarum* as the anvil.

FOOTNOTES

1. Thomas Bokenkotter, *A Concise History of the Catholic Church*, pp. 253-54.
2. *Ibid.*, p. 58, Para. 1.
3. *Ibid.*, pp. 299-304.

The Catholic Church and Popes in the Twentieth Century

35

At the dawn of the twentieth century, we see a fully different Europe, compared to the previous two centuries. Several factors contributed for this transformation.

Europe's population of 188 million in the year 1740 has grown to around 400 million by the year 1900.

Growth of literacy consequent on the rise of popular education was another important factor. Illiteracy was almost wiped out, especially in Northern and Western Europe. With the growth of mass literacy, there arose popular journalism, daily newspapers feeding the appetite of the masses for excitement and sensational news.

Science revolutionized transport and communication. By 1851, Railways linked major cities of Europe. Electric telegraph has come into existence. These facilitated better mutual contact among the people.

In many countries, people's representative governments, giving political power to the people, replaced monarchies. The right to vote for adult males in most European countries created a new awakening enhancing individual prestige and liberty.

Upsurge in Socialist Ideals

Mechanisation of methods of production accelerated industrialisation bringing up prosperity for the nation and the entrepreneurs. An age of industrial barons emerged. The most crucial problem generated by industrialization was that of the oppressed and exploited factory workers. The conditions in the factories and slums were abominable. Children under eighteen and women were forced to work twelve to fifteen hours a day for very low wages, not enough even for their modest diet consisting of bread and potatoes with an occasional dose of cabbage. The Damocles' sword of lay-off, virtually meaning starvation for the labour, was hanging over them. In this pitiable situation, no avenues for remedy were open to the workers, except socialism. Socialist parties generally committed to Marxian ideology sprang up all over Europe, one in Germany in 1875, in Austria and Switzerland in 1888, in Sweden and Holland in 1889 and in Italy, Poland and Finland in 1892. By 1880, the working class was almost lost to the Church in France. The Church leadership was generally reactionary. They refused to accept the idea of class-conflict and therefore they desired to wean away the workers and use them against socialism.

Some outstanding initiatives were taken in Germany, Italy, France and Belgium under the leadership of German Catholics. German bishop Wilhelm Kittler prepared a catholic solution sorted out from both socialism and liberalism. He argued for State intervention to control liberal capitalists and the totalitarian tendencies of the socialists. In England, Cardinal Henry Edward Manning, a convert from Anglicanism, successfully identified himself with the labour publicly. He personally attended a meeting of the farm workers. It was a courageous act as it was the first time in England that a Roman Catholic prelate had openly sided with the labour. In 1874, he delivered a lecture on 'Rights and Dignity of Labour' defending forcefully the right of the worker to organize, demanding laws to regulate working hours of the labourer and pleading to stop the abuses associated with child labour.

Social Catholicism

In America, 'the Knights' was the most powerful labour union with its president and two-third of the members Catholics. The conservative American and Canadian bishops approached Rome to condemn the 'Knights'. Cardinal Gibbons of Baltimore with the support of Cardinal Manning obtained from Rome a successful verdict favouring the 'Knights'. In the eighteen eighties there emerged a profound Catholic sociology which offered a pragmatic alternative to the ideologies of both economic liberalism and socialism. In 1891, Pope Leo XIII summarized this progressive social thought and issued the encyclical *Rerum Novarum*, the Magna Carta of social Catholicism urging Catholics to be involved in the struggle for social justice and charity. The encyclical went unheeded by many Catholics. But, it helped to prevent the spread of Marxian socialism among the workers and exerted a positive influence on two manifestations of social Catholicism, the Christian trade unions and the Christian Democratic parties.

As it was a period of totalitarian governments, Pope Leo XIII did not favour State intervention. The Popes in the twentieth century developed the ideas in *Rerum Novarum* into a coherent social philosophy, which could on its own hold against both materialistic Marxism and the materialistic liberal capitalism. The encyclicals *Quadragesimo Anno* of Pope Pius XI, *Mater et Magistra* of Pope John XXIII and *Popularum Progressio* of Paul VI were all advanced thinking of the Church on social order taking into consideration the developments in the social and political situations in the world. All these documents show a gradual recognition of democracy as a form of government most in harmony with the innate dignity of man and basic human rights. The second Vatican Council summed up the most beneficial elements in social Catholicism in its Constitution 'On the Church in the Modern World'.

The twentieth century had been an age of tremendous advances in science and technology, new ideologies, war and destruction, waning influence of religions and development of a materialistic outlook. Science ensured efficiency, speed, accuracy, better health and longevity. At the same time, it provided the modern world with nuclear devices capable of wiping out human race. Now, humanity is at the threshold of conquering planets and creation of a superman through cloning or some other artificial means. Secular humanism (a product of the enlightenment), individual materialism (selfish pursuit of possessions) and economic and political ideologies like capitalism, socialism and communism were eclipsing religions by promising salvation in this world itself. The repercussions of these developments posed a very serious threat to Christianity. Two world wars killed more people than those died in all the wars in human history.

Christianity, which comprised half of world population in 1850 shrunk to less than one third by 2000 AD. An increasing number of Christians in Europe and North America have thrown off the mask of external religious conformity and ceased participation in the worship and spiritual life of the Church. Now, few young people are visible in the worshipping services of the Western Church. There is every reason to fear that a whole generation is being lost to Christ. It is not a question of losing some believers, but the problem of all-embracing materialism gnawing the very marrow of the Church, its doctrines, faith and practices.

The twentieth century produced the largest number of martyrs since the early centuries. In fact, far more Christians have been put to death for their faith than in any other century. From a Christian point of view, the twentieth century deserves to be evaluated differently. Many developments, which changed the course of world history, some foreseen and many others unforeseen at the dawn of the century, took place in the twentieth century with consequential impact on the human race in general and on Christianity in particular. They were:

The World War I	– 1914-1918
Bolshevik Revolution in Russia	– 1917
Fascism in Italy under Benito Mussolini	– 1922
Nazism in Germany under Adolph Hitler	– 1933-1945
The World War II	– 1939-1945
Fall of Communism in Eastern Europe and USSR and the death of Colonialism	– 1993

Eight Popes occupied the throne of St. Peter in the twentieth century. All of them were of exemplary character, men of extraordinary calibre and vision, one better than the other and good captains to navigate the Church ship through the stormy high seas, as listed below:

Pius X	–	1903-1914
Benedict XV	–	1914-1922
Pius XI	–	1922-1939
Pius XII	–	1939-1958
John XXIII	–	1958-1963
Paul VI	–	1963-1978
John Paul I	–	1978 (Aug. 26th to Sept. 23rd)
John Paul II	–	1978-2005
Benedict XVI	–	2005 (continuing)

Pope John XXIII convoked the second Vatican Council, the new Pentecost in the Church, on October 11, 1962. On the death of John XXIII, Pope Paul VI continued the council till December 8th, 1965. Now, we shall look into the periods of each of these Popes.

Pope Pius X (1903-1914)

The main thrust of Pope Pius X was on strengthening catholic worship and protecting the Church against modern errors. He introduced a series of reforms in this respect. The age for first receiving the Holy Eucharist was fixed around seven years. "Confraternity of Christian Doctrine" was established for religious education of the youth. All Catholics were encouraged to receive Holy Communion at Mass every week. Through the movement known as Catholic Action, he brought out the catholic faith into the modern world. Music was introduced in the liturgy to make it more attractive and inspirational. Pius X took the initiative to codify the canon law enabling its publication in 1917. Modernism, a new school of thought that arose in the nineteenth century advocating examination of the Bible using methods of historical and literary criticism was condemned by the Pope in his encyclical *Pascendi dominici gregis*. A very bold step taken by Pius X was the surrender of all Church property in France to the hostile French government to free the Church from government control, that later benefited the Church in a large measure. His period was one of great spiritual revival in the Church.

Pope Pius X was declared a saint in 1948, the first Pope canonized after the sixteenth century.

Pope Benedict XV (1914-1922)

World War I and the Bolshevik Revolution in Russia bound up the period of papacy of Benedict XV with the conflagration that swept Europe in 1917. When Pope Benedict ascended the throne of St. Peter, the people were looking for a peacemaker Pope. He did not disappoint them. He, from the very beginning, pursued the path of peace and conciliation. When the World War I broke out, he was absolutely opposed to war as morally and totally unjustifiable and rejected outright the ancient theory of 'Just Wars' of St. Augustine. But, he never made a public statement condemning the war as Catholics on both sides were theologically and emotionally not prepared to take such a radical decision. But the Pope and the Church remained neutral all along. This was widely criticised by both sides. In 1917, the Pope issued "Note to the Heads of States" at war urging the suspension of hostilities, regulated disarmament, arbitration etc. Though his ideas were realistic and farsighted, his note fell on deaf ears. Holy Mary's appearance in Fatima was during the papacy of Benedict.

Pius XI (1922-1939)

Pius XI followed a unique path to the papal throne. He spent the first thirty years of his priestly life as a Librarian, at first in Milan and later in Vatican where he gained recognition for his research. This helped him to keep himself away from controversies over the then prevailing modernist ideas. Thereafter, he became apostolic visitor and nuncio in Poland. There, he succeeded in his assignment by securing the rights of the Catholic Church in Poland (became independent in 1919). On return from Poland he was appointed Archbishop of Milan in 1921 and made a Cardinal. On the death of Benedict XV, he was elevated to the papal throne in 1922.

Reconciliation with Italy was one of the major objectives set forth by him. Pius XI, smoothened Mussolini's way to power by withdrawing Vatican's support to the Catholic Popular party. Mussolini rewarded the support by signing the Lateran Concordat in 1929 whereby the Church gained a munificent sum of money and sovereignty over 109 acre complex around St. Peter's basilica in return for the surrender of the papal territories in Italy. The Concordat also accorded a privileged status for Catholic teaching in Italy.

The tenure of Pope Pius XI coincided with the rise of dictators to power in many European nations. He never hesitated to come to terms with them to secure full freedom and rights for Catholics. In 1933, Pius negotiated a Concordat with Adolph Hitler. In 1937 he issued the encyclical *Divini Redemptoris* scathingly condemning atheistic communism. In 1935, Vatican reached a *modus vivendi* with the republican government of Spain, realizing that monarchy was dead. Only two conditions were attached: the Republicans should maintain law and order and stop the anti-religious excesses of the extremists. But they were unable to do either. The fanatics destroyed the churches and convents, murdered priests and nuns and at last destroyed the Spanish republics. Vatican thereon went over to the side of Franco's nationalists facilitating the rise of another dictator, General Francisco in Spain in 1936. The Pope's handling of the *French Action Francaise* by condemning Maurras' movement helped to maintain the French church safe for the democrats. All these go to show that Pope Pius was a pragmatist in his political views with no ideological preferences either for Fascism or Nazism. He negotiated altogether eighteen Concordats, the main objective being the safeguarding of the freedom of Catholic Action; to obtain legal status for church marriages and to give the Holy See the exclusive control in the appointment of bishops. His pontificate was a period of impressive accomplishments, 128 residential Sees, new Institutes and Ecclesiastical Colleges in Rome, canonization of thirty-three Saints etc.

When Hitler showed belligerence towards the Church, the Pope decisively met the challenge by issuing his encyclical *Mit brennender Sorge* criticizing Nazism, one of the greatest condemnations ever issued by Vatican. In retaliation, the Nazis took numerous vindictive measures including a series of immorality trials of the Catholic clergy. The Pope was very much distressed by the treatment of the Church by Hitler and Mussolini and their vicious racist policies. While preparing an explosive encyclical denouncing Fascist crimes and racism, the Pope passed away on February 10, 1939.[1]

Pius XII (1939-1958)

Eugenio Pacelli (Pius XII) was the only Pope of the 20th century who did not hail from Northern Italy. Earlier, he was the Secretary of State under Pius XI. He impressed every one by his aristocratic bearing, personal piety, affability, holiness and experience gained from unprecedented global travels. He was a born Roman, tall with aquiline nose, deep-set eyes and long bony fingers.

Two weeks after Pius' coronation, Hitler sent his army to Czechoslovakia bringing the world into the brink of a global war. The Pope made strenuous efforts, even risking his life, to avert the catastrophe. Italy's declaration of war put Vatican, a small island in the Axis Sea situated in between Germany and Italy, in a very delicate situation of being attacked as an accomplice of the Allies. Pius' policy was to maintain an appearance of neutrality. When the Nazis invaded Russia, the Pope, in spite of his hatred of communism, did not lend support to the attempts of the Nazis to portray their invasion of Russia as an anti-Communist religious crusade. Pius was fully aware of the atrocities and crimes of the Nazis against the Jews, the Poles, the Serbs and others. But he preferred silence except for some vague generalized references. This silence and inaction on the part of the Pope was criticized by several quarters. A complexity of reasons motivated the Pope to refrain from publicly denouncing the Nazi crimes. Threat of terrible reprisals against the Church, fear of more savage measures, the experience of Dutch bishops who spoke against the Nazi deportation of Jews, realization that nothing would deter the hysterical Hitler from his determination to exterminate the Jews and the unwillingness of the Pope to leave aside his calculated neutrality motivated the Pope to be more prudent by being publicly silent and helping the victims behind the backs of the Nazis. In Rome alone, more than five thousand Jews were given asylum in monasteries and convents. Pinchas Lapide, former Israeli consul in Italy in his book "The Last Three Popes and the Jews" credited the Church with saving four hundred thousand Jews from sure death. Anthony Rhodes in his book *The Vatican in the Age of the Dictators* endorses the fact that the Pope did much in private to save the Jews.

By the end of the war, the conditions in Italy deteriorated. Vatican joined the efforts of the anti-Mussolini forces in Italy to get out of the war and took part in the armistice negotiations. This effort was not fruitful, but armistice was arrived at through other channels. While Pius was maintaining impartiality during the war, communism had an upsurge in the West. Italy and Rome itself came under the verge of a communist take-over. Pope thereupon issued a decree in 1949 by which all Catholics belonging to the Communist party were automatically excommunicated. He also influenced the dominant Christian Democratic Party to strive for a ban on the Communist party in Italy.

When the war ended, the prestige of papacy remained very much elevated. Many nations including the US sent ambassadors to Vatican. At the time of the celebration of Jubilee in 1950, the number of pilgrims to Rome was estimated at millions. The number of Catholic dioceses increased from 1696 to 2048 during the period of Pius XII. In his encyclical *Humani Generis* (1950) he warned the Catholics against possible dangers of the new historical theology. He published his famous *Mystici Corporis Christi* (1943) revolutionizing the Catholic view of the Church as the mystical body of Christ, against the general view of seeing the Church as a human institution or a pyramid-shaped hierarchy. In the same year he published another encyclical *Divino Afflante Spiritu* allowing catholic biblical scholars to apply the methods of form criticism in their exegesis (explaining and interpreting the Bible). In 1942, he consecrated the world to the Immaculate Heart of Mary and declared Mary the 'Queen of the World'. Pius declared the infallible dogma of 'Assumption of Mary'. His rejection of communism was related to the appearance of 'Our

Lady of Fatima'. Pope Pius was known as the Pope of Peace as well as Pope of Mary. He expanded the College of Cardinals by including many from countries other than Italy. When the Cardinals assembled after Pius' death, to elect a new Pope, their number was 58 out of which only 17 were from Italy.[2]

A better part of his long reign for 19 years was one of stress and strain for the Church as well as its Supreme Pontiff caused by the threats of inhuman massacres and wars unleashed by Fascism, Nazism and Communism. Diplomacy and holiness of the Pope played a significant part to bring the Church out of all dangers with a new prestige.

John XXIII (1958-1963)

On the death of Pope Pius XII, the conclave of cardinals to elect the new Pope was evenly divided between those who felt the need of a break with Pacelli's triumphalist church and those in favour of continuing it. At last, a compromise candidate was chosen, seventy-six-year-old Angelo Roncalli, Patriarch of Venice, known to be moderate and conciliatory. No one on either side had an inkling of a revolutionary mind hidden behind the old man's peasant face. The first surprise came when he chose the name John XXIII, a name chosen by no one after the notorious anti-Pope John XXIII was tried and deposed by the Council of Constance. The new Pope was a jolly and spontaneous person who loved life and people and not at all hesitant to show it. He invited friends to dinner, wandered thro' the streets of Rome, heedless of papal etiquette, speaking with all and sundry, visiting hospitals and prisons, speaking jokes, that soon were repeated all over the world. At first, the world was astonished. The Church had almost forgotten that Popes were also human beings. But they took him to their hearts and poured out their affection for him.

Though his pontificate was one of the shortest in history (four years and seven months), it happened to be one of the most important turning point, which revolutionised and ended the siege mentality of the Catholic Church, often described as a New Pentecost. He addressed his *Paecm in Terris* and *Mater et Magistra* to all men of goodwill and spoke in terms of values respected by all and appealed to all to work together to build up a better world. He reversed dramatically the approach to the communist world in his quest for establishing harmonious relations with all. His dreams and ideas would have been lost in oblivion, had he not convoked the General Council of Vatican II (1962-65) where the whole church assembled for a heart-to-heart conversation, bypassing the conservative Curia.

Paul VI (1963-1978)

On the death of Pope John XXIII, John Baptist Montini, Archbishop of Milan, a progressive committed to the Johannine Revolution was elected Pope with the title Paul VI. He led the Church during one of the most crucial periods of history. His father was a Northern Italian, a journalist and a member of the Italian parliament during the Pre-Fascist era and very much involved in the defence of the Church against socialists and anti-clericals. He served in the Secretariat of State for long thirty-two years, also acting as chaplain for a time to the federation of Italian Catholic University students. He also worked in close association with the then Cardinal Pacelli (later Pope Pius XII). In 1954 he was appointed Archbishop of Milan. Pope John made him his first Cardinal and dropped broad hints of his desire to have him as a successor.

Pope Paul VI opened the second session of Vatican II on September 29, 1963 with a magnificent address reiterating his goals, renewal of the Church, unity of all Christians and dialogue with the world. By virtue of his office, the new Pope was entrusted with the onerous responsibility of executing the monumental changes decreed by Vatican II. He opted a cautious path in implementing the changes by moving slowly, gradually and prudently. He was fully conscious of the fact that maintenance of continuity with the past should be an essential component in all changes as the Church he was dealing with was not a new one but a church with a long history and tradition. Though Paul VI was criticized for his slow and cautious approach, the Pope struck on to his own wisdom, which was subsequently proved right.

Pope Paul VI was a powerful teacher. His mission was not confined to Vatican II alone. Like St. Paul, he believed in a mission to the world. He personally went to the United Nations and addressed them on World peace. He travelled to the Holy Land and greeted the Eastern Orthodox Patriarch with the "Kiss of Peace". He attended the Eucharistic Congress in India, Colombia and Italy and visited the sites of the Natural Disaster in Pakistan. He met Michael Ramsey, the leading bishop of the Anglican Church to seek unity of Churches. Through all these travels, he proved himself an apostle of peace. He issued three encyclicals, *Ecclesiam Suam* (1964) on the true nature of the Church, *Popularum Progressio* (1967) on the 'Development of Peoples' dealing with Social Catholicism and *Humanae Vitae* (1968) on Christian morals, condemning contraceptives including 'the Pill'.

He introduced several reforms in the Church, raised the number of members in the College of Cardinals giving international representation, added the first woman religious in the Roman Curia, restored the status of the permanent deacon in the early church, convened frequent synods of bishops and so on. His encyclical *Humanae Vitae* invited criticism from several quarters of the Church for not complying with the collegiality of bishops. Pope Paul VI will be remembered in church history as the key figure, who maintained the balance between the changes of Vatican II and the faithfulness to the traditions in the Church.

Pope John Paul I (1978 August 26th-Sept. 23rd)

He passed away thirty-three days after his accession to the throne of St. Peter.

Pope John Paul II (Oct. 16, 1978-April 3, 2005)

On the sudden death of Pope John Paul I, the College of Cardinals elected the first non-Italian Pope after 1522 and that from a Communist nation, Karol Cardinal Wojtyla, the Archbishop of Krakow, Poland. His name, John Paul II embodying the names of his three predecessors, indicates his intention to continue their liberal policies. He was considered a theological moderate, liberal on social issues and an active participant in Vatican II. He was dedicated to a strategy of "restoration" – a concerted effort to recuperate the great Catholic tradition lost or neglected in the aftermath of the Vatican Council. His penchant for abstractions and deductive logic indicated that he was very much influenced by the scholastic modes of thought characteristic of his professors in Rome where he pursued his theological studies. His papacy has been dedicated to spread the good news of Jesus Christ, the Redeemer of mankind. In his first encyclical *Redemptor Hominis*, he projects Jesus as the ultimate solution to the problems of the world. He travelled to more nations than any other Pope in history to spread the message of Jesus Christ. (Visited 129 countries during his 98 trips abroad and has made 142 trips within Italy till Oct. 16, 2002.)

In 1986, Pope John Paul promulgated an encyclical on Holy Spirit, *Dominum Vivificantum* (Lord and giver of life) completing a set of three letters, one on the Father (*Dives in Misericordia*) and the other on the Son (*Redemptor Hominis*). In 1985, Pope John Paul convened an Extraordinary Synod of bishops for two weeks to evaluate the implementation of Vatican II in twenty years. In the final statement, the bishops expressed their concern regarding the Church and their hopes of a future direction for the Catholic Church on the basis of a proper understanding of Vatican II. Some of the recommendations of the bishops echoed the need to recognize the Church as a mystery formed by God's grace and not just another human organization.

Pope John Paul II had to deal with several vexed problems during his papacy, especially the nuclear arms race, the clamour for liberation among peoples of the world, crimes against human rights and dignity, threats of war in several parts of the world etc. A Pope from the Communist world had the distinction of witnessing the fruits of his prayer and efforts, the fall of communism in Russia and East Europe. He consecrated the world again to the Immaculate Heart of Mary, the mother of God and speaks of the present time as a new advent, a time for the preparation for the coming of Jesus Christ.

A few months after his enthronement, he visited Santo Domingo on the island of Hispaniola, Pueblo, Mexico, Poland and New York and addressed the UN General Assembly, where, he championed the primacy of spiritual values and applauded the Universal Declaration of Human Rights. At the Yankee Stadium, the Pope exhorted the Americans to share their wealth with the poor in the Third world. His ecumenical overtures are specially noteworthy – visit to the Lutheran Church in Rome (1983), Second visit to Germany (1987), World Council of Churches in Geneva (1984), Jewish Synagogue in Rome (1985), Muslims in Morocco (1985), Animists in Togo (1985), India (1986) addressing Hindus, Muslims, Sikhs, Buddhists, Jains and Parsees and participated in the World Day of Prayer in Assisi along with 150 representatives of a dozen world religions. As to the enduring value of the Pope's initiatives, John Paul II has undoubtedly kept in the forefront the Catholic consciousness while winning the respect and admiration of the world and magnifying the diplomatic clout of Vatican.

The Pope's strategy of 'Restoration' is to strengthen loyalty to papal authority by projecting the image of an energetic leader, fully in command with determination to lead. In this perspective, John Paul II is a visible head of the Church and indeed more visible on the world stage than his predecessors as the undisputed leader not only of the Catholic church but of the Christians all over the world.[3]

FOOTNOTES

1. C. Falconi, *The Popes of the Twentieth Century*, p. 117.
2. Thomas Bokenkotter, *A Concise History of the Catholic Church*, p. 354.
3. Alan Schreck, *The Compact History of the Catholic Church*, pp. 140-44.

The General Council of Vatican II

36

(Oct. 11, 1962 to Dec. 8, 1965)

On January 25, 1959, Pope John XXIII announced his intention of calling a General Council, attributing the idea to an inspiration of the Holy Spirit. The call for the Council was the response of the Church to the question "How could an ancient Church that prided itself as anti-modern and unchangeable survive in a world undergoing social, political, cultural and scientific transformations of an unprecedented magnitude."[1] The Roman Curia was wonderstruck by the announcement. They feared the outcome when thousands of bishops go out of hand and therefore girded themselves for the battle. The Curial officials monopolized the key positions in the preparatory Commissions for drawing up the Schemata (proposals) to be placed before the Council. After examining the suggestions from bishops all over the world, they drew up seventy proposals covering a variety of conventional subjects ranging from revelation to ecclesiastical benefices so that the bishops need only affix their stamp of approval. Had everything went on as preplanned by the Curial officials, the Council would have ended up as another Roman pageant. But, God willed otherwise.

The opening ceremony was marked by a dazzling procession of bishops vested in copes (long loose garment) and mitre (the conical hat symbolizing authority) and the Pope borne aloft on his portable throne. After intoning the opening liturgy, the Pope mounted the rostrum and delivered the papal address, the most remarkable in the history of the Church. In unmistakable language, the Pope disassociated from the Curia's outdated and ludicrous proposals and exhorted the bishops to undertake a renewal and updating of the Church with a pastoral approach without engaging in unproductive academic controversies. In the opening session itself, the bishops under the leadership of Cardinal Lienart upset the apple cart of the Curia. 69 out of the 70 schemata proposed by the Curia were rejected and the bishops themselves took up the responsibility of constituting their own preparatory commissions to draft each schema. The one accepted schema of the Curia – on the liturgy – was an ideal document, which provided a starting point for the discussions. The reform of the liturgy allowing the use of local languages helped the average Catholic to feel the meaning of the Council. The debate on the liturgy revealed the growing progressive mood of the bishops.

When the document *Sources of Revelation* was introduced, Cardinal Suenens of Belgium suggested that if Vatican I was remembered as the Council on the 'Pope', let Vatican II were remembered as the Council on 'Church'. He suggested studying the Church in its inner mystery and constitution and then its relation to the world. This meant a triple dialogue, one among the faithful themselves, then with the separated brothers and finally with the world outside. This blueprint was hailed with immense outburst of applause (against Council rules). In other words, the aims of the Council were set in unambiguous terms, the renewal of the Church, unity of all Christians and dialogue with the world. Having found and set forth the direction, the fathers were happy to have their first recess on December 8, 1962. Before they reconvened, Pope John who captivated the world was taken from the world, leaving the Church and the world to doubt whether his successor would carry forward Pope John's adventurous initiative.

The progressives, the so-called liberals, not only heaved a sigh of relief but also were in a jovial mood on learning the news of the election of John Baptist Montini (Paul VI), a progressive committed to the Johannine revolution, as the successor to the throne of St. Peter. Under his able leadership, the Council opened the second session on September 29, 1963 with a magnificent address by the Pope reiterating the goals set forth by Cardinal Suenens.

The Second Vatican Council, the twenty-first in the history of the Church, undoubtedly a most important religious event in which 2500 top religious leaders participated in four three-month sessions spanning over four years, concluded on December 8, 1965. It issued sixteen documents and four constitutions, which won virtually unanimous consensus of the participants and likely to produce, when implemented far-reaching changes in Catholic communities around the world. Two significant features noteworthy about Vatican II are non-interference by secular governments and attendance of other Christians as official delegates representing their respective Churches.

The decrees and constitutions of Vatican II, though not presented as infallible definitions, the Catholic Church believes that the contents of those documents were guided by the Holy Spirit as a word for our age, a direction for the Catholic Church and the world.

The documents issued by the Council can be classified into two categories: those concerned with the life of the Church itself, including its relationship with other Churches and those concerned with the relationship of the Catholic Church with the world at large including the non-Christians.

Documents on the Life of the Catholic Church and Relationship with Other Christians

The Dogmatic Constitution on the Church (Lumen Gentium)

This constitution deals with the essential elements of the Church's understanding of itself, an authoritative summary of the official teaching in the area of doctrine. It also completed what Vatican I had begun; the people of God, laity, religious and so on.

The Mystery of the Church

The Church is not primarily an institution, but a work of God. It is a mystery in the same way as Jesus Christ is a mystery, a union of the human and divine. The Church is a sacrament, a visible continuation of Jesus in this world.

The People of God

The Church is primarily not an organized structure, but the people of the New Covenant chosen by God to be his own, his body in the world.

The Church is Hierarchical

This affirms that the Church Jesus founded does possess ordained leaders who are a gift to God's people to lead them in carrying on Jesus' mission in this world through the ministries of pope, bishops, priests and deacons.

The Laity

This addresses the sharing in the priesthood, kingship and prophetic role of Jesus Christ with those that are not ordained, nor dedicated by vows to religious life. This is a breakthrough in recognising the active role and full dignity of lay persons in the Church. They are not second-class citizens, but full participants in the mission of Jesus Christ.

The Religious

The value and relevance of the religious life to the modern world based on the vows of poverty, chastity and obedience are stressed.

The call of the whole Church to Holiness

All Christians are called to holiness and each vocation possesses its own way to achieve holiness.

The Pilgrim Church

The Church is a pilgrim on the earth; its goal being union with the Lord in heaven. The present union or communion of the Church on earth is being purified in purgatory with those who already attained glory of heaven. This fellowship is known as 'the communion of saints'.

Our Lady

The document is devoted to the special role of Mary as mother and model of the Church and her role in God's plan of salvation. It is emphasized that Mary is first and foremost a member or part of the Church and not above the Church. She is a member of the community of believers saved through the grace of Christ.

The contents of this decree is further expanded and developed in several other decrees namely:

(i) Decree on the apostolate of lay people (*Apostolic Aetuositatem*).

(ii) The Decree on the ministry and life of priests (*Presbyterorum Ordinis*).

(iii) The Decree on the training of priests (*Optatam Totius*).

(iv) Decree on the appropriate renewal of religious life (*Perfectae Caritatis*).

(v) And the Decree on the pastoral office of bishops (*Christus Dominos*).

These decrees were essential to complete the full understanding of the different ways of life and vocations that make up the entire people of God.

Decree on Eastern Catholic Churches (Orientalium Ecclesiarum)

This decree proclaims the beauty and importance of the Eastern Catholic churches subject to the governing authority of the Pope, but with rites other than the Roman Rite, very often overlooked or not properly understood in the past. These churches demonstrate the diversity of the Catholic Church and enhance its beauty. Unity does not mean uniformity.

Constitution on the Sacred Liturgy (Sacrosanctum Concilium)

As we have seen, this is the first document discussed and approved by the Council. A key word used in it is 'active participation'. Lay people, who hitherto remained spectators at the liturgy were to be involved in worshipping God. For this purpose, the Council approved practical changes to make it possible or easier for the laity to understand and participate in the worshipping practices. One such change that had universal impact was the adoption of vernacular, people's language in the liturgy.

This Constitution also clarified the Catholic belief about the liturgy, it explained Mass as a perpetuation or re-presentation of the one eternal sacrifice of Christ on Calvary and not as re-sacrificing Christ.

Dogmatic Constitution on Divine Revelation (Dei Verbum)

This constitution states that God reveals His truth through human beings. So the Bible may be considered "the word of God in the words of man". It encourages scholars to use modern methods of biblical exegesis but final validity of the judgment shall rest with the teaching office (*magisterium*) of the Church – the pope and the bishops. It exhorts all Catholics, especially priests and religious to study and read the Bible constantly by 'immersing themselves in the scriptures by constant sacred reading and diligent study'.

Declaration on Christian Education (Gravissimum Educationis)

Approaches to Christian education from the perspective of the Catholic Church are examined in this declaration. Religious freedom for Christian schools and same status and opportunity as public schools are emphasized.

The Decree on Ecumenism (Unitatis Redintegratio)

In this document, a new era was begun on the relationship of the Catholic Church with other Christians. Throwing aside the Constantinian and Tridentine triumphalism, the Catholic Church openly acknowledged its share of blame for the division of Christianity. The document advises Catholics to regard other Christians as brothers and sisters even though they are separated by differences of beliefs and practices. Though the decree examines the differences separating Catholics from Protestant and Orthodox Christians, emphasis was laid on those beliefs that all hold in common. In the chapter 'Catholic Principles of Ecumenism', some practical guidelines are issued to the Catholics that they should take the initiative and first approach for unity, avoiding 'false conciliatory approach'. The constitution highlights that the Catholic Church alone possesses the fullness of the means of grace and salvation brought to mankind through Jesus Christ. As genuine unity is based on truth, all Christians must continue to be faithful to what they truly believe, trusting in the grace of God and the guidance of the Holy spirit to bring us together as He wills. The Decree encourages Catholics, until full unity is achieved, to join with other Christians in service, in praying together and sharing our Christian lives in other ways to promote the unity of God's people.

Documents on the Catholic Church's Relationship to the World (including Non-Christian Religions)

Pastoral Constitution on the Church in the Modern World (Gaudium et spes)

This document is the only one called by the Council 'a pastoral constitution'; 'constitution' indicating its great importance for the life of the Church and the term 'pastoral' denoting that it is not primarily concerned with doctrine, but practical guidance. The basic desire of Pope John XXIII for *aggiornamento*, updating the Church with the situations and needs of the modern world, is fulfilled through this document. It is divided into two parts, the former a general presentation of Church's understanding of man's situation today and its relationship with modern man and the latter an examination of some specific areas of special urgency in the life of mankind today.

The dignity of the human person created by God in His own image is the basic premise of the first part. The consciousness of the Church, that it is a part of the world and its problems and needs and its desire to work together with all men of goodwill to seek solutions, is unambiguously admitted. Along with this admission, the Church boldly proclaims that the ultimate solution to all predicaments and problems is to be found only in Jesus Christ, God's only begotten son, who emerged victorious over all evil, sin and death, giving the hope of sharing the same victory with man.

The second part provides principles to guide Catholics as to how to relate to the modern world and how to approach certain areas of special concern. The Constitution discusses specific areas such as dignity of marriage and family life, culture, economic and social life of mankind, the political community, peace and the establishment of community of nations.

The Declaration on Non-Christian Religions (Nostro Actate)

This declaration states that the Catholic Church respects whatever is true and good in other religions and points out that God, in his mercy, can grant salvation to those who have not accepted Christianity but those who follow the truth as it is known thro' their conscience. A large portion of this declaration is concerned with Judaism – reproduced elsewhere in this book.

Decree on Church's Missionary Activity (Ad Gentis)

To dispel the mistaken notion among Catholics that missionary activity is no longer required among non-Christians, the Decree clarifies the implication of the 'Declaration on Non-Christians' that the command of Jesus to 'make disciples of all nations' (Mt. 28:19) is absolutely true and necessary today. The declaration exhorts a vibrant missionary outreach to all that have not heard or accepted the gospel and gives practical instructions on how the missionary work is to be organized and carried out effectively.

Declaration on Religious Liberty (Dignitatis Humanae)

This declaration advocates that all persons should have the liberty to hold and practise any religion they wish without coercion as long as they respect the common good and right of others to practise other beliefs. The basis of this document, a landmark in Catholic thought, is the recognition of the dignity of human person whose freedom of choice of religion, God fully honours.

Decree on Social Communication (Inter Mirifica)[2]

This Decree enunciates few important principles and moral guidelines on the use of means for social communication. It serves only as a beginning. Much more teaching is required in this sphere, in the light of the exploding growth of the communications media in the modern age.[3]

The Christian Church – A Communion of Churches

In a landmark declaration, the Council asserted that the Christian Church is not a monolith but a communion of churches, beautified by unity in diversity rather than uniformity.

Vatican II – Achievements

Viewed in any angle, Vatican II stands unique and conspicuously separate among the twenty-one General Councils in the history of the Catholic Church. The dreams and ideas of Pope John XXIII were acceptable to a vast majority of the Fathers. The progressives outmanoeuvred the traditionalists. The Council departed from the past and approved a series of measures to renew the Catholic Church and to put it in a more positive relationship with other Christians and non-Christians in the modern world. Some of the remarkable features of Vatican II are summarised below:

No interference by any Government.

Unlike previous Councils, it was never Curia-ridden.

Representation of Non-Catholic Christians.

The role of the laity in the Church – the whole people of God – was recognized.

The seeds of a democratic revolution were sown.

The Church shed its siege-mentality and came out to the open.

Opened the doors of the Church for dialogue with Non-Christian religions and the modern world.

An about-turn from the anti-modernism of Pius IX to modernism.

A definite advance in the Church's self-understanding.

Greater regard for the historical dimension in the Church's faith and life.

The Hildebrandine papacy claiming position above the Church was brought down into the Church.

Assertion of the collegiality of the Pope and bishops.

Shift from the Church as the pyramidal structure to the Church as the whole people of God.

Change in attitude and practice as regards Non-Catholic Christians.

The end of the Tridentine Triumphalist Church.

Ecumenism-Dialogue for the unity of Christians.

Thomism was no longer considered the only Catholic approach to theology.

Reform of the Liturgy, especially the introduction of vernacular.

Freedom to catholic historians and biblical exegetes and other scholars to explore and pursue new approaches.

Erection of priests' Senates and Pastoral Councils that would include laity at Diocesan level.

Frequent synods of bishops and National Conferences of Bishops introduced.

A new image for the Catholic Church – A transformation from the conservative and traditionalist church to a church of openness and modernity.

Aftermath of Vatican II

The Church leaders who attended the Second Vatican Council were, generally speaking, fully conscious of the necessity of change within the Church and the relations of the Church with the outside world undergoing rapid and sweeping changes in all aspects of human life. They applied their mind and in their wisdom and good faith arrived at conclusions to renew the Church and its relations with the outside world, gave concrete shape to their ideas for revolutionary changes and published them in black and white in the form of 'constitutions' or 'decrees' or 'declarations' of the Council. On the other side, the picture was entirely different. The average Catholic was not prepared intellectually or spiritually or emotionally for the change. He was not taught or trained to think of any change. He considered the authoritarian structure of the Church as a dictate of divine revelation. He looked upon the Pope as a superhuman entity whose every word was a command with supernatural authority. Even the bishops were regarded with extreme reverence and awe. The typical Catholic had no difficulty in being compatible even with the liturgy in an unknown language.

In this situation the question of reconciliation of the two positions has become a cumbersome impasse confronted by the Church in implementing the decisions of the Council. Consequently, many problems and crises cropped up mainly due to misunderstanding or false application of what the Council actually taught. Some people commented that when Pope John XXIII 'opened the window' of the Church, some undesirable things blew in along with the Holy Spirit. The decade after the closing of the Council in 1965 appeared as the most tumultuous period in the whole modern history of the Church. The typical Catholic was left in a state of complete bewilderment and sense of uprootedness. In his book *Future Shock* Alvin Toffler says that the change affected every aspect of life, not only religion but also all old roots, family, nation, community, profession etc. "shaking under the hurricane impact of the accelerative thrust". In many countries, the Bishops were reluctant to move down the line.

Liturgy

When the new liturgy was introduced shortly after the Council, the myth of the mass as an unchangeable rite was exploded. Some people felt betrayed and refrained from going to the Church. Some others continued the Tridentine Latin mass with the help of sympathetic priests. A few others took it as a licence for one's own improvisation and introduced innovative ideas. But most Catholics however accepted the changes with grace but with little enthusiasm. They took in their stride the changes not only in the mass but in the other sacraments as well.

Authority

Authority was another central issue. The emphasis of Vatican II on the Church as the whole people of God, collegiality of bishops, Pastoral Councils etc. had a revolutionary impact.

The basic structure still remained pyramidal, power flowing downward from the Pope. The Vatican Council took pains to safeguard the absolute power of the Pope. The concept of collegiality gave the bishops only a consultative position, the Pope enjoying discretionary powers as to the calling of synods and as to the topics to be discussed there. This invited a lot of criticism from the liberals who found little change in practice.

When Pope Paul VI issued the encyclical *Humanae Vitae*, a strong body of opinion critical of the Pope was gradually formed for not conforming to the principle of collegiality of bishops. This question was discussed in the second synod of bishops in 1969, wherein the bishops reaffirmed full freedom for the Pope to act on his own, both in governing and in the exercise of his teaching authority. Since then, it seemed obvious that the Vatican is determined to keep the bishops in line.

Priests

By emphasing the nature of the Church as the whole faithful community, a democratic trend was set in motion whereby the medieval caste system of priesthood was becoming no longer needed. The Church was gradually becoming an affair of the personally committed, rather than that of the born Catholic. The priest alone was not to bear the whole burden of the mission of the Church. This weakened the historical reason for the priest being set apart (sacred). In view of the affirmation of Vatican II that all faithful participate in the priesthood of Christ, the priest, in this age of specialization, often found himself challenged by lay persons who may be better informed, on certain topics, than the priest. The laymen have begun to take over much of the job of administration. In this situation, many priests suffered from some sort of confusion about their role. The question of the priest's identity has become a cause for concern.

No post-council trend has been so disturbing to the bishops as the spectacular decline in vocation and the exodus of large number of priests, brothers and nuns. Between 1966-74, around 8000 priests in America left the public ministry. The number of seminarians decreased by 31.4 per cent during the period

1962-74. The situation in Europe was no better than in America. Statistics released in 1974 show that while the Catholic population increased from 530 million in 1960 to 659 million in 1974, the number of priests remained static. The Dutch Pastoral Council in 1970 with overwhelming majority voted that the compulsory link between celibacy and ministry be abolished. The Dutch bishops agreed to work in consultation with the universal church for changes whereby married priests could be admitted to service in the Latin Church and priests who are married could be reinstated under certain conditions. But their brother bishops, in the Synod of 1971 reaffirmed to maintain the law of celibacy for priests, quickly shut this door opened by the Dutch church.

Ecumenism and Dialogue

One of the most evident signs of Christian renewal was the progress towards Christian unity. Roman Catholics and Protestants, at the local level, worked out to remove the age-old barriers between them and arrived at doctrinal agreements. Until second Vatican, ecumenical movement was the work of Protestants at the world missionary conference at Edinburgh in 1910. Later in 1937, the Edinburgh conference approved the proposal for a World Council of Churches, which was organized in 1948 at Amsterdam. It proclaimed their faith in Our Lord Jesus Christ, God and Saviour and commitment to "help the Church penetrate the Churches and make them one". In 1971, Pope Paul visited the headquarters of the World Council of Churches in Geneva and recited the Lord's prayer with the leaders. Officially commissioned groups of theologians worked out consensus-building measures aimed at eventual official approval. The main theological differences involved in the process were relation of scripture to tradition, the role of Mary in man's salvation, the true meaning of Lord's supper, the nature of the ordained ministry, papal primacy and infallibility. On all these points, the theologians were able to arrive at a consensus, previously considered impossible. The issue of valid ministry was much discussed. The Roman Catholic Church insisted that for a valid ministry, a bishop who was linked by imposition of hands with the historic episcopacy stretching back to the apostles must ordain one. The other groups insisted on viewing the valid ministry in a broader context. They point out that apostolic succession cannot simply be identified with the historical chain of bishops but depends also on fidelity to the Gospel and conformity with life and word to the teaching of the apostles. But most Catholics still hold that the Protestants lost contact with the historic chain due to rupture in the sixteenth century and that episcopal ordination is something that all Christian communities should strive for. Some prominent catholic and protestant theologians in Germany refused to place so high a value on episcopal ordination.

Papal primacy, the main issue that split the Christian church in both the Eastern Schism and the Reformation movement, is another thorny question confronted in the process for unity of Churches. There has been some progress on this issue, but no breakthrough. The two significant dialogues on this issue were one involving the American Lutheran Church and the Roman Catholic Church in 1974 and another involving the Anglican and Roman Catholic theologians in 1975. In the Lutheran-Catholic dialogue, both sides agreed that a trajectory of images in the New Testament indicates that Peter exercised a ministry involving responsibility for unity of the Church and that for many centuries, the bishop of Rome validly succeeded to this Petrine office. It was also agreed that Christians need such a Petrine office and the papacy, despite its failures, has the best claim to such an office. But, the Lutherans were prepared to accept any kind of papal primacy only after extensive restructuring to eliminate its autocratic and bureaucratic features.

In the Anglican-Roman dialogue also, the conclusions were similar. The Anglicans recognized the value and necessity of such a Petrine Office and the claim of the Bishop of Rome to that office. But, some difficulties still remained. These included their fears of abuse of papal power and their reservations in accepting two infallibly defined dogmas, the Immaculate Conception and the Assumption of Mary.

On the issue of Mary's role in the salvation of Man, there was not much dialogue. The Catholic approach to Mariology had some distinct dimensions. Vatican II decided not to issue a separate treatise on Mary but confined its statement in a separate chapter in the Dogmatic Constitution on the Church (*Lumen Gentium*).

The implications were significant. The bishops wanted to emphasise the fact that Mary is still a member of the Church and not a semi-divine being exalted above the Church. There was a distinct biblical emphasis in the Council's text on Mary that helped the bishops to produce a very sober treatise free from excesses often characterized even in the official documents on Mary.

The issue of Mary's virginity came to the fore in the Dutch Catechism that appeared in 1966. The critics pointed out that the book sidestepped the question. A Commission of Cardinals appointed by the Pope asked the Dutch bishops to issue a revised edition, but the Dutch bishops refused. At last, a compromise was reached when they agreed to add an appendix containing Vatican's instructions on the traditional doctrine of the Church. A few years ago, no Catholic would have dared to debate the issue in view of the emotional aspects of the subject. But the statement shows the sophistication and maturity of the Catholic community of scholars after the Council. Fr. Rene Laurentin, one of the outstanding defenders of the traditional position, points out that the school favouring only a symbolic interpretation of the Virgin birth is the dominant one among European Catholic theologians at present. "The pendulum has swung so sharply that there is difficulty for getting a hearing for the traditional view," he says. The net result was the opening up of an entirely new chapter as in other areas. There has been a sharp decline in the traditional forms of piety towards Mary, rosaries and medals have been tossed away, statues of Mary were removed, hymns praising Mary faded and May Day celebrations disappeared.

Through dialogues on doctrinal positions, both sides found common grounds giving hopes of a final agreement in due course. But, no serious dialogue has been started so far on the morals. Moral theologians were expressing contradictory views on many issues such as sexuality in marriage, use of contraceptives, the pill, pre-marital sex, abortion, homosexuality, divorce, remarriage, masturbation and so on.

Grave Problems within the Catholic Church

The Church in its long history survived many storms threatening to overwhelm and destroy it. The latest one is the gale-like winds of change unleashed by the Second Vatican Council. Momentous changes that have affected the doctrinal-moral-liturgical arrangement has struck hard at the Catholic sense of identity. One of the most difficult changes for the average Catholic to digest was the call for openness and dialogue with other churches and religions. Hitherto, they believed that the Protestants and other non-Catholics might be saved by reason of their ignorance only and not by the power of their institutions as such. But, the Vatican II did a 180-degree turn by recognizing the merits and salvation potential of the other churches and even other religions. By doing so, it broke the Catholic boundaries of faith and opted for a strategy of openness and dialogue. It was a difficult challenge for the Catholic to find a new identity.

No side has offered official approval on any point of agreement so far. But initiation of dialogue has produced a positive result – Christians keenly felt the necessity of dialogue leading to an eventual unity, generally speaking, all over the world. This has led to an emotional affinity among almost all groups, providing a base for further advancement of the efforts.

Resultantly, two great supports of Catholic identify were rocked by the increase in mixed marriages and Catholic Schools with fewer Catholic students. The leakage in Catholic population is the apparent result of the breakdown of these supporting factors. A poll by *New York Times* revealed that one out of five persons brought up as catholic no longer considers himself/herself an adherent to the faith and the loss through such defections was three times larger than the gains through conversions.[4]

The impact of the changes severely affected the identity of the priests, being more involved with the Church every day.

Vatican statistics show that out of 3,68,000 parishes in the world, 1,57,000 have no resident priests.[5] A Dutch study showed that against the requirement of 100 replacements of priests through ordination for 100 losses due to death or resignation, the number registered is – Netherlands 8, Belgium 15, Germany 34, France 17, Italy 50, Ireland 45, Spain 35 and Portugal 10. The same is the case with seminarians.[6] In the diocese of Chicago, almost half of those ordained have resigned and married. In such a crisis situation, it seems likely to become necessary to install leaders of community – male or female, married or unmarried – as priests with the prior permission of the authorities. Another alternative is to do away with the requirement of celibacy. As to enforced celibacy, the arguments in its favour no longer seem persuasive. As to the ordination of women, the door stands slammed shut at present. The present Pope is dead set against such changes. The possibility of a change of this policy in future cannot be ruled out, considering the demand of circumstances.

Liberation Theology

Liberation theology is one of the most significant developments in the last few decades. While classical theology aims at a deeper understanding of faith, liberation theology aims to transform the world, echoing in this respect Karl Marx's famous dictum – the task of philosophy is not to understand but to change the world. Classical theology is removed from day-to-day experience – the experience of the sufferings of the poor. Liberation theology emanated and grown out of the experience of some Catholics with the harsh reality of life of the miserable poor. Moreover, while classical theology interprets Jesus' message of 'Kingdom' as a guide to personal morality, liberal theology sees it as, above all, a call to struggle against the forces of social oppression. Advances in social justice and love are partial realization of the Kingdom, steps towards its final consummation.

A crucial event that gave rise to liberation theology was the meeting of the Latin American bishops at Medellin in 1968. In the documents of the meeting, prominence was given to the themes of this thinking: the injustice meted out in Latin America by the Neocolonialism and imperialism and the reinterpretation of salvation to include liberation from servitude and the Kingdom of God as beginning in this world. The God revealed through Jesus Christ is not a Greek "unmoved mover" but a God whose very essence consists of love. They prefer the word liberation to salvation. Therefore, they insist the Church must again become poor in solidarity with poor if it is to be an authentic sign.

A gentle Franciscan padre from Brazil, Leonardo Boff, one of the leaders stresses five features that distinguish liberation theology from traditional theology.

The primacy of the anthropological element over the ecclesiological element as the focus is on the person rather than on the Church.

The Utopian perspective is placed over the factual – the future over the past as the social process is permanently open to transformation – a possibility opened by Jesus.

The critical over the dogmatic to counteract the tendency of institutions to fossilize.

The social over the personal in view of the increasing misery of the masses.

Orthopraxis over orthodoxy as Christ has come not to give intellectual concepts to master, but a new way of acting and living.[7]

No one accuses the Liberation theologians of subscribing to Marx's atheistic dialectical materialism but they were charged with using Marxist analysis as a tool. But they deny the charge. They admit that in so far as Marxist concepts entered into the social sciences, they naturally make use of them. Closely connected with liberation theology is the grass-roots movement called base communities – loosely organized small groups of Catholics drawn from poor urban and peasant masses coming together to pray, worship and to apply the gospel to their situation of poverty and exploitation. A dialogue type sermon at mass is one of the means they employ for this. They felt that they were on the right track and fully in line with the direction of the bishops after Vatican II. Their bishops in their synod declared in 1971 "action on behalf of justice and the transformation of the world fully appear to us as a constitutive dimension of the preaching of the gospel". This position was repeated in the Synod in 1974. The Latin American bishops meeting in 1979 stated that the Church should have a "preferential option for the poor".[8]

Boff in his book *Church, Charism and Power* summoned the Church to a conversion, to forsake the path of power and return to the Church Jesus had in mind, one that would embrace "poverty, rejection of false security, acceptance of the inability to control the future". Boff wanted to restore the respect for the many gifts or charisms promised by Jesus to all members of the Church. He finds the Church's present way of exercising power and control abusive and a cancer in its body, most evident in the inquisitorial spirit that, he claims, still dominates Vatican. But, at the same time, he favours some form of authority to prevent the possible anarchy when charisms are given a free reign. But, Cardinal Joseph Ratzinger, Prefect of the ccngregation for the Doctrine of the Faith, Vatican singled out Boff, his student, for the temerity to apply liberation theology to the Church itself. While Boff wanted a decentralised church, the Cardinal favoured more centralization. Anyhow, Boff was invited to Rome for a conversation. But, before both met, Vatican fired a warning shot. "Instruction on certain aspects of the Theology of Liberation" charging the liberationists with an uncritical use of Marxist modes of analysis. In the meantime Cardinal Arns intervened in favour of Boff. Arns' intervention highlighted the fact that the debate was over the future of the Church in Brazil. Arns and Boff were leaders of the 'new church' being forged in the bloody turmoil of revolution and counter revolution in Latin America, a church no longer subservient to the dictators but a friend of the poor, a church where priests and religious work in the slums. At last, Boff was ordered to be silent for an indefinite period. Boff accepted the reprimand saying that he preferred "to walk with the Church rather than to walk alone with my theology".

But the events took a happier turn soon when the senior bishops held a meeting with the Pope. It revealed that the Pope was much better disposed towards the theology, than people thought. Boff was released from the silencing order. Vatican on 5th April, 1986 wherein Marxism was rejected for its recourse to violence and its doctrine of class warfare issued a more positive critique of Liberation theology "Instruction on Christian freedom and Liberation". At the same time, the document does not reject the basic ideas of liberation theology but seeks to correct certain exaggerations.

The Instruction refers to the real progress made in the cause of human liberation like abolition of slavery, strides towards equality etc. Without mentioning Marxism by name, it warned against collectivist solutions to poverty. Solidarity is necessary if the grave socio-economic problems of our times are to be solved, it pointed out. It condemns recourse to violence, as it will only lead to greater solitude. Recourse to armed struggle is admitted only as a last resort. Moreover, the refinements of technology available to tyrants make non-violence a preferable option. Finally, the instruction insists on the need for the clergy to stay clear of direct involvement in the political process, which should be left to the domain of the laity.

Arns and most of the bishops welcomed the document in Brazil. Boff applauded Vatican for giving a universal dimension to "values that were initially only those of the Third World". A later papal letter to the Brazilian bishops referred to their "dear base communities" and spoke of the chance the bishops had "to renovate all of Catholic theology".

Nicaragua is perhaps the best example of the liberation theology in action, where 2 per cent of the families owned 46.6 per cent of the land while the bottom 43 per cent had to eke out a living from sub-family-size portions of land. It was members of the base communities who began to identify themselves with the liberation of the people with the armed struggle led by the Sandinistas. The local church became the centre of the resistance movement. A number of young Christians entered directly as combatants while others helped by establishing communication network. Many priests advised parents to allow their children to join the guerillas as a legitimate option for the Christians. At times, even the priests, pastors and religious would help make the bombs while also teaching first aid. At the last stage when the Sandinistas were preparing for their last offensive, the bishops issued a statement reaffirming the traditional doctrine of a just insurrection when all other means have failed. Later, victory came for the Sandinistas. A civil war that had cost fifty thousand lives and brought ruin to the country was over. The Marxist Sandinistas gained near total political control. One of the major irritants of the bishops was that the priests who held high government posts disobeyed orders to resign.

In the 1990 elections, the Sandinistas faced a stunning defeat. Even then, they remained the largest political party. But the Church remained divided between pro- and anti-Sandinistas.

El Salvador

El Salvador was another testing ground for liberation theology. The uprising in Nicaragua was against a corrupt dictator. But, in El Salvador, it was a struggle against an oligarchy supported by the military and the powerful United States. In 1932, there was an eruption of violence by the peasants against brutal exploitation that was brutally repressed with the slaughter of 10,000 people. In 1960s, the Christian Democratic Party was formed in El Salvador with anti-communism and land-reform in the agenda.

In 1977, Oscar Romero, a conservative not favourably disposed towards confrontation tactics, was installed as Archbishop of El Salvador. A few days after his installation, the landholding oligarchy, in a fraudulent election, installed one General Romero (similarity only in name) as President. The government forces massacred thousands who gathered to protest against this election. In a few months following the installation of General Romero, the toll on the clergy has become dreadful. A terrorist group named 'White fathers' was organized by the Oligarchy. They issued a handbill with the message 'Be a patriot, kill a priest'. The Jesuits were asked to leave the country. Many priests were expelled from the country or jailed or beaten or threatened or killed. Archbishop Romero in his radio sermon urged the soldiers to stop firing at their own unarmed brothers and sisters and that the soldiers are not obliged to obey an order against God's law. The next day when Bishop Romero was celebrating mass, he prayed that the Eucharist would "feed us so that we may give our body and our blood to suffering and pain as Christ did, not for himself, but to give ideas of justice and peace to our people". At the very moment, the bishop was shot dead by a sharpshooter miscreant. This led to an upheaval in the struggle, increasing the number of martyrs, from among the priests, nuns, catechists, etc. The number of victims rose to seventy thousand, many of them dying at the hands of the right wing death squads. In November 1987, six Jesuits working at the Central American University were dragged from their beds and gunned to death. In effect, the struggle has become a war between the Church and the Oligarchy for the rights of the exploited peasants and labour.

Role of Women in the Church

When the bishops were wrestling with economic and social issues, they were hard pressed to deal with one of the volatile issues in the Church – the ordination of women. Committed feminists argue that the major documents of church tradition are shot through with anti-female prejudices. The critics of Christian tradition point out the misinterpretation of scripture relating to creation of Eve from Adam's rib and Eve's part in Adam's fall. St. Augustine held a dualistic view of the body as antagonistic to the spirit, seeing women as dominated by bodiliness compared to man who stands for the predominance of the spirit. Hence, the predominance of bodiliness, sensuality, pettiness and maliciousness are seen in women. According to Augustine. "This definition of femaleness as body decrees a natural subordination of female to male as flesh must be subject to the spirit in the right ordering of nature." St. Jerome was obsessed with the dress, adornment and physical appearance of women. According to him, the virgin must blot out whatever was specifically female in her visual image by eschewing all adornment, veiling her face and limbs and wearing unshapely dress.

According to St. Paul, the coming of Christ has abolished all inequality including that between men and women. But he forgot his radical theological vision in his practical dictates as the subordination of women became normative, only as a concession to the social order of his day. For St. Thomas Aquinas, the inferior and subordinate status of women was not only one of the most obvious facts of existence, it was also divinely ordained condition whose origins were fully explained in the scripture and he therefore interpreted the Genesis and the Pauline epistles in this perspective. He also found a confirming explanation in Aristotle who defined women as a misbegotten male. Biological reason was also advanced to substantiate the inferiority of women. The male seed carried in its potency the total genetic structure of the offspring and therefore should produce by nature the image of its origin – another male – unless some accident happened to the male sperm in which case a female is begotten more properly misbegotten. This attributes a subhuman form for women.

In the Incarnation, God assumed a male form because only in the male is the image of God that is, intellectually, seen in its fullness. For the same reason, women were to be excluded from the priesthood.

But, the feminists see the deep-rooted anti-female prejudice of the Church as the main obstacle for the ordination of women. According to the Declaration of Vatican in October 1976, the Church refuses to ordain women not because of anti-female prejudices but because it wants to remain faithful to the example of Jesus Christ himself who did not choose to bring women into the ranks of the Apostles despite the fact that he showed a singular lack of prejudice towards women. The document says that the symbolism inherent in the sacramental role of the priest demands that only males be ordained, as the priest takes the part of Christ himself when he consecrates the bread and wine at the altar.

Pope John Paul II in his encyclical 'On the dignity of women', preaches that women should find their identity in motherhood or virginity and pays little attention to other possible ways women might find fulfillment. But, the number of Catholics favouring ordination of women is on the increase.[9]

As we have seen, the Post-Second Vatican Church is burdened to find solutions for a series of problems in the 21st century such as celibacy of clergy, ordination of women, accomplishing the unity of churches, liberation theology, faith and morals including ethics in sexual behaviour, divorce, dearth of priests in the developed world, the estrangement of youth, devotion to Mary and so on.

FOOTNOTES

1. Thomas Bokenkotter, *A Concise History of the Catholic Church*, p. 356.
2. Alan Schreck, *The Compact History of the Catholic Church*, pp. 123-32.
3. St. Paul's publications, *The Documents of Vatican II.*
4. *The New York Times*, Sept. 10, 1987.
5. Thomas Bokenkotter, *A Concise History of the Catholic Church*, p. 388.
6. *Ibid.*, p. 389.
7. *Ibid.*, pp. 411-12.
8. *Ibid.*, p. 412.
9. *Ibid.*, pp. 427-29.

Non-Catholic Christians

37

We observed heresies and schisms haunting the Catholic Church in different periods of history resulting in the emergence of separate Christian communities not in communion with Rome. Many of them faded away in the course of history and a few of them retraced to the Catholic fold. But, several of them exist today in organized form in different parts of the world with their own doctrines of faith, liturgy and practices. These churches follow different administrative systems, the Episcopal system (governed by bishops, e.g., the Orthodox and Anglican churches), the Presbyterian system (governed by presbyters or elders of equal rank, e.g., the Church of Scotland) and the congregational system (a union of congregations in which each congregation looks after its affairs, e.g., the Pentecostal churches). In faith and practices also, these churches differ from one another, from those following the Catholic faith excluding papacy to those at the extreme other end not accepting even the divinity of Jesus Christ. These denominations outside the Catholic Church are broadly classified under four categories: (1) the Heretical Churches, (2) the Orthodox Churches, (3) the Anglican Church, and (4) the Protestant Churches with hundreds of divisions and subdivisions born and grown within them. A recent estimate shows that the number of denominations in Christianity is thirty-three thousand eight hundred and twenty, but the figure is likely to be more as independent denominations arise every day in the nook and cranny of all continents. Here, we are attempting a cursory view of these groups.

1. Heretical Churches

The Nestorian Church

The founder is Nestorius, the Patriarch of Constantinople (428 to 431 AD), who shared the views of the extremists in the Antiochian school that conceived the distinction in the two natures in Christ as of two persons. His teaching is that Christ was a human person to whom the divine person was united. In other words, Christ was a unique figure, the 'Word of God' dwelling in Christ as in a temple. Anastasius, the chaplain of Nestorius, in one of his speeches, presumably influenced by Nestorius, declared that Mary is not the 'Mother of God', but only the 'Mother of Christ'. This teaching raised much hue and cry in the Church. St. Cyril of Alexandria (376-444) took cudgels against Nestorius for challenging the true faith of the Church. In 431 AD, the General Council at Ephesus condemned Nestorianism and deposed Nestorius. This was later confirmed by the General Council of Chalcedon in 451 AD. Though condemned, Nestorian faith spread to many parts of Persia and Syria. Edessa, the highest seat of learning in Persia became a centre of Nestorianism. From there, it spread to several countries including India and China.

Nestorians, expelled from the Roman Empire by Emperor Zeno (474-491), were welcomed, protected and encouraged by the Persian non-Christian Kings for political reasons. Those Christians who were already there in Persia from the early periods of Christianity also joined them. The theologian bishops, Theodore of Mapsuestia and Deodore of Tarsus became the accepted teachers of this Church, next to Nestorius. In 652 AD, Muslims conquered Persia and murdered the Persian King. The persecution unleashed by the Muslims and Persians forced the Christians to migrate to other countries. There, they propagated their faith and converted many. In one of their early documents, it is recorded that twenty thousand Turks and Mongols accepted their faith. Traveller Marco Polo (1256-1323) testifies the presence of Nestorians in China. This group in India, known as the 'Chaldean (Assyrian) Syrian church of the East', who were originally Nestorians is now reported to be not enthusiastic about Nestorian faith.

In the 16th century, as a result of a split among them, one group returned to the Catholic Church. The Chaldean patriarch titled 'Simon' residing in a village named K'dhaneese from 18th century was exiled to the Cupros (Cyprus) island by the Muslim Government in Iraq and his followers migrated to New Guinea under the auspices of the United Nations. There is no monasticism in this church. Anyhow, the Nestorian church known under different names such as Assyrian church, Persian church, Chaldean church etc. which once flourished under the Persian Kings is now only a splinter group scattered all over the world.

Monophysites or Eutychianism

Founder is a monk named Eutychus.

Teaching: The human nature of Christ was absorbed by the divine nature and hence Christ has only one nature, the divine.

The General Council of Chalcedon condemned this teaching. Therefore, the monophysites who opposed the decision at Chalcedon are also known as anti-Chalcedonians. The Churches which accepted monophysitism are mainly the Churches in Armenia, the Church in Syria later known as the Jacobite church, the Coptic church in Egypt and the Church in Abyssinia (Ethiopia). Later, it spread to other countries including India, in the course of time, for different reasons.

(i) The Churches in Armenia

Armenia, the source of Euphrates and Tigris rivers, is situated in West Asia, west of the Caspian Sea and north of Khurdistan culminating in Mount Ararat. The people are of Aryan race converted to Christianity in the last quarter of the third century through the missionary activities of Gregory the Illuminator supported by King Theridotus (AD 261-317). In the fourth century, this Church, on some confrontation with their mother church in Kaisarieh, erected a separate Catholicate for them. From the 5th to the 9th century, Armenia was under Persia. It is during this period that this church accepted the faith of monophysitism to appease the Persian Kings. In the early times, the Armenians migrated to adjoining and even remote countries for commercial pursuits, the wealthier ones engaged in banking. The Armenian streets that we find in some cities in India were once the abode of these migrants. They established two churches and one college in Calcutta. Armenians were subject to one of the most brutal massacres in modern history by the Turks (1894-96); more than a million of them perished during the Great War and the race was almost exterminated.

(ii) The Jacobite Church in Syria

One of the prominent Monophysite churches is the Jacobite Church in Syria. This church derived its name from Jacob Bhurdhana, earlier a monk in a monastery near Edessa, well-versed in Arabic, Syriac and Greek languages, who later became a bishop and staunch supporter of monophysitism. He adopted a peculiar *modus operandi* to propagate his mission. In his ecstasy and zeal, he dressed in coarse clothes (used to cover donkeys and hence known as Bhurdhana), wandered through the streets of Syria propagating his faith. During his efforts lasting 35 years, he converted a large number of people, ordained thousands of priests, consecrated 88 bishops and two Patriarchs of Antioch: Sergius of Tella (543-546) and Black Paul (547-565). Bizantine Emperor Justinian I, opposed to the anti-Chalcedonians, resorted to oppressive measures to suppress them. But Empress Theodora was sympathetic towards monophysites and did whatever possible to help them. Many migrated to Persia during the period of persecution. In the seventh century, the Jacobite Church spread from Syria to Asia Minor and Cupros (Cyprus) Islands. In the 12th and 13th centuries, several religious scholars like Patriarch Michael I (1166-1199), Syriac Scholar Gregory Bar Hebraeus (1226-1286), Divannasios Barslibi, the bishop of Amida etc. provided the Jacobite Church with distinct doctrines of faith that served as a fillip for its structural and administrative compactness. After the disappearance of these scholars from the scene, this Church began its decline due to internal conflicts and persecution by the Muslims. In the 16th century, there were only fifty thousand people in this Church in Syria. In the 17th century, a group among them embraced the Catholic Church. Another important event in the seventeenth century is its contact with a section of the St. Thomas Christians in India. Due to the vicissitudes of history, a Jacobite Church was accidentally established in India about which we have dealt with in Part Four on 'Christianity in India'. This Church, though later underwent a vertical split, still remains the major component of the Jacobite Church in the world. The dialogue for unity initiated by the Catholic Church with the Jacobite Church has not yet borne fruit, but a positive result, within not distant a future, is on the cards.

(iii) The Coptic Church of Egypt

The emergence of the Monophysite Coptic Church in Egypt is closely associated with the origin of the Orthodox Church in Alexandria. During the period of persecution by the Turks, thousands of Coptic Christians became martyrs. The present state of affairs of this church is really pitiable. Lack of educated priests is the main drawback. National language is Arabic, but liturgy is in Coptic language not known even to the priests. Now, efforts are on to replace Coptic language with Arabic. This ancient church owns several monasteries in Egypt.

(iv) The Church in Abyssinia

Abyssinia, earlier known as Ethiopia, is situated in Africa on the Western side of the Red Sea. Christianity entered Abyssinia during the period of Emperor Constantine through the efforts of the Church in Alexandria. When the Coptic Church accepted monophysitism, the Church in Abyssinia followed suit through the efforts of Coptic monks. The head of this church is a bishop under the Coptic Patriarch. Some Jewish practices like circumcision, Sabbath etc. are found in this Church along with several other pagan and superstitious rituals. Though living amongst Muslims, this Church upheld Christianity in the face of hardships, for several centuries.

2. The Orthodox Churches

The word 'Orthodox' is derived from two Greek words 'ORTHO' meaning straight, correct, true etc. and 'DOXA' meaning glory. Thus, the word 'Orthodox' means a community worshipping and glorifying God in the true and correct spirit.

After the division of the Roman Empire by Emperor Constantine, a system of naming the Churches based on the division of the Empire developed. The Churches in the Western Empire were known as the Western Church and those in the Eastern Empire were known as the Eastern Church. The Churches that originated later due to the missionary efforts of the respective churches were also known under the name of the mother churches. The independent churches in the East that were having a separate origin and existence were known as the Oriental churches. These churches can be regrouped on the basis of languages used in their liturgies, Syrian, Greek, Coptic, Ethiopian and Armenian. On the basis of patriarchates and liturgies, these churches are divided into five liturgical families, Antiochean, Alexandrian, Bizantine, Armenian and Assyro-Chaldean. Thus the total number of liturgical families is six including the Roman liturgy of the West.

In the chapter on Eastern schism, we have seen the emergence of Orthodox churches in the Eastern Church. These churches having uniformity in faith and practices are commonly known as the 'Orthodox Church of the East' with the liturgy in the respective vernacular. As regards faith, they accept:

The Holy Bible.

The seven sacraments.

The canons of the first seven General Councils, Nicaea I & II, Ephesus I, Chalcedon and Constantinople I, II & III.

The teachings of the Holy Fathers, especially the book of John Damasus on 'Orthodox Faith'.

The Creed (Rule of faith) of Nicaea.

The intercession of Saints.

The prayer for the dead.

The twelve churches under this category are dealt with below:

(i) The Patriarchal Church of Constantinople

Roman Emperor Constantine in 330 AD made Bizantium (renamed as Constantinople) the capital of the Eastern Roman Empire (present name is Istanbul). The General Council of

Constantinople in 381 AD made the Bishop of Constantinople the ranking prelate of the East with primacy next to Rome, a position till then enjoyed by the Church in Alexandria. The political preponderance of the capital city known as 'New Rome', the royal patronage and the leadership of efficient prelates like St. Gregory of Naxianzen (328-389) and John Chrisostum (397-407) enhanced the prestige and status of the Church of Constantinople. In the sixth century, the Patriarch of Constantinople designated himself the 'Ecumenical Patriarch' and brought the Churches of Alexandria, Antioch, Jerusalem and the Churches in the Balkan countries within the circumscription of Constantinople with spiritual and temporal authority over them.

But, the tussle between the Bishop of Rome and Patriarch Photius (878-886) finally led this 'Great church' to become independent in 1054 (see details in the Chapter 30 on "The Orthodox Churches"). The decline of this predominant church of the East started with the conquest of Constantinople in 1453 by the Turks, aggravated by the separation of the Greek Church in 1850 and completed by the Treaty of Lucien in 1923. This church, much dwindled in size and authority, now remains a small Orthodox Church following Bizantine liturgy, with majority of people Greeks.

(ii) The Patriarchal Church of Alexandria

Alexandria, the chief port of Egypt, built by and named after Alexander the Great of Macedonia, is an ancient city of commerce, learning and philosophy. St. Mark is believed to be the founder of the Church in Alexandria. Origen and Clement, the eminent leaders of the ancient church, were the teachers in the Alexandrian seminary. Dynasius the Great (247-264), Alexander who deposed Arius (313-328) and Coorilos, the great theologian (412-444) were eminent patriarchs of the Alexandrian church. Monophysitism and the invasion of Islam were the factors instrumental in the decline of this church. After the General Council of Chalcedon, the Church was divided into two groups, those accepting the canons of the General Council of Chalcedon called 'Melkites' and the other anti-Chalcedonians known as the Coptic, who accept the monophysitism of Diascoros (condemned by the General Council of Chalcedon). Later, when Muslims invaded Alexandria, the Coptic Church supported the Muslims against the 'Melkites'. With the growth of the Church of Constantinople to a position of authority, the Melkite Patriarch became a puppet of the Eastern Roman Emperor and many of his followers embraced Islam. Today, though Egypt, Libya, Arabia, etc. come within the jurisdiction of the Patriarchate of Alexandria, this is a small Church following the Orthodox faith and Bizantine Liturgy.

(iii) The Patriarchal Church of Antioch

The city of Antioch was built in 301 BC by Seleucus Nicator, the founder of the Seleucian dynasty in Syria and one of the commanders of the army of Alexander the great of Macedonia. During the period of Roman Emperors Trejan (97-117 AD), Marcus Orillius (161-180 AD) and Diocletian (284-305 AD), Antioch was the third city of importance in the Roman Empire. Even if we do not admit the traditional belief that St. Peter was the first bishop of Antioch, the Church in Antioch is one of the most ancient Christian Churches in the world. It was in Antioch that the disciples of Christ were first named 'Christians'. Martyr St. Ignatius and several other bishops of Antioch were famous and well-known personalities in the Church of those days. But, the perverted teachings of the successors of Ignatius like bishop Paulose of Samosta, Theodore of Mopsuestia etc. tarnished the image of the Church of Antioch. Consequently, the Churches in Jerusalem and Persia severed their relations with Antioch. The persecution unleashed by the Turks further weakened the Church, which was once ruling over the Churches in Siberia, Jerusalem, Cyprus and Edessa in Persia. Seven churches, which considered the Church in Antioch as their mother church, embraced the Catholic faith. The Orthodox Patriarch in Damascus, the Latin Rite Patriarch in Rome, the Jacobite Patriarch in Murdeen, four other patriarchs – Maronite, Greek, Armenian and Syrian – altogether seven are now using the title 'Patriarch of Antioch'. But, the real heir and successor of the ancient patriarchate of

Antioch is the Orthodox Patriarch at Damascus who has followers in Cilicia, Mesopotamia, Syria and Isaria. All the orthodox Patriarchs till recently were Greeks while the language of the ordinary people was Arabic.

(iv) The Church in Jerusalem

The Patriarchate of Jerusalem occupied the fourth rank among the Patriarchates of the East. The traditional belief is that St. James was the first bishop of Jerusalem. After delinking its relations with Antioch, the General Council of Chalcedon in 451 AD decided to erect a separate patriarchate for Jerusalem with 14 bishoprics (dioceses) including Bethlehem, Kaiseriah (Caesaria), Nazareth, Lida, Ghasa, Tabore, Philadelphia and Acre. More than fifty monasteries (excluding the one especially devoted to guard the Sepulchre) that look after the welfare of the tourists to Jerusalem were under the care, protection and control of the Patriarch of Jerusalem.

(v) The Church in the Cupros (Cyprus) Island

Cyprus is a fertile, mountainous and the third largest island in the Mediterranean, 145 miles long and 60 miles broad. This church is believed to have been established by St. Paul and St. Burnabas in around 46 AD. It remained under the Church of Antioch for four centuries. Later, it was reconstituted as an autocephalous church according to Canon No. 8 of the General Council of Ephesus in 431 AD. The Patriarch of this Church uses the title 'the most blessed Archbishop of Cupros and Novojustinia'. They still use with honour the symbols of dignity granted by Emperor Zeno: bishops wearing red-coloured silk apparel, holding of monarchical sceptre and signing in red ink. In 1878, the Sultan of Turkey handed over Cyprus to Britain as per the Berlin treaty. In 1959, Cyprus became an independent nation.

(vi) The Church in Mt. Sinai Monastery

Mt. Sinai is one of the ranges of three mountains in the Sinai Peninsula between the Gulf of Suez and Gulf of Akaba at the head of the Red Sea. Moses received the Ten Commandments at the summit or slopes of Sinai. The monastery in Sinai was for long under the Patriarchate of Jerusalem. Some dispute between the Patriarchate and the monastery culminated in the monastery obtaining the status of an independent church and the prior of the monastery the status of an archbishop, who now resides in a branch of the monastery in Cairo.

(vii) The Church in Russia

Russia accepted Christianity during the period of Emperor Vladimir I (984-1015) as a result of the missionary efforts of the Church of Constantinople.

Hence, the Church in Russia depended on the Church in Constantinople for a long time. In 1589, the bishop of Moscow was elevated to the dignity of Patriarch of entire Russia, due to the efforts of Emperor Ivanovich. Thus, Moscow became the fifth patriarchate in the Eastern Church. The modern age in the political history of Russia began during the period of Emperor Peter the Great. He abolished the Patriarchate and instead constituted in 1721 a twelve-member Synod consisting of the bishops and the representatives of the Emperor. From thence onwards till the Bolshevik Revolution in 1917, the Church in Russia remained a shadow of the Emperor without any freedom. But it undertook exemplary mission work in the USA, Alaska, Siberia, Persia, Syria, Manchuria and Japan. The services to the Church by eminent personalities like Innocent Veniaminov, the founder of Orthodox Missionary congregation (1868-1879), Nicholas Kosatkin, the bishop of Tokyo (1880-1912), Pleton, the great evangelist and public speaker (1775-1882) Philaret, the scholar who translated the Bible to Slavonic language (1821-1867), Historian Makari etc. are specially noteworthy.

The persecution by the Bolshevik Government in 1917 crushed the Church. 28 bishops and 1215 priests were brutally murdered, the properties of the Church were confiscated, religious teachings were banned and the church buildings were turned into theatres. After the fall of communism in 1993, the Church in Russia is being gradually revived.

(viii) The Greek Church

The Churches in Bulgaria, Yugoslavia, Romania and Greece were once under the Church of Constantinople. But, after Muslim occupation of Constantinople, these churches gradually became independent. The Turkish Government unleashed a series of measures against the members of the Orthodox Church. In the beginning of the 19th century, Greece became politically independent. In AD 1834, a synod of 34 bishops declared the independence of the Greek Church but the Church of Constantinople was initially reluctant to approve the decision. In 1850, the Patriarch conceded. Even now, the Patriarch, as a symbol of authority, continues the practice of consecrating and supplying 'Chrism' to the Greek Church ('Chrism' is a mixture of olive oil and balm or spices consecrated and used in the Catholic and Orthodox Churches for anointing ceremonies in 'confirmation', 'extreme unction' etc.). The administration of this Church is vested in a Synod consisting of the bishops and a layman as the representative of Parliament and presided over by the Metropolitan of Athens. This is a Church very rich in monasticism.

The Synod has the right to elect the bishop, but it is the Government that appoints and pays them. Married men, after the death of wife, can hold episcopal positions. There is a minimum age limit of thirty for priests and twenty-five for deacons. Lent is observed for 40 days before Christmas and 48 days before Easter in addition to all Wednesdays and Fridays and days after Pentecost, day of remembrance of St. Mary and Apostles etc. This is one of the Orthodox churches in dialogue with the Catholic Church for unity. A faction within the Orthodox Church in Greece still owes their allegiance to the Church in Constantinople.

(ix) The Church in Bulgaria

The position of this Church amongst the Orthodox churches is a peculiar one as its mother church in Constantinople considers it a schismatic church. The Bulgarians (the Slav tribe, an important branch of the Aryan race-stock) were converted to Christianity due to the efforts of their King (Tsar) Boris I (882-868), influenced by his close friend Emperor Michael III of Constantinople. For a long time, Greek bishops under the Church of Constantinople ruled this Church. Bulgarians and Greeks were always engaged in hostilities. The Bulgarians stood for an independent church, but the Greeks and the Church in Constantinople were opposed to it. The Bulgarians, in liaison with the ruling Turks, acquired in 1870 the status of an independent church and the heads of the Church were titled 'Exarch' (the administrator) by the Sultan of Turkey. The Patriarch of Constantinople immediately convened a synod and excommunicated the Exarch. But, the churches in Jerusalem, Russia, Romania and Serbia did not accept this decision of the Synod. Therefore, the Church in Bulgaria is in communion with these churches, though it remains condemned by the Church of Constantinople. Today, the Bulgarian Church has jurisdiction over Thrace and Macedonia besides Bulgaria with the palace of the Exarch in Ortakeki.

(x) The Church in Yugoslavia

Yugoslavia is a federation of four small States – Serbia, Montinigro, Bosnia and Herzgovinia – of Slavs in Austria-Hungary before World War I. The efforts of two missionaries named Methodius and Koorilos of Constantinople, considered the Apostles of Slavs, were instrumental in converting the Slavs in the 9th century. This Church continued under Constantinople for nearly five centuries. The Slavs desired to sever the communion with Constantinople and created a separate Patriarchate for Serbia in 1351. The mother church in Constantinople reluctantly approved the new patriarchate in 1375. But the Turks lost the control of this church. The Slavs again came back under the Greeks and Constantinople. After several centuries, the Ecumenical Patriarch himself took the initiative to grant freedom for this church in 1879. In 1920, Belgrade was made the capital of the Patriarchate of Yugoslavia. After the fall of communism, the four component States of Yugoslavia became politically independent and the Churches in these four States are in the process of revival.

(xi) The Church in Romania

History shows that along with political freedom, the Balkan countries acquired freedom of their church as well. In 1885, the Ecumenical Patriarch of Constantinople approved the freedom of the Church in Romania. In the Romanian church, both the priests and the laity are backward in education. Out of 12.5 million people in the Romanian church, Russians and Bulgarians form a sizable component.

(xii) The Church in Georgia

The Church in Georgia, earlier a part of the Russian church, became independent in 1919 with a constitution of their own. But, the Synod in Russia had no occasion to assemble and approve the freedom of the Georgian church due to the post-revolutionary turmoil and strife in the Russian church. But, the Georgian church is generally approved as the twelfth Orthodox Church.

All these twelve churches except the Bulgarian church are in mutual communion. There is uniformity among them in matters of faith, worship, rituals and administration. But there is no uniform language for liturgy, each church following their own vernacular and separate rubrics with some alterations. Festivals are classified into three groups:

(i) Those relating to the Lord (Maranaya),

(ii) Those relating to Mother Mary, and

(iii) Those relating to Saints.

Sermon is not of much importance in worship. Monasteries are not independent, but under the control of the bishops. In administration, episcopal system is followed on the basis of the Canons of the early General Councils (Synods).

In later years, the Orthodox Church spread to many other countries like Poland, Albania, Czech and Slovak republics, America, Finland, Japan, China, and Canada. Though the Church is named after the country, it does not mean that the entire church in the respective countries accepted the Orthodox faith. A faction of the Church remained in communion with Rome following their original rites, Armenian, Alexandrian, Antiochian, and Bizantine. Till 1952, the Orthodox churches were following the Julian calendar. From 1953 onwards, they also follow the Gregorian calendar.

Detailed lists of the Churches within the Catholic communion and those not in communion with Rome are given below:

Churches within the Catholic Communion

1. Roman Catholic Church.
2. Antiochian:
   The Syrian Catholic Church.
   The Maronite Catholic Church.
   The Syro-Malankara Catholic Church.
3. Church of the East:
   The Chaldean Catholic Church.
   The Syro-Malabar Catholic Church.
4. Armenian Catholic Church.
5. Alexandrian:
   The Coptic Catholic Church.
   The Ethiopian Catholic Church.
6. Byzantine:
   The Greek Melkite Catholic Church.
   The Romanian Catholic Church.
   The Ruthenian Catholic Church.
   The Slovak Catholic Church.
   The Russian Catholic Church.
   The Italo-Albanian Catholic Church.
   The Ukrainian Catholic Church.
   The Greek Catholic Church.
   The Krizevcian (Yugoslavia) Catholic Church.
   The Bulgarian Catholic Church.
   The Albanian Catholic Church.
   The Hungarian Catholic Church.
   The Byelorussian Catholic Church.

Churches not in Communion with the Roman Church

1. The Assyrian Church of the East.
   The Assyrian Church of the East with two Patriarchates in Baghdad and USA.
   The Assyrian Church of the East in Trichur.

2. Oriental Orthodox Churches:
   (a) Armenian:
   The Armenian Apostolic Church.
   The Catholicosate of Etchmiadzin.
   The Catholicosate of Cilicia.
   The Patriarchate of Jerusalem.
   The Patriarchate of Constantinople.
   (b) Alexandrian:
   The Coptic Orthodox Church.
   The Ethiopian Orthodox Church.
   The Erithrean Orthodox Church.
   (c) Antiochian:
   The Syrian Orthodox Church.
   The Malankara Syrian Orthodox Church.
   The Malankara Orthodox Syrian Church.
   The Thozhiyoor Church.
   The Mar Thoma Church.
   (d) Eastern Orthodox Churches (Byzantine Orthodox Churches).

(i) The Autocephalous Orthodox Churches

The Patriarchate of Antioch.

The Patriarchate of Jerusalem.

The Orthodox Church of Russia.

The Orthodox Church of Serbia.

The Orthodox Church of Romania.

The Orthodox Church of Bulgaria.

The Orthodox Church of Georgia.

The Orthodox Church of Cyprus.

The Orthodox Church of Greece.

The Orthodox Church of Poland.

The Orthodox Church of Albania.

The Orthodox Church in the Czech and Slovak Republics.

The Orthodox Church in America.

The Autonomous Churches.

The Orthodox Church of Mount Sinai.

The Orthodox Church of Finland.

The Orthodox Church of Japan.

The Orthodox Church of China.

(ii) The Canonical Churches Under Constantinople

The American Carpatho-Russian Orthodox Greek Catholic Church.

The Ukrainian Orthodox Church of America.

The Russian Orthodox Archdiocese in Western Europe.

The Albanian Orthodox Diocese in America.

The Belarussian Council of Orthodox Churches in North America.

The Ukrainian Orthodox Church in Canada.

The Ukrainian Orthodox Church in the United States.

The Churches of Irregular Status.

The Church of the Old Believers.

The Russian Orthodox Church outside Russia.

The Ukrainian Orthodox Church-Kiev Patriarchate and Ukrainian.

The Autocephalous Orthodox Church.

The Belarussian Autocephalous Orthodox Church.

The Macedonian Orthodox Church.

The Old Calendar Orthodox Churches in Greece and Romania.[1]

3. The Anglican Church

It is reasonable to call the early church in England before reform as 'Anglican Church'. The name 'the Anglican Church' generally refers to the body of episcopal churches all over the British Empire and colonies as well as America sprung from the Church of England after the reform.

Though there was scattered presence of Christianity in England even in the early centuries, large-scale organized conversion took place in the sixth century under the leadership of Augustine (the first Archbishop of Canterbury), a Roman monk of the Benedictine congregation, specially commissioned by Pope Gregory the Great (590-604) for conversion of Angles and Saxons. This church remained till the fifteenth century as a strong arm of the Catholic Church with unshakeable loyalty to the Pope and exerting considerable influence in the political sphere of England. The Archbishop of Canterbury became the chief celebrant who crowns the King in the coronation ceremony of the monarch.

A turning point that changed the entire course of history of the Church in England occurred in the sixteenth century during the reign of Henry VIII, the King of England from 1509-1547. In 1521, the Pope conferred on the King the title 'Defender of Faith' for his published treatise in defence of the sacraments, against the attacks of Martin Luther. But when the King sought permission to divorce his first wife Catherine of Aragon and to marry Anne Bolyn, the Pope refused. A breach with the Pope ensued. The King defiantly married Anne Bolyn and secured himself against appeals to the papal court by declaring himself the supreme head of the Church in England. Thereafter, he married several times, altogether six, first wife Catherine and Anne of Cleaves divorced, Anne Bolyn and Catherine Howard executed, Jane Seymour died during childbirth and Catherine Parr survived him. He left behind three successors to the throne, Mary, daughter of Catherine of Aragon, Elizabeth, daughter of Anne Bolyn and Edward, son of Jane Seymour. In 1534, the Parliament passed the *Supremacy Act* accepting the monarch as the head of the Church of England. The suppression of the defiant monasteries and the confiscation of their properties followed (1536-40). The reforms were continued by drawing up *Ten Articles of faith* and publication of an authorized translation of the *Bible*. Three years later, the *six Articles* reiterating the Catholic faith in the 'real presence of Christ in the Eucharist', 'clerical celibacy', 'private masses', 'auricular confession' etc., were adopted to pre-empt the spread of protestant faith. In 1541, Henry was declared the King of Ireland also. In the following two years, he waged successful wars against Scotland and France. He passed away in 1547 after crushing with an iron hand all those who desired to continue the loyalty to Pope and at the same time without deviating from the faith and practices of the Catholic Church.

Edward VI, the son of Henry VIII who ascended the throne in 1547 continued the efforts of his father to strengthen the Anglican Church. The *Book of Common Prayer*, that binds together all the different groups and departments of the Anglican Church even today, was published in 1549. Mary, the daughter of Henry VIII in Catherine of Aragon, succeeded Edward. After her mother's divorce, she was treated with aversion and hence lived in retirement during Edward's reign clinging to her Catholic faith. On her accession to the throne in 1553, the Protestants plotted to put Lady Jane Grey on the throne, but failed. Mary cautiously began to restore Catholicism by imprisoning reformers and reinstating the old bishops. On her choosing Philip of Spain as her husband, a revolt broke out, but it was suppressed, paving the way for execution of Jane Grey and imprisonment of Elizabeth. After the marriage of Mary, religious reaction gained strength. Submission was made to Rome and persecution began resulting in the death of many eminent leaders of the reform movement. But, before achieving anything substantial, Mary breathed her last in 1558 due to ill health, cruelties of Philip, her childlessness and defeat in the war against France resulting in the loss of Calais.

Queen Elizabeth, the daughter of Anne Bolyn, who ruled England for long 45 years (1558-1603), ascended the throne after the death of Mary. The Pope's opposition to her succession on grounds of illegitimacy of birth strengthened her attachment to the Protestant faith. During her reign, the power of Spain crumbled by the defeat of the Armada, maritime enterprise flourished, commerce was extended and literature reached its zenith of perfection. In 1563, the *39 Articles of Faith* were published. Later, the Parliament approved the Anglican Church as *The Established Church of England*. Thus, from sixteenth century onwards, the Church has become one of the departments of the Government. The appointment of new archbishops, payments to the office-bearers of the Church, upkeep and maintenance of churches etc. were brought within the domain of the Government. Bishops were granted the privilege of becoming members of the Upper House – the House of Lords. In those days, there were 43 and 13 dioceses respectively under the Archbishops of Canterbury and York. The administration of the Church was vested in two bodies, *the Convocation* consisting of the Diocesan bishops and the representatives of the clergy and the *National Assembly* consisting of people's delegates. Now, efforts are on to free the Church from State control.

In the early period itself, many missionary societies emerged in the Anglican Church for propagation of gospel and evangelisation. The Church Missionary Society (CMS), the London Missionary Society (LMS), the Society of St. John the Evangelist, Oxford Mission, SPG 1701 etc. are some among them who were instrumental in propagating the gospel in British colonies and other countries. The Churches established by these missionaries in different countries were known by both names, the 'Anglican Church' and the 'Church of England'.

The influence of Protestantism gave rise to the emergence of three groups in the Anglican Church on the basis of faith and practices. Freedom from the strict disciplinary framework of the Catholic Church accelerated the growth of groups known as the High Church, the Broad Church (also known as the 'Middle Church' or 'Moderate Churchmen's Union') and the Low Church. The High Church also known as Anglo-Catholics advocated continuance of the traditional Catholic faith and practices. The Low Church party emphasised the evangelical side of Protestant teachings. They wanted to reduce the importance of rituals and the role of the priestly office. The Middle Church was in favour of a middle path in between Catholicism and Protestantism. Here, a salient feature to be noted is that all the three groups accepted the Archbishops of Canterbury and York as their ecclesiastical heads and the *39 Articles of Faith*.

Consequent on the passing of the *Act of Uniformity* during the reign of Queen Elizabeth, requiring all to conform to Roman Catholic doctrine and rituals, the clergymen of the Church of England formed a body called 'Puritans' who insisted on the simplicity envisaged in the Holy Scriptures.

Under the Stuart Kings James I (1603-1625) and Charles I (1635-49), the strife between 'the Episcopalians' and 'the Puritans' became bitter and the Kings favoured the anti-puritans. With the Restoration of Charles II in 1660 as King of England, the Puritans became unpopular and the name fell out of use.

In the subsequent years, due to the influence of Protestant ideas, many ideological groups emerged in England and became independent denominations such as Presbyterians, Weslians, Methodists, Congregationalists, Baptists, Society of Friends, Salvation Army etc.; all independent groups of Protestant churches. We shall deal with them when we take up Protestantism.

4. Protestant Churches

There is no church named 'Protestant Church'. The word Protestantism derives from the protestation of a section at the Imperial Diet of Speyer in 1529. Five princes and delegates from fourteen cities took part in this protest. As the Roman Catholic Church was the official religion in the West, the Protestant revolt assumed a politico-religious character. It divided Europe into Protestant and Roman Catholic camps leading to political and religious polarisation. Today the word is commonly applied to all Non-Catholic Churches established in the Western countries by the reformers subsequent to the Reformation Movement.

The supremacy of the Bible, justification by faith alone and universal priesthood of believers are the three cardinal principles of Protestantism. Three systems of Church Government, Episcopal, Presbyterian and Congregational are found among them. When everyone enjoyed the freedom to interpret the Bible in one's own way and in the absence of a final authority to distinguish between right and wrong, innumerable denominations sprang up among the Protestants. Though the Anglican Church was not Protestant in its origin, Protestant ideas crept into that church giving birth to several denominations, some of them like the Salvation Army not deserving to be considered as Christians as they do not believe in Baptism and 'Last Supper'.

(i) The Episcopal System

The word 'Episcopal' is derived from the Greek word Episcopa, *Epi* (meaning 'on' or 'over') and *Skopee* (meaning 'to look'). In the Episcopal system, the Episcopa (called bishop) is the head of the local Church. One of the bishops becomes the head of the whole church. The presbyters and other office bearers down below in the order like deacon, subdeacon, acolytes etc. come under the bishop. Thus, a pyramidal nature of church government is formed in the episcopal system.

(ii) The Presbyterian System

Presbyterianism is the form of church government that regards all ministers in conclave as on the same level in rank and function. It does not recognise the office of bishop. The Church is governed by a gradation of Courts, the 'Kirk Sessions' of office bearers at the level of the congregation, 'Presbyteries' at the level of the district, 'Synods' at a larger level and finally a 'General Assembly' or Synod of the whole Church. The head of the Church is an 'Elder' or 'presbyter' called 'Moderator' elected by the people.

John Knox, the disciple of John Calvin, first introduced the Presbyterian system in Scotland when the Church in Scotland severed its relations with Rome and accepted the reforms. In 1572, when both Scotland and England came under one King, the Church in England made a futile attempt to introduce the Episcopal system in Scotland. But, the *Westminster Confession, Directory of Worship, Shorter and Larger Catechisms,* the pillars of faith of the Presbyterian church were later approved by the Government of England. A salient feature of the Presbyterian system is the recognition of the rights of the lay people, the representative of the faithful is treated on par with the presbyter. This system spread from Scotland to England,

France, Switzerland, Netherlands, Hungary and America and later to India and China through the efforts of the missionaries. In 1661, the Parliament by an Act accepted the Presbyterian Church *as the Established Church of Scotland.*

In addition to the Church of Scotland, there existed in Scotland an independent church by name 'Free Church of Scotland' a union of some subsidiary groups of Presbyterians. In 1928, both churches joined together and now there is only one Presbyterian Church in Scotland.

(iii) The Congregational System

The literal meaning of the word 'Congregation' is a body of people actually or habitually attending a particular church, an assemblage of people.

Congregationalism denotes a form of church government in which each congregation is independent in the management of its own affairs. All the members of the congregation are having equal rights, privileges and status. No synod or government or superiors have any authority over the congregation. The ministers or other ordained people have no right for any reward other than those the faithful are eligible. Robert Brown (1550-1638) in England first introduced this system. The London Missionary Society is the missionary wing of the Congregationalists. The relation between the different congregations is one of fellowship or friendship. The Congregationalists established Yel and Harvard Universities in America.

FOOTNOTE

1. Xavier Koodapuzha (Dr.), *Christianity in India*, pp. 25-30.

The One Church and Many Churches

38

The Church of Jesus Christ is a Communion of Churches

In the post-Reformation period, the Bible acquired a position of primacy enjoyed by the Church and the Pope in the pre-Reformation days. An infallible book – the *Holy Bible* replaced the role of the infallible church as the foundation of faith and Christian life. In the absence of a teaching office, everyone interpreted the *Bible* according to one's own choice and separate churches emanated according to each one's convictions. As the congregations of many of these churches were independent, there exist thousands of churches. It is neither necessary nor practicable to introduce all of them. Hence the main denominations alone are introduced below, highlighting the general features.

1. Society of Friends

In the 17th century, a group of Christians appeared in England advocating that every Christian is expected to live on the basis of one's own 'Inward Light' and not on the basis of literal interpretation of the *Bible* or creed or sacraments or ecclesiastical set up. The leader of this group was a pious Englishman named George Fox (1624-1691). They initially called themselves 'Children of Light' but subsequently changed their name as 'Society of Friends' on the basis of Christ's words "But I have called you friends" (Jn-15: 15). They were often known by the name 'Quakers' as they shivered, stuttered and their voice choked with emotions while praying. In their collective prayer and worship, silence plays an important part to pave the way for the Holy Spirit to work and inspire them. In spiritual matters, men and women enjoyed equal freedom and rights in the Society of Friends. They pray or preach only when the Spirit inspires them. They do not accept any creed or sacraments.

In 1656, the Society started a community in the USA (Pennsylvania) under the leadership of William Pen, one of their leaders. The Society of Friends, though limited in number, exert much influence in the Christian world as a moral force very near to the teachings of Christ and also for their social service, opposition to war, efforts to establish peace among races and communities etc. Friends' House, Easton Road, London is the headquarters of the Society.

2. Methodist Church

The Methodist church, the biggest in number among the Protestant churches, was the result of a reform movement initiated by John Wesley (1703-1791), the son of an Anglican priest. The history of this church is closely linked with the life of Wesley and therefore this church is often known as Weslian Church. Wesley, born in 1703 in Epworth in Lincolnshire, after education in Oxford, was ordained priest in the Anglican Church. Initially he worked in his father's parish, but later (1729) joined as a Tutor in Oxford. There, he gathered his friends as a group for collective prayer, study of the New Testament and visit to the sick. His brother and poet musician Charles and inspiring public speaker Whitfield were members of Wesley's prayer group. Noticing their zeal and alertness in following their methods, the students in Oxford jokingly called them 'Methodists' that later became the name of this community. In their enthusiasm for evangelisation, John Wesley along with his brother Charles went to America but returned to England when they failed in their mission as Wesley, according to his own admission, was not fully 'converted'. Wesley was born and brought up as a High Church Anglican and he wished to continue as a member of the Anglican Church. But, when he appealed to his bishop in the Anglican Church to ordain a priest to be deputed to America, the bishop declined. Thereupon, Wesley, with the help of another priest ordained a presbyter, appointed a superintendent and deputed both of them to America. This episode compelled Wesley to sever his relations with the Anglican Church. But, thoughts on 'Fellowship with God', 'Redemption from sin', 'Certainty of salvation', etc. were haunting him. At this juncture, he accidentally attended a meeting where the speaker was giving a discourse on Martin Luther's commentary on St. Paul's epistle to the Romans. There he found answers to his misgivings – justification by faith alone. At the very moment, he gave his heart to Jesus and was fully convinced of his salvation.

After conversion, John Wesley along with his brother Charles and Whitfield went all over England preaching about their methods and salvation. They established several Methodist communities in England. Later, its branches were set up all over the world with different names such as Methodists (England), Methodist Episcopal (America), Primitive Methodists, United Methodists, Methodists New Connection etc. Only 'born again' people were admitted as members. Faith is uniform in all branches, but there are differences in administrative systems. In 1907, three groups among them, 'Weslian', 'Primitive' and 'New connection' joined together to form the United Methodists. In 1932, the other groups also joined to form the Methodist Church. The speeches of John Wesley and his notes on New Testament are followed as scriptures. Each community is named as 'class system'. Travelling evangelists and local preachers look after the missionary work. The hymns written and composed by the Weslian brothers emphasizing the salvation through Jesus Christ were capable of inspiring all Christians irrespective of denomination, colour, caste or tribe.

3. The Baptist Church

Compulsory adult baptism is the main distinction between the Baptist church and the Congregationalists. According to the Baptists, the original word *'Baptisma'* means a bath by immersion and not by sprinkling. Baptism is, therefore, the sign of internal rebirth and the symbol of witnessing Christ before the world. As such, they claim that their church alone is the true church of Christ.

In the Baptist church, there are two functionaries, the Pastor and the Deacon. For public worship, there are no procedural rules. Normally, the items include hymns, spiritual reading (Gospel), sermon and prayer; much importance being attached to music and sermon. Study of Bible and propagation of faith have prime significance.

John Banyan, the author of 'Pilgrim's Progress', C.J. Spurgan, the great public speaker, William Carey, the founder of the Baptist church in India, Robinson, Rendel Harris etc. were all famous Baptist leaders.

Several groups are found among them; the Disciples or River Brothren, Mennonites, Adventists, Winnie Brennarians, Particular Baptists, Strict Baptists or Plymouth brothers etc. It is rather difficult to define the distinction between them. In 1905; all the Baptist groups have formed a union known as the 'Baptist World Alliance'.

Anabaptists were the Swiss Brothren who were radically opposed to Swingly. They preached Adult Baptism and organised independent congregations.

Disciples of Christ is the result of a reform movement started in America at the beginning of the 19th century. They insist on rigorous adherence to the New Testament as the only model of Christian faith and practice and reject all kinds of credal formulae and traditions. The members are allied in a kind of conventional relationship. They accept baptism by immersion only.

Mennonite church is an offshoot of the Anabaptist movement of the sixteenth century. Menno Simons (1496-1561), a Dutch priest who deserted the Catholic Church led the reform movement. He was a good writer. He did not establish any church or wished his name to be adopted by any church. Two ministers, Martin Boehm and Philip William first used the title 'Mennonite Brothers' at their evangelistic meeting at Baltimore. Persecution compelled them to flee to Russia in 1860. The Mennonite Brothren church was born out of widespread evangelistic and pietistic awakening in the German, Lutheran and Dutch-Prussian Mennonite settlements in South Prussia. They insist on three immersions during baptism. Today, Mennonites are found around the world with large congregations in Angola, Austria, Brazil, Canada, China, Colombia, Germany,

India, Japan, Mexico, Panama, Paraguay, Peru, Russia, USA, Uruguay and Zaire.

The units of the Church are divided into field associations that elect five representatives each to the Governing Council, the supreme body of the Church. The Governing Council elects the President and other office-bearers for a period of two years.

Seventh Day Adventists are doctrinally heirs of the Mellerite Movement of the 1840s. They celebrate the Sabbath, the day of rest and worship, on Saturday. Although the name 'Seventh Day Adventists' was chosen in 1860, the denomination was organised only in 1863. At the initial stages, work was confined to North America. From there they moved to Africa, first in Gold Coast (Ghana) and later to South Africa. The publication and distribution of literature were major factors in the growth of the movement. This Church has units in a large number of countries at present.

The distinctive message is the everlasting gospel, the basic Christian message of salvation through faith in Jesus Christ based on threefold message of Revelation, the call to worship the Creator and that 'the hour of His judgment has come'. This message is epitomized as 'the commandments of God and the faith in Jesus'.

Plymouth Brothers – Plymouth is the largest town of Devonshire, England. This community founded by Nelson Darby in 1830 is also known as Darbyites. They accept the Calvinistic view of the Christian religion and exclude all unconverted men from their communion. As they believe in the common priesthood of all the faithful, they have no separate office-bearers or functionaries like presbyters or deacons. They assemble in the homes of the faithful for breaking the bread as was done during the days of the Apostles. Now, there are six groups among the Plymouth Brothers.

Free Will Baptist Church was started in America in the 17th century. The earliest work for this church is credited to Paul Palmer who organised a church in North Carolina. Today this group carries out active denominational programmes in missions, education, childcare etc. This organisation is purely religious, social, charitable and autocephalous.

4. The Presbyterian Church

The Presbyterian Church is the outcome of the religious awakening in England and Wales in the 18th century. A church named 'Welsh Calvinistic Methodist or Presbyterian church of Wales' emerged in Wales. The Assembly is the supreme body of the Church exercising authority over all churches within its fold and the authorised body to effect changes or to modify its constitution. Matters between the Presbyterian Church and other world bodies like the Council of World Missions, World Alliance of Reformed Churches, Christian Conference of Asia etc. are dealt with by the Assembly renamed as synod. In the North-East India, the Presbyterian Church has a good number of followers.

5. The Evangelical Church

In 1846, an alliance of Christians of all countries and denominations holding evangelical principles was founded in London to fight religious indifference and the power of the Pope. The Oriental Missionary Society International founded the Evangelical Church in the East. They emphasize the establishment of Bible Seminaries, intensive and extensive evangelism and the planting of indigenous national churches. They work in partnership with other national churches. The Oriental Missionary Society started missionary work in Japan in 1901. Today, it is the fourth largest protestant body in Japan. Later, they founded churches in India. Their units are called Area Conferences. They run a lot of educational institutions, social service centres and children's homes.

6. The Salvation Army

As the Salvation Army has forsaken Baptism and Holy Supper (Holy Eucharist) many consider them as a non-Christian denomination. General William Booth (1829-1912), an Englishman born in 1829 in Nottingham is its founder. Booth, though not concerned with any religion in his young days, later enrolled himself as a minister and an evangelist in the New Connection Baptist Church. In this period, he was engaged in the uplift of the orphans and downtrodden people of London with the help of two voluntary organisations named 'East End Mission' and 'Christian Mission'. This humble work combining evangelism with charity to serve the poor and sick gradually grew from its low beginning to a very big institution, now serving millions of poor all over the world under the name and banner 'Salvation Army'. In 1878, this movement was organised on semi-military lines with distinctive uniform and military degrees of ranks with such accessories as brass bands and banners. Bound up with religious propaganda, Salvation Army conducts enormous work for social amelioration including care for the sick, education, assistance in natural disasters etc. They run homes of rest, hostels, workshops, farms, schools, hospitals, leper colonies etc. all over the world. Its chief official publication is *War Cry*. On the death of General William Booth, his son Bramwell Booth (1912) succeeded as General. After Bramwell being superseded, E.J. Higgins and on his death Evangeline Booth, the daughter of William Booth became Generals (1934).

The work of the Salvation Army, already done and still doing for the poor and the downtrodden, especially among the outcastes in all parts of the world, deserves to be recorded in golden letters in the history of mankind.

7. The Lutheran Church

The Lutheran Churches emerged from the Protestant reformation in Germany. Martin Luther broke with the Catholic Church over the issue of attainment of salvation by mankind. According to Luther, the death of Jesus Christ absolved mankind from the penalty for its disobedience to God. According to him, humanity no longer required to live in fear of God's punishment. This teaching jeopardised all aspects of faith and practices of the Catholic Church and paved the way for the emergence of Lutheranism. The Lutherans rejected the notion that the Catholic Church alone was the only channel of God's grace. They also rejected the authority of Pope over all peoples and held that all Christians were equal before God as shareholders of the priesthood of Christ. There is no special status for priests in the Lutheran Church except by being called to exercise specific ministries on the basis of ability and training. The Lutherans believe only in two sacraments instituted by Jesus, baptism and communion as against seven sacraments in the Catholic Church. Celibacy is not mandatory for priesthood in the Lutheran Church.

Lutheranism came to North America from Europe through the colonialists and immigrants. The Lutheran Church assumed different names in different areas such as Evangelical Lutheran Church, Gossner Evangelical Lutheran Church. Good Samaritan Evangelical Lutheran Church etc. depending upon ethnic heritages and local customs. To co-ordinate the activities of all Lutheran Churches, the Lutheran World Federation, an international co-operative body was established in 1947.

The basic unit of administration in the Lutheran practice is the congregation. It is normally administered by a council headed by the senior pastor or layman elected from the council. The council consists of elected representatives of the congregation and the clergy.

8. The Unitarian Church

This is a term applied to those of the Protestant faith who profess belief in one God denying the Church doctrine of the Trinity and in particular the divinity of Christ, though they acknowledge his paramount importance as a teacher and inspired prophet. In England, the clergy expelled by the Act of Uniformity in 1662 largely increased their membership. Eminent persons like Emerson, Holmes, Longfellow, Lovell, Martino etc. were members of this denomination.

9. The Universalists

The 'Universalists' is a protestant denomination among Christians who profess belief in the final harmony of all souls with God and the ultimate triumph of good over evil in each individual soul. Rev. J. Murray founded this movement in the USA in 1770 to protest against the doctrine of endless punishment. This idea was largely developed by Hosea Ballou

(1771-1852) under whom it took on a Unitarian tendency. In 1926, there were 500 Universalist Churches in the USA.

10. The Brethren Assembly

The Brethren Assembly was neither a new church nor a novel teaching but a reawakening within the Reformation of the 16th century. The move of a number of believers to return to the form of worship and prayer of the early days of Christianity resulted in the formation of an association. They gave up their social disparities and differences to form a brotherhood of themselves, later known as Brethren. The first assembly of these brethren was held at Dublin, Ireland in 1825 with the initial endeavour to reform the Churches in which they were members. But a major change in strategy occurred when four of them assembled in Dublin in 1827 to break the bread without the presence of an ordained priest. This was based on the teaching of St. Peter on the royal priesthood of all those who recognise Jesus Christ as their saviour. They held that an ordained priest was not a prerequisite for the worship of God. On that day, all the four that assembled there – Cronin, Darby, Bellect and Hutchinson – constituted a congregation.

Later, similar congregations were held at Plymouth and thence it spread to other countries and continents. Within a short span of time, J.N. Darby initiated the setting up of 1400 similar congregations in England, USA, New Zealand, West Indies, Switzerland, France and Holland. By 1829, it spread to Arabia and Egypt and in 1835 to India. These 'Brethren' Assemblies had no centralised administration. Every regional church had become almost autonomous. Elders carry out day-to-day work or service persons recognised by believers as men of God-given talents. However, members of the Church of a region usually organise informal conventions, activities for women and children, youth meetings, prayer meetings, Bible classes etc.

Some minor groups like Jerusalem Church founded by Zwedenberg, Christian Socialists, and Christian Scientists etc. are not mentioned here for want of space.

11. The Pentecostal Churches

There is no agreement among the Pentecostalists as to when and where the movement actually began. But the main roots of the movement are in the Holiness Movement, which was a puritan reaction against the growing institutionalism and ritualism in the mainline churches. Those who think that the Baptism in the Spirit accompanied by the gift of tongues is the central characteristic of Pentecostalism generally consider Charles Parham (1873-1929), an American Holiness preacher as its founder. According to them, the origin of the movement is traced to Parham's Bethel Bible School in Kansas, USA where one of his students spoke in tongues on receiving the baptism in Spirit.

Those who wish to highlight the Movement's Black roots, interdenominational character and ecumenical spirituality attribute the origin of the movement in the religious revival initiated by William Seymour (1870-1922), a black ecumenist, son of a former slave and the student in Parham's Bible school for a while.

The movement soon spread to the rest of the United States and to other parts of the world. The apostle of the movement in Europe is considered to be Thomas Baratt, a Norwegian Methodist Minister. Though the movement entered South America, Africa and Asia in the first decade of the 20th century itself, it gathered momentum only after World War II. It is difficult to positively identify all the Pentecostals in the World because the groups are numerous and often amorphous.

The *World Christian Encyclopaedia* estimates the Pentecostals in the World in 1980 as over one hundred million. It has grown fourfold in number in less than twenty years. In 1996, their number was estimated as 400 million.

Scholars divide the Pentecostals into three mainstreams:

Classical Pentecostals and their missions.

Charismatic Movements within the mainline churches.

Indigenous non-white churches in the Third World.

Classical Pentecostals are those who left the mainline churches and joined autonomous Pentecostal denominations like the Assemblies of God, the Apostolic faith Movement, the Church of God etc.

The Charismatics, also called Neo-Pentecostals, are those who have accepted certain elements of Pentecostal spirituality, but continue to remain in their traditional churches. Charismatic prayer groups existed in the mainline churches even before the emergence of Pentecostalism. But, it became popular only in the 1960s. Today it attracts large number of adherents from the traditional churches. It experienced massive growth in the Catholic Church in the wake of the Catholic Charismatic revival originated in 1967 in two universities in America. Charismatics claim that Pentecostal spirituality does not in any way militate against the prevailing tradition. On the other hand, it helps to understand and appreciate traditional faith better. According to Hollenweger (1986:9) "Charismatic spirituality does not change any of our melodies, but it changes the rhythm and sometimes the key. It does not change our churches, but it lights them up. It does not change our ministry; it makes it more credible. It does not change our ecumenical commitment; it makes it more alive."

The third category, the non-white indigenous Churches, is found in Asia, Africa and Latin America. They have no historical links with the Pentecostal Churches or their founders in the West. Yet, they are regarded as part of the Pentecostal movement because in their theology, spirituality and worship, they resemble the early Pentecostals. But all Pentecostals do not accept these indigenous churches as part of the movement as some of their beliefs and practices appear 'heretical' and non-Christian. There were 82 million non-white Pentecostals in the world in 1980. This is the fastest growing segment of Christianity in the world today.

Basic Features

Pentecostalism is not monolithic in doctrine or practice. A wide variety of beliefs, practices and organisational pattern known as Patchwork quilt, Rainbow, Kaleidoscope, Mosaic and Umbrella exist among them. But, several threads binding these churches together into a unified movement are visible.

Emphasis on Experience

Pentecostalism emphasises experience rather than doctrine. Justification, sanctification and baptism in the Holy Spirit, three most significant episodes in Christian life are not mere articles of faith but physically palpable experiences. "For them, the medium of communication is, as in Biblical times, not the definition but the description, not the statement but the story, not the doctrine but the testimony, not the book but the parable, not a systematic theology but a song, not the treatise but the television programme, not the articulation of concepts but the celebration of banquets" (Hollenwager 1986:10).

Centrality of the Bible

Unquestioning acceptance of the Bible is another common trait of Pentecostalism. The Assemblies of God says "The Bible is the inspired word of God, a revelation from God to man, the infallible rule of faith and conduct and is superior to conscience and reason, but not contrary to reason" (Bloch-Hoell, 1964-97).

Almost all the Pentecostals believe that "whatever is said in the Bible is literally true" and that "the Bible has answers to all our problems". They oppose all attempts to interpret the Bible critically.

Baptism in the Holy Spirit

Baptism in the Holy Spirit is the most distinctive characteristic of Pentecostalism. According to the British Pentecostal Fellowship, "their only distinctive doctrines and practices centre around being Pentecostal in that they believe in the baptism in the Holy Spirit as a definite experience for Christians, received subsequent to conversion, accompanied by the manifestation of the spirit as inaugurated by the Grace of God on the day of Pentecost and still possible in the Church" (Bloch-Hoell). Most Pentecostal groups believe that the 'initial physical sign' of Glossalia or speaking in tongues always accompanies the Spirit Baptism. However, there is no unanimity among them in this respect. Some believe that other visible supernatural signs, not necessarily glossalia, could accompany the Spirit Baptism.

Charisms

They believe that the nine charisms or spiritual gifts mentioned in Corinth 12: 8-10 are today available to those who are baptised in the Spirit. All charisms are, however, not accorded equal importance. The general tendency is to highlight the more sensational charisms like speaking in the tongue, healing and prophecy.

Puritan Morality

Pentecostalists enjoin a very strict moral code. They disdain the culture of modernity, its technological achievements and consumerist orientation. Use of tobacco and alcohol is forbidden. Watching Television, seeing movies and wearing jewellery are wrong. Some are even opposed to medical treatment.

Eschatology

They are convinced that the end is near. Few are prepared to predict when exactly it would happen. Natural calamities, wars, terrorism, growing consumerism and immorality are signs of imminent Second Coming of Christ when only the born again will be saved. Therefore, they display urgency and zeal to convert as many as possible to their faith.

The Pentecostal movement has achieved phenomenal growth in India in the last two decades. The growing appeal of this phenomenon points to a new spiritual awakening in India.[1]

FOOTNOTE

1. The Deepika, *Indian Christian Directory*, 2000.

Short Notes

39

1. Canonisation in the Catholic Church[1]

There was no formal canonisation in the early centuries. But, public cult was given to the martyrs and recognised by the local bishop. Canonisation was reserved to the Apostolic See during the time of Pope Alexander III (1159-1181).

Pope Sixtus V (1585-1590) created a special congregation to deal with the process of canonisation. Pope Urban VIII and Benedict XIV introduced legislations giving the process a legal framework. This was later codified in the Canon Law. According to the present law, four stages prescribed are:

(i) Informative process whereby the local bishop, where the servant of God died, after enquiry submits the report to the Roman Curia.

(ii) Introduction of the subject in the Curia.

(iii) Apostolic process and judgments on validity of Apostolic process.

(iv) Heroic virtues practised by the 'Servant of God'. Authenticity of the miracles and approval by the Pope.

After successful completion of these four processes, the Pope declares the servant of God 'Blessed' – Beatification. After beatification, if two miracles through the intercession of the 'Blessed' are proved beyond doubt and approved by the 'congregation' for the cause of saints (after Vatican II) the 'Blessed' is canonised by the Pope.

Up to the stage of Beatification, the declaration is not ex-cathedra and hence it does not attract infallibility. But, canonisation is an ex-cathedra declaration and therefore infallible. Now, the number of miracles has been reduced from two to one and the apostolic process stands dispensed with by Pope John Paul II. For 'Beatification', the cult and liturgical practices are restricted to the diocese or congregation of the 'Blessed' while Canonisation applies to the whole church.

2. College of Cardinals[2]

Cardinals in the Catholic Church are advisers and assistants to the Pope in the governance of the Church. The Pope chooses them. They form the supreme Council or the Senate of the Pope and on the death of the Pope, the college of cardinals known as conclave elect the successor Pope subject to the restriction that none of them, at the time of entry into the conclave should have passed their 80th birthday. The maximum number of cardinals is now fixed at 120.

There are three divisions or orders of cardinals:

Cardinal bishops – they are the bishops of the suburbicarian Sees, viz. the bishops of the seven dioceses adjoining Rome.

Cardinal priests formerly the Rectors of the ancient 'titular churches' of Rome. Now they are in fact archbishops and bishops of dioceses outside Rome, and

Cardinal deacons formerly deacons in charge of the divisions of Rome. Now they are archbishops or bishops holding important posts in the Roman Curia.

The first cardinal is the Dean of the Sacred College and always the bishop of Ostia. Till the 19th century, only those from the countries in Europe were chosen as Cardinals.

3. Encyclical

'Encyclical' is a letter addressed by the Pope to the bishops all over the world either condemning prevailing errors or counselling them on how to act or react concerning public questions of the day. In the early centuries, many bishops used this term for their pastoral letters. But, in modern days, this term is used only for the official letters of the Pope. An encyclical is different from 'Bull', 'Brief', 'Constitution', 'Rescript', 'Decrees' etc. issued by the Pope on specific occasions and for specific purposes. Pope Benedict XIV (1740-1758) is the first Pope who used this term for his letter *'Ubi Primum'*. After Benedict XIV, many Popes widely used this medium as a part of the responsibility of their teaching office (*Magisterium*) as listed below:

Name of Pope	Year	Number of Encyclicals
Benedict XIV	1740 – 1758	29
Clement XIII	1758 – 1769	10
Clement XIV	1769 – 1774	5
Pius VI	1775 – 1799	12
Pius VII	1800 – 1823	11
Pius VIII	1829 – 1830	3
Gregory XVI	1831 – 1846	12
Pius IX	1846 – 1878	36
Leo XIII	1878 – 1903	84
Pius X	1903 – 1914	16
Benedict XV	1914 – 1922	12
Pius XI	1922 – 1939	30
Pius XII	1939 – 1958	39

These letters are written in Latin, the official language of the Church and the first two or three words are considered the title of the Encyclical.

4. The Padroado

The role of 'Padroado' can be understood only in the context in which it was necessitated. Islam was rapidly spreading in the East and the cradle of Christianity came under Muslim occupation. The ancient patriarchates of Antioch, Alexandria, Jerusalem and later Constantinople came under the control of the Saracens. They threatened the European countries on all the three sides. The Crusades failed to achieve tangible results. After a long struggle extending centuries. Portugal freed their homeland from their Mohammedan masters.

In the 15th and 16th centuries, two adventurous nations in the Iberian Peninsula, Portugal and Spain, discovered vast new lands in the East and West. The sovereigns of these nations were Christians with ardent faith, zeal and valour. They had financial resources, means of transport and competent priests, navigators and sailors. This situation posed a challenge to the Church as to how to evangelise the 'New World' without adequate wherewithal. The Roman Pontiffs could not overlook the mandate of the gospel to "go into all the world and preach the gospel to the whole creation" (Mk 15:16).

In this context, Pope Nicholas V in 1455 issued a Bull declaring that all lands and seas already discovered or would be discovered in future belong forever to the respective Kings. This is the founding document of the Padroado. Subsequent Popes enlarged its scope by reserving more and more ecclesiastical rights and privileges for the Kings. Pope Alexander VI made an imaginary division of the earth into two parts, East and West passing about 160 Kms west of Azores and entrusted the Western part with Spain and the Eastern part with Portugal for conquest and evangelisation. Pope Callixtus III established the diocese of Funchal. Pope Leo X renewed the concessions in 1514. He granted to the King the right of patronage and presentation of personnel for dioceses and other benefices. In 1533, Pope Clement VII erected the Goa diocese with jurisdiction extending from Cape of Good Hope to India and up to China. The net result was that the Kings enjoyed the following rights and privileges:

To present candidates for ecclesiastical benefices.

To erect and maintain churches, monasteries and institutions.

To provide the above with all accessories.

To maintain the clergy, bishops and seminarians.

To depute clerics abroad for missionary work.

In short, the cross accompanied the sword. Political power played its role in the evangelisation process. The net result was atrocities galore. The post-reformation inquisition aggravated matters. In 1580, Portugal lost its independence by its annexation to Spain. Protestant countries like England, Holland, Denmark etc. appeared as competitors in the mission field. Spain had to confront its own problems. Complaints against atrocities increased day by day. In the changed scenario, the idea of direct control of mission work all over the world by Rome gained acceptance. Pope Gregory XV by Bull *Inscrutabili* established the Congregation for Propagation of Faith (*Propaganda Fide*) with jurisdiction over the whole world. The padroado was not annulled, but met with a natural death. Ignacio Ting Pong Lee remarks, "Padroado was a legitimate existing institution which had its credentials in order – an institution rich in merits and good works, notwithstanding its deficiencies and shadows."[3]

5. The Lambeth Conference

As a result of missionary expansion, colonialism and migration of people to other countries, the Anglican Church spread to Asia, Africa, USA, Canada, Australia and several other parts of the world. Several of these churches in other countries, in the course of time, became independent in administrative and ecclesiastical matters, weakening the bond of communion among these churches.

In 1865, the Synod of the Anglican churches in Canada proposed to have a Synod of all the bishops of the Anglican Communion under the chairmanship of the Archbishop of Canterbury. The immediate need was some problems in the Churches in Canada. In 1867, Archbishop C.T. Longley convened the first conference at Lambeth, the headquarters of the Canterbury Archbishop. Later, it became a regular decennial programme with much significance. Thus, the Lambeth Conference is the decennial meeting of the bishops of the Anglican Communion under the chairmanship of the Archbishop of Canterbury. From 1968 onwards, the representatives of other churches were also invited to attend the meeting as observers.

The decisions of the Lambeth Conference are not legally binding on the Churches. But, they are widely accepted as the opinion of the Communion. The last Lambeth conference was held in 1998 wherein the opinion of the Church was formed on several vital issues such as homosexuality, euthanasia, international debt etc. The most Rev. Dr. George L. Carey presided over the 1998 meeting attended by 736 bishops from different parts of the world, inclusive of 11 women bishops, besides 40 observers from other churches and ecumenical bodies. The formation of the Church of South India and the Church of North India uniting several protestant churches in the respective areas was based on the constitution of the Lambeth quadrilateral (four principles laid down by the Lambeth Conference for unity of Churches).

6. The World Council of Churches

The World Council of Churches was constituted in 1948 at the General Assembly of 147 (Protestant) churches from 44 countries held at Amsterdam. The World Council of Churches is a fellowship of churches which confess the Lord Jesus Christ as Lord and Saviour according to the scriptures and therefore seek to fulfill together their common calling to the glory of the one God, the Father, the Son and the Holy Spirit.

Any church having 25000 or more members can become full member of the Council. Churches with more than 10000 and less than 25000 members can become associate members with no voting right. The World Council of churches is not a church above the member churches, certainly not the Church universal. It is an instrument to bear witness together in their common allegiance to Jesus Christ and to achieve greater communion among churches. The Council shall not legislate for the churches. Nor shall it act for them except as may be specified by the constituent churches. The Council offers counsel and provides opportunity for united action in matters of common interest.

The Assembly shall be the supreme legislative body of the Council. It usually meets at seven years interval. The Assembly shall be composed of delegates elected by member churches. The Assembly elects a President or Presidents, a Central Committee, an Executive Committee, and a Programme Committee. The Central Committee elects four advisory commissions for:

Faith and Order,
Mission and Evangelism,
Education and Ecumenical Formation, and
International Affairs.

The Central Committee also elects a General Secretary who is the Chief Executive of the Council. There is a Deputy General Secretary and support staff to assist the Chief Executive. Today the Council has 336 member churches. The Head Quarters of the World Council of Churches is at Geneva, Switzerland. There is an additional American office in New York. The Catholic Church always preferred to keep away from such Protestant organisations. But, we see a marked change in this attitude of the Catholic Church after the ascendancy of John XXIII to the throne of St. Peter; Pope John Paul II visited the World Council of Churches at Geneva in 1984.[4]

7. The Bible

The word 'Bible' is derived from the word *Biblia* meaning 'books'. The *Bible*, the scripture of Judaism and Christianity, is a collection of books, which according to scholars took 1600 years for compilation. These books were originally written on either ceramic planks or papyrus or leather scrolls in three languages, Hebrew, Aramaic and Greek. A manuscript of the Bible first discovered in a cave in the Sinai Mountains in the fourth century BC known as *Codex Sinaiticus* is kept in the British museum. Another manuscript discovered from Alexandria known as *Codex Alexandria's* is also kept in the British museum. In this book, the first forty sheets are missing. A third manuscript with few worn out pages known as *Codex Vaticanus* is available in the Vatican Library.

The Bible has two parts, the Old Testament and the New Testament. The word 'Testament' is the translation of the Greek word 'Canon' meaning law. From among the books available, the Christian Churches accepted as scripture those books found authoritative, reliable and God-revealed. In between the Old and the New Testaments, there is a gap of four hundred silent years. In the second century AD, the whole Bible was translated to Syriac. Fourteen books believed to have been written after the period of the Prophets in the Old Testament were not included in the Bible as they were treated as not authoritative. But, these books were widely used in Western

Europe till the Reformation period. The Reformists did not incorporate these books in the Protestant Bible on the ground that Jesus Christ never quoted from these books in his speeches. But, the General Council of Trent in the Catholic Church (1545-1583) found seven of these *duetero canonical* books as authoritative and included them under *Proto canonical* category. They are Machabees I & II, Tobit, Judith, Baruch, Sirach (Ecclesiasticus) and Wisdom, altogether making the number of books in the Old Testament 46, on the basis of the Greek *Sapthathy* (*Septuagint*). Thus, the Catholic and Greek Bible have 46 books in the Old Testament, while the Protestant Bible has only 39 Books in the Old Testament on the basis of the Hebrew translation. (Further details are given under the title Latin Vulgate given below.)[5]

The Old Testament was originally written in Hebrew. The prophecies of Prophet Isaias written on leather scrolls in Hebrew in the second century BC were discovered in 1947 from a cave near the Dead Sea. The Old Testament in Hebrew was translated to Greek in the second century BC at Alexandria. The New Testament was originally written in Greek, as it was the language in Palestine in those days, though Christ spoke only in the Aramaic. The main language in Europe in the 5th century AD was Latin. Hence, the Bishop of Rome asked Jerome (later Saint) in 410 AD to translate the *Bible* into Latin. He accomplished the task with ardent dedication by residing for 25 years in the underground cell of the Church of Nativity in Bethlehem. The Catholic Church approved this Latin *Bible* as the official version of the *Bible* known as Latin Vulgate. (Please see separate notes on Latin Vulgate.)

The use of Latin in Europe gradually waned. By the seventh century, it has become the language of scholars and the elite. Hence, Venerable Bede translated *Bible* from Latin to Anglo-Saxon, the then prevailing language in Europe. Christianity is believed to have entered England through the Roman soldiers, probably in the second or third century AD. In those days, persecution of those who hear, read or teach *Bible* was in vogue. It was John Wycliff who first ventured to translate the *Bible* into English. Despite the attempts of Church leaders to dissuade Wycliff from his endeavour, he succeeded in completing the translation of the New Testament in 1380. Later, Wycliff's *Bible* became very popular in Europe. Under the directions of the General Council of Constance, Wycliff's remains were exhumed 31 years after his death, burnt and the ashes were thrown into the River Swift in 1415.

Martin Luther translated the *Bible* from Greek and Latin to German; he completed the translation of the New Testament in 1523 and the Old Testament in 1534. In the course of time, several translations in English appeared, the first one was that of William Tindale. Johannes Gutenburg, who invented the art of printing with movable types, printed a Latin *Bible* in 1456. It was printed at Germany, as there was prohibition in England. When Tindale was engaged in the translation of the Old Testament, he was caught and murdered. But Milescover Dale completed the work of the Old Testament. In view of the big size of the Book, it was called 'The Great Bible'. To prevent theft, this book kept on the pulpit in the Church was chained and locked. In 1537, one Thomas Mathew prepared English translation of the *Bible*. This became the basis for subsequent revision or translation of the English *Bible*.

Queen Mary Tudor of England banned the public use of *Bible* in England. Consequently, many religious scholars went to Geneva, scrutinised the Greek and Hebrew manuscripts and published a handy *Bible* in 1560 known as the Geneva *Bible*. A speciality of this *Bible* was that it was the first time that each verse (sentence) in the *Bible* was distinctly separated. In 1568, another English *Bible* named Bishop's *Bible* was published.

Consequent on the publication of a large number of translations, the ideas in the original texts underwent a series of variances, deviations and distortions. In order to rectify these anomalies, King James of England convened a meeting of scholars and constituted a high-level committee to prepare a genuine translation of the *Bible*. The *Bible* prepared by the Committee is known as King James *Bible*. This authoritative translation of the *Bible* in England is popular all over the world today.

The Bible in Oriental Languages

The first translation of the Bible into oriental languages was in Tamil. A few Christian missionaries, under the leadership of Bartholomew Zeigenbalg settled at *Tranquebar* (Tharangampady in Tamilnadu, India), studied Tamil language and published the Tamil Bible in 1714. One J.B. Francis published an improved version of this Bible in 1772. William Carey, a Baptist evangelist who settled down in Serampore, translated the *Bible* into Bengali and published it in 1793. Later, Carey and his associates translated the Bible into thirty Indian languages. A Malayalam translation of the Bible was published in 1806 by a committee headed by Bishop Mar Divannasios with Cladius Buchanan, a foreign missionary, Ramban Philipose of Kayamkulam and Pulikkottil Ittoop Ramban as members. Later, the Catholic Church and the Protestant Churches published many versions in Malayalam, separately, i.e. The Catholic Bible with 73 books and Protestant Bible with 66 Books. Today, the Catholic *Bible* with 73 (46+27) books, 1189 chapters and 3,11,173 verses and the Protestant *Bible* with 66 (39+27) books remain published in the largest number of languages in the world, currently estimated as 165.

8. The Latin Vulgate[6]

Vulgate is a version of Bible in Latin executed by St. Jerome (331-420 AD), which was adopted universally in the Western Christian Church as authoritative for both faith and practice. Consequent on its general acceptance as authentic, it became known as the Vulgate (meaning commonly accepted Bible of the Church) and accepted by the Roman Catholic Church under sanction of the General Council of Trent.

The Jews determined their Canonical books in the *Bible* in the Yamni meeting held between 80-100 AD. They accepted the books directly translated from Hebrew only as canonical. Other books translated from Greek and Aramaic languages were not accepted even though those books were also in use among some Jewish communities. Non-Catholic Christians followed the Jewish stand. But, the books known as *Deutero Canonical,* Jobith, Judith, Wisdom, Sirach (Ecclesiasticus),

Baruch, 1 Maccabees, 2 Maccabees, a part of Daniel (3:24-90 and 13-14) and Esther 11-16 were accepted by the General Council of Trent as Canonical (De Canonicis Scriptures 1546). Lamentations, which was a part of the book of Jeremias, was later treated as a separate book. Thus, the Latin Vulgate has 73 books, 46 in the Old Testament and 27 in the New Testament.[7]

Jerome, one among the doctors or teachers (Ambrose, Augustine, Jerome and Gregory the Great) of the early Christian church, well-versed in Roman Classics (Vergil, Cicero, Terence, Sallust, Horrace etc.) and an erudite scholar in Hebrew was a quarrelsome and quick-tempered person. The following sentence can provide a deep insight into his multifaceted personality:

> "The dark side of his personality – his ferocious intolerance and bigotry, his nasty explosions of temper, his uncouth displays of vanity, his delight in putting down his enemies by fair means or foul – was some how glossed over; and posterity even accorded him the title 'saint' – rightly perhaps, for at least no one could deny the burning sincerity and steadfast devotion he manifested in carrying out his commitment to Christ."

Conclusion

The Catholic Church is an institution with a history spanning two thousand years. Here, the attempt was to give a summarized version of the main events in its long history. The facts and names not mentioned here are more than those mentioned. What is more important is not to remember all the facts and figures given but to view things in its proper perspective. Judging it according to the failings and weaknesses of the members, especially the Popes and the bishops, the leaders of the Church, is like the blind seeing the elephant. God entered into a covenant with His chosen people. He promised He would not break this covenant even if some of His chosen people become unfaithful or betray Him. Judas betrayed Jesus. The result of that betrayal was the resurrection. In the history of the Church, we see intermittent failures and successes, fall and resurrection. After every fall, we see the Church rising up with more vigour and vitality, establishing repeatedly the guidance of the Holy Spirit in periods of crisis, as promised by God Jesus Christ.[8]

(Faiths of various Christian denominations are given in Annexure III.)

FOOTNOTES

1. *Indian Christian Directory*, Deepika Publications, 2000, pp. 75-77.
2. *Ibid*., p. 147.
3. George Menachery, *St. Thomas Christian Encyclopaedia*, Vol. 1, p. 23.
4. *Indian Christian Directory*, Deepika Publications, 2000, p. 133.
5. Vettom Mani, *Puranic Encyclopaedia* (Mal.), pp. 851-53.
6. Thomas Bokenkotter, *A Concise History of Catholic Church*, p. 69.
7. Joseph Kottackal (Dr.), *Athmabothanam* (Mal.), pp. 24-25.
8. Alan Schreck, *The Compact History of the Catholic Church*, p. 151.

PART SIX

JUDAISM (ISRAEL)

Origin and Growth

40

1. Introduction

Judaism, the religion of the Jews, is one of the oldest (nearly 4000 years old) religions in the world. It is based on the 'Old Testament' in the Bible, particularly the 'Law of Moses' as set forth in the *Pentateuch* (also called *Torah*), the first five books of the Old Testament, viz. Genesis, Exodus, Leviticus, Numbers and Deuteronomy. The family of the Hebrew Patriarchs (Abraham, Isaac and Jacob) traces its origin in Mesopotamia, then belonging to the Hurrian Kingdom of Mittani. The Hebrews were semi-nomadic herdsmen and occasionally farmers ranging close to towns and living in houses as well as tents.

The distinctive features of Judaism are strict ethical monotheism, the Sabhat Rest, circumcision, an elaborate dietary and sanitary code and the celebration of certain festivals, especially the 'Pass Over' and the 'Day of Atonement'. Israelite tradition identified YHWH (by convention pronounced 'Yahweh'), the God of Israel with the Creator of the world who had been known and worshipped by men from the beginning of time. Abraham did not discover this God, but entered into a covenant with him in which he was promised the land of Canaan and a numerous progeny. God fulfilled that promise through the Hebrew leader Moses who liberated the people of Israel from slavery in Egypt, imposed covenant obligations on them at Mt. Sinai through the Ten Commandments and brought them to the promised land.

Before the fall of Jerusalem in 70 AD, Judaism in Palestine practised sacrifice offered by an organised priesthood supported by *tithes* (an ecclesiastical tax practised by the Jews). Worship is carried on in *Synagogues* (see notes). The *Talmud* (see notes) a commentary on the law, supposed to be inspired by God, is second to the Bible.

The circumcision, the sign of the covenant commanded by God, is scrupulously observed by the Jews even today, wherever they are. They believe themselves as the chosen people of God and the Government of the Jewish State under the original Mosaic dispensation is always treated theocratic, professed in the name and under the direction as well as the sanction of heaven as commanded by God. "And you shall be to me a priestly Kingdom and a holy nation" (Exodus 19:7). The corporate life of the chosen community was a summons to the rest of mankind to recognise God's presence, sovereignty and purpose – the establishment of peace and tranquility in the universe and mankind.

The concept of Messianism, the expectation of the coming of a Messiah (a Redeemer or Saviour) in one form or another, permeated Jewish thinking throughout the ages and under various guises and variations, influenced and coloured the outlook of many secular-minded Jews. According to the messianic idea, at the advent of the Redeemer, all nations would see the light, give up war and strife and follow the guidance of the *Torah* (divine guidance, teaching or law) emanating from Zion (a hill in Jerusalem having a spiritual significance). The ideas of 'chosen people', 'theocratic nationhood' and 'Messianism' deepened their faith, instilled courage and invigorated their valour to defend their religion at any cost.

2. Growth and Adaptation

In nearly 4000 years of historical development, the Jewish people and their religion have displayed remarkable adaptability and continuity. In their encounter with ancient civilizations like Babylonia and Egypt down to Western Christendom and modern secular cultures, they have assimilated and integrated foreign elements into their socio-religious system, simultaneously maintaining an unbroken line of ethnic and religious tradition. Each period of Jewish history left behind it a specific element of Judaic heritage that influenced subsequent developments. As such, the total Jewish heritage at any time is a combination of successive elements and adjustments and accretions inevitable in each generation. Consequent on adaptability, the strict following of the Mosaic laws is much relaxed among many 'reformed' and 'liberal' Jews, especially in the USA and Western Europe.[1]

In the history of the Jews, we find a galaxy of eminent personalities who contributed to shape Judaism as a religion with a concrete form and structure, independence, faith, theology, scripture, philosophy etc. The prominent among them are:

Moses – the father of Western monotheism and rescuer of the Jews from bondage, one of the most influential figures in world history.

David – the great King who gave political existence to his homeland and to its people.

Solomon – a great King of the Jews, pious, wise and just, who outshone all thinkers and philosophers of his times in wit, knowledge and sophistication. He constructed the Jerusalem Temple and made Jerusalem a Holy city.

Elijah – The greatest of the Jewish prophets. Though his warnings were ignored by the community, he 'went up' by a whirlwind into heaven. He was the forerunner of the Messiah.

Philo of Alexandria – Born in Alexandria around 20 BC, a brilliant Jewish scholar who bridged the Greek philosophy and the Old Testament and created a new approach to Jewish theology.

Akiba (1st century AD) – A poor illiterate shepherd who was destined to become one of the greatest teachers of Judaism and the most revered martyr.

Maimonides (1135 AD) – Full name Raffi Moses Ben Maimon (known as Maimonides) was a scholar, physician, and leader of people in exile who exerted great influence in Western thought and important role in Jewish thought and tradition.

Nachmanides (Born in 1195 in Spain) – Teacher, philosopher, physician and poet. His teaching was that the Jewish resettlement of the land of Israel was a biblical injunction.

The Baal Shem Tov (Born in 1700 in Poland) – Founder of the Hasidic movement, a mystic, who taught that God should be worshipped joyfully in work and play as well as in study and prayer.[2]

3. Different Periods of Development

The history of development of Judaism is viewed as falling into four distinctive periods classified as: (a) Biblical Judaism, (b) Hellenistic Judaism, (c) Rabbinic Judaism, and (d) Modern Judaism.

(a) Biblical Judaism

The period of Biblical Judaism is from its origin (migration of Abraham to Canaan), in around 20th century BC to Alexander's conquest of Palestine in 332 BC. Canaan comprises roughly the regions of modern Israel and Lebanon. In those days there prevailed a mixture of West Asian, Egyptian and Mediterranean ethno-culture. After the period of Abraham and Isaac, we see a turbulent period in the life of the Jews involving migration to Egypt, servitude, Moses, Exodus, Ten Commandments, return to Canaan, Rule of Judges and Kings, division into two kingdoms, Assyrian and Babylonian domination and destruction of the Jerusalem Temple, Babylonian captivity, Persian domination and freedom from captivity etc. This period ended in the 4th century BC with the conquest of Palestine by Alexander the Great.

The initial Israeli culture was neither primitive nor wholly original. The Canaanite component of Israeli culture consisted the Hebrew language and a rich literary heritage. Judaism in its growth during this period had interacted with the high civilizations of the day. Situated on the land bridge between Asia and Africa, it was exposed to the crosscurrents of foreign thought throughout its history. Identification of Yahweh with the Creator of the World and the concept of monotheism distinguished Judaism from the Pagan religions of those days.

The lessons they learnt from their experiences of sinning and punishment, atonement and rescue by Yahweh made their faith in Yahweh unshakeable. Messianism, the expectation of the coming of a Redeemer instilled hope and courage to witness this faith by enduring pains and sacrifices and even death. The fierceness of the revolt led by an old priest Mattathias and his five sons, the so-called Maccabees or Hasmoneans, against the rigorous measures imposed on Jews by Antiochus IV Epiphanes described in the Dead Sea scrolls is a thrilling example of Jewish faith, hope and courage. The figure of the *martyr* as known in Judaism and Christianity dates from this event.

(b) Hellenistic Judaism

Hellenism denotes the adoption of Greek manners, culture and language by the peoples of Near-East, Asiatics, Egyptians, Jews etc. after the conquests of Alexander the Great and lasted until the rise of Mohammedanism – in the case of Jews it refers only upto the 2nd century AD. After the conquest by Alexander the Great, Palestine became part of the Hellenistic Kingdom of *Ptolemaic* Egypt, the policy of which was to permit religious and cultural freedom to the Jews. In 198 BC, Palestine was conquered by King Antiochus III of the Syrian Seleucid dynasty. He treated the Jews more liberally and gave a charter to govern them by their own laws – the *Torah*. Even at that time, Greek influence was becoming manifest. *Philo*, the Hellenistic philosopher of Alexandria encouraged it. In the early part of the 2nd century BC, Hellenistic Jews occupied the position of High priests. *Jason*, as high priest established Jerusalem as a Greek city, Antioch-at-Jerusalem with Greek educational institutions. During this period, the priests became the wealthiest class and the strongest political group among the Jews in Jerusalem. The fact that the Hasmoneans, in their counter-attack against the Hellenistic Jews, forcibly circumcised the children of Hellenistic Jews shows the inroads made by Hellenism. While the Hellenists derived their strength from the wealthy urban population, the Hasmoneans (or Maccabees) derived strength from the peasants and urban masses. The ruthlessness exhibited by the Hasmoneans towards the Greek cities in Palestine (22 in number) proved that the origin of their cause was more political than cultural and that their fight was for personal ambitions and not for *Torah*. The influence of Greek reached its zenith during the period of King Herod I of Judaea (37 to 4 BC) who built a Greek theatre, amphitheatre and hippodrome near Jerusalem. The birth of Jesus was during the period of Herod I.

A salient feature of this period was that conversion to Judaism has become increasingly numerous both in Palestine and the Diaspora (Jews outside Palestine). The Jewish population in this era ranged between seven hundred thousand and five million in Palestine and between two million and five million in the Diaspora. In Palestine, literature was composed in Hebrew, Aramaic and Greek (the exact language is still a subject of dispute among the scholars). Though most of the works were composed in Hebrew, many of the existing ones are in Greek. E.g.: Ecclesiasticus, I Maccabees, Judith, Testament of Twelve Patriarchs, Baruch, Psalms of Solomon, Prayer of Manasseh etc.

After the Greek period comes the Roman period from 63 BC to 135 AD. Under the Romans, a number of new groups – largely political – emerged in Palestine. Their common aim was the establishment of an independent Jewish State. They were all zealous for the strict observance of the *Torah*. The *Zealot's* party among them even refused to pay tribute to the Romans and advocated overthrowing the Romans on the ground that God alone is their master. Several groups, the *Essenes*, the *Theraputae*, the *New Covenanters*, the *Dead Sea Sect*, the *Gnostics* etc. emerged during this period. When Paul (St.) proclaimed his *antinomianism* (against *Torah* observance as a means of Salvation) many Jewish followers of Jesus became Jewish Christians, but continued to observe the *Torah*. There were two main groups among the Jewish Christians, the *Ebionites* who accepted Jesus as *Messiah*, but denied his divinity and the *Nagarenes* who regarded Jesus as both *Messiah* and God. Both these groups regarded *Torah* as binding upon all the Jews. Here, it may be noted that though Jesus criticised Pharisaic legalism, he proclaimed that he was not for abrogating the *Torah* but for fulfilling it. The percentage of Jews converted to any form of Christianity in this period was very small, except in Alexandria. In the Hellenistic Age, both in Palestine and the Diaspora, we can envision a line between Jewish currents and Christianity, especially in the traditions of martyrdom, proselytism, mysticism, liturgy, the doctrine of the Logos (Word) as an intermediary between the God and the world, the synthesis of faith and reason and a religious philosophy.

(c) Rabbinic Judaism (2nd Century to 18th Century AD)

Rabbi is a title applied to a teacher of law or scholar among the Jews honoured for their knowledge of *Talmud*. Rabbinism is a programme devised by the Rabbis providing an alternate ideology and practice for the Jews independent of the age-old system based on temple, priesthood and political independence. This was not the result of a conscious reform but a necessity of the times after the fall of Jerusalem and the growing hostility between the Jews and the Romans. After the collapse of active Jewish resistance to Roman rule, politically moderate and *quietist* (quietism is the religious theory that man should seek perfection by remaining purely passive under the working of Divine Grace, without seeking the active display of the practical virtues) rabbinic elements remained the only cohesive group within Jewish society. With Jerusalem outside the limits of the Jews, rabbinic ideology and practice provided a viable alternative for their community life and filled the vacuum created by the suppression of all other leaderships. The Romans, confident that the will for opposition or insurrection against them had been shattered, relaxed the restrictions on Jewish ordination, public assembly and regulation of the calendar and permitted the Rabbis who fled from the country to return and re-establish an academy in the town of Usha in Galilee. The strength of the Rabbinate was its peculiar position of representing the interests of both the Jews and the Romans simultaneously, as the religious and political interests of both coincided. The Romans regarded the Rabbis as politically submissive to be used for influencing the Jews to translate the *Pax Romana* (the peace imposed by Romans) into Jewish religious precepts. At the same time, the rabbinic ideology provided the Jews with the appearance of continuity to Jewish self-rule and freedom from alien interference. It substituted sacrifice and pilgrimage to the temple with study of scripture, prayer and works of piety. The necessity of a central sanctuary at Jerusalem was eliminated. Thus, Judaism has become a religion capable of fulfilment anywhere in the world. To all intents and purposes, Judaism became a diaspora religion even in its homeland.

Mishna (a collection of rabbinic laws) emerged as the primary source of reference in all Rabbinic schools around which the Talmud was compiled. This literature, fundamentally legal in character, was designed to regulate every walk of life – agriculture, festivals, family life, purity, sacrificial and dietary laws etc. encompassing all areas of Jewish day-to-day experience. The promulgation of the *Mishna* initiated the period of the *Amoraim* (lecturers and interpreters).

The adoption of Christianity as the religion of the Roman Empire had no direct effect on the freedom of the Jews for worship and other rites. But the mounting hostility between Christianity and Judaism resulted in some restrictions like curtailment of disciplinary rights of Jews over their co-religionists (by this, the Sanhedrin was deprived of its rights to award capital punishment and hence the charges against Jesus were referred to Governor Pontius Pilate), interference in the collection of patriarchal taxes and abolition of patriarchate after the death of Patriarch Gamaliel VI, restrictions on building Synagogues, diversion of Jewish taxes to the Imperial Treasury etc. Due to the growing animosity towards Christendom, many Jews migrated to Babylonia (then under Persian Rule) where they could live under a network of autonomous institutions. In order to regulate Jewish affairs and to ensure the steady flow of taxes, the Parthian Rulers (247 BC to 224 AD) created the post of an *Exilarch* (head of the Jews in exile) who claimed more Davidic descent than the Palestinian Patriarch. They cultivated a native Babylonian Rabbinate. Though tension between religious and temporal authorities erupted in Babylonia also, both the Exilarchate and the Rabbinate existed side by side uninterruptedly upto the middle of the eleventh century. In this period, Judaism acquired strength and vitality in faith and spread their missionary activities to the entire Middle-East. Proud Jewish tribes living in proximity to each other were visible in the vicinity of *Yathrib* (later Medina, the birthplace of Prophet Mohammed) engaged in agriculture and commerce. The Abyssinian army, through the connivance of Christianity, defeated even King Dhu Niwas of Yemen who proclaimed himself a Jew. The rivalries between Jewish and Christian missionaries paved the way for the emergence of an indigenous Arabic monotheism called Islam that later altered the course of world history.

The lightning conquests in the Middle-East, North Africa and the Iberian Peninsula by the armies of Islam in the 7th and 8th centuries changed the religious environment in the Middle-East and Europe. In Muslim Spain, Jews served in the government as officers and took active interest in political affairs. In the period between 950 and 1750 AD, two major branches of Rabbinic system developed in Europe: the *Ashkenazic* (Franco-German) and the *Zefardic* (Andalusian-Spanish). The Ashkenazim (plural of Ashkenazi) traced their cultural affiliation to Italy and Palestine while Zefardim (plural) maintained cultural affiliation to Babylonia.

(d) Modern Judaism (1750 AD to the Present)

According to most scholars, the end of a passive waiting on the Messiah and the beginning of an active pursuit for fulfilment on this earth, preferably in one's lifetime, marks Jewish modernity. The 18th century *Haskala* (enlightenment) among the Ashkenazim of Central and Eastern Europe is treated as the starting point of modernism in Judaism. But, the process of Westernisation began earlier among the Zefardim in Western Europe and Italy. Despite the efforts at religious reform, the majority of the Jewish establishments in Western and Central Europe remained orthodox (a term first used by reform leaders to designate their traditionalist opponents). Consequently, a more modern and militant form of orthodoxy emerged under the leadership of Samson Raphael Hirsch. They advocated the living of a virtually and religiously full life while being totally integrated in to the Western society. This happened to be an attractive and influential thinking. In Eastern Europe, they preached the virtues of secular culture and used Hebrew as a vehicle to introduce this culture. But, the German *Haskala* abandoned the use of Hebrew in the place of German and gradually disintegrated. The immediate descendants of *Mendelssohn*, the champion of the Hebrew, failed to strike a balance between secular and Jewish culture. Their Western education undermined their religious faith and they perceived their identity as Europeans rather than as Jews.[3]

The *Haskala* when played out in Europe, they attempted to continue their failed ideals in Russia. But, as a result of the programmes in 1881, the Jews lost faith in the goodwill of the Russians to accept the enlightened Jews. In the 19th century, Jewish-Christian relations strained erupting into open conflicts. Established Christianity, especially the Roman Catholicism, the staunch supporters of the old order, identified Jews as the major beneficiaries of the French Revolution and as the bearers of a liberal, secular, anticlerical and often a revolutionary threat. To the Church in Russia, the Jews were the enemy seeking to undermine Russian orthodoxy and the Tsar, the very foundations of Russian tradition.

The most striking of the Jewish life is *Zionism*, a phenomenon to return to Zion (a poetic term for the Holy Land); an attempt to revive old religious themes. It stressed the national concentration of the Jews in Secular State, yet another example of secularisation of the Jewish life and Messianism. Zionism attempted to complete the emancipation of the Jews by transforming them into a nation like all other nations.

The story of Judaism in the United States is the story of several fresh beginnings. In the colonial period, the small Jewish community in America was officially orthodox, but unlike Jewish communities in Europe. The East European Jews who migrated to America in large numbers from 1881 to 1914 were profoundly different from the older elements in the Jewish community there, both in culture and manners. It is they and their descendants who made American Judaism as we see it today. The present American Judaism is a continuum from the most traditional orthodoxy to the most radical 'Reconstructionism'. As religious identification became increasingly respectable in American life, the Jews followed the American norm, affiliating with synagogues for ethnic and social reasons rather than for religious reasons.

In Anglo-Jewish life in the last decades of the 19th century, the most pronounced modernist tendencies were 'moderate romantic traditionalism' and the *renewed Karaism* whose religious reform was 'Back to the Bible'. In other places where European Jews arrived later than in the United States, modernity appeared only in the 20th century. Among the Jewish communities in the Arab lands, in North Africa and the Middle-East living on traditional lines, modernity came very late depending upon immigrant scholars and intellectuals.

The Gas Chambers and Concentration Camps in Germany in the 20th century killing millions of Jews known as the 'Holocaust' was the beginning of a resurrection of a transformed Judaism. Eversince, Judaism has become a Non-European religion. Now, 75 per cent of the world Jewry live in three major centres, the Israel, the Slavic region in the erstwhile Soviet Union and the United States. Even though Judaism constitute only a small fraction of the U.S. population, it occupies a position far surpassing its numerical strength and regarded as one of the major American faiths equal to Roman Catholics and Protestants. In the international realm of the Western religions, Judaism is being welcomed as a partner able to deal with other world religions as an equal on issues like human rights, anti-Semitism and world peace. The world Jewish community decimated and horrified by the holocaust in 1945 feared disappearance from the world scene. But, Judaism survived the holocaust and persecution and remains a strong world religion today, relieved of fears of annihilation. In the closing year of World War I, the European powers were grabbing whatever territories they could. Britain took Egypt, Cyprus, Eden and Gulf sheikdoms. They badly needed Palestine also, then under the control of Turkey. To gain international support for their claim, Britain tactfully wooed the powerful Jewish lobby. The Balfour Declaration of 1917 recognised the

Jewish aspirations for a separate 'homeland for the Jewish people' in Palestine. Five years later, Britain took over Palestine under a mandate from the League of Nations and the present State of Israel, in the midst of Arabs, came into existence rendering the Arab locals virtually landless and homeless. Almost the entire Jews migrated to the new State were citizens of European States and automatically their leaders were also Europeans, Hertz from Hungary, Weizman from Belarus (settled in England), Ben Gurion and Menachem Begin from Poland, and Golda Meir from America. Here begins the Palestinian problem now snowballing into a crisis threatening the world peace. The creation of an independent 'Israel' nation helped Judaism in a very large measure to regain its lost glory as an ancient world religion and also to fulfil their long-cherished aspirations of nationhood duly acquiring the recognition of world nations as one among them with a strong will and determination. As on today, the Islamic nations surrounding Israel view Israel as a threat to their unity and peace and conversely Israel look upon them as a threat to their existence. What is in store for the future, no one is sure. Let us wait and see.

4. The Jews in India

All scholars, historians and the Government unanimously agree on the presence of a Jewish community in India from ancient days till the latter half of the 20th century. They were God-fearing, industrious, strict in the observance of religious rituals and good warriors as well. During the period between the early centuries of AD till the coming of the Portuguese, they flourished and led a happy and contented life, spread to different parts of South India and even Bombay, under the patronage of the Hindu Kings of South India and the co-operation and goodwill of other communities in India. According to a survey report of the Dutch in 1686, there were ten synagogues in and around Cochin. King Parkavan Eravi Vanmar granted to the Jews a Copper Plate describing 72 rights and privileges including right over a village named 'Anjuvannom'. The historians do not agree on the year of granting the Copper

Plate by the King. The Cochin Jews believe it as 379 AD while the Dutch Governor Moens puts it as 426 AD, the Protestant Missionary Dr. Buchanan puts the year as 490 AD, Adolf Edwin Medlycott, the first Bishop of Trichur puts it as 508 AD, Lawson consider it as 750 AD and so on. However, there are several stray pieces of evidences confirming the presence of Jews in India in the early centuries of AD. Mr. A. Sreedhara Menon, the Kerala historian has stated in his book 'A Survey of Kerala History' that the Jews who came to Cranganore in 68 AD found a Christian community at Cranganore (Please see Pages 97 & 98 of his book). But, there is no other concrete evidence to prove the first migration of the Jews to India.

Some customs and rituals followed till recently by the Jews confirm that the Jews first landed and settled down in Shingly (the Jewish name for Kodungalloor or Cranganore).

(a) Even today some of the hymns chanted in the synagogues are called Shingly melodies.

(b) A handful of Shingly sand found place in the coffin of every Jew along with the sand from the Holy land.

(c) Majority of the Jews avoided visiting Cranganore and if for any purpose a Jew goes there, he hurriedly leaves the place before sunset.[4]

Anquitil du Peron first brought to light the existence of the Jews in India before the Christian era. In the early centuries of BC, a Roman ship regularly plied between the ports on the Red Sea and Arabia, Ceylon and Malabar Coast. Many travellers have testified the presence of articles made of Indian teakwood and ivory decorating the palace of Solomon, proving the trade relations between India and the kingdom of Solomon. Some historians, therefore, argue that the first migration was during the rule of Solomon (970-931 BC). But, Jewish history says that the period of Solomon was one of plenty and prosperity in Palestine. As such, an exodus during that period is not conceivable.

According to the history of Christianity, St. Thomas came to India in 52 AD. The disciples of Jesus Christ always gave priority for the evangelisation of Jews, the Gentiles were only second in priority. From the sailors, he would have learnt about a Jewish settlement in Malabar coast and set out to reach Shingly, the only port in Malabar coast known to the outside world and where the Jews were settled in those days. History also reveals the influx of Jews into India in different periods of the Christian Era from Spain, Portugal and other European countries. Some of these groups would have landed in Bombay. This would have misled some historians to consider those migrations as the first. Anyhow, when St. Thomas came in the first century AD, there were Jews in India.

When Cyrus of Persia freed the Jews from Babylonian captivity and allowed them to return to their homeland, some Jews preferred to stay in the Persian Kingdom. It is likely that some amongst them would have migrated to other countries in later years, subsequent to the death of Cyrus or during the conquest of Persia by Alexander the Great. The history of the Jews also mention about many Jews fleeing from Palestine during the initial days of Roman Rule (63 BC to 135 AD) to escape from Roman repression.

The darkest period in the history of the Jews in India is said to be the one hundred and sixty years of Portuguese occupation of Cochin. The spirit of that age is revealed from a letter written by Alphonso Albuquerque, the Portuguese Viceroy in which he brought to the attention of the King of Portugal the large influx of Portuguese and Castilian Jews (the Jews of Castile, a District in Spain, at one time occupied by *Moors* which later became a kingdom and in 1469 united to the crown of Spain) and sought permission of His Majesty to exterminate the Jews one by one as and when they come across them. The Portuguese not only destroyed the already shattered principality of Jews in Cranganore but also sacked the Jew town in Cochin with its houses and synagogues. When the Dutch appeared in Cochin in 1661, the Jews openly supported them paying a heavy penalty in blood, but the Dutch were forced to retreat to Ceylon. In 1663, the Dutch reappeared and put the Portuguese to rout from Cochin. During the 132 years of Dutch supremacy, the Jews regained their lost glory and continued their march towards prosperity.

After the creation of the State of Israel, almost the entire Jews returned to their homeland leaving in India a nominal number of families who hesitated to return for some reason or other. A statement of the Jews in Kerala on the eve of their departure to Israel reads as follows:

"Unlike their brothren in Europe and elsewhere, the toleration of Hindu rulers and the fraternal feeling of all the communities in Malabar enabled the Jews in Kerala to weather the stormy events of history and survive for nearly two thousand years."

"After some years, the story of the Jews of Malabar which has marked an interesting episode in the chequered history of the Jewish people may come to an end. If this happens, history can record that their emigration was not motivated by intolerance or discrimination by Government nor by external political or social pressure but their deep sense of religious fervour to live and die in the Holy Land."[5]

It is learnt that the descendants of the Jewish settlers in India who migrated to Israel had to face problems due to their deviation in some *Halakhic* matters from the present orthodox consensus.

FOOTNOTES

1. *Encyclopaedia Britannica* – Internet – *Judaism.*
2. *Reader's Digest*, Published by Maxwell Associates 1983-1984, Printed in Hong Kong, *The Great People of Faith and Wisdom*, pp. 9-52 & 83-120.
3. *Encyclopaedia Britannica* – Internet – *Judaism.*
4. A Publication of the Cochin Synagogue, *Mattanchery*, 2000.
5. A Publication of the Cochin Synagogue, *Kerala and her Jews*, 2000.

Israel – A Peep into History

41

Early History

Today Israel is a tiny independent theocratic nation carved out of the ancient motherland of the Jews after World War I. The word 'Israel' first appears in the Bible in Genesis. God, after a wrestling with Jacob, the grandson of Abraham changed Jacob's name as 'Israel'. It reads as follows: "But he said, Thy name shall not be called Jacob, but Israel, for if thou hast been strong against God, how much more shall thou prevail against men?" (Gen.: 32:28). Literally, the word means one who fights against God. Jacob had twelve sons. They and their succeeding generations were known by the name 'Israel'.

After the death of Solomon, the Kingdom of the Jews was divided into two. Ten out of the twelve tribes revolted against the then King Rehoboam and set up a separate kingdom in the North named 'Israel' with its capital at Samaria. Two tribes, Judah and Benjamin remained in the original kingdom of Judaea with their capital at Jerusalem. Thus, the word 'Israel' is used for the Jewish community as well as for their nation.

It is interesting and informative to peep into the Old Testament of the Bible to learn the chequered history of Israel extending more than two millennia in the BC with intermittent ups and downs, victory and defeat, freedom and slavery, prosperity and famine, destruction and reconstruction, war and peace, joy and sorrow and sin and atonement.

In the third millenium of BC, two distinctive cultures with separate forms and practices, faith and worship and art and literature emerged in the surrounding areas of the Mediterranean Sea, (i) the Mesopotamian culture on the banks of the twin rivers of Tigris and Ufratees, and (ii) the Egyptian culture on the banks of the Nile. According to the Bible, the story of man begins in Eden Gardens, supposed to be somewhere in Mesopotamia. The history of Jews begins with God's covenant with Abram, changed by God as Abraham, the grand Hebrew patriarch of the Jewish community. Circumcision of every male member of the tribe is the physical symbol of the covenant, commanded by God.

Abram was the eldest son of Thareh (Therah) who hails from the genealogy of Noah and his sons rescued by God from the universal deluge. Thareh and family were shepherds by occupation and therefore led a semi-nomadic life. Thareh set out from the city of Ur in Chaldees along with grandson Lot, son Abram and Abram's wife Sarai. After a sojourn in Haran (where Thareh died) they proceeded to Canaan and settled there. God changed the names of Abram and Sarai as 'Abraham' and 'Sara' respectively and blessed them with a son named Isaac. Abraham proved his faith and obedience to God by his readiness to sacrifice Isaac, his most loved and coveted son. God entered into a covenant with Abraham whereby he was made the Grand Patriarch of the God's chosen tribe. As a physical symbol of the covenant, God demanded circumcision of all male members. When there was a famine in Canaan, Abraham went to Egypt but returned to Canaan. He died at the age of one hundred and seventyfive. His son Isaac succeeded him.

Isaac had two sons, Esau and Jacob. At the instigation of their mother, Jacob impersonated Esau and obtained from Isaac, through deceit, the blessings, rights and privileges due to the eldest son according to custom.

God changed the name of Jacob as Israel. Through the succeeding generations of the twelve sons of Jacob through two wives, Lia and Rachel and their handmaids, Israel was divided into twelve tribes. The sons of Jacob also went to Egypt during famine in Canaan and settled in Goshan in Egypt. They remained there in slavery and misery for 400 years. God chose a leader from among them called Moses to lead Israel out of Egypt. En route, God gave Ten Commandments to Israel through Moses. This forms the ethical code of conduct of the

Jewish community. Before reaching Canaan, the Promised Land, Moses passed away. Thereafter, Josue led them to Canaan. He defeated all neighbouring enemies, consolidated the motherland of the Jews and laid the foundations of a prosperous nation.

After the death of Josue, Judges (eminent warriors who enjoyed spiritual and temporal leadership) protected Israel. When Samuel, the last among the Judges, was old, the people requested him to nominate a King for them. When his attempts to dissuade the people failed, Samuel coronated Saul as the King of Israel. In the early period of his reign, he was a good King. But, later on he became arrogant and unpopular. Neither Saul nor his son Jonathan could continue the rule of the dynasty. He was compelled to accept David as King. David consolidated the Kingdom of Israel. He captured Jerusalem from Jebusites, annexed it to his kingdom and made it the capital. The period of David is considered the golden age of Israel. Solomon succeeded David. His wisdom and love of arts and architecture are famous. He constructed the Jerusalem temple. Though he taxed the people heavily, his period was one of plenty and prosperity. He gave shape to a just administrative system. The people loved and admired Solomon as their favourite leader.

Rehoboam, the successor of Solomon rejected with contempt the appeal of the people to relax the burdensome taxation. Unrest and disappointment led to a revolt. Ten tribes of Israel in the North established a separate kingdom named Israel with capital at Samaria and raised Jeroboam as their King. Rehoboam continued as the King of two tribes of Israel (Judah and Benjamin) with capital at Jerusalem. Thus, in 931 BC the unified kingdom of Jews was divided into two, Judaea and Israel; one inimical to the other. The division of the country, emergence of weak kings and the rivalry between the Kingdoms facilitated alien countries to conquer both. The Assyrians who became powerful at this point of time conquered them, destroyed the ruling dynasties and took away many as slaves in 722 BC. Later, they found it difficult to maintain their Empire. In 614 BC, the Medians invaded the city of Ashar and in 612 BC the Babylonians invaded the city of Ninive. These invasions witnessed the scattering of the Assyrian Empire. They retreated to Haran for safety but were chased from there by the Babylonians. The Egyptians, sensing danger for their Empire through the advancement of the Babylonians, sent their army to stall the Babylonians. But, Josias, the then King of Judaea confronted the Egyptian army at Megido. The Egyptians defeated Josias and annexed the Kingdom of Judaea. In 605 BC, the Babylonians defeated the Egyptians which led to the rise of the Babylonian Empire. The attempts of the Egyptians to seek revenge with the help of Judaea miserably failed. In 586 BC, the Babylonians laid siege to the city of Jerusalem for eighteen months, destroyed the Jerusalem temple and exiled all healthy people in Jerusalem. The Jews remained in Babylonian captivity till 539 BC. Henceforth, we see the emergence and domination of the Persian Empire. Cyrus of Persia conquered Persia and Media, two countries on the east of the Babylonian Empire. He continued his military expedition upto India in the east. By 539 BC, the entire Babylonian Empire lay under the feet of Cyrus. He conquered Egypt and the present Turkey, consolidated his Empire and reorganised its administrative system and appointed local rulers. God responded to the prayers of Israelites in captivity. Cyrus freed the Jews from captivity, instructed them to return to their motherland, reconstruct the Jerusalem temple and pray for him.

Darius I, the Persian Emperor from 522 to 486 BC, was a popular and able ruler. He established his capital at Persopolis and conquered countries upto North India. In 513 BC, he conquered Macedonia in Greece, but the Greeks defeated Persia in 490 BC at the battle of Marathon and recovered their territory. (A messenger named Pheidippedes ran from Marathon to Athens, a distance of 21 miles to convey the news of victory in the battle. Marathon Race, an event in the Olympic Games and similar races wherever held derived its name from this event.) The subsequent years witnessed several battles with Egypt, Media, Greece etc. All these wars ended with the coming of Alexander the Great of Macedonia. He conquered Palestine in 332 BC. He liberated almost all countries including

Egypt from Persia. As a memorial of victory, he constructed a port named after him as Alexandria. Alexander passed away in 323 BC at the young age of 33. After his death, the Empire was divided into four provinces, each ruled by one of the commanders of the army of Alexander. Seluquius (or Seleucus) ruled over Palestine with his capital at Antioch. The Ptolemy dynasty (the name derived from Ptolemy I, another commander of Alexander's army) ruled Egypt from 323 BC to 30 BC with the capital at Alexandria. Even though there was no political unity in the Greek Empire, culture and language of the Greek Empire held sway over all the provinces.

The New Testament era begins 500 years after the return of the Jews from Babylonian captivity. During the rule of the Greeks, the Jews had to pay tributes to Ptolemy dynasty of Egypt. Greek became the language of the Jews. The Greek King Antiochus of Syria defeated the Ptolemies and captured Palestine in 198 BC. In 190 BC, the Romans captured Palestine and made it their territory but Antiochus was entrusted with the reign of Palestine on payment of a heavy tribute to the Roman Emperor. Antiochus taxed the Jews very heavily. Antiochus Epiphanus plundered the Jerusalem temple and took away all the valuables. To irritate the Jews further, he constructed in the heart of the Jerusalem city a temple dedicated to Syus, the God of the Greeks. The various anti-Jewish steps adopted by Antiochus Epiphanus provoked the Jews to unitedly revolt against him under the leadership of Maccabees. They confronted Antiochus in guerilla war and sanctified the temple of Jerusalem in 165 BC. Aristobulus, the high priest of the Jews personally led the army and declared himself the King of the Jews in 104 BC. This led to resentment and disunity among the Jews. Capitalising on the confused state of affairs, the Romans interfered, murdered the King of the Jews and made Judaea a part of the Syrian division of the Roman Empire. But, the Romans were magnanimous enough to grant religious freedom to the Jews and to permit them to have a king of their choice. Thereupon, Herod became the King of Judaea and ruled from 37 BC to 4 BC. The birth of Jesus Christ took place in 7 or 6 BC when Herod was the King of Judaea and Augustus Caesar was the Roman Emperor (BC 31 to 14 AD). Modern historians put the birth of Jesus as 4 BC.

Tiberius succeeded Augustus Caesar as Roman Emperor (14 AD to 37 AD). After the death of Herod, the country was divided into three divisions, ruled by the three sons of Herod. One of them, who ruled Judaea was inefficient and unpopular. The Emperor removed him and appointed Pontius Pilate as the Governor of Judaea. The public life, death and resurrection of Jesus Christ took place when Pontius Pilate was the Governor of Judaea and Tiberius was the Emperor of Rome.

The Christian Era (*Anno Domini*) begins 6 or 7 years after the birth of Christ.

Chronology of Events – History of Jews

1850 BC	Abraham in Canaan
1700 BC	Israelites in Egypt (Hiksos Dynasty in Egypt 1720-1560)
1550 - 1250	Slavery in Egypt (Hiksos chased away Pharaoh in Egypt 1550)
1250 - 1200	Liberation from Egyptian slavery (Exodus)
1200 - 950	Philistine occupation of Canaan (Philistines earlier driven out from Egypt, occupied Canaan)
1200 BC	Israel re-entry into Canaan under Josue
1200 - 1025	Rule of Judges
1030 - 721	Monarchy (From Saul to Assyrian occupation)
1030 - 1010	Saul
1010 - 970	David
970 - 931	Solomon
931 BC	Division of the Country into Judaea and Israel

	JUDAEA		ISRAEL
931 - 913	Rehoboam	931 - 910	Jeroboam I
926	Conquest of Jerusalem by Sheshak	910 - 909	Nadab
		909 - 886	Basha
913 - 911	Abia	886 - 885	Ela
911 - 870	Asa	885	Simri
870 - 848	Jehoshophat	885 - 874	Omri (Construction of the city of Samaria)
848 - 841	Jehoram (Joram)	874 - 853	Ahab (Prophet Elia)
841	Ahasia (Osias)	853 - 852	Ahasia
841 - 835	Athalia	852 - 841	Joram (Elisaus)
835 - 796	Joas	841 - 814	Jehu
796 - 781	Amasia	814 - 798	Joachez
781 - 740	Usia (Azarias)	798 - 783	Joas
741 - 736	Joatham	783 - 743	Jeroboam II
736 - 716	Achaz	743 - 738	Menahem
		738 - 737	Pekahia
		737 - 732	Pekka
		732 - 724	Osee (Treaty with Egypt)
		721	Fall of Samaria

Assyrian Domination (721 to 612 BC)

721 - 705	Sargan II
704 - 681	Zennacherib
680 - 669	Essarhadon
668 - 627	Azar Banipal
614	Medians conquered Ashur
612	Fall of Ninive to Babylonians

Babylonian Domination (612 to 539 BC)

586	Destruction of Jerusalem Temple by Babylonians
586 - 539	Jews under Babylonian captivity.

Persian Domination (539 to 332 BC)

539 Cyrus, the King of Persia defeated Babylonians
539 - 530 Cyrus (Release of Jews from captivity - 538)
530 - 522 Cumbisus
522 - 486 Darius I (Battle of Marathon in 490 BC)
486 - 465 K'cerxus I (Aharswerus)
465 - 423 Artha K'cerxus I
423 K'cerxus II
423 - 404 Darius II
404 - 358 Artha K'cerxus II
358 - 338 Artha K'cerxus III
336 - 330 Darius III
332 Alexander the Great conquered Palestine

Greek Domination (332 to 190 BC)

332 - 323 Alexander the Great of Macedonia
323 Death of Alexander & Division
320 - 200 Palestine under Egypt (Ptolemy dynasty)
200 - 142 Palestine under Syria

	EGYPT		SYRIA
323 - 285	Ptolemy I (Sother)	312 - 280	Selucquius I
285 - 246	Ptolemy II (Philadelphus)		(300 BC capital
246 - 221	Ptolemy III (Evu Ergethes)		at Antioch)
221 - 205	Ptolemy IV (Philopather)	280 - 261	Antiochus I
205 - 180	Ptolemy V (Epiphanus)	261 - 246	Antiochus II
	(Syria conquered Palestine	246 - 226	Selucquius II
	200-198)	226 - 223	Selucquius III
180 - 145	Ptolemy VI (Philomethor)	223 - 187	Antiochus III
145 - 116	Ptolemy VII		(Conquered Palestine)
		190	in the war at Magnesia, Romans Conquered Palestine.
165	Sanctification of Jerusalem temple	187 - 175	Selucquius IV

165 - 160 Revolt of Maccabees
160 Death of Judas Maccabees
160 - 143 Joanathan
143 - 134 Simon (Hasmonian dynasty)
134 - 104 John Hircanus
104 - 103 Aristobulus I (High priest of Jews' self-declared King)
103 - 76 Alexander Jeneus
76 - 67 Alexander Hircanus
67 - 63 Aristobulus II

75 - 164 Antiochus IV (Epiphanus)
164 - 162 Antiochus V
162 - 150 Demetrius I
145 - 138 Demetrius II
145 - 142 Antiochus VI & 142-138 Thriphon)
138 - 129 Antiochus VII
129 - 96 Antiochus VIII
83 - 69 Nigranus
64 Syria became Roman province

Roman Domination (63 BC to 135 AD)

Palestine Kings

63 - 40 Hircanus Antipathar
40 - 37 Anthigomus of Rome
37 - 4 Herod (King of Palestine) (Birth of Jesus in 6 or 7 BC)
4 BC Death of Herod
4 BC Herod Anthipas
6 AD Galilean rebellion
6 - 15 AD Hannas, High Priest
18 - 37 AD Kayyaphas High Priest
26 AD - 36 AD Pontius Pilate - Governor of Palestine[1]

Roman Emperors

37 BC - 14 AD Octavian Augustus Caesar, Emperor
14 AD - 37 AD Tiberius

The New Era (AD) commenced 6 or 7 years after the birth of Christ. Jesus Christ was born when Octavian Augustus

---

Notes: 1. The years given are approximate.
2. The names of persons are spelled and pronounced differently in different languages.

Caesar was the Emperor of Rome and Herod was the King of Palestine. He was crucified when Tiberius was Emperor and Pontius Pilate was the Governor of Palestine.

FOOTNOTE

1. *Chronology from the Bible.*

Judaism and Christianity and Short Notes

42

Judaism and Christianity

The Christians consider Judaism a prelude to Christianity and claim themselves as the 'New Israel'. According to Christianity, Jesus Christ is 'God Incarnate', the Redeemer promised to the Jews through the prophets. In the 8th century BC, Prophet Amos expressed it "You only have I known of all the families of the earth, therefore I will punish you for all your inequities." Christianity recognises that her roots are firm and deep in the fertile earth of the ancient Israel. Her origin goes back to the Patriarchs and the Prophets, particularly to the day when Abraham was called from among the pagans to set out through the unknown path of faith. In her, the Jews and pagans have become one children of God. This oneness is a reality that proclaims the reconciliation of the whole world in Christ. Jesus, the Redeemer of the world lived and died as a member of that chosen community of God. The Christian Church cannot forget that Mary, the mother of Jesus was from the House of David and that Apostles, the first disciples of Jesus came from the race of Abraham and spent their childhood amongst the children of Israel. Moreover, there is a spiritual patrimony common to the Jews and the Christians. The mysticism of Christians traces its origin in the *Hassidic* tradition in Judaism. The Jewish mysticism is bound up with Moses and Elias. The Christian mysticism is also partly bound up with them. The Jewish prophecy continues to influence the Christian theology.

The Christian world believed that until the rise of Christianity, Judaism was but a preparation for the Gospel, followed by the manifestation of the Gospel as revealed by Christ and the Apostles. This formulation could be theologically reconciled with the assumption that Christianity had been preordained even before the creation of the world. The earliest Christological profession and faith expressed in three concise formulae 'Jesus is the Christ', 'Jesus is the Lord' and 'Jesus is the Son of God' emerged from this assumption. A further development in the Christian church is the evolution, which was already latent in the Christological profession, of the Trinitarian profession of faith based on the teachings of the Apostles.

Judaism could not reconcile with these professions of faith. According to them, Jesus was neither the promised Messiah nor the Redeemer but a Messianic pretender and false prophet misleading the people of Israel. His claim to unique authority was regarded as blasphemy and his words against temple were considered sacrilege. Jesus antagonised the priests, the most influential class among the Jewish community, by publicly criticising them for their misdeeds and exploitation of the masses. When the size of the followers of Jesus was bulging, the priests heard the ringing of the alarm bells. They conspired with the extremist elements in the community and the Romans to annihilate Jesus, the greatest threat to their vested interests, by hook or crook. When the charges they brought out against Jesus were not convincing enough to Pontius Pilate to award death penalty, they levelled fresh charges of treason and even ingeniously threatened the Governor of dire consequences for actions against the interests of Caesar. Finally, they succeeded and Jesus was crucified. Thenceforth, we see the antagonism between Christianity and Judaism growing and appearing in various forms in the course of history.

A few Christian writers have lamented over the attitude of the Jews towards Jesus on the ground that Islam accepted Jesus at least as a Prophet, but the Jews failed to recognise him at least as a human being. Bishop Fulton J. Sheen, the famous scholar, orator and writer counter these arguments by a simple logic. Christ is a person who claimed himself as 'the Way, the Truth and the Life'. Any man of common sense has only two options left before him, either to accept the words of Christ as true and follow him as God or to ignore him as a liar or lunatic. Any middle course in the acceptance of Christ is illogical. The Jews accepted the latter course.

From a historical point of view, those who actively took part in Christ's passion were a small group of the Jews, Romans and Syrians. To accuse the entire Jewish people of yesterday or today, of the exclusive responsibility of the crucifixion of Jesus is baseless, erroneous and unjust. A Christian, who would put the entire blame on the Jews and at the same time pronounces his own acquittal and innocence, disavows the saving action of Christ, refuses His offer of salvation and insults the mercy of God.

The Christians, conscious of this modern thinking, today view Judaism in a changed perspective, which is well reflected in the Declaration of Vatican II, reproduced below:

"As this Sacred Synod searches into the mystery of the Church, it remembers the bond that spiritually ties the people of the New Covenant to Abraham's stock.

Thus the Church of Christ acknowledges that, according to God's saving design, the beginnings of her faith and her election are found already among the Patriarchs, Moses and the prophets. She professes that all who believe in Christ – Abraham's sons according to faith – are included in the same Patriarch's call, and likewise that the salvation of the Church is mysteriously foreshadowed by the chosen people's exodus from the land of bondage. The Church, therefore, cannot forget that she received the revelation of the Old Testament through the people with whom God in His inexpressible mercy concluded the Ancient Covenant. Nor can she forget that she draws sustenance from the root of that well-cultivated olive tree onto which have been grafted the wild shoots, the Gentiles. Indeed, the Church believes that by His cross, Christ, Our Peace reconciled Jews and Gentiles, making both one in Him.

The Church keeps ever in mind the words of the Apostle about his kinsmen: 'Theirs is the Sonship and the glory and the covenants and the law and the worship and the promises; theirs are the fathers and from them is the Christ according to the flesh' (Rom. 9:4-5), the Son of the Virgin Mary. She also recalls that the Apostles, the Church's mainstay and pillars, as well as most of the early disciples, who proclaimed Christ's Gospel to the world, sprang from the Jewish people.

As Holy Scripture testifies, Jerusalem did not recognize the time of her visitation, nor did the Jews, in large number, accept the Gospel; indeed not a few opposed its spreading. Nevertheless, God holds the Jews most dear for the sake of their Fathers; He does not repent of the gifts He makes or of the calls He issues – such is the witness of the Apostle. In company with the Prophets and the same Apostle, the church awaits that day: known to God alone, on which all peoples will address the Lord in a single voice and 'serve him shoulder to shoulder'. (Soph. 3:9)

Since the spiritual patrimony common to Christians and Jews is thus so great, this Sacred Synod wants to foster and recommend that mutual understanding and respect which is the fruit, above all, of biblical and theological studies as well as of fraternal dialogues.

True, the Jewish authorities and those who followed their lead pressed for the death of Christ; still, what happened in His passion cannot be charged against all the Jews, without distinction, then alive, nor against the Jews of today. Although the Church is the new people of God, the Jews should not be presented as rejected or accursed, as if this followed from the Holy Scriptures. All should see to it, then, that in catechetical work or in the preaching of the word of God they do not teach anything that does not conform to the truth of the Gospel and spirit of Christ.

Furthermore, in her rejection of every persecution against any man, the Church, mindful of the patrimony she shares with the Jews and moved not by political reasons but by the Gospel's spiritual love, decries hatred, persecutions, displays of anti-semitism, directed against Jews at any time and by anyone.

Besides, as the Church has always held and holds now, Christ underwent His passion and death freely, because of the sins of men and out of infinite love, in order that all may reach salvation. It is, therefore, the burden of the Church's preaching to proclaim the cross of Christ as the sign of God's all-embracing love and as the fountain from which every grace flows."[1]

Dialogue

A dialogue between Judaism and Christianity is learnt to be in progress. But nothing tangible has so far turned out.

Short Notes

(a) Pharisees

The word 'Pharisees' literally means separatists or specially elected persons. Here, it denotes a Jewish sect, which arose about 150 BC, in opposition to the *Sadducees*, who insisted on the authority of tradition as well as the written law. They strictly adhered to the law literally rather than in its spirit and maintained the reality of a spiritual world and kept aloof from nationalist politics. They were liberal and their regard for the public won considerable support amongst the masses and stressed the importance of complying with all commandments including those which appeared insignificant and the observance of all Levitical Rules. They believed in the providential guidance of the universe, reward and punishment in the world to come, angels and the resurrection of the dead. The eagerness of the Pharisees to win converts is beautifully illustrated in the statements of many Jews that the Pharisees would traverse sea and land to make a single proselyte. A result of their work is that they earned many sympathisers for Judaism, who observed one or more Jewish practices without being fully converted.

In the New Testament, we see them questioning Jesus to test his views and knowledge, very often to trap him through his answers and Jesus repeatedly denouncing them for their hypocrisy and reproving their blindness in attributing his miracles to Satan. They prevented the Sadducees from entering the Temple that soon resulted in the disappearance of Sadducees from Jewish life.

(b) Sadducees

A sect of the Jews supposed to be the descendants of Sadok, the high priest during Solomon's period. They were very prominent during the period of Jesus for their opposition to the Pharisees. Compared to the Pharisees, they were in higher strata in social grading. They were identified with the wealthy landowners and families of priests in the community. They acknowledged the obligation only of the written law and refused to accept tradition or oral laws and rejected the idea of a revealed oral interpretation of the Torah, inspiration of the prophetic books of the Bible, belief in angels, rewards and punishments in the world to come, providential governance of human events and the resurrection of the dead. According to them, Judaism is centred on the temple. But, about ten years before the destruction of the temple in 70 AD, the Sadducees gradually disappeared from Jewish life due to the opposition of the Pharisees.

(c) Samaritans

Samaritan denotes the people of Samaria, the capital of Israel, the Northern Kingdom of Palestine. King Omri built the city of Samaria in 875 BC. Assyrians destroyed it in 772 BC but rebuilt by Herod I and named it as 'Sabasthe', the Greek name of Augustus, the Roman Emperor. The Southerners, especially the people of the Jewish kingdom of Judaea considered the Samaritans as an uncivilised sect. The Samaritans are the descendants of the northern Israelites who had their own Torah and their own sanctuary. Just like the Sadducees, the Samaritans also refused to recognise the validity of the Oral Law and they were opposed to the Jewish priesthood and the cult of the temple (for a long time the Southern Kingdom of Judaea prevented the Northerners from entering the temple at Jerusalem situated in Judaea), regarded Moses as a messianic figure and forbade the revelation of esoteric doctrines to the outsiders. Earlier, they were identified with the Sadducees, but the break occurred later after the conquest of Shecham by John Hercanus in 128 BC. In the New Testament, Jesus presents the Samaritans as people of virtue, a Good Samaritan as the symbol of his new commandment 'Love thy neighbour' (Lk: 10:30-37). Another leper who came to express his gratitude to Jesus was also a Samaritan (Lk: 17:11-19).

(d) Sanhedrin

Sanhedrin is the judicial council of the Jews consisting of 71 members including priests, popular leaders and experts in law. It held its sittings in Jerusalem and claimed jurisdiction over the entire Jewish people. The High Priest presided and the Vice-President conducted the trial. The legal advisers sit beside the Vice-President to advise him on legal issues. 23 votes in favour are enough for decisions. In the early period, Sanhedrin enjoyed unlimited authority of punishment over their co-religionists, including death penalty. The Romans seriously curtailed this power about the time when Jesus was arraigned before it for trial. The Council found Jesus guilty for capital punishment for which it was not competent and therefore transferred the case to the Governor Pontius Pilate.

(e) Synagogue

Synagogue is a place of Jewish worship and prayers. The idea of a synagogue first arose in the Diaspora during Babylonian captivity when the Jewish people were cut off from the temple where they usually met together on the Sabbath, festivals and other solemn occasions for public worship. After the first destruction of the Jerusalem temple by the Babylonians, the Jews in Palestine also had to suffer a lot for want of a place for them to assemble, pray and worship. Therefore, they also encouraged the idea of synagogues. It soon grew into a place of study as well, and by the time of Jesus, in spite of restoration of temple, local synagogues were firmly established not only in Palestine but also in Rome, Alexandria and Antioch and wherever Jews were to be found. After the second destruction of the temple in 70 AD, they had no difficulty for collective worship and prayers due to the existence of synagogues. The chief features of the synagogues are Ark or receptacle for the Scrolls of the Law, the almemor or pulpit, the reading desk and (except in modern reformed synagogues) the gallery for women who are strictly separated from the male worshippers. In the New Testament, we find Jesus teaching and preaching in synagogues. In later years, synagogues came up in all places where there were Jewish congregations, big or small.

(f) Talmud

Talmud is the collection of texts and commentaries on Jewish religious law as developed from the *Pentateuch*. It consists of two parts, the *Mishnah* and the *Gemara*, the former being a commentary on the matters dealt with in the Mosaic legislation and the latter a commentary on the *Mishnah* itself. Two versions of the Talmud exist, one the Palestinian version compiled about the end of the 4th century and the other the Babylonian version compiled about two centuries later. The portions dealing with law proper are called *Halakah*, those consisting of illustrations, anecdote, history, legend etc. are called the *Haggadah*. In orthodox jury, the authority of the Talmud is held second to that of the Old Testament. The Christians attacked the Talmud as anti-Christian.

FOOTNOTE

1. Declaration of Vatican II on the relation of the Church to non-Christian religions.

PART SEVEN

OTHER WORLD RELIGIONS

Mohammedanism (Islam)

43

Mohammed the Prophet

The founder of Mohammedanism is Mohammed, the great prophet of the Arabs, born in Mecca, the son of Abdullah of the tribe of *Quraysh*, left an orphan, brought up by uncle Abu Talib, became steward of a rich widow *Kadeejah* (40) whom he married at 26, spent much time in solitary meditation and prayer and at last claimed to have received a series of divine revelations on the basis of which he formed a religious system. His preachings offended the influential people of the times, they plotted to murder him and he fled to Medina at the age of 53 (622 AD). There also, his enemies took sword against him, but he survived the murder attempts. He died at the age of 64 and was buried at Medina. By the time of his death, the entire Arabia accepted the new faith. His supposed revelations form the *Koran* (Qur'an), the sacred book of the Islam religion.

Their Creed is "there is no God but God and Mohammed is His Prophet". The religion insists on prayer, five times a day, fasting in the month of Ramadan, alms giving to the poor (according to old conceptions) and pilgrimage to Mecca as the chief obligations of the devout follower. It also emphasises ritual cleanliness, forbids alcohol, inculcates circumcision, recognises the divine origin of the teachings of the Old Testament and Jesus as a prophet, though it considers them as superseded by Mohammed's revelations. Now, its profession extends over Western and Central Asia, North, East and Central Africa, much of Malay countries and Indian subcontinent covering a population of 1155 million. The members of the religion are staunch believers and generally zealous, conservative and rigid in the enforcement of the laws of the religion and observance of rituals. Almost all nations, where the religion can exert influence on Government either through the ruler or through a majority of the people, are theocratic States with Islam as the State Religion and the law of the religion as the law of the Government.

The God, whose name in Arabic is *Allah* for whom Mohammed warred, was eventually the same divinity, Jews and Christians already worshipped. According to Mohammed, Allah had in the past revealed himself to Adam, Abraham, Moses and Jesus. But men had corrupted these revelations – Jews by their pride and refusal to listen to the warnings of the prophets and the Christians by believing in the Holy Trinity, making the oneness of God a mockery. Now, God has chosen to reveal himself once more, the last time, by giving his holy word, the *Koran* to His prophet Mohammed. The need to follow the *Koran* is the central tenet of the faith called *Islam* (an Arabic word describing the state of grace born out of submission to God). The adherents of this religion called *Muslims* (those who submit to Allah) now constitute one of the major religions in the world.

One night, 15 years after his marriage, an extraordinary event befell Mohammed that marked the beginning of his prophetic mission. It is recorded in the *Hadith,* a series of writings about Mohammed's life and works that are second in importance in Islam only to the *Koran. Hadith* records Mohammed as saying: "He (Gabriel) came to me while I was asleep with a piece of brocade and said 'Recite' and I said 'what shall I recite?' He pressed me with it so tightly that I thought it was death: then he let me go and said 'Recite' I said 'what shall I recite?' He pressed me with it again so that I thought it was death, and then he let me go and said 'Recite'? I said but 'what shall I read'? And this I said only to deliver myself from him lest he should do the same again, but he said 'Recite'? In the name of thy Lord, who created, created man from blood clotted Recite? Thy Lord is the most beneficent who taught by the Pen."

Taught that which they knew not unto men "So I recited it and he departed from me. And I awoke from my sleep, and it was as though these words were written on my heart."

The experience devastated Mohammed. Many such visions followed and more of Allah's words vouchsafed to him.

Guided by Angel Gabriel, Mohammed had the vision of Abraham, Moses, Jesus and Adam.

It is from the time of Mohammed's *Hijrah* (Hegira) or flight from Mecca and the establishment of the community at Medina in 622 AD that the Islamic calendar is dated. When the Arabs and the natives demanded to attack the Jews who controlled the market and the land, he resented, but later he appropriated the wealth of the Jewish clans and distributed it among the Arabs.

Earlier Mohammed considered Jerusalem a holy city and asked his followers to face Jerusalem while praying. He led *Razzias* (raids) against commercial caravans twice. When news reached him that a large army of nomads were approaching to destroy him, he himself led an army of 2000 men, overran the nomad camp, captured all the women and children and confiscated all the livestock, tents and stores. When the Byzantine Empire finally defeated Persia, the Arabs lost the protection of the Persians. Thereupon, the Prophet, with thirty thousand men, marched and reached the borders of the empire. He established alliances with several settlements en route, but a war never took place.

In 628, Mohammed with 1600 followers and a herd of sacrificial animals arrived outside the walls of the city of Mecca, but he did not enter the city by force. The Meccans sent a delegation to him for negotiations. The result was a non-aggression treaty in return for which Mohammed secured right for his followers to make pilgrimage to *Ka'bah* in the spring season. In 630, Aabu Sufian formally surrendered the city to Mohammed. The Prophet instructed his followers to face Mecca and the Ka'bah, Allah's temple, while praying instead of facing Jerusalem.

"The century of his revelations, the seventh century AD, was a time of bloodshed and chaos throughout Arabia. Old societies and traditions were dying and new ones had not yet come to take their place. The two most powerful civilizations of the region, Zoroastrian Persia and Christian Byzantines had nearly depleted themselves in war. The 1000-year supremacy of Yemen over Southern Arabia had been challenged by a Christian-Abyssinian invasion from across the Red Sea. Although the major Arabian oases still harboured some orderly commercial centres, the immense stretches of desert between them held little but danger and death. For, they were controlled by Bedouin nomads, who saw no evil in murder and plunder, who automatically preyed upon the helpless; who had no loyalties beyond those of their own tribes; and who were embroiled in blood feuds that were handed down with undiluted bitterness from one generation to the next.

Only one place in this unstable land was safe from the looters – the city of Mecca, a prosperous enclave of trade fairs, markets, warehouses and counting houses, which was also a stage for the outfitting of spice-trade caravans."[1]

Caliphate

'Caliph' is the name assumed by the successors of Mohammed in the government of the faithful and in high priesthood. The holder of the title is supreme in both civil and religious matters. The principal Caliphates were: (1) the Caliphate of the East established at Mecca but later transferred to Baghdad by the Abassides (632-1258), (2) the Caliphate of Cordova established at Cordova by Abd-el-Rehman (756 to 1031), and (3) the Caliphate of Egypt established by the Fatimites. The most celebrated of the Caliphs of Baghdad was Haroun-al-Rashid (Aaron the Just) (786 to 808) under whom learning, science and art flourished. The most brilliant period of the Western Caliphate was during the 9th and 10th centuries. The Eastern Caliphate lingered on till 1258 AD, when the Mongols sacked Baghdad. The title was abolished by Turkey in 1924 when Mustafa Kamal was re-elected President.

Sunnites and Shiites

The dispute over the succession to Caliphate and Imamate led to a split in Mohammedanism resulting in the emergence of two groups, Shiites and the Sunnites. Shiites rejected the

'Sunna' or traditions, championed the case of Ali, the son-in-law of Prophet Mohammed, to succeed to the Caliphate and to maintain the divine right of his descendants to represent the Prophet in the Islam religion. Shiaism is the national religion of Iran. A majority (65%) in Iraq follows it. There is no doctrinal difference between these groups. Political and historical factors led to the differences, essentially of a social and cultural nature.

"The distinctive institution of Shia Islam is the Imamate – a more exalted position than the Sunni Imam, who is primarily a prayer leader, in contrast to Sunni Muslims, who view Caliph only as a temporal leader lacking a hereditary view of Muslim leadership, Shias believe that Prophet Mohammed designated Ali to be his successor as Imam exercising both temporal and spiritual leadership. The Shia school considers the first Caliph Abu-Bakr as one who came through election by a limited number of people. This dispute eventually resulted in the schism.

The Shias traditionally used the term 'Imam' only for Ali and his eleven successors, but none of them, except Ali, ruled an Islamic government. Caliph Mamun, in the eighth century, in order to close the dispute, invited Imam Reza (765-816), who was designated as Mamun's successor, to Medina. Reza's sister Fatima, who journeyed to Medina died en route and her tomb in Qom Iran later developed into a major pilgrim centre.

Imams usually are men of importance in their communities, but they need not be descendants of the Prophet. Before the Iran-Iraq war in 1980, the Shias used to visit the Shrines of Imams both in Iraq and Iran. The Iranians made it a central aim of their war with Iraq."[2]

The Sunnites are orthodox Mohammedans. The name Sunni derived from their acceptance of 'Sunna', the traditional teachings of the Prophet as of the same authority as *Koran* in matters of both faith and morals. The greater part of the world of Islam accepted the Sunni system, Persia alone being an exception. The Sunnis are divided into four sects. According to the UN statistics 83 per cent of world Muslim population are Sunnites, 16 per cent are Shias and 1 per cent other schools.

The Islamic army of the Arab countries conquered the North African people in 647 AD and converted them to Islam. The North African Mohammedans, whether Arab or Berber, were generally known as *Moors*. These Moorish people seized and settled in the Iberian peninsula (Spain) in the first half of the 8th century. They introduced a civilization further advanced than that in Europe in the fields of science, art and industry alike and maintained a strong rule till the 11th century. Later, the Christians gradually recovered the peninsula through a series of wars ending with the fall of Grenada, the last Moorish stronghold in 1492. The last Moorish inhabitants were banished from the country in 1609 AD.[3]

In the early stages of the birth and growth of Islam, the Christians treated Islam as a heresy in Christianity. This naturally gave rise to hostilities between the two religions. In the 7th century, the Islamic army under Abu-Bakr and his successors as Caliphs conquered North Africa, Persia, Syria, Iraq and India and converted the people there. Later, in the 8th century, they invaded Spain and threatened the entire Southern Europe. All these aggravated the hostilities between the Christians and the Islam.

'Saracens' is the name given in the medieval times to the Arabs or Mohammedans and extended to all non-Christian races with which the Crusaders or the Christian people came into contact. The word seems to have originated among the Greeks and the Romans and probably derived from 'Saraskene', a place in the Sinaitic peninsula. In the world history, we see eight military expeditions from the 11th century to the 13th century (1096 AD to 1270 AD) led by the European Christians against the Saracens for the recovery of the Holy Land from Muslim occupation. In Indian history also we see several invasions of India by the Muslims of the neighbouring nations. Ghazni Mohammed, Shahabudeen Mohammed Gory, Jalaludeen Firoz Khilji, Giyasudeen Tuglaq, Timur, Babur etc. were all well-known Muslim invaders who succeeded in their conquests as well as in the spread of Islam in India.

Muslims and Christians

Though the relation of the Muslims with the Christians throughout history was one of enmity, mistrust and hostilities, a marked change is noticed in the second half of the 20th century as revealed from the Declaration of the Vatican II General Council of the Catholic Church, reproduced below:

"The church regards with esteem also the Muslims. They adore the lone God, living and subsisting in Himself, merciful and all powerful, the Creator of heaven and earth, who has spoken to men; they take pains to submit whole-heartedly to even His inscrutable decrees, just as Abraham with whom the faith of Islam takes pleasure in linking itself, submitted to God. Though they do not acknowledge Jesus as God, they revere Him as a Prophet. They also honour Mary, His virgin mother, at times they even call on her with devotion. In addition, they await the Day of judgment when God will render their deserts to all those who have been raised up from the dead. Finally, they value the moral life and worship God especially through prayer, alms giving and fasting.

Since in the course of centuries, not a few quarrels and hostilities have arisen between Christians and Muslims, this sacred synod urges all to forget the past and work sincerely for mutual understanding and to preserve as well as to promote together for the benefit of all mankind social justice and moral welfare, as well as peace and freedom."[4]

(Declaration of Vatican II on the relation of the Church to Non-Christian Religions.)

The Muslim-Christian Dialogue

The declaration of Vatican Council II, reproduced above, expresses a significant deviation on the part of the Church in its relations with other religions, especially Islam. Three distinct aspects are discernible in the tone and tenor of the declaration: a perceptible change in the age-old relations of the Church towards other religions, willingness to admit the partial responsibility for the past hostilities and a desire to establish a new relationship of universal brotherhood and fellowship. To set right the future path, the Council advises a positive approach of 'forgive and forget' and urges both parties to come around the table, discuss, elucidate and sort out issues. In the light of this mandate, the Church exhorts its adherents to enter into dialogue with Islam.

Dialogue is a word that has ample scope for being misunderstood. It is likely to be misconstrued as attempts either for conversion or to shake the ardent religious faith of the Muslims. The Council does not envisage any such hidden agenda. The dialogue visualised by the Council is simple, straightforward, practical and beneficial not only to both the religions but also to the world at large. Its scope is confined to meetings to identify areas of misgivings through interaction and to overcome sceptical attitudes through reasonable explanations. Conversations between individuals aimed at exchange of views for better understanding of each other are also helpful. The aim of this exercise is not achieving convergence of views but to facilitate an atmosphere of understanding, peace and brotherhood under the fatherhood of God – the one and only God of Israel, Christianity and Islam.

Dialogue can take place only between human beings; not between systems or ideologies. As such, the fruitfulness of a dialogue depends upon the individual participants. The approach to the dialogue gathers a more significant dimension than that of the subjects discussed, especially in view of the hostilities prevailing among the two religions from the very day of inception of Islam. A peep into history of these religions can amply testify the widening dent in their relations.

In the early stages of the birth and infancy of Islam, the Christians mistook it as a heresy in Christianity and adopted all means at their command to suppress it. In the seventh century, the Islamic militia under Abu-Bakar and his successors conquered North Africa, one of the strongholds of Christianity and forcibly converted many to Islam. The success of their operations in North Africa emboldened them to conquer Persia, Syria, Iraq and India and to repeat the same practices in those countries. In the eighth century, the Moors (the North African Muslims) invaded Spain, occupied a major portion of the

Iberian Peninsula and threatened the entire Southern Europe. Grenada, the last Moorish stronghold was recovered only in 1492, after a series of wars. In between the eleventh and the thirteenth centuries, the European Christians led eight military expeditions against the Saracens to recover the Holy Land from Muslim occupation. The Turkish conquest of Constantinople, the genocide in Armenia, the Mohammedan conquest of Abyssinia (Ethiopia) and several other battles between Christian and Arab nations aggravated the rivalry between Islam and Christianity. Though happenings in the modern age in Libya, Afghanistan, Iraq, Palestine etc. were more political than religious, all of them added fuel to the fire and ended in flaring up hatred, rancour and revenge between Muslims and Christians. In this backdrop, there is no cogent reason to expect a positive response from Islam for the call to dialogue, unless and until they are convinced of the intentions of the Christians; a Herculean task.

Preparation for a Dialogue

Dialogue is something, which has deep-roots in our culture, civilization and faith. Participation in a dialogue is more a question of overcoming ourselves than that of confronting others. In the background of vitiated relations, mis-understandings, prejudices, acts of injustices etc., the role of each participant becomes all the more difficult and cumbersome. The first task is to remove the beam from one's own eyes before taking the mote in other's eyes. Therefore, the vital prerequisite for a fruitful dialogue is to get rid of one's own worst prejudices.

The participant must have a fair knowledge of one's own religion: its basics, theology, philosophy, canons, liturgy, rituals, practices etc.

Willingness to admit injustices committed against the other party in the past is a sign of one's sincerity and open heartedness.

A general complaint of the Muslims is that many Christians, who think highly of them and fond of them as individuals, despise and dislike their community. In such a situation, a Christian is bound to make amends and shed such misconceptions.

A Christian who enters into a dialogue with Islam has to bear in mind some salient features of Islam. The following points will be helpful in this respect:

- Islam is fatalistic in outlook. Muslims believe in the Divine Decrees of Allah (God) without doubt or murmur. The inscrutable will of God is beyond question (Fatalism).
- Muslim piety, which is fundamentally reverential fear, can all too easily become a rigid compliance with the duties of worship that makes faith perfect (Legalism).
- Islam is a religion of fear. But, of the 99 'most beautiful names of God', only two refer to him as 'the Terrible' and 'the Omnipotent' and context makes it clear that He only manifests himself, as such, towards those guilty of impiety (Fear of Allah).
- There is a moral law in Islam based on *Koranic Akhlaq* (customs), which lies scattered throughout *Koran*, the equivalent of the commandments in Exodus and Deuteronomy. In fact, there is no separate moral code as such in Islam (Laxity).
- Islam is a static religion. The Muslim mind is averse to changes (Static).
- Islam is both a religion and a community. Islam is a religion. Yet, it is inextricably bound up with the notion of a community, culture and civilization (It is the Prophet's community – *Ummat al nabi*).[5] A Muslim in any part of the world finds it easy to acquaint and assimilate with another Muslim community in any other part of the world. Language, prayer, moral laws, customs, worshipping practices etc. bind him/her as one among that community with the desire to live together. This sense of community colours the values of the Muslim faith (community).
- Islam is a religion of a book, explained by tradition. Islam is centred on this book, its scripture – the *Koran*

(Qur'an), the revealed word of God (*Kalimat Allah*) – whereas Christianity is centred on a person, Jesus Christ. According to the Muslim faith, the author of the *Koran* is God, not Mohammed. Every Muslim feels its incomparable charm and beauty. The awe-inspiring force of this text will, nearly always, elude those unable to enjoy it in Arabic. The message of the *Koran* is the absolute monotheism of the transcendent God. The *Koran*, read over again and again, learnt by heart, meditated upon and put to music is the first formative element of the Muslim community (Scripture).

- Islam is testimony and witness. "I testify (or witness) that there is no divinity outside of God; and I testify or witness that Mohammed is the one sent by God." This is the *Sahada* (witness), which incorporates one to Islam and makes one a believer (Witness).
- "Man does not have faith unless he believes in four things:
  1. He must witness that there is no divinity outside God.
  2. He must accept that I am God's envoy, charged with teaching the truth.
  3. He must believe in resurrection after death.
  4. He must believe in the divine decrees for good or evil, for pleasant or unpleasant things." The Prophet said.[6]

These are further clarified as 'Faith in God', 'The Divine Decrees', 'the Message of the Prophets' and 'Four Major Prophetical Messengers' – Abraham, Moses, Jesus and Mohammed. Among them, Abraham was the father of the line of Prophets, who existed before Moses and Jesus, the founders of Judaism and Christianity respectively. Abraham was neither Jew nor Christian. He is believed to have built the Temple (*Kab'ah*) at Mecca. Moses is the one, who redeemed Israel from Egypt. He is the one to whom God spoke in the 'burning bush' in the Sinai and to whom He gave the Torah (the Law). Mohammed is the one who brought a new religious law from God to men (the Muslim Creed).

- Jesus and Mary form part of this line of Prophets but have special privileges of their own. Mary, who was consecrated to God while still in her mother's womb and who is innocent of all sin, is the Virgin who accepts with faith the message of the divine joy (*ruh*) telling her of the miracle of her maternity. Against the calumnies of the Jews (Qur'an 4:156) the Qur'an, and all Islam, in consequence, protests in favour of her virginal motherhood. She is "the one who guarded her virginity", "she who believed in the word of the Lord" (Qur'an 66:12).[7]
- God is inaccessible in his divinity, but simultaneously close to the faithful (nearness to God).

Muslims' View of Christianity

1. Christianity corrupted the concept of monotheism by believing in Trinity – three gods or godheads. The Muslim is likely to seek an explanation on Christian monotheism and Islamic monotheism.
2. The Christian Church is both a religion and, at the same time, a political institution.
3. Christianity is a fusion of spiritual and temporal matters.
4. Vatican Council's formula defining the Church as 'the Universal Sacrament of Salvation' is acceptable to Islam. This brings Islam closer to Christianity.
5. Jesus and Mary are acceptable to Islam, Jesus as Prophet (not God) and Mary as virgin mother who was consecrated to God while still in her mother's womb (Immaculate Conception) and one who guarded her virginity.
6. Christianity forsook circumcision, the symbol of God's covenant with Abraham.

7. Divorce is permitted in Islam, while it is forbidden in Christianity.
8. The gap between preaching and practice in Western Christianity is the most irritable element in the entire Islam.

Dialogue in the Indian Context

India has the second largest Muslim population in the world, 12.1 per cent of the nation's population, spread over in almost all States in India. In the Indian context, both Islam and Christianity are minority communities; Islam, the largest minority and Christianity, the second largest. Four sects in Islam are found in India: Sunnites form the most widespread and predominant in number, a sizable number of Shiites are found in the States of Uttar Pradesh and Andhra Pradesh, Ahmediyyas have scattered presence in the States of Jammu and Kashmir and Punjab and Ismailies are concentrated in certain portions of Maharashtra and Gujarat.

A number of issues figure prominently in any discussion on Muslims in the post-partition India. They are:

1. Communal riots and disturbances.
2. Obstacles in the field of religious preaching and propagation.
3. Secular ideals in the Constitution are not honoured. Consequently, the area of education is jammed with the teachings of the majority community.
4. In the sphere of Muslim Personal Law, no freedom is allowed.
5. The question of Urdu language remains a traumatic affair.
6. The Waqf Board enjoys no freedom to exercise executive powers.

All these issues are likely to crop up in a dialogue. As regards many of these grievances, the Christians are also sailing in the same boat. Several minority rights protected by the Indian Constitution are in the cold storage due to the hostile attitude of the majority community.

Conclusion

In short, the Muslim-Christian dialogue aims at development of human personality and working towards a more fraternal society. Even the most 'temporal' kind of dialogue is destined to become spiritualised, as it progresses, because everything a man does brings into focus his relations within the society and with God. When the dialogue happens to be between two major religions of the world, it inevitably leads to the realm of spirituality.

"Dialogue is not merely an appeal from the heart, it is first and foremost an act of understanding. One of the principal tasks is to clarify ideas we have of one another, by getting rid of prejudices and correcting the ideas if they are inexact."[8] Without truth, there can be no meeting of hearts. When it becomes a meeting of hearts, success is assured.

(Of late, some Hindu leaders are reported to have taken the initiative for a dialogue between Hinduism and Islam. No further details are available.)

FOOTNOTES

1. *Reader's Digest*, Published by Maxwell Associates 1983-1984, Printed in Hong Kong, *Great People of Faith and Wisdom*, p. 75.
2. *Shia-Sunni of IRAQ – Internet.*
3. *Encyclopaedia Britannica – Internet – Mohammedanism.*
4. St. Paul's Publications, *The Documents Vatican II*, pp. 548-51.
5. Albert Nambiaparambil (Fr.), *Guidelines for Dialogue between Muslims and Christians*, pp. 22-35.
6. *Ibid.*, p. 33.
7. *Ibid.*, p. 40, Para. 3.
8. *Ibid.*, p. 90.

Zoroastrianism (Religion of Parsees)

44

Zoroaster

The founder of this religion is Zoroaster (the Greek form of his name Zarathustra), an Iranian religious reformer and preacher and a historical personage. Nothing certain is known about his childhood except that he was born in Bactria in a family with a royal lineage called Spitama (white). The earliest source of information about Zoroaster is the *Avesta*, the Zoroastrian book. Some parts of this book are believed to have been written by Zoroaster himself, but a major portion of the book is supposed to be written later by his followers. Besides *Avesta*, the writings of Greek and Roman classical writers like Plutarch and Plini the Elder are other sources of information about the Prophet. Some writers have gone to the extent of placing his period of life as far back as 6000 BC. But, a reliable guess accepted by most historians is that Zoroaster lived in the seventh century BC. Whether fact or fiction, we find a lot of legends about his miraculous birth and life.

A 15-year-old virgin conceived Zoroaster after a divine light shone on her and throughout her pregnancy; she radiated the lustre that emanated from the child in her womb.

Unlike ordinary infants, the child was born smiling and at the time of his birth all the demons went underground.

He lived in a cave in Mount Sabalan for about 15 years subsisting on one piece of cheese which miraculously replenished and renewed itself after his each bite.

In the cave, he had an encounter with Satan, who tried to lure him into doubt and despair and to chase him from the path of truth, but he succeeded in turning to the Supreme God he was searching for.

The vast Persian Empire extending from the Greek Islands and Egypt to India was established 75 years after the death of Zoroaster. By that time, the adherents of Zoroaster became a dominant force not only in the Persian Empire but also in a considerable area of the civilized world. The conversion of King Vishtaspa happened in 618 BC when Zoroaster was 42. The King not only named him as the high priest of his court but also became a vigorous crusader of the new faith. From Bactria, Zoroaster and an army of his dedicated followers carried the message of the new religion to Persis, the home of the Persians. They animated the new religion they embraced, conquered the powerful Babylonia and launched a series of military campaigns that made them masters not only of the present Iran but also of territories far beyond it.

The Prophet himself was the most effective of all crusaders of his faith. One story tells that a learned *Brahmin* from India, who approached the Prophet for a debate, became a convert even before the Prophet had a chance to utter a word. Zoroaster unrolled a document prepared by him that contained all the answers to the questions the *Brahmin* had planned to raise. Convinced of the extraordinary powers of Zoroaster, the Indian became a Zoroastrian missionary and converted to the new faith 80,000 souls in Hindustan. It is likely that the Parsis in India are the descendants of those early converts.

At the age of seven, Zoroaster was deputed to Azerbaijan for training under a wise man named *Burzin Kurus*. There he remained for eight years learning skills in cattle rearing, farming and healing the sick as well as delving into the mysteries of polytheism. When he returned home at the age of 15, his father wanted to put him in charge of farming. But Zoroaster, moved by the appalling misery and poverty all around, wanted to set right all grievous wrongs in the community misled by deceitful priests to worship false gods. To accomplish these objectives, he went off to a cave in Mount Sabalan to devote himself in solitude to ponder over the ways of God and man. It was during his years in the cave that Zoroaster evolved his religious concept. Zoroaster concluded that polytheism was profoundly a wrong conception; there could be only one

Supreme Being, one creator of the entire universe, omniscient, immutable, unchanging, undeceiving and undeceived, benign and bounteous and the personification of all that was good. Among the gods worshipped by the Iranians, there was one called Mazda, the God of wisdom and knowledge. By adding the word *Ahura* to this title, he coined a new name *Ahura Mazda* (all wise God) for the single Supreme God. This name was later shortened to *Ormazd*.[1]

Good and Evil in the World

Then, the next question arose. If *Ahura Mazda* was the abode of pure goodness, why there was so much evil in this world? To this perplexing question confronted by humanity, Zoroaster found an answer. According to him, *Ahura Mazda* had two sons, *Spenta Mainyu* and *Augra Mainyu*. These two had free will to choose between good and evil. *Spenta Mainyu* chose good and *Augra Mainyu* chose evil. Thus, we see the birth of an evil deity, the full-fledged figure of 'Satan'. In the Old Testament, we see Satan appearing, but not always with the same character. In the books written before Babylonian captivity, the Lord was supposed to be the source of both good and evil. We see Satan inflicting sufferings on Job with the permission of the Lord. Here, Satan was no more than the servant of the Lord. On the other hand, in the books written after the exile, Satan is pictured as Lord's adversary rather than his minion. The difference is visible in the description of the sufferings of Israel during King David's reign. In chapter 24 of 11 Solomon we read "And again the anger of the Lord was kindled against Israel; and he moved David against them." In chapter 21 of 11 Chronicles (a post-exile version) we read "And Satan stood up against Israel; and provoked David to number Israel." Zoroaster's view of evil had radical influence on Judaism and also Christianity through Judaism as is revealed in the presentation of Satan in two distinctive manifestations, one subservient to God and the other independent of God.

Zoroastrian Ideology

Zoroaster told his followers about Messiahs and of redemption. He mentions three Saviours – *Aushadar*,

Aushadar-Mah and *Saoshyant* – each appearing on earth at thousand-year intervals hinting his own rebirths. Though he introduced a number of religious concepts, he was careful not to depart from the past rituals. The rapid spread of Zoroastrianism was not only due to conquest and missionary zeal but also due to the fundamental appeal of his doctrines. A religion which placed *Ahura Mazda*, one all-good God in charge of the entire universe, the concept of Satan and the existence of evil, the eventual victory of *Ahura Mazda* by eating evil – all these were new precepts acceptable to the people of those days who had not yet emerged from predatory nomadism. *Ahura Mazda* is reported to have told Zoroaster "You will come under my friendship by helping your poor fellow men – Relieve those who have fallen in distress." He summed up this ideology in a three-word dictum, *Humata, Hukhta* and *Hvarstha* (Good thoughts, Good words and Good actions). The social responsibility and necessity for co-operation implied in his teachings were entirely new to the Iranians and had its mass appeal and impact.

Jesus on the cross spoke to the thief beside him 'Today shall thou be with me in paradise.' The very word 'Paradise' is the Persian name '*Pairidaeza*' (abode of the righteous after death) used by Zoroaster.

Zoroaster regarded *Atur* (Fire) as the element closest to God and called it a 'Son of *Ahura Mazda*'. He insisted that constant fires be aired in houses, as messengers from earth to the high throne of *Ahura Mazda*. Fire, according to him, represented the divine spark that flows in the heart of every human being, and also the symbol of divinity, bright and powerful, far more preferable to idols or any other creation of man. Thus worship of Fire became a ritual among his followers.[2]

Another ritual introduced by Zoroaster is regarding the disposal of the dead, on which he consulted *Ahura Mazda* who replied "O! Spitama Zarathushtra, on the most elevated place." He, therefore, instructed his followers to retain the ancient Aryan custom of leaving the bodies of the dead on the tops of hills or on towers later called 'towers of silence'. A cardinal principle underlying this practice is that dead matter does not defile the four great elements – earth, air, fire and water.

In his last days, Zoroaster persuaded King Vishtaspa to send an ultimatum to Arjasp, the King of Turan to give up idol worship and accept *Ahura Mazda* as the true God. Arjasp declined and asked Vishtaspa to renounce Zorostrianism or face war. But a soldier of the Turan army stabbed Zoroaster in the back while he was worshipping. Though Zoroaster killed the soldier, the wound he received was fatal. At the age of 77, the Prophet of the one wise Lord breathed his last.

The religion of Zoroaster flourished for more than 100 years under Kings Cyrus, Darius I and Zerxes 1 of Persia. The victory of Alexander the Great in 330 BC in the conquest of the Persian Empire dealt a severe blow to Zorostrianism. The copies of the book *Avesta* were destroyed. For the succeeding five centuries, Iran was under foreign occupation and the faith of Zoroaster became corrupted by Sun worship and polytheism. But after 226 BC the religion again flourished under King Ardashir I. But total destruction of Zoroastrianism occurred in the 7th century AD with the victorious march of Islam through the Middle East. A small section in Iran continued to practise the religion in secret. Their descendants are now known as Parsis. Some others who hesitated to change fled to India. Their descendants known as 'Parsis' still practise Zoroastrianism.

This revolutionary faith which substituted one God (Monotheism) for the worship of many, introduced the concept of a devil as the evil adversary of God, preached last judgment, resurrection of the dead, immortality of the soul, paradise as the abode of the righteous after death and Fire as the symbol of *Ahura Mazda* (Supreme God) exerted significant influence on Judaism and many other religions which originated later, especially Christianity and Islam.[3]

FOOTNOTES

1. *Reader's Digest*, Published by Maxwell Associates 1983-1984, Printed in Hong Kong, *Great People of Faith and Wisdom*, p. 56.
2. *Encyclopaedia Britannica - Internet - Zoroastrianism.*
3. *Reader's Digest*, Published by Maxwell Associates 1983-1984, Printed in Hong Kong, *Great People of Faith and Wisdom.*

Confucianism

45

Confucius

Founder is Confucius, the great sage and philosopher of China (Kyung fu-taze) who lived from 550 BC to 479 BC. His religion is based on the worship and practice of morality as exemplified in the lives and teachings of the earlier wise men who, as he conceived, have made the world as it is and have left it to posterity to build up on the same basis. After his death, he became an object of worship. Now, the followers of his philosophy number about 62,53,000 mainly in Asia and with scattered presence in Europe and Oceania. Many other major religions in the modern world consider this not as a full-fledged religion but only as a Socio-Ethical system.

Although Confucius claimed no supernatural origin or powers, his ethical system has dominated Chinese thought over the centuries. His essentially humanist philosophy dominated the thought and day-to-day life of the Chinese people, providing the basis for the conduct of family life. The earliest biography of Confucius (meaning *Kung the Master*), written some 300 years after his death by Czema Ch'ien (145-85 BC), is considered the most trustworthy account of the philosopher.

Confucius established his reputation as a teacher. In his teaching, he told a great deal about his philosophy of education that he specifically designed to produce good men who would lead their people in righteous ways. The words uttered by him in different contexts on different topics reproduced below will give us a better insight into his philosophy.

Teachings

"I won't teach a man who is not anxious to learn and will not explain to one who is not trying to make clear himself. And if I explain one fourth and the man doesn't go back and reflect and think out the implications in the remaining three fourths for himself, I won't bother to teach him again."

"Reading without thinking gives one a disorderly mind and thinking without reading makes one flighty (unbalanced)."

"Wake yourself up with poetry, establish your character in *li* (ritual) and complete your education in music."

Poetry, according to him, is a basic tool for increasing perceptiveness and stimulating the emotions. It has a more pragmatic use as a rhetorical device. In conversation, the Chinese frequently quoted verse to support their statements. Ready acquaintance with a wide body of poetry would greatly strengthen the arguments of a gentleman.

"Music expresses the harmony of the universe, while rituals express the order of the universe...music rises from heaven, while rituals are patterned on the earth."

"A gentleman is ashamed to die without having accomplished something."

At the centre of Confucian vision is a moral order of which the well-oiled patriarchal family is the microcosm. The social order should always be based on primary relationship within the family, the son being properly dutiful to the father who in turn must be a worthy authority figure. If the family order is secure, it provides a model for all hierarchical relationships up to the Emperor and the basis for national harmony and stability.

"When the ruler himself does what is right, he will have influence over the people without giving commands and when the ruler himself does not do what is right, all his commandments will be of no avail."

"If a man can just for one day realize his true self and restore complete moral discipline, the world will follow him. To be a true man depends on yourself. What has it got to do with others." Very often, he stresses the basic chord of humanism. "It is the man that makes truth great and not truth that makes man great."

"What is the right thing to do?" To this question, he answers "Anyone who tries with an open heart to do what is good, and who is willing constantly to question and think through his actions, will find the way. The measure of man is man."[1]

It is said that, in relatively good times, Chinese is a Confucianist who deals with day-to-day problems with Confucianist solutions. But in bad times, when the world's burdens seem too much to be borne, the same Chinese becomes a *Taoist*.

FOOTNOTE

1. *Reader's Digest* Publications, "Great People of Faith and Wisdom."

Shintoism

46

Shintoism began around 2500-3000 years ago. It is the native religion of Japan, a highly nationalistic creed. The word 'Shinto' is derived from the Chinese characters *Shin* and *Tao* signifying the 'way of the spirits'. The highest manifestation of Shintoism is in the expression of the worship of the Emperor (*Mikado*) and loyalty to the State and family, combined with ancestor worship. There are two main divisions, one is the Thirteen Ancient Sects, all very similar, with separate founder for each sect, and the other is known State Shinto. The primary works on Shintoism are *Kokiji* (Record of Ancient Things), *Nikong* (Chronicles of Japan) *Yengishiki* (Institutes of the Period of Yengi) and the collections of ten thousand leaves. These are not regarded as revealed Scripture as in other religions.

Shintoism is claimed to be a racial religion belonging to all Japanese by birth. There is no question of any foreigner converting to 'Shintoism'. Shinto is as much cultural as it is religious, having developed along with the Japanese culture from the ancient period. Shinto has no texts, no scripture, no dogma, no organized teachings, no regular worship services, no sermons, no rules or commandments. The Shinto belief is that Nature is divine, all things in nature are parts of the divine and worthy of our respect and care; even people are divine.

Shintoism is rich in mythology. The history of the Japanese race and the Imperial line that are traced back to the gods are combined with the oral myths. In the 8th century AD under the initiative of political leaders, some historians have recorded the history of Japan. These chronicles reflect Shinto, but do not embody any official teaching of Shintoism. On the top of the classical stories come the animal and object deities of spirits (called *Kami*). To show reverence to the divinity in Nature, they single out some entities of nature like sun, moon, mountains, trees, stones, deceased relatives etc. for worship. They believe that this sort of respect will bring forth some help or co-operation from them or at least accomplish harmony with the spirits of nature. Peoples of all cultural and religious traditions can follow this. There is every reason to conclude that the Shinto has an inward belief in the sacredness of the universe and that man ought to be in tune with this sacredness. Here, there is special emphasis on truthfulness and purification through which man can remove the 'dust', which conceals his inherently divine nature, and receive the blessings of the *Kami*.

Buddhism came to Japan from China through Korea around the 5th century AD, replete with written teachings developed in almost one millennium. With language, literature, architecture, higher education, system of government and above all the practitioners coming from China and Korea with this new culture being highly educated, Buddhism represented a culture superior to that prevailed in Japan at that point of time. It soon became the religion of the elite, eventually the ruling class in Japan. Gradually, its influence percolated down to the common people. Now this Mahayana Buddhism is the predominant religion in Japan. It is interesting to note that out of the 27,78,000 Shintos at present in Japan, more than 50 per cent are Buddhist followers. The Japanese find no difficulty in simultaneously following both Shinto as their native culture and Buddhism as their religion, one not in conflict with the other. The place of worship of the Shinto is called 'shrine' and that of Buddhism is called 'Temple'. It is very often difficult to distinguish between the two because the architecture is also very often the same. It is not uncommon to find both Shinto shrines and Buddhist Temples situated in the same compound side by side. It is said that at times, Buddhist images are found within Shinto shrines.

In the shrines, no images are worshipped; it is considered that the presence of *Kami* is already there. Fresh foods, water, incense etc. are offered daily upon the altar in the shrine. In the middle ages, the politically influential Buddhist culture never outlawed Shintoism as both traditions assimilated with each other, but Shintoism did not regain official acceptability till 1868. Now, it is in the process of popular come back.

On a true analysis, it is observed that Shintoism is primitive animism. Their ardent love of the motherland finds its expression in the loyalty and devotion of the Japanese people to their State institutions and to their Emperor.

Baha'i Religion

47

Baha'i religion is of very recent origin. But, within a short span of 151 years, it has grown and acquired the status of a world religion accepted by the UN. According to a publication of the religion, it is a world community comprising more than 2112 ethnic groups in different countries, representing a true cross-section of the human race. Baha'i literature has been translated into more than 800 languages. They have seven houses of worship (magnificent edifices) in different parts of the world, Wilmette in Illinois (USA), Kampala in Uganda, Sydney in Australia, Frankfurt in Germany, Panama City in Panama, Apia in West Samoa and Delhi in India, each with its distinctive design inviting people of all races and religions to worship the Creator of the Universe and to express the love between God and man. It upholds the unity of God, recognises the unity of His prophets and inculcates the principle of oneness and the wholeness of the entire human race.

Origin

The central figures of the *Baha'i* faith are the Bab (1819 to 1850), *Baha'U'llah* (1817 to 1892) and *Abdu'l Baha* (1844 to 1921). A radiant youth in Persia known as Bab (meaning 'Gate') on 23rd May 1844 proclaimed that he was the fore-runner to prepare the way and herald the appearance of a spiritual figure. His teachings were profound and widely accepted. The religious orthodoxy considered it heresy, persecuted him and murdered (martyred) him in 1860. Nearly 20,000 of his followers were also killed within the succeeding two decades.

Baha'U'llah

Baha'U'llah (meaning 'the Glory of God') born in a noble family was distinguished from early age for his extraordinary wisdom, intelligence and knowledge. For espousing the cause of the Bab, he suffered torture and imprisonment. In 1853, while in prison Baha'U'llah had intimation (revelation) that he was the one foretold by the Bab. In 1863, while in exile in Baghdad, Baha'U'llah publicly proclaimed that he was the promised one. He was also continuously persecuted by the religious fanatics and later on banished to Constantinople and thence to Adrianople and finally to *Akka* in Palestine in 1868. He passed away in 1892 and his remains were laid to rest at Bahji, facing Mount Carmel. During the lifetime of Baha'U'llah, his religion spread beyond Persia and the Ottoman Empire to the Caucasus, Turkistan, India, Burma, Egypt and Sudan. During his years of imprisonment, he revealed thousands of inspired writings which together with the writings of the Bab and Abdu'l Baha represent the extensive scriptures of the Baha'i faith. For the first time, the holy writings of a major religion are authentically available in the handwriting of its founder or in the handwriting of his secretary duly signed by the founder.

Abd'ul Baha

Baha'U'llah in His will and testament named his eldest son Abd'ul Baha (meaning 'servant of God') as the leader of the Baha'i community and the sole authorised interpreter of his teachings. He from the age of nine onwards accompanied his father throughout his exile. During his period, the Baha'i faith spread to the United States, Canada, Britain and Europe. Before his death in 1921, he appointed his grandson Shogi Effendi as the guardian of the faith.

Principles of Baha'i Faith

The Principles of the Religion are:

1. The Oneness of mankind.
2. Independent investigation of Truth.

3. The common foundation of all religions.
4. The essential harmony of religion and science.
5. Equality of men and women.
6. Universal compulsory education.
7. Elimination of all prejudices.
8. Universal peace.

Other principles:

1. Universal auxiliary language.
2. Abolition of extreme wealth and poverty.
3. World Tribunal for adjudication of disputes between nations.
4. Glorification of justice as the ruling principle in human society.
5. Exaltation of 'work in the spirit of service' to the rank of worship.
6. Religion to be a bulwark for the protection of all peoples and nations.
7. Spiritual solution to economic problems.
8. Obedience to the government of one's country.

The Baha'i Houses of worship are spacious, beautiful and magnificent edifices, each one distinctively designed and exquisite examples of modern architecture. Entry is allowed for all religionists. The temple at Delhi is designed in the form of a lotus flower, the symbol of purity according to Indian conceptions, surrounded by extensive lawns and gardens, popularly known as 'Lotus Temple' which attracts a lot of tourists every day. According to the followers of the faith, theirs is a world religion, divine in origin, all-embracing in scope, broad in outlook, scientific in methods, humanitarian in principles and dynamic in its influence over men of all religions, castes and nations and a fast growing religion with 69,32,000 followers in 1998 (UN Statistics).[1]

FOOTNOTE

1. Publication of Baha'i House, 6, Canning Road, New Delhi.

PART EIGHT

HINDUISM VS CHRISTIANITY (ACCORD & DISCORD)

Kingdom of God and *Dharma*

48

Introduction

Hinduism and Christianity are two prominent religions in the modern world embraced by nearly half of the world's population, precisely speaking, 2900 million (Christianity 2000 million and Hinduism 900 million as per UN Statistics corrected upto September 2002). A number of instructive parallels and similarities are noticed in these two religions. This does not necessarily mean equivalence. It is a blunder to jump into conclusions that the faith and teachings of two religions of long traditions are theologically equivalent or that one religion borrowed or copied its ideas from another religion. Deeper analysis reveals that even in the use of same technical terms, the conceptions and practices often differ. Even in comparisons between Hinduism and traditions like Buddhism and Jainism, originated from the same background of Hinduism, we notice the use of identical terms with different connotations. Similarly, there may be obvious conceptual affinities between Hinduism and Christianity, but we ought to be cautious about presumptions of equivalence. A mutual understanding between these two religions is of immeasurable worth in the present context of increasing *Adharma* (vices) in the modern world. Here, the attempt is to pave the ground for a dialogue to find out areas where Hinduism and Christianity can agree or agree to disagree on fundamentals.

If Christianity is a big anthology, Hinduism is a great Encyclopaedia. Both these religions have a long past extending several millennia. [Christianity, claiming itself as 'new Israel', believes and presents its founder Jesus Christ pre-ordained by Yahweh (God) to redeem his chosen people from all inequities.]

Jesus said, "Amen, amen, I say to you, before Abraham was made, I AM" (Jn. 8: 58). According to the Christian world, until the rise of Christianity, Judaism was only a preparation for the gospel.

Many parallels and similarities noted in these religions are:

- *Dharma* in Hinduism and 'Kingdom of God' in Christianity.
- The *Om* in Hinduism and 'the Word' in Christianity.
- *Trimurthy* in Hinduism and 'Trinity' in Christianity.
- *Moksha* in Hinduism and 'Salvation' in Christianity.
- *Bhakti* in Hinduism and 'Love' in Christianity.
- The story of the birth of Sri Krishna and the story of the birth of Jesus.
- *Ahimsa* in Hinduism and 'Non-violence' in Christianity.
- *Avatar* in Hinduism and 'Incarnation' in Christianity.

Relation between *Jeevatma* and *Paramatma* in Hinduism and relation between 'man' and 'God' in Christianity.

Revelation

Both Hinduism and Christianity are revelation-based religions.

The Scripture

In the *Bhagavad Gita* and the *Bible*, the scriptures of Hinduism and Christianity respectively, we notice identical terms with identical meanings.

Krishna says in the *Gita*,

- "God is Love. Pure love generates sweetness in all its excellence. Love expresses as bliss. Supreme bliss is divinity itself."
- "God is Light. What shines through the human frame is none other than the inextinguishable Cosmic Light."
- "God and Truth are identical."
- "Blessed are the distressed in heart, they shall be comforted in enlightenment."

Corresponding verses are seen in the Bible. (Please see Jn. 1:4:8, Jn. 1:1:5, Jn. 14:6 and Mat: 5:3-12 – The Beatitudes.)

What was the mission of Jesus, the God Incarnate? To put the answer in capsule form, it is the establishment of the 'Kingdom of God' among His creations. St. Mathew says, "do penance; for the Kingdom of Heaven is at hand" (Mt: 3: 2) (The terms, 'Kingdom of heaven', 'Kingdom of God' and 'Reign of God' are synonyms). To put in other words, the gospel exhorts: 'Jesus, the God Incarnate is near at hand. Repent for your past actions, change your life style with a break from the past, turn to God and co-operate with Him to establish His Kingdom.' The entire public life of Jesus was devoted to attain that end – the establishment of His Kingdom. His sermons, services, miracles, feeding, healing, parables, sufferings and his death were means to attain that end. The kingdom of God is one that encompasses all virtues: It is the path to salvation. The Christian Church is the instrument of Jesus to continue the above mission of Jesus.

Correspondingly, what is the mission of Sri Krishna, the God Incarnate, according to Hinduism? He himself has answered the question.

Parithranaya Sadhoonam
Vinasayacha Dushkrutam
Dharma Samsthapanarthaya
Sambhavami Yuge Yuge

(B.G. 4: 7-8)

Meaning: 'Whenever there is decline of *Dharma* and rise of *Adharma*, O! Bharata, then I send forth myself. For the protection of the virtuous, for the destruction of the wicked and for the establishment of *Dharma*, I come into being age after age.'

The mission of Sri Krishna is the establishment of *Dharma.* The content of the *Bhagavad Gita* is the sermon of Sri Krishna to Arjuna in the battlefield at Kurukshetra. 'The Kauravas' action in denying what was legitimately due to the Pandavas was *adharma.* Anyone who upholds *Dharma* has to oppose

Adharma. Opposing *adharma* is *Dharma*, Krishna says. By his sermon, Krishna invigorated the despondent Arjuna. He fought the battle and won it. *Adharma* was wiped out. Similarly, the central theme of Epic Ramayana is Vishnu's *Avatara* as Sri Rama for the establishment of *Dharma*. According to Hindu faith, all *Avataras* of Vishnu, either in human form or subhuman form, were for destruction of *Adharma* and establishment of *Dharma*. The form of manifestation differs according to the necessity of the context, but the mission is the same – the establishment of *Dharma*. The Implications of the terms 'Kingdom of God' in Christianity and *Dharma* in Hinduism are discussed in the following pages:

The Kingdom of God

The *Bhagavad Gita*, the revealed word of God in Hinduism, is the prominent among the three books constituting the Hindu Scripture. Similarly, the Bible, the scripture of Christianity, is also revealed word of God. The basic message contained in these scriptures is the integral welfare of mankind. While the *Bhagavad Gita* concentrates on 'the establishment of Dharma', the Gospels concentrate on the establishment of 'the Kingdom of God'. "When *Dharma* reigns in the universe, the Kingdom of God really comes. The contents of the synoptic gospels are the illustration of the nature and the meaning of the Kingdom of God. Similarly, the essence of the message of the *Bhagavad Gita* consists in the explication of the real meaning and nature of the reign of *Dharma* in the universe. In details, the nature and meaning of the Kingdom of God and the nature of *Dharma* do differ. At the same time, there is fundamental unity of the good news of these two religious traditions and their scriptures. This aspect of unity can be spelled out as the establishment of the Kingdom of God or the establishment of *Dharma*."[1]

The Gospels presented the theme of the kingdom of God as understood by Jesus, his disciples and the early Church. Jesus began his public ministry when Herod was the Tetrarch of Galilee. Palestine and all neighbouring areas in those days were under Roman domination and the Jewish people in all walks of life suffered either economically or politically or socially or religiously due to the oppression and exploitation by the Romans. Social upheavals were common in Palestine and the Jews were under very high expectation of a Messianic King promised to them in the Old Testament. Jesus' proclamation of the Reign of God had a very big impact among the Jews in the given context. But, Jesus refused to politicise his vision of the Kingdom of God. His life of service created a 'New Hope' among the Jews. The Jews understanding of the 'Reign of God' was irreconcilably distant from the vision of Jesus.

What is the Kingdom of God?

What is the Kingdom of God proclaimed by John the Baptist, the herald of Jesus and taught by Jesus during his life on this earth? This term is etymologically derived from a Greek word that corresponds to *Malkuth Samayim* and the term *Malkutha dismaya*. Equivalent English translations are 'Kingship of God', 'Rule of God' and 'Sovereignty of God'. St. Mathew used the term 'Kingdom of heaven' 30 times in his gospel. Contemporary interpretations of the term by the theologians vastly differ, as detailed below:

The kingdom of God is a gift as well as a task. Just waiting for the other world to come is a negative approach.

Kingdom of God is something that the humans have to achieve through their moral efforts.

Eschatology of the kingdom of God is concentrated upon the present. (R. Bultmann)

The kingdom of God is the transition from the temporal to the eternal. (P. Tillich)

The eschatology of the kingdom of God is a Christian hope for the future. (J. Moltman)

Not only Jesus' preaching about the kingdom of God, but also his ministry is of eschatological character. (A. Schweitzer)

Jesus' proclamation of the Kingdom of God has two stages; in the first stage the prophecies of the kingdom of God are fulfilled and in the second stage the consummation of the present age is visualised. (G. Ladd)

Others including St. Luke contend that the kingdom of God has come in the person of Jesus. (Lk. 17:20).

The latest interpretations by J.B. Metz and A. Kee present the teachings of Jesus from the perspective of political theology, considering the message of the Kingdom of God as a social and political Utopia governed by justice, freedom, equality, love and compassion.[2]

Perspective in the Old Testament Period

In the Old Testament, we find an element of eschatological expectation of the Reign of God. "Yahweh is the sovereign, victorious, exalted and the just King of Israel" (Ps. 22, 28, 47 and 84).

The human kings were only covenant administrators, totally depending on Yahweh. Though the doctrine of creation is only a later development according to the theology of Israel, the Old Testament begins with the story of creation. Israel's experience of God as the creator, sustainer and saviour is the basis of the biblical tradition of Yahweh's divine kingship (Ps. 82:1) and eternal reign.

The idea of covenant appears for the first time in the *Bible* when God entered into a covenant with Noah after saving him from the deluge. God promises in this covenant that He would preserve the creation. This covenant applies not only to Noah, but also to every living creature. God called Abraham and entered into a covenant with him and promised to continue the covenant with the posterity of Abraham. Thus, the covenant has become a gift of God to Abraham and his posterity. Thereafter, God's dealings with his chosen people were governed by the covenant. God sends Moses to Egypt to liberate the children of Abraham. After the liberation from the Egyptian bondage, God re-establishes his covenant. Yahweh reminds this experience of covenantal relationship between God and Israel in the following words:

"If you will hear my voice and keep my covenant, you shall be my peculiar possessions above all peoples; for all the earth is mine, and you shall be to me a priestly kingdom and a holy nation" (Ex: 19:5-6).

This traditional relation reminds the people of Israel of their covenantal obligation that demands loyalty to the laws of the covenant. This covenantal law and morality rest on Israel's consciousness of God's everlasting righteousness. Just like Yahweh exercises His righteousness in just judgment, the people of Israel are expected to practise justice in their social and moral life. In this mutual righteousness, the wholeness of the community is maintained. "This unique covenantal relationship between Yahweh and the people of Israel has gradually developed into the experience that Yahweh is their king who reigns over them, brings justice to them, protects them, leads them into prosperity and destroys their enemies" (Ex.15: 18-21). Later, the people of Israel asked Prophet Samuel to grant them a King. As this was against their covenantal obligation, Samuel prayed to the Lord. Then Yahweh said to Samuel "for they have not rejected you, but they have rejected me from being King over them" (Sam 8: 7&8 and 10:19). But, Yahweh, later gave His consent for a human King for Israel. When that kingship failed in Israel due to constant infidelity by the Kings to the covenant, Yahweh took over the kingship. At the time of Jesus, the kingdom of God was in vogue in Judaism. This was universal in its character, a form of Government based on the principles of justice, righteousness, holiness and charity. Thus, the concept of the kingdom of God was familiar to the contemporaries of Jesus.

Kingdom of God in the Gospels

The concept of the Kingdom of God was the central theme of all Synoptic Gospels with a significant role in their theology. Many parables of Jesus are centred on the 'Kingdom of God'. Jesus tells his people "The Kingdom of God is not coming with signs to be observed; nor will they say, lo, here it is! Or there, for behold, the Kingdom of God is in the midst of you" (Lk. 17: 20 & 21). It is given and appointed by the Father.

"Fear not, little flock, for it is your Father's good pleasure to give you the Kingdom" (Lk: 12:32). Humans are to seek and respond to the Kingdom of God and His righteousness.

"But, seek first his Kingdom and his righteousness, and all these things shall be yours as well" (Mt. 6: 33).

Jesus' proclamation of the Kingdom of God reveals God's righteousness that promotes values. These values promoted by the proclamation dealt with in the Synoptic Gospels are:

- The dignity of the Human person. The Kingdom of God gives respect to all persons, the righteous as well as the sinners.
- The greatest demand the Kingdom of God makes is to 'Love God with all one's heart and love of one's neighbour as oneself.' The first one is found in the Deuteronomy and the second one is found in the Leviticus.

"The Lord our God is one Lord; and you shall love the Lord with all your heart, and with all your soul and with all your might" (Deut. 6: 4 & 5).

"You shall love your neighbour as yourself: I am the Lord" (Lev. 19: 18).

The Kingdom of God is associated with *fellowship*. It is the immediate outcome of love. In fellowship, every person enjoys equal rights and privileges.

The reign of God ushers in freedom from sin and guilt. The Kingdom of God invites humans to total freedom so that one may be free to love.

Justice is re-established when humans respond positively to the Kingdom of God and live in love. This results in liberation from all dehumanising and oppressive powers.

The Kingdom of God is good news to the poor. A significant aspect of the approach of the Gospels to the Kingdom of God is that the poor and needy are specially invited to accept it. Here we see the fulfilment of the promises of the Old Testament.

"Blessed are you poor, for yours is the kingdom of God" (LK. 6: 20). In the biblical perception, the poor are the destitute who lack the minimum necessaries of life. At the time of Jesus, the poor were the impoverished, the oppressed, the sick, the social outcasts and the religiously illiterate. Poverty is in itself an evil. In the kingdom of God, the poor are blessed because of their dependence and trust in God's promises. In their helplessness, the poor absolutely and exclusively depend on God. In this sense, the poor of the New Testament are the pious of Yahweh of the Old Testament.

The kingdom of God is a *challenge to the rich*. Jesus challenges and exhorts the rich to give up compulsive attachment to the worldly riches and possessions.

"A person who accepts the reign of God in his life becomes liberated from the slavery of Mammon" (Lk. 19: 1 to 10).

Each author of the synoptic gospels presents their theology of the kingdom of God.

Mark says "The time is fulfilled, and the kingdom of God is at hand; repent and believe in the gospel" (Mk. 1:15).

He emphasises the present aspect of the kingdom. According to him, repentance is openness to the new reality of the kingdom of God and readiness to give up everything opposed to it.[3]

Mathew used three phrases in his Gospel, 'kingdom of Heaven', 'kingdom of the Father' and 'kingdom of God'. The Jews preferred to use euphemistic substitutes for God such as 'Heaven', 'the Blessed One' etc. Scholars are of the view that all his phrases denote one and the same idea. It has to be noted that Mathew's Gospel is predominantly intended for the Jewish Christian community. He purposefully avoids the phrase 'kingdom of God' to guard against politico-military repercussions in the context of the anti-Roman feelings that prevailed in Palestine in the first century AD. He preferred to use a term that gives no scope for being misconstrued with political overtones or sedition. (Please note that Pilate asked Jesus "Art thou the King of the Jews.") (Lk. 23:3). According to Mathew, the ethics of social life and the relationship between the disciples of Jesus are to be based on the values of the 'kingdom of Heaven'. He summarises the contents of his Gospel in the words 'Repent, for the kingdom of heaven is at hand'.

Jesus sent out his disciples by saying "And preach as you go, saying, 'the kingdom of heaven is at hand', heal the sick, raise the dead, cleanse lepers, cast out demons" (Mt. 10:7 & 8).

Liberating the mankind from Satan is an essential prerequisite for the inauguration of the 'kingdom of God', he points out.

According to Luke, the public life of Jesus begins with the Nazareth declaration and not by the announcement on 'Kingdom of God' as we see in other Synoptic gospels.

"Today this Scripture has been fulfilled in your hearing" (Lk. 4:21).

"I must preach the kingdom of God to the other cities also; for I was sent for this purpose" (Lk. 4:43).

The Good News of the Kingdom of God in Luke's Gospel is the good news of liberation for all from all sorts of sins and enslavements. Many parables in Luke's Gospel point towards reversal of values and judgments in the Kingdom of God.

All the parables, miracles and Sermon on the Mount emphasise the 'Kingdom of God'. The long awaited reign of God is an imminent reality. The command to repent and change shows the urgency of the issue. To expect to repent and change now to obtain something happening in an unknown future is against human psyche. When the life of humans synchronises with the commandments and teachings of Jesus, when human thoughts, words and actions reconcile with God's reign, when love and fellowship between God and the humans and between the humans are established, when humans repent and attune their life in conformity with God's plan, it is the Kingdom of God. When 'Love' becomes the fulcrum around which human activity moves, all theological virtues will follow. Peace, fellowship, prosperity, righteousness, contentment and other virtues will prevail in the community. That is the gift promised to mankind by Jesus, envisaged in the phrase 'Kingdom of God' for the coming of which Jesus exhorted the humans to pray 'Let thy Kingdom come'.

Dharma in Hinduism

Hinduism sets forth four goals in human life, *Dharma, Artha, Kama* and *Moksha*, together known as *Purusartha*. For generations Hindus live in the lively tension of *Dharma* and *Moksha*. *Artha* (Wealth or Worldly possessions) and *Kama* (Pleasure including sex) are essential for life, but they are to be gained according to *Dharma* with *Moksha* (liberation or salvation) as its destination. The concept of *Dharma* has exerted very powerful influence on Indian thought and life for the last several millennia that dates back from Vedic times. The earlier name of the present Hinduism was *Arya Dharma* or 'Dharma' alone. This word is derived from a Sanskrit root *dhr* literally meaning 'to sustain', 'to uphold', 'to support', 'to nourish', 'to carry' etc. Dictionaries give different meanings such as duty, responsibility, charity, justice, moral obligations, virtue, religion, function, ordinance, good works and so on. Philosophically, it has a different meaning. A thing, in its own characteristic essence, has its *Dharma*. This characteristic essence of *Dharma* is the function of holding a thing together in its wholeness. It is the essence of nature of each being that continually supports and sustains it.[4]

Rta, *Satya*, *Karma* and *Dharma*

The meaning of the word *Dharma* becomes lucid and clear when examined in association with other relative words in Hindu scriptures like *rta* (A Rig Vedic term meaning 'to order', 'to regulate', 'to arrange' etc.), *Satya* (truth or static order) and *Karma* (right conduct). R.T.H. Griffith interprets *rta* as follows:

"The word used to denote the conception on the order of the world is *rta*. Everything in the universe that is conceived as showing regularity of action may be conceived as *rta* for its principle. In its most general application, the conception expressed by the word occupied, to some extent, the place of natural and moral law, fate or will of the Supreme God."[5]

Originally, *rta* had a wider meaning than *Satya*. Later it has been replaced by the word *Dharma*. '*Satya*' signifies truth in the sense that all things have their foundation on *Dharma*.

Karma implies a uniform moral law, governing the actions of humans and rewards and punishments that are appropriate to such actions. Right conduct maintains the *Dharma* of the universe.

Types of *Dharma*

Though not comprehensively, *Dharma* is classified into different categories, attributing different shades of meaning, in Hinduism.

Sanatana Dharma

It is universal, eternal and permanent righteousness. In the moral realm, it holds the cosmos and mankind together.

Yuga Dharma

The validity of this *Dharma* is only for a particular age or era. Hence, it is of a temporary character.

Varna Dharma

The division into four castes in the Hindu Society is known as *Chathurvarna* (Chathur = four, Varna = colour). Each caste has its own *Varna Dharma,* which has a sacred character as each caste is supposed to have originated from the limbs of the Creator. *Bhagavad Gita* followed the Rig Vedic and Upanishadic dictates of the *Varna* system. *Gita* indicates the hereditary character of caste.

Asrama Dharma

The *Dharma* of each individual is determined by the stages of life known as *Asrama.* (Hinduism divides the life span of humans into four stages, *Brahmacarya, Garhasthya, Vanaprastha,* and *Sannyasa.*)

Svadharma

This is determined on the basis of the *Svabhava* (the personal potentiality of each individual). Each one has responsibility to act according to his personal calling to promote *Dharma* in the Universe.

Sadharana Dharma or Manava Dharma

It is *Dharma* in its universal perspective. *Manavadharma* binds together the humans in the bonds of mutual rights and duties, of causes and consequences of actions in relation to each other for the maintenance of the society at large.

Dharma in Hindu Scriptures

The word *Dharma* appears in almost all philosophies, scriptures and theology in Hinduism. The canons of Hinduism are named as *Dharma Sastras* (Here, Dharma means law). In the *Rig Veda*, *Dharma* is personified as one of the gods. It is also seen applied to various other gods. E.g.: *Svadharman, Satyadharman, Vidharman* etc.

Satapatha Brahmana states (14: 12: 26) that *Dharma* is the King of kings, nothing can be higher than *Dharma*. The term *Dharma* is generally used in the *Upanishads* to mean privileges, duties, obligations, standard of conduct etc. It is seen often identified with truth. In the *Vaiseshika* philosophy, it means quality or good quality. In the epics *Ramayana* and *Mahabharata*, the incarnations of God as Sri Rama and Sri Krishna were for the destruction of *Adharma* and establishment of *Dharma*. The *Brihadaranyakopanishad* states that the Absolute God brought forth *Dharma* when the Absolute felt those humans did not prosper even after giving origin to the four castes.

Sage Vatsyayana, a fourth century logician analysed *Dharma* and its opposite *Adharma* as follows: "*Dharma* consists in *Dana* (charity), *Paritrana* (succour to the distressed), *Paricarana* (service), *Satya* (truthfulness), *Hitavacana* (talk with good intentions), *Priyavacana* (gentle talk), *Svadhyaya* (recitation of scripture), *Asphra* (detachment or disinterestedness), and *Sraddha* (faith or devotion). When such qualities are found in the lives of the human beings and in the society, *Dharma* reigns. Correspondingly, *Adharma* reigns when qualities such as *Himsa* (violence), *Steya* (theft), *Pratisidha maithuna* (unlawful sexual indulgence), *Mithya* (falsehood), *Parusa* (caustic talk), *sucana* (calumny), *asumbandha* (absurd talk), *Paradroha* (ill-will for others), *Paradravyabhipsa* (covetousness) and *Nastikaya* (irreligious) dominate the lives of human beings and the society.[6]

The God of the Bhagavad Gita is the abode and guardian of Dharma. Sri Krishna says:

"For I am the abode of *Brahman*, the Immortal and the Imperishable, of the eternal *Dharma* and of absolute bliss" (B.G. 14:27).

"Thou art the Imperishable, the Supreme to be realised. Thou art the ultimate resting place of the universe; Thou art the undying guardian of the eternal *Dharma*. Thou art the Primal Person, I think" (B.G. 11:18, B.G. 9:17-18).

The God Himself has descended from heaven to earth to establish *Dharma*. "Using *Dharma* and *Bhakti* as wings, the devotee can rise higher and higher in the path of God-realisation."[7]

The *Bhagavad Gita* handles the concept of *Dharma* in all its shades of meanings. For Arjuna, *Dharma* is his *Varnasrama Dharma*. At the same time, the Lord asks the people to undertake all actions without desire and attachment to fruits of their actions. Having completed their mission, they are invited to abandon everything and to take refuge in the Lord for *Moksha* (salvation).

Conclusion

Yahweh established the social order in the biblical society through a covenantal relationship with the people. The social order in the Hindu society is maintained by the Absolute God through descent to the universe as an *Avatara* to establish *Dharma*, which is the very nature of the Absolute. It is a fundamental difference that has to be taken note of. In the Christian tradition, the reign of God is established through a covenant between God and his chosen people. In the Hindu tradition, the reign of *Dharma* is established through periodic intervention of God in the history of mankind. The common and ultimate goals of both traditions are the universal welfare, liberation and the maintenance of the wholeness of humankind. This leads us to the conclusion that a theological understanding of the unity of this unique religious experience is essential for peace and harmony in the universe and among the humans. The ultimate aim of both these traditions is the same: the establishment of the 'Reign of God' in the Universe.

In the preceding pages, we have examined the complementarity of the themes, the 'Kingdom of God' and 'Dharma'. All religions are based on the religious experiences of individuals and the community at large in a given context of time, history and culture. The religious traditions of Hinduism and Christianity therefore differ due to the influence of the history, culture and time of their origin and growth. The languages of the scriptures of these religions and the cultures and times of their origin stand wide apart. We have to transcend these external elements to arrive at understanding and trust. Dialogue is futile in the absence of mutual trust. Theological investigations into the religious experiences are required to get hold of the essence of these religions. Now we shall look into the complementary aspects of the themes of the 'Kingdom of God' and of the *Dharma*. They are:

(a) Belief in the Absolute Being.

(b) Preservation of the wholeness and well-being of God's creation.

(c) The World as the realm of God's reign.

(d) Proclamation of the Good News of the Kingdom of God and *Dharma*.

(e) Necessity of Divine action to achieve the aims.

(f) God's reign and *Dharma* as signs of God's love for this world and all beings.

(g) Righteousness as an essential aspect of the kingdom of God and *Dharma*.

(h) Free human response and support.

(i) Faith in God and loving devotion.

(j) Kingdom of God and *Dharma* as human goals.

(k) Inclination to live under the Sovereignty of God.

(l) Undue attachment to this world as obstacle.

(m) The Reign of God and establishment of *Dharma* are identical with the persons of Jesus and Sri Krishna respectively.

(n) Kingdom of God and *Dharma* are a march towards eschatological salvation. (Moksha)[8]

The establishment of the Kingdom of God and *Dharma* herald the vision of a new world, a society living in peace, in conformity with the commandments of God – a march to salvation or *Moksha*. The battle at Kurukshetra was not meant to conquer or to acquire power over someone, but it was the battle for the establishment of *Dharma*. The humans are exhorted to participate in this battle for the establishment of *Dharma* in the whole universe. The concepts 'Kingdom of God' and 'Dharma' emanated in the context of people's sufferings from spiritual, social, political and economic enslavements and when their hope for liberation from those vices reached its zenith. In other words, the proclamation of these ideals came, when *adharma* had become rampant in the society, as a talisman to cure the ailments, the Universal Society was afflicted with.

FOOTNOTES

1. Sudil, I.M.S. (Rev. Dr.), *The Reign of God and the Establishment of Dharma*, pp. 11-12.
2. *Ibid*., pp. 46-48.
3. *Ibid*., pp. 84-89.
4. *Ibid*., pp. 115-16.
5. Griffith, R.T.H., *The Hymn of Rig Veda* (Eng.) 1:1.8.
6. Sudil, I.M.S. (Rev. Dr.), *The Reign of God and Establishment of Dharma*, pp. 142-43.
7. Date, V.H., *Brahma Yoga of the Gita*, IX–X.
8. *Ibid*., pp. 192-215.

49

Hinduism and Christianity – Mutual Perceptions

At the outset, a clarification on the above topic seems necessary. As already observed, Hinduism is a religion based on individual experience. Resultantly, Hinduism attaches utmost importance to uphold and maintain the freedom of the faithful in matters of religious faith and practices. Man is, by nature, endowed with the divine faculty to search for 'truth'. In the course of this quest, he may perhaps go astray to the extent of landing himself in atheism. Even in such situations, external interference or correctives are neither advisable, nor warranted. The individual is left to oneself to correct by one's own experience in the current life or successive lives in the cycle of births and rebirths. The cumulative effect of this approach is that Hinduism evolved into a religion with many incomparable specialities; it has no founder, no head, no apex body, no organisational structure, no teaching office, no control mechanism and no enforcement of discipline.

The inevitable and obvious outcome of these premises is the unlimited and unrestricted freedom of the individual in the sphere of religion. In this context, the quotations in this chapter have no official sanction or sanctity. They are only the personal opinions of the leaders, thinkers, philosophers, theologians etc. in Hinduism, in the absence of any authority for official pronouncements.

Non-Hindu religionists may wonder as to how such a religion can sustain itself in its cohesiveness. But, Hinduism survived hundreds of generations, sustaining its cohesiveness in tact and its members spontaneously following their faith and practices, of course, subject to one's own choice and discretion, reflecting their faith in daily life, thereby transforming Hinduism into a life-oriented religion. (Had a fraction of this freedom been allowed in other religions like Judaism, Christianity, Islam etc., what would have been the result? It is left to the wisdom of the readers to imagine.)

Christianity also has another handicap. Today it stands divided into hundreds of denominations with irreconcilable differences in the area of faith and doctrines. In a comparative study or dialogue with non-Christian religions, there is no scope to accommodate multifarious faiths and interpretations. Christianity has to be projected as a single entity. To tide over this handicap, the Catholic Church, with compactness in structure, faith and canons, is representing the whole Christianity in this study; though not fully logical, it is the pragmatic solution.

Doctrines of Faith

The doctrines of faith of Hinduism can be grouped under three heads, 'God', 'World' and 'Man'.

God: The metaphysical notion of an Impersonal and static Absolute (*Nirguna Brahma*) and the religious notion of a dynamic Personal God (*Saguna Brahma*) are both acceptable to Hinduism. In relation to the world, the *Saguna Brahma* assumes three distinct forms, the *Brahmav*, the *Vishnu* and the *Siva*, together known as *Trimurthy*. Another doctrine inseparable from *Trimurthy* is the doctrine of *Avatara*, God's descent to the universe as and when necessity arises. The concept of Love (*Bhakti Yoga*) received its impetus from *Avatara*.[1]

World: Cosmos is eternal, but periodically disappears at the end of each cycle known as *Kalpantha* (the end of *Kalpa*) and reappears at the beginning of a new cycle. (Please see measurement of time in Part Two – Hinduism.)

Man: Human soul is eternal, passing through successive births. This leads to rebirth and transmigration of soul known as *Karma-Samsar*. Hinduism prescribes methods (*Yogas*) for liberation from rebirths. This liberation is known as *Mukti*.

From very early centuries, Hinduism had contact with Christianity. Several Hindu leaders have gone to the extent of publicly expressing willingness to accept Jesus Christ as Incarnation and His teachings, though historical Christianity is not acceptable to them. Many Hindu scholars claim Hindu influence in Christianity. Leaders like Dr. S. Radhakrishnan and Swamy Vivekananda share this view.[2] Several legends go around in India in this respect; few of them asserting Christ's visit to India for learning Hindu spirituality from Indian sages. The arrival of Western scholars in India to study Sanskrit and Hindu literature strengthened the relationship between these two religions. But with the arrival of the Portuguese, the Dutch, the English etc. for colonization, the relations became seriously strained, as the Hindus found no influence or trace of Christ's teachings in them.

The Hindu Conception of Religion

(a) *Oneness:* Religion, according to Hinduism, is essentially one, oneness based on experience; not a creed or doctrine. It is eternal and ineffable, a direct apprehension of the Supreme, attainment of a state of illumination. Dr. Radhakrishnan says, "It is not true religion, unless it ceases to be a traditional view and the basic becomes a personal experience."[3]

(b) *Religious Pluralism:* Pluralism is an essential feature of Hinduism. Different people approach the same Being in accordance with their spiritual and mental evolution. All religious traditions have a sacredness of their own to the people concerned because it is an integral part of their inner soul. Vivekananda says "My idea is that all these religions are different forces in the economy of God, working for the good of mankind; and that not one can become dead, not one can be killed." Mahatma Gandhi says "All the great religions of the world are God-given and hence all of them are necessary for the people for whom they are revealed. They all have something special to contribute to the spiritual evolution of humanity."[4]

(c) *No religion is absolute:* Hinduism considers no religion as absolute. All religions are imperfect. Absolutism is inconsistent with an all-loving universal God. Dr. S. Radhakrishnan says "It is not fair to God or man to assume that one people are the chosen of God, that their religion occupies a central place in the religious development of mankind and that all others should borrow from them or suffer spiritual destitution."[5]

(d) *Validity of all Religions:* All religious leaders in Hinduism endorse the view that all religions are valid. Gandhiji says "Looking at all religions with an equal eye, we would not only hesitate but would think it our duty to blend into our faith every acceptable feature of other faiths."[6]

According to Vivekananda, "different religions are different attempts at embodying and typifying one particular aspect of the inexhaustible universal truth".[7] Dr. S. Radhakrishnan graded the religions in a hierarchical order. The highest in rank is the worshippers of the Absolute. Worshippers of the personal God, worshippers of Incarnations and worshippers of ancestors occupy the second, third and fourth ranks respectively.

(e) *Tolerance:* The Hindus are, by nature, tolerant towards other religions. According to Dr. S. Radhakrishnan "toleration is the homage which the finite mind pays to the inexhaustibility of the Infinite".[8] Mahatma Gandhi admonishes that toleration should not imply a gratuitous assumption of the inferiority of other faiths to our own, but a sincere respect for all faiths. Swamy Vivekananda accepted all religions. He had no hesitation to worship God in the Christian Church or Muslim Mosque or Buddhist Temple along with the respective religionists. In short, Hinduism by its very nature is intolerant towards religious intolerance.

Dr. S. Radhakrishnan went to the extent of declaring that this world would be a much more religious place, if all religions were removed from it. Referring to Christianity, he says "unfortunately Christian religion inherited the Jewish creed of the 'Jealous God' and in the case of Christ 'the only begotten Son of God' and so could not brook any rival near the throne".[9] According to Prof. N.K. Devaraj, "the Christian intolerance towards other religions is due to the fact that Christianity misunderstood and misinterpreted, restricted and compromised the content of Christ's commandment of 'Love' because of its insistence on the dogmas".

(f) *Disgust to organised religion:* The Hindu mind, being individualistic and liberal in religious life, has an instinctive antipathy towards organised religions. Dr. S. Radhakrishnan comments "When religion becomes organised, man ceases to be free. It is not God that is worshipped, but the group or the authority that claims to speak in His name."[10] There is something inherently secular and unspiritual in any organisation. It tends to create vested interests and breed corruption. This is the general view of the Hindus and hence they are repugnant to organised religions.

Hindu Approach to Christianity

The Hindus, in the past, not only welcomed Christianity, but also shown willingness to imbibe certain values from it. The Reform Movement in Hinduism, vastly influenced by the Christian missionaries, was instrumental in abolishing several social evils like *Sati*, Caste system, Child marriages etc. The concerns for humanism, charity, services to the community etc. developed in modern-day. Hinduism were the expressions of the willingness of the Hindus to imbibe Christian ideals and examples. They had no hesitation to publicly acknowledge these facts as the results of the positive approach towards Christianity. But, the present-day Hindu approach to Christianity is more negative than positive. This negative approach, a more acceptable option to the Hindu majority, is the cumulative effect of many contributory factors enumerated below:

(a) Gap between Christ and Historical Christianity

The Hindus generally are of the view that dogma, authority, corruption etc. found in the Church do not reconcile with the spirit of Christ. According to Dr. S. Radhakrishnan, the Christian victory over Rome is the sad moment of the beginning of the failure of the Gospel of Christ. Prof. R.C. Zahner seems more forthright in his words. "The greatest disaster that has befallen Christendom was perhaps the conversion of Constantine and the consequent involvement of Caesar in the affairs of God and of God's Church in the affairs of Caesar."[11] According to Gandhiji, what is often labelled Christian is not in line with the spirit of the Sermon on the Mount. The Jewish spirit of exclusiveness, Greek dogma and Roman organisation are the hallmarks of Christianity, according to Dr. S. Radhakrishnan. The most stinging invective came from Swamy Vivekananda while addressing a Christian audience in his discourse at Boston, "Stop your bragging! What has your Christianity ever accomplished without the sword? Your religion is preached through pomp. I can hear nothing but hypocrisy in all your preaching. All these heaped up riches bespeak Christ! Christ will not find among you a stone to lay his head on. You are not Christians. Return to Christ."[12]

(b) Existence of Many Churches

The credibility of Christianity remains a puzzling question in the Hindu mind by the existence of many churches. K.M. Panicker says, "The wide variety of Christian sects extending from the Catholic Church to the Seventh Day Adventists, each proclaiming the errors and superstitions of others, was naturally a source of embarrassment."[13]

(c) Revelation

For the Hindu, Revelation is a process that continues incessantly. The Christian claim of finality of divine revelation is contrary to the faith and experience of the Hindus.

(d) Incarnation

Similar is the case with incarnation. According to Hindu faith, divine incarnation is not unique as claimed by Christianity.

In the *Bhagavad Gita*, Lord Krishna explicitly affirms that *Avatara* takes place whenever *adharma* (vices) become rampant. Sri Ramakrishna says, "*Avatara* is always the same having plunged into the ocean of life, the one God rises up at one point and is known as Krishna, and when, after another plunge, He rises up at another point, He is known as Christ.[14] Vivekananda exhorts "to find God not only in Jesus of Nazareth, but in all the great ones who proclaimed Him, in all who have come after Him, and in all who are yet to come".

Mahatma Gandhi, though the message and life of Christ influenced him, could not accept Christ either as the most perfect incarnation of God or at the most perfect man ever born. He even believed that Buddha was greater than Christ in the aspect of love in the sense that Christ's love was confined to mankind whereas that of Buddha extended to all living beings.[15]

(e) Historicity

The absence of a historical sense in Hinduism is a cause for a negative attitude to Christianity that presents Christ as a historical personage and his redemptive work as a historical event. Gandhiji says, "I must say that I have never been interested in a historical Jesus, I should not care if it was proved by someone that the man called Jesus never lived and that what was narrated in the Gospels was a figment of the writer's imagination. For the Sermon on the Mount would still be true to me."[16]

(f) Karma Theory

The imperfect condition of humanity linked to the fall of the first parents is altogether not acceptable to Hinduism. Salvation and bondage depend solely on the effort of each individual. The Redeemer's blood is not needed for atonement of man's deeds. In the light of the theory of *Karma Samsar*, the Christian doctrine of eternity of hell cannot withstand reason.

Dr. S. Radhakrishnan says "An eternity of torment is inconsistent with a God of love while the best of us are not quite prepared for the sudden splendour of bliss, the worst of us are not so bad as to be cast aside into eternal doom."[17]

On the question of the creation of soul, Dr. S. Radhakrishnan thinks that if God is to create souls, we will have to attribute the difference of nature and character of men to the 'caprice and cruelty' of the creator. It is difficult for them to attribute immortality to man's soul if it begins to exist only for a definite point of time. As such, Hinduism stands for pre-existence and eternity of the human soul.

(g) Nationalism

Nationalism is a very prominent factor influencing the Hindu mind towards a negative attitude to Christianity. According to a good number of Hindus, Christianity is an alien religion and an unwelcome intruder. In spirit and form, it is non-Indian, an imported one and their mission work was part of 'aggressive imperialism'. K.M. Panikkar says, "Inevitably national sentiment looked upon missionary activity as inimical to the country's interests." This hostile sentiment began with the landing of the Portuguese in 1498, in the Indian soil.

(h) Proselytisation

Theoretically, Hindus are not opposed to conversions born out of conviction. But, practically they are against conversions brought about by proselytizing religions as they fear the eventual tampering of their culture and the integrity of their motherland. The Hindus envisage conversion as one that should take place in one's own religion and not a change from one religion to another. This is the Hindu attitude towards all other religions. Gandhiji says, "I want the Christians to be good Christians, Muslims to be good Muslims, the Sikhs to be good Sikhs and the Hindus to be good Hindus under all circumstances. That, to me, is real conversion."[18] Dr. S. Radhakrishnan endorsed this view.

Modern Hinduism is thinking of starting a mission to give something worthwhile to the world at large, especially to Christianity. The chief aim of this mission is to purify Christianity and other religions like Judaism and Mohammedanism from external ritualism, closed dogma, centralised authority and to convert them to the *Advaidic* spirituality of the *Upanishads*.

The sponsors of this idea of mission visualize a World Religion, in a near or distant future.

Hinduism-Christian Perspective

In the preceding pages, we had a glimpse of the Hindu perceptions on religions in general and on Christianity in particular. Now, let us examine the Christian perspective of Hinduism.

In the first century AD, Christianity was comparatively a small community with no organisational structure. The Jews mistook it as a heresy in Judaism and employed all methods at their command to crush it. The imperial Rome took it as a seditious group challenging the authority of a statutory government, by frequently mentioning about 'Kingship', 'Reign', 'Kingdom' etc. The Roman citizen viewed it as a threat to the Roman religion headed by the Emperor. The Empire with the support of the Roman religionists savagely persecuted them. This atrocious persecution continued till the period of Emperor Constantine in the 4th century AD. The mystery religions and the philosophers of the days held Christianity upto ridicule and derision. Circumstances forced it to remain a religion confined to the boundaries of the Roman Empire. (Even the coming of St. Thomas to India was accidental.) In the peculiar circumstances, Christianity preferred a policy of exclusiveness till the 5th century AD. This exclusiveness later developed into a self-imposed siege-mentality.

Early Church fathers like Justin and Tertullian were never sympathetic towards other religions. The attitude of the Church towards pagan philosophies showed strong dislike and contempt. The remark of Tatian, the disciple of Justin, against the Greeks is a classic example of the intolerance of the Church. He says, "The theology of the Greeks was folly, their theatres were schools of vice, their philosophy full of deception, their games, music and poetry sinful."

The general impression prevailed in the West on the religions in India, in the early centuries of the Christian Era, was that of a pagan conglomeration based on myths, legends, astrology, superstitions, idolatry etc. Though it was a vague, casual and superficial assessment, the Church also naturally shared this view. By the 5th century AD, the Christian Church shaped an organisational structure, a creed and a theology formulated by St. Augustine, imbued by the theology of St. Paul. The doctrines of 'Divine Grace', 'Free Will', 'Original Sin' etc. were also developed. The Church initiated attempts for a deeper understanding of Hinduism only in the colonial period in India, from the 15th century. Many European scholars visited India from the 16th century onwards to study Sanskrit and to conduct research and investigations on the ancient Indian literature, history, culture, civilization, religion etc. The results of their studies appeared in the Western markets in the form of very valuable books on the above mentioned subjects. This helped to create awareness in the West on the rich cultural, literary and religious heritage of India. The facts brought to light by the European scholars, historians, philosophers and others were an eye-opener to the Church to correct the contrary notions maintained for centuries and to initiate independent research on the religions in India. Now, hundreds of books dealing with Indian culture and Indian religions are available not only in Europe, but also all over the world, with startling information on similarities and instructive parallels in Hinduism and Christianity. It was in this backdrop, the august General Council of Vatican II was convoked in the Catholic Church. It marked the dawn of a new era of openness, fraternity, humanism, sincerity, unity and dialogue in Christianity. The Council paved the way for revolutionary changes not only in the Church, but also all over the religions and nations in the world.

General Council of Vatican II

The General Council of Vatican II was a turning point in the history of the Church. Unlike the previous councils, wherein the agendas were drawn up by the *Roman Curia* (Church Secretariat), the agenda of Vatican II was set forth by the Council itself. In the beginning, the Council declared its aims in unambiguous terms as below:

(i) The Renewal of the Church.

(ii) Unity of all Christians.

(iii) Dialogue with the World.

Item (iii) alone is relevant in our context. On this item, the Council approved a document titled "Documents on the Catholic Church's Relationship to the World" (including non-Christian religions). It is the only one document classified as 'Pastoral Constitution' among a series of documents approved by the Council, indicating its great importance for the life of the Church. The word 'pastoral' indicated that it is not primarily concerned with doctrine, but practical guidance. To clarify the implications, the Council issued at the end of the sessions, two declarations:

1. The Declaration on Non-Christian Religions (*Noctro Actate*)

This declaration states that the Catholic Church respects whatever is true and good in other religions, and points out that God, in His mercy, can grant salvation to those who have not accepted Christianity, but those who follow the 'truth' as it is known through their conscience. The Church itself further amplified this position as reproduced below:

"From ancient times down to the present, there is found among various peoples a certain perception of that hidden power, which hovers over the course of things and over the events of human history; at times some indeed have come to the recognition of a Supreme Being, or even of a Father. This perception and recognition penetrates their lives with a profound religious sense."

"Religions, however, that are bound up with an advanced culture have struggled to answer the same questions by means of more refined concepts and a more developed language. Thus, in Hinduism, men contemplate the divine mystery and express it through an inexhaustible abundance of myths and through searching philosophical inquiry. They seek freedom from the anguish of our human condition either through ascetical practices or profound meditation or a flight to God with love and trust. Again, Buddhism, in its various forms realises the radical insufficiency of this changeable world; it teaches a way by which men in a devout and confident spirit, may be able either to acquire the state of perfect liberation, or attain, by their own efforts or through higher help, supreme illumination. Likewise, other religions found everywhere try to counter the restlessness of the human heart, each in its own manner, by proposing 'ways' comprising teachings, rules of life, and sacred rites."

"The Catholic Church rejects nothing that is true and holy in these religions. She regards with sincere reverence those ways of conduct and of life, those precepts and teachings which, though differing in many aspects from the ones she holds and sets forth, nonetheless often reflect a ray of that Truth which enlightens all men. Indeed, she proclaims and must ever proclaim Christ, 'The Way, the truth, and the life' (Jn. 14:6) in whom men may find the fullness of religious life, in whom God has reconciled all things to Himself."

"The Church, therefore, exhorts her sons, that through dialogue and collaboration with the followers of other religions, carried out with prudence and love and in witness to the Christian faith and life, they recognize, preserve and promote the good things, spiritual and moral, as well as the socio-cultural values found among these men."[19]

2. The Declaration on Religious Liberty (*Dignitatis Humanae*)

This declaration advocates that all persons should have the liberty to hold and practise any religion they wish without coercion as long as they respect the common good and right of others to practise other beliefs. The basis of this document, a landmark in Catholic thought, is the recognition of the dignity of the human person, whose freedom of choice of religion, God fully honours.

The Church further elaborated this, as below:

"The Vatican Council declares that the human person has a right to religious freedom. This freedom means that all men are to be immune from coercion on the part of individuals or social groups and of any human power, in such wise that no one is to be forced to act in a manner contrary to his own beliefs, whether privately or publicly, whether or in association with others, within due limits. The Council further declares that the right to religious freedom has its foundation in the very dignity of the human person as this dignity is known through the revealed word of God and by reason itself. This right of the human person to religious freedom is to be recognized in the constitutional law whereby society is governed and thus it is to become a civil right."

"It is in accordance with their dignity as persons – that is, being endowed with reason and free will and therefore privileged to bear personal responsibility – that all men should be at once impelled by nature and also bound by a moral obligation to seek the truth, especially religious truth. They are also bound to adhere to the truth, once it is known, and to order their whole lives in accord with the demands of truth. However, men cannot discharge these obligations in a manner in keeping with their own nature unless they enjoy immunity from external coercion as well as psychological freedom. Therefore, the right to religious freedom has its foundation, not in the subjective disposition of the person, but in his very nature. In consequence, the right to this immunity continues to exist even in those who do not live up to their obligation of seeking the truth and adhering to it; and the exercise of this right is not be impeded, provided that the just public order be observed."[20]

The decisions of the Council were a break from the past, revolutionary in character and a green signal to the Church to pave the way for a new approach, not only towards non-Catholic Christians, but also towards all non-Christian religions.

The *Bible* on Other Religions

As described in the preceding pages, the attitude of the Church, in the early centuries of the Christian era, towards non-Christian religions was one of characteristic aversion, polemic and seclusion. Resultantly, the approach of Christianity towards Hinduism was unsympathetic, hypocritical and outstandingly motivated to point out their flaws and drawbacks. Vatican Council II turned this attitude upside down by creating a new spirit, a new self-awareness and a positive and constructive approach. Resultantly, mutual respect, openness and necessity of diologue replaced the erstwhile scepticism, suspicion and conservatism. In the words of Pope Paul VI, who visited India in 1964, "the ever-growing tree of the Church is capable of producing 'new leaves, new flowers and new fruits' when matured and nurtured by the rich age-old cultures of the East, especially of India, the land of sages and Saints, Seekers and Seers, where monasticism flourished in a sublime manner and where prayer and contemplation reached the high mark of mysticism".[21]

This magical transformation was brought about by Vatican II not on the basis of any new philosophy or theology, but on the lines of the scripture of Christianity – the *Bible*. Now, let us examine what the *Bible* says on this subject. Though the *Bible* references remain elusive and more often inconclusive, a common trend can be noticed. Here, the attempt is to examine briefly what scholars usually consider as Biblical teaching relating to Christian attitude towards other religions. Though our main concern is to see the *New Testament* attitude, the *Old Testament*, being the basis of the *New Testament*, has to be considered first.

The *Old Testament*

The Jewish attitude towards the Gentiles and their religions, in general terms, was one of hostility. The historical and prophetic literature of Israel explicitly encounters pagan religions. But, an outlook of universalism can be noticed in the Psalms and the Isaiah. Pagan Saints of *Old Testament* like Abel, Henoch, Daniel, Noah, Job, Lot and Melchizedec were treated by Danielou as 'Saints of Cosmic Religion' and 'Priests of Cosmic Religion' common to all men. The approach of Israel to the Nations was positive. The institution of 'Kingship' that gave rise to the messianic ideal was due to the impact of the Canannite 'Nature Worship' (Ps. 29). This enrichment was achieved through a long process of selective cultural assimilation and not by changing religion.

Prophet Micah says, "For all people will walk every one in the name of his god: but we will walk in the name of the Lord our God forever and ever" (Mic. 4:5). This is a clear recognition of others' right to live loyal to their god. In Sam 26:19-20 the Lord says, "Go serve other gods." It is natural for anyone outside the land of Israel to worship other gods. The book of Jonah shows that God's merciful love extends to the gentiles, but it also implies that Ninavites can find salvation in their own religion. They were being asked to forsake their wicked ways and to convert to God, but not to become Jews.

The *New Testament*

The *New Testament* is a telling example of inculturation or adaptation, which tantamount to openness to non-Christian cultures. The attitude of Jesus to the non-Judaic religions is apparently positive but at times negative, John says that Jesus considered the religion of the Samaritans inferior to Judaism. But Jesus often singled out Samaritans for special commendations (Lk. 3:7, 17 and 16 and Jn: 4:39). The criterion for the final judgment is the practice of brotherly love, not racial or religious superiority (Mt. 25:31-46).

Once, Jesus warned his apostles against going into the way of the gentiles and into the city of Samaritans. A little afterwards, Jesus says "Into whatever city or town you shall enter, inquire who in it is worthy and there abide." The reason behind this prohibition by Jesus, who stayed two days with the Samaritans, was not actually due to any exclusiveness. Had the disciples gone also to the gentiles and Samaritans, the Jews, who considered it below their dignity to be taught by such men, would, in all good faith, have considered the disciples unfit to teach them. On the basis of this clarification Robert De Nobilee argues as follows:

"When our Lord Jesus Christ in his condescension for the Jews, took into account their weakness by forbidding the Apostles to go to the Gentiles and Samaritans, which in itself would have been but an act of charity, should not the preacher of the Gospel in this part of India take into account the weakness of the high-born Indians, do away with what makes him unwelcome to them and embrace that way of life which will conciliate the hearts of the Indians and make them amenable to his preaching."[22]

The Attitude of the Apostles

The attitude of the Apostles is ambivalent. According to St. Paul, the faith once offered to the Christians abolishes for them, through the judgment of God, the value of all religions (Rom: 6: 6, 2 Cor: 5:17. Eph: 4: 22, Col. 2: 9). If this is the purport of the affirmations of St. Paul, it need not be taken as to imply the denial of values to other religions. It only shows that Paul was always ready to adapt to the needs of the people.

In the Acts of the Apostles, at times, a positive evaluation of the pagan religions is discernible. St. Peter led Cornelius, the centurion, a man of prayer and kind-heartedness to Jesus. He accepted the Gospel. Here, the pagan religion of Cornelius served as a preparation to the acceptance of Gospel.

A classic example is available in St. Paul's relations with the Athens. He addressed the Athens:

"Men of Athens, I perceive that in every way, you are very religious. For, I passed along and observed the objects of your worship, I found also an altar with this inscription, 'To an unknown God' what therefore, you worship as unknown, this I proclaim to you" (Acts. 17:22-23). According to Karl Rahner, this passage is a basis for Christian openness. The Church will go out to meet the Non-Christians of tomorrow with the attitude of St. Paul 'What therefore you do not know and worship (and yet worship) that I proclaim to you.' On this basis one can be tolerant, humble and yet firm towards all non-Christian religions. But, the Church is not only the second Israel, she is also the Church of the incarnated God, who came to make all things one in himself, reconciling the world into Himself (2 Cor: 5:19). According to the sacred scripture, to adhere to the Christian faith is a decision, which implies a break with the past. The *Bible* offers a foundation for a positive approach to all religions.

FOOTNOTES

1. Mahabharata – 3 – 292.
2. Radhakrishnan, S. (Dr.), *Eastern Religion and Western Thought*, pp. 152-72.
3. Radhakrishnan, S. (Dr.), *An Idealist View of Life*, p. 69.
4. Shriman Narayan, *Selected Works of Mahatma Gandhi*, 1968, Vol. VI, p. 264.
5. Radhakrishnan, S. (Dr.), *The Hindu View of Life*, 1968, p. 43.
6. *Selected Works of Mahatma Gandhi*, Vol. VI, p. 241.
7. Zacharias Paranilam, *Christian Openness to World Religions*, p. 133.
8. Radhakrishnan, S. (Dr.), *Eastern Religion and Western Thought*, p. 317.
9. *Ibid*., p. 324.
10. *East and West, Some Reflections*, London, 1955, p. 51.
11. Zaehner, R.C., *Concordant Discord*, Oxford, 1970, p. 222.
12. Justinan Cherupallikkal, *Witness Potential of Evangelical Poverty in India*, 1975, p. 2.
13. Panikkar, K.M., *Asia and Western Dominance*, 1953, pp. 4-6.
14. *Sriramakrishna and His Unique Message*, p. 140.
15. Zacharias Paranilam, *Christian Openness to World Religions*, p. 139, Para. 3.
16. Gandhi, M.K., *The Message of Jesus Christ*, 1940, p. 35.
17. Radhakrishnan, S. (Dr.), *An Idealist View of Life*, pp. 233-36.
18. *Selected Writings of Mahatma Gandhi*, p. 199.
19. St. Paul's Publications, *Documents of Vatican–II*, pp. 549-50.
20. *Ibid*., pp. 549-50.
21. Zacharias Paranilam, *Christian Openness to the World Religions*, p. XI.
22. *Ibid*., p. 11.

Hinduism vs Christianity – Accord & Discord

50

The word 'Religion' *prima facie* gives the notion of a group of people or community united together in a broad uniformity of faith in certain precepts and practices. This yardstick applies to Hinduism only as a square peg in a round hole. Unity in Hinduism is confined to the areas of Indian cultural ethos, traditions, natural environment and nationalism. Uniformity in faith and practices is not only conspicuously absent but also reprehensible to the Hindu, just because it is contrary to one of the basic tenets of Hinduism – freedom of the individual. Judged on this premise, Hinduism does not deserve to be reckoned as a religion. In the strict sense of the term, it can only be treated as a culture interwoven with spirituality or at the most, as an eclectic religion.

In the preceding chapter, we already had a glimpse of Hinduism and Christianity; their doctrines and mutual perceptions. An appraisal of the major world religions of today shows Hinduism and Christianity in closer proximity to each other in the realm of doctrines. These religions, in the course of centuries, developed their doctrines of faith and theological and philosophical visions in the respective backgrounds of their culture, civilization, language etc. Hence, it is a fallacy to presume that the doctrines and practices of one religion are borrowed from the other. Buddhism, originated from Hinduism, acquired fantastic growth in India to the extent of eclipsing even Hinduism. But Hinduism not only survived the threat by its own renewal, assimilation and acceptance of a middle path through the *Madhyamika* (middle path) theory of Nagarjuna, but also succeeded in the gradual absorption of Buddhism in India, without any fuss or confrontation.

A comparative analysis of the doctrines of Hinduism and Christianity brings to light three distinctive characterestics: (i) full concord, (ii) similarities and parallels with differing connotations, and (iii) contradictory teachings. Now, let us have a bird's-eye view of them.

1. Full Concord

(a) 'The Logos', 'The Word' and 'Om'

'Logos' is a Greek term, which represents the manifestation of God as the creative reason of the world, according to Neo-Platonic and Christian philosophies. St. John, in his Gospel translated 'Logos' as 'The Word'. In order to avoid ambiguity, he himself clarified that 'the Word was God' (Jn: 1:1). The corresponding word used in Hinduism is *Om*, the sound of respiration (*Pranava*). *Om* is a combination of the English syllables 'a', 'u' and 'm' representing Vishnu, Siva and Brahmav respectively, the three deities in the *Trimurthy*. Hinduism insists on uttering *Om* at the commencement of study of Hindu scripture or Holy Books, as invocation. Detailed explanations on *Om* are found in *Mandukyopanishad* and several *Puranas*. The terms 'The Logos', 'The Word' and *Om* are synonyms. On this basic theological concept, both religions are in perfect harmony.

(b) Revelation

In the 'revelation', God reveals His 'plan of loving goodness'. In His goodness and wisdom, God is pleased to reveal himself and to make known the mystery of His will. Here, God comes to meet man. Christianity claims its scripture, the *Bible*, as the revealed word of God. Hinduism also claims its scriptures as the revealed word of God. Both are revelation-based religions.

(c) Tradition

'Tradition' literally means the passing of beliefs or customs from one generation to the next. In the religious context, tradition transmits in its entirety, 'the Word of God' revealed to man, to the succeeding generations. In both Hinduism and Christianity, Scripture and Tradition are accepted and honoured with sentiments of reverence. Tradition facilitates the transmission and interpretation of revelation. In Hinduism, the first Revelation – the Vedas – transmitted through tradition remained in the memory of ordinary, illiterate village folks for centuries, without understanding the meaning. Hence, tradition and scripture are closely bound together, 'both flowing out from the same divine well-spring, come together in some fashion to form one thing, and move towards the same goal'.[1] Hinduism and Christianity accept this position, without any reservation.

(d) Scripture

The *Bible*, the revealed word of God, is the scripture of Christianity. The *Vedas*, the *Bhagavad Gita* (the Lord's song) and the *Brahma Sutra* together constitute the Hindu scripture, known as *Prasthanathrayam* (the triple march). *Veda* is the revealed word of the unseen God, heard and remembered by the people, without recording, and hence classified as *Smriti* (memory). Later, Sage Veda Vyasa divided and compiled the *Vedas* into four texts (Veda Vyasa means – he who divided the *Vedas*). *Bhagavad Gita* is the sermon of Sri Krishna, the God Incarnate, in the battlefield at Kurukshetra, recorded by Sanjaya, the Minister of King Dhritarashtrar, the blind father of the *Kauravas*. *Brahma Sutra* is the book compiled by Sage Vyasa incorporating the scriptural dictates in the *Vedas* and the *Bhagavad Gita*. It contains 555 *Sutras* (Principles or dogmas) on the *Brahma*, the Supreme God.

(e) Incarnation

Incarnation is God's descent to earth in the form and time of God's own choice. According to Christianity, there is only one and final incarnation, that of Jesus Christ. The Hindus have no hesitation to admit Jesus Christ as God Incarnate. But, they do not subscribe to the Christian view of uniqueness of incarnation. *Avatara*, the term in Sanskrit, corresponding to incarnation, is a recurring feature, ceaselessly occurring and recurring age after age (*Sambhavami Yuge Yuge*), according to Hinduism. Sri Krishna is the ninth *Avatara* of Vishnu, the Deity conserving the universe.

(f) God is Love

The *Bhagavad Gita* says, "God is Love. Pure love generates sweetness in all its excellence." Love is the inspiration and impetus for *Bhakti* (devotion or piety) in Hinduism and *Bhakti Yoga* is one of the paths prescribed for Liberation (*Mukti*). The *Bible* says, "He that loveth not knoweth not God; for God is charity (Love)" (1 Jn 4:8). Here, the *Bible* and the *Bhagavad Gita* are in full harmony and agreement.

(g) God is Light

The *Bhagavad Gita* says, "God is Light. What shines through the human frame is none other than the Inextinguishable Cosmic Light." A famous prayer in Hinduism reads "Lead me from darkness to light" (*Thamaso ma Jyotir Gamaya*) (Briha, 1:3:28). The *Bible* says, "God is Light and in him there is no darkness" (1 Jn. 1:5). Here, both religions are in full accord.

(h) Monasticism

Both Hinduism and Christianity give due respect and recognition to spiritual exercises like asceticism, prayer, meditation, fast, lent, contemplation, abstinence, renunciation, continence, monasticism etc. Though ascetic life (*Sannyasa*) is prescribed obligatory in the last *Asrama* (Stage of Life) in Hinduism, monasticism acquired popularity after the coming of *Vihars* (monasteries) through Buddhism. Both Hinduism and Christianity recognise matrimony and celibacy with respectful equanimity.

(i) Mysticism

'Mysticism' literally means the belief that the knowledge of God and of real truth may be reached by directing one's mind or through spiritual insight, independently of reason and the senses. The remarks of Pope Paul VI, during his visit to India in 1964 that "India, the land of Sages and Saints, Seekers and Seers, where monasticism flourished in a sublime manner and where prayer and contemplation reached the highest mark of mysticism" shows the appreciation of the Church for the advancement made by Hinduism in the realm of mysticism. As regards monasticism and mysticism, both Christianity and Hinduism are in perfect harmony and mutual respect.

(j) Priesthood

Priesthood is prevalent in both religions. In the *Bible*, Jesus Christ is projected as High Priest (Heb: 9:11). Though all the faithful in Christianity are endowed with the faculty of priesthood according to the *Bible*, trained and ordained priests perform priestly functions. Being earmarked for specific functions of a sacred character, priests form a sacred class in Christianity. In Hinduism, priesthood is caste-based, the prerogative of the *Brahmins*, the highest caste in the hierarchical order. In the early days of Buddhism, many Hindus accepted Buddhism solely for relief from the burdensome rituals imposed by priests in Hinduism. Today, this caste base of priesthood is gradually losing its grip.

(k) Realisation of God (Salvation or moksha)

The words 'Salvation' in Christianity and *Moksha* in Hinduism denote 'realisation of God', the ultimate goal of human life. Realisation means the eternal enjoyment of heavenly bliss (*ananda*) in the beatific vision of the Creator – The Beginning and the First Cause. Hinduism stipulates four goals in life (known as *Purusartha*) – *Dharma*, *Artha*, *Kama* and *Moksha*; *Artha* (wealth) and *Kama* (pleasure including sex) are to be acquired with *Moksha* as the end and *Dharma* as the means to achieve that end. Both religions reconcile on this aspect. But there is disagreement on the path to achieve realisation of God. This is dealt with separately in the succeeding pages.

(l) Monotheism

In practice, we notice in Hinduism, Polytheism, Pantheism, Monism, Ancestor worship, Nature worship, *Isthtadevatha* worship (worship of a god of one's choice) and so on. This is due to several factors like multiplicity of *Avataras*, unrestricted freedom of choice for the faithful, absence of corrective mechanism, the existence of the primitive system of idolatry, myths, legends, traditional worship of forces of nature and so on. But, all these mini-gods and semi-gods have to accept human life, at one stage or other, to attain realisation of God (*Moksha*) as man is the crown of creations. A closer analysis reveals that all these mini-gods are below the one Supreme God.

In theory, Hinduism is absolutely monotheistic. The scripture says *Ekam Evam Adwiteeyam Brahma* – Meaning: God is one, unrivalled and unparalleled one.

They address God *Paramatma*, *Parabrahma*, *Parameswara* etc., meaning Supreme Soul, Supreme God, the Ultimate, the Absolute etc. In theory, there is no discord between Hinduism and Christianity in the faith in one Supreme God.

(m) Teachings of Christ

The 'Sermon on the Mount' and other teachings of Christ are acceptable to Hinduism. Equivalent teachings are available in *Yama* the first branch of *Ashtanga Yoga*; the cardinal principles of Hindu life. They are (i) *Ahimsa* (absence of hostility towards other beings), (ii) *Satya* (truth or essence), (iii) *Asteya* (non-stealing or non-covetousness and avoidance of exploitation of others), (iv) *Brahmacariya* (self-control and freedom from sexual desires), and (v) *Aparigraha* (non-accumulation of wealth more than that required for sustenance of life).

(n) Morality and Ethics

In the areas of morality and ethics in life, there is no contradiction in the teachings of both religions. In this respect, we find full concord in theory.

(o) Dharma and Kingdom of God

Detailed explanations are given in Chapter 48 (Part Eight).

(p) Prayer and Rituals for the Dead

Prayer and rituals for the dead are prevalent in Hinduism from time immemorial. A large section of Christian Churches – Catholics, Orthodox and few other churches – believe and practise prayer and mass for the dead, the only difference being that Christians substitute 'mass' for the rituals in Hinduism.

In the sixteen items enumerated above, we find concord between Christianity and Hinduism, in the realm of dogmas, despite differences in details.

2. Similarities and Parallels

(a) Trimurty in Hinduism and Trinity in Christianity

The 'Trimurty' and the 'Trinity' are parallel terms in two distinct languages. But, the connotations vastly differ.

(b) Birth of Sri Krishna and Birth of Jesus

Parallel stories of attempts to murder Baby Krishna and Baby Jesus at the time of birth of these babies do not attach much significance in the economy of salvation upheld by these religions. But, they help to project the divinity in these births and to proclaim God's descent to earth.

3. Contradictory Teachings

(a) Path to Attain Realisation of God (Transmigration of Souls)

On this doctrine of faith, there is wide gap between Hinduism and Christianity. In Christianity, salvation is based on purification through penance, reconciliation, absolution of sins and the Last judgment of God. There is another school of thought among the Christians emphasizing 'Justification by faith in Jesus Christ alone' propounded by Martin Luther, the German Reformer. The Protestant churches generally accept this Lutheran concept.

Hinduism prescribes purification through transmigration of soul (*Karma samsar*), a cycle of rebirths, wherein the soul forsakes one body and accepts another body, either human or non-human, till the attainment of liberation (through successive rebirths). The basic doctrine behind transmigration is that the soul of all living beings is an integral part of the Supreme Soul and therefore, it is eternal. An eternal soul is beyond annihilation. Rebirth is another chance for reconciliation with God. If it fails to utilize the first chance, a series of chances are given through a cycle of rebirths until ultimate realisation of God is achieved.

Hinduism provides different paths (*Yogas*) for liberation (*Mukti*) of the soul from rebirths. Asceticism is one of the prescribed paths.

The element of fatalism, the human endeavour and the role of God in this concept require deeper investigation and study.

The doctrine of transmigration is an area where the teachings of Christianity and Hinduism stand irreconcilably apart.

(b) Casteism

The division of people into different castes based on ethnic origin or occupation or colour etc. is a practice prevalent in Hinduism from pre-historic period. According to the Hindus, it is God who ordained casteism. Lord Krishna endorsed this practice. Each caste is metaphorically described as the members of the hypothetical body of the Infinite, which endows casteism with divine sanction. The religious literatures of Hinduism insist on *Varnasrama-dharma*, the obligations on the basis of *Varna* (Caste) and *Asrama* (stage or station) in life. Though casteism is banned in India under the law of the land, this age-old practice still persists in the minds of the people and resultantly exists in the society at large. Christianity teaches that all men are children of God and therefore equal in the eyes of the Lord. Hence, discrimination or segregation of the humans on grounds of caste is untenable from the Christian point of view.

(c) Idolatry

Idolatry literally means the practice of worship of idols or images set up as representations of gods or supernatural beings, developed in primitive religions. In other words, it is a system devised by primitive man to worship the invisible God in a visible form. With advancement of civilization, the idols are made of stone, wood, metals, clay etc. The priests invoke the Deity with chants and rites, sanctify it with water, incense, flowers and flames and erect them in public view in temples and other places for worship. This system is in vogue in Hinduism even today, though the literate and enlightened Hindus and many reformist movements in Hinduism are opposed to this practice. This system was absent in the Vedic Age, but became popular after the period of the *Ithihasas* (epics). A section in Christianity believes in veneration of relics and images, but does not worship them in the light of the Christian teaching that worship is only for God. But the possibilities for perversions and corruption in this practice cannot be ruled out.

Another section in Christianity vehemently opposes even the making of idols and images in the light of Biblical strictures.

(d) Redemption

Hinduism does not subscribe to the theory of redemption of mankind with the blood and death of the Redeemer, upheld by Christianity. The Hindu view is that no Redeemer can help mankind in this respect, as redemption has to be achieved by individuals themselves by their own endeavour.

(e) Astrology (Jyotisha)

Most Hindus consider *Jyotisha* as an accurate science. The entire life of an individual is predetermined and it can be identified and foretold by precise astrological calculations, they argue. According to Christianity, astrology is a superstitious fiction, a clarion call for human inaction, reliance on destiny and negation of divine intervention in human life.

(f) Some Unique Features of Hinduism

The Hindu concept of 'Religion' stands far apart from other religions, especially Christianity (Please see "The Hindu Concept of Religion" in the preceding chapter). The unique features noticed are:

- Hinduism does not claim itself as the only true religion in the world. No religion can claim absoluteness according to Hindu perceptions.
- Hinduism accepts the plurality of religions and upholds the validity of all religions. As such, their approach towards other religions is remarkably tolerant.
- Hinduism does not endorse the desirability of an organisational structure for religion. As organisation is the breeding ground of vested interests and corruption, the Hindu attitude towards organised religions is one of inherent antipathy.
- The members of Hinduism enjoy unrestricted freedom in matters of faith and practices.
- The Hindu religion is inseparably mixed up with Indian culture, Indian environment and Indian nationalism.

Consequently, Mount Himalayas, River Ganges, the Banyan tree, the Cow, the Snake etc. are sacred in their view.

- The Hindus do not object conversion from one religion to another, born out of convictions. But they abhor proselytisation and proselytizing religions.

Christianity has contradictory views on most of these practices.

The points of accord and discord between Christianity and Hinduism enumerated above are neither comprehensive, nor deep. They are only tips to serve as advance information in a process of dialogue for both sides.

Dialogue

In the early centuries, precisely in the post-Constantine era, the approach of Christianity to the so-called pagan religions in the East, especially Hinduism, was one of hypocrisy, dissidence and contempt. In the evaluation of the Church, Hinduism was a pagan religion founded on myth and legends, superstitious in faith and primitive in rituals and practices. Without understanding the salvific worth of the Hindu religion or realizing the rich cultural heritage of India, the only solution the Church offered to them was the acceptance of visible membership in Christianity, the only repository of all virtues and salvific potential. In the medieval period, this approach assumed the characteristics of neglect or indifference. But, in the colonial period, money, power and superiority complex played a decisive role in the shaping of an aggressive approach.

In the pre-reformation and post-reformation periods, the controversial issue of salvation of those outside the visible structure of the Church came up as a puzzling question before the Church. God, the father of all, not only of 'Abraham', 'Isaac' and 'Jacob' wishes all His children to be saved or at least be provided with the means appropriate and essential for salvation, without disturbing their inborn right for liberty to choose or discard the means placed at their disposal. In its quest for an answer to this question, Vatican II inaugurated a new era of Church's openness to all non-Christian world religions. Dialogue was the medium prescribed by the Council to initiate a search for the salvific worth of those religions.

In pursuance to the dictates of the Council, the Church started a process of dialogue with those religions, particularly with Hinduism. Being an open religion always prepared to accept and assimilate worthy ideas, Hinduism responded positively to the call for dialogue. But the Church is put into a disadvantageous situation on two specific counts; firstly, the Church is incapacitated to speak in one voice even on doctrines, save rituals and practices, due to the existence of innumerable churches in Christianity with wide-ranging interpretations of dogmas and practices. This is rather incomprehensible to the Hindu mind. Secondly, as Hinduism is a religion with no organisational structure, dialogue cannot assume an official character and even if consensus is arrived at, how far it can percolate to the grass-roots level and find acceptance by the devotees remains a puzzling question with no immediate answer. Transformation of external forms and practices may be comparatively easy, but as far as doctrines are concerned, it may not be easy to bring forth changes.

Prerequisites for a Fruitful Dialogue

The second Vatican Council has rekindled the minds of Christians with new hopes, aspirations and enthusiasm for a meaningful dialogue. To make it effective and fruitful, it is utmost essential to carry out it in an atmosphere of trust, sincerity, humility, mutual understanding, an unfeigned openness to truth, in a level-playing field and above all in a spirit of mutual give and take. In the words of Pope Benedict XI, an all out venture for adaptation will show the real Catholic nature of the Church, which is 'neither Latin, nor Greek, nor Slav, but universal'. The universal and open character of the Church is in itself a step in the right direction to foster good relations with Hinduism, which is visualizing a World Religion. Whatever truth and goodness are found among other religions should be viewed as a preparation for the Gospel; a guidance to God. Many prominent Hindus have acclaimed the spirit behind the services to the poor by Christianity in India. This can facilitate and foster a positive approach.

Christian attitude towards openness demands a witnessing life. The most irritant aspect noticed by the Hindus in the historical Christianity is the wide gap between preaching and practice. In the infant stage of the Church, it was not dogma that attracted many to the Church, but the life of the Christians; the depth of their faith, their fraternal love and service and their commitment to Christ reflected in daily life. Authority, dogma, corruption etc. found in the Church had only a repulsive effect among others, especially Hindus. Luxury and waywardness cannot go hand in hand with religion. A break from the past is the hallmark of Christianisation. A witnessing life can do wonders. It is the absence of this witnessing Christian life that provoked many Hindu leaders to comment, 'there is no space for Christ in Christianity' 'we have come across only one Christian, that is Jesus Christ' etc. The establishment of a life-oriented Christianity devoid of pomp and power is the need of the hour and a prerequisite for a fruitful dialogue.

The conciliar approach encouraged the adoption of mystical practices of the Hindus in the Christian Church. Bede Griffith is of the view that prayer and contemplation can provide a Hindu-Christian meeting point. Here, one point to be taken note of is the fact that modern Hinduism is a bit different from the classical Hinduism of the Vedic-Upanishadic period. Humble service with love by the Christians is likely to garner more appreciation on the part of the Hindus, as expressed by few Hindu leaders. Now there is more and more awareness among the Christians on the necessity of a transformation in the Christian Church. In Christians' relations with Hinduism, the superiority complex pattern of relations have to disappear. In the modern age, this is an important task of the Indian Church.

In pursuance to the declarations of Vatican II, the Church constituted a commission for dialogue in India. The commission undertook two important steps titled 'Get Together' and 'Live Together'. Under the 'Get Together', delegates from different local dioceses came together for two or three days for preliminary studies on the nature, scope, difficulties, risks and possibilities of the dialogue in the particular region. *Bible* study, exposition of Hinduism by Hindu leaders, life sharing etc. came up in the first meet for sharing mutual viewpoints. The first meeting under 'Live Together' was held at Benares in February 1973. The programme consisted of common prayer, meditation and sharing of reflections. Much time was consumed by songs, readings from scriptures, *bhajan* (Hindu Hymns) and sharing of insights on the readings etc. Along with it, few topics were identified for initiating the dialogue; (i) What my religion means to me? (ii) What is my attitude towards other religions? (iii) Prayer-religious experience in life, (iv) Religion and social concern, and (v) Sufferings of neighbour. 15 centres in 13 monasteries were selected as venue and eight dialogue groups were put in position to continue the process. Both the groups shared the costs of these meetings.

India's glorious culture is deep-rooted in religious and spiritual values. Buddhism and Jainism share these values as well. A methodology has to be worked out to ensure participation of those religions also in the process of dialogue.[2]

The study on the dimensions of the Christian attitude of openness to religions brought out three directions. The search for the foundation of openness led to Revelation and Traditions, where very valuable insights of positive attitude lie embedded. Enquiry about the availability of salvific values was the second concern. Fellowship was the third perspective. The availability of salvific values in religions shows that a union of complementarity and fellowship is possible, despite differences. In the course of this study, some ecclesiological and missiological problems are likely to crop up.

In a dialogue between two age-old religions with comprehensive theological and philosophical visions and long traditions encompassing millions of people, a consensus is just a mirage. Insurmountable obstacles may come in. It is only natural. No one need be frustrated on this score. If two religions can arrive at genuine fellowship with all their differing views, it is a real success, which can later lead to a missiological union or federation. Let man propose and leave it to God to dispose.

The discovery and recognition of salvific values in non-Christian religions are the greatest contributions of the Second Vatican Council in the area of the relation of the Christian Church with non-Christian religions. This provides the dialogue with an authenticity. Karl Rahner puts it "man is a Christ-Centred being, that is, he possesses an ontic and spiritual capacity for community with Jesus Christ".[3]

Now let us conclude this attempt to find the wide horizon of openness of the Church inaugurated by the Second Vatican Council in the words of Joseph Cardinal Parecattil:

"We shall not abandon our quest for a 'New World'. 'By a new world', I do not mean a new religious syncretism or an amalgamation of religions, but a new era of understanding and co-operation based on the brotherhood of men under the fatherhood of God."[4]

Let us pray and offer our humble might for the establishment of a New World of peace and tranquility.

FOOTNOTES

1. Veritas, *Catechism of the Catholic Church*, p. 25 item 80.
2. Zacharias Paranilam, *Christian Openness to World Religions*, pp. 164-65.
3. Rahner, K., *Theological Investigation*, Vol. II, p. 241.
4. Joseph Cardinal Parecattil, *Unitive Understanding*, Speech at the World Parliament of Religions (24 Mar. 1971).

ANNEXURES

ANNEXURE I

Bibliography

Sl. No.	Author	Book
1.	Abraham, C.E. (Dr.) Rev.	Sabha Charithra Samgraham (Concise History of Church)
2.	Acharya Narendra Bhushan	Hindu Encyclopaedia
3.	Advaita Ashram, Calcutta	Vivekananda – His Call to Nation
4.	Alan Schreck	The Compact History of the Catholic Church
5.	Alangaram, A.	Christ of the Asian Peoples
6.	Albert Nambiaparambil C.M.I. (Fr.)	Guidelines for Dialogue Between Muslims & Christians
7.	Alexander Marthoma Metropolitan (Dr.), Rev.	The Marthoma Church, Heritage and Mission
8.	Baha-i's House	Baha-i's House of Worship
9.	Bengt Sundkler	Church of South India
10.	Bernard Haring, C.S.S.R.	The Law of Christ
11.	Bible League, U.S.A.	The Greatest is Love
12.	Brodov, V.	Indian Philosophy in Modern Times
13.	Catholic Bishops Conference of India	Catholic Directory of India 1998 (Jubilee 2000 Publication)
14.	Catholic Truth Society	The Holy Bible
15.	Chandy, T.	101 Thoughts
16.	Cheriyan, C.V. (Dr.)	A History of Christianity in Kerala
17.	Cyril Mar Basselios (Dr.), Archbishop	Syro Malankara Church
18.	David Daniel	The Orthodox Church of India
19.	Deepika Publications	The Indian Christian Directory
20.	Delhi Gurudwara Management Committee	What is Sikhism?

Sl. No.	Author	Book
21.	Delhi Gurudwara Management Committee	Guru Granth Sahib
22.	Devi Book Stall	Srimad Bhagavad Gita
23.	Doug Burke and Paul Knowles	New Direction – Bible Reading Guide
24.	Fulton, J. Sheen (Bishop)	The Life of Christ
25.	Gandhi, M.K.	My Experiments with Truth
26.	George Karter	History of England
27.	George Koruthu, C.M. (Rev.)	The Milton Hall Controversy on Episcopacy
28.	George Menachery (Dr.), Prof.	The St. Thomas Christian Encyclopaedia of India, Vol. I
29.	George Menachery (Dr.), Prof.	-do- (Vol. II)
30.	George Onakkoor	Mar Ivanios
31.	Gopalakrishnan, N. (Dr.)	Indian Scientific Heritage
32.	Gopalakrishnan, N. (Dr.)	Ancient Indian Scientific Thoughts for the Third Millennium
33.	Internet	Encyclopaedia Britannica
34.	Jacob Kollaparambil (Dr.), Rev.	St. Thomas Christian Revolution 1653
35.	Jacob Kollaparambil (Dr.), Rev.	Knanaya Community in Kerala History
36.	Jawaharlal Nehru	Autobiography
37.	Jawaharlal Nehru	The Discovery of India
38.	John Pallathu, OCD (Fr.)	The Christian Church in the Portugal Age (Mal.)
39.	John Patrick Brennan	Christian Mission in a Pluralistic World
40.	John Renaurd	Responses to 101 Questions on Hinduism
41.	Joshua Mar Ignatios (Rev. Dr.)	Malankara Catholic Directory, 2001
42.	Justin Panackal (Dr.) OCD	Intimacy with God
43.	Justin Panackal (Dr.) OCD	In the Other Hell
44.	Karl Adam	The Spirit of Catholicism

Sl. No.	Author	Book
45.	Kerala Language Institute	Christu Darsanam
46.	Mahajan, V.D.	Ancient India
47.	Mahajan, V.D.	Medieval India
48.	Mahatma Gandhi	Collected Works of Mahatma Gandhi, Vol. I
49.	Mahatma Gandhi	Collected Works of Mahatma Gandhi, Vol. II
50.	Majumdar, R.C.	An Advanced History of India
51.	Malayala Manorama	Manorama Year Book – 1999
52.	Margaret Gibbons	Mar Ivanios, Apostle of Church Union
53.	Martin, P. Joseph	Sree Yesu Christuvum Sree Ramanum (Mal.)
54.	Mathew, K.V. (Dr.)	The Faith and Practices of Marthoma Church
55.	Muzhoor, S.J.	Bible Encyclopaedia
56.	Nair, P.S. (Dr.)	Sree Maha Bhagavathom (Mal.)
57.	Neuner, S.J. and Dupis, S.J.	Christian Faith
58.	Orthodox Church	The Malankara Orthodox Church Directory
59.	Pandey, J.N.	The Indian Constitution (with commentaries)
60.	Placid, C.M.I. (Dr.)	Our Rite (Mal.)
61.	Rajagopalachari, C.	Ramayana
62.	Ramakrishna Mission	Swamy Vivekananda's Address
63.	Reader's Digest	The Great People of Faith and Wisdom
64.	Readers Digest	Vanishing Civilizations
65.	Richard, P. Johnson (Dr.)	Spiritual Vitality
66.	Rozario, A.J. (Msgr)	Kollam Christians (Mal.)
67.	Sachidanandan, V.	A. Toynbee Anthology
68.	Sree Ramakrishnasramom	The Collected Works of Swamy Vivekananda
69.	Sreedhara Menon, A.	A Survey of Kerala History
70.	Sreeramakrishnasramom	Vivekananda Sahitya Sarvam Part VI

Sl. No.	Author	Book
71.	St. Paul Publications	The Documents of Vatican II
72.	Sudil, I.M.S. (Dr.)	The Reign of God and Establishment of Dharma
73.	Sukumar Azhikode	Tatvamasi
74.	Swamy Chidbhavananda	The Bhagavad Gita with Commentaries
75.	Swamy Mridananda	Isavasyopanishad
76.	Swamy Mridananda	Kenopanishad
77.	Swamy Mridananda	Katopanishad
78.	Swamy Mridananda	Prasnopanishad
79.	Swamy Mridananda	Mundakopanishad
80.	Swamy Mridananda	Mandukyopanishad
81.	Swamy Mridananda	Aitareyopanishad
82.	Swamy Mridananda	Taittiriyopanishad
83.	Swamy Mridananda	Chandogyopanishad
84.	Swamy Mridananda	Brihadaranyakopanishad
85.	Tatas	Statistical Outline of India
86.	Thiruvalluvar	Thirukkural
87.	Thomas, A. Kempis	Imitation of Christ
88.	Thomas, Arukalil (Fr.)	The Indian Catholic Directory, 2001
89.	Thomas, Boken Kotter	A Concise History of the Catholic Church
90.	Trichur Diocese	Jubilee Souvenir
91.	Universal Publications	The Great Encyclopaedia of Universal Knowledge
92.	Varghese Kilichimala (Fr.)	The Truth and the Life
93.	Varghese Kilichimala (Fr.)	Ecumenism
94.	Varghese Kilichimala (Fr.)	Ecumenical Thoughts and Dialogue in Malankara Church
95.	Verapoly Diocese	Jubilee Souvenir
96.	Veritas	Catechism of the Catholic Church
97.	Vettom Mani	Puranic Encyclopaedia
98.	Victor, O.C.D. (Fr.)	A Manual of Christian Sociology
99.	Warder, A.	A Course in Indian Philosophy
100.	Xavier, Koodapuzha (Dr.)	Christianity in India

Sl. No.	Author	Book
101.	Youhanon Marthoma Metropolitan (Dr.)	The Christian Church in India and Concise History of Marthoma Church
102.	Zacharias Paranilam	Christian Openness to the World Religions

ANNEXURE II
Chronology of Events

Year		Events
3102	BC	Epoch of the Kaliyuga and the ascension of Sri Krishna
3100	"	Indo-Iranians settled at Mesopotamia
2700	"	Indus valley seals found
1500	"	Second group of Aryans settled in Northern and Western Punjab
1500 to 1000	"	The Vedic Age
1200 to 600	"	The period of Upanishads
973	"	Jews came to India with the trade fleet of Solomon
931	"	Division of Jewish Kingdom into Judaea and Israel
817	"	Traditional date of birth of Parsvanath, 23rd Theerthankara of Jainism
605	"	Fall of Assyrian Empire
586	"	Babylon conquered Judaea and destroyed the Jerusalem city and temple
563	"	Birth of Siddhartha, later known as Buddha, the founder of Buddhism
558	"	Accession of Cyrus the Great in Persia
540	"	Birth of Vardhamana Mahavira, the 24th Theerthankara of Jainism
539	"	Conquest of Babylon by Cyrus of Persia
483	"	Death of Buddha and the beginning of Buddha Age
332	"	Conquest of Palestine by Alexander the Great and beginning of Hellenism
326	"	Conquest of India by Alexander
324 to 184	"	Maurya dynasty in India
322	"	Chandragupta Maurya ascended the throne in India

Year		Events
305	BC	Indian expedition of Seleucus Nicator
273 - 232	"	Emperor Asoka
206	"	Indian Expedition of Antiochus III, King of Syria
198	"	Syrian domination in Palestine
185 - 149	"	Pushyamitra rule in India
73 - 28	"	The Kanvas ruled India
63	"	Roman domination in Palestine
27	"	Establishment of Roman Empire by Augustus Caesar
26 - 20	"	Indian Embassy in Rome
4	"	Birth of Jesus Christ
29 OR 30	AD	Death of Jesus Christ
47	"	Takht-I-Bahi record of Gondophornes
48	"	Jerusalem Synod of Apostles
52	"	St. Thomas landed at Kodungalloor (India)
64	"	Death of St. Peter and St. Paul
70	"	Destruction of Jerusalem City and Temple (the sanctuary of Jews) by Romans
72	"	Death of St. Thomas at Calamina (Mylapore) and burial
78 - 123	"	Kushana dynasty in India (Kanishka)
96	"	Presbyter system asserted in Church by Pope Clement
186	"	Montanus, the proponent of Montanism (heresy)
195	"	Roman Emperor Septimus Seravus prohibited Romans accepting Christianity
276 - 293	"	Sassanian Conquest of N-W India
280-336	"	Arius, the proponent of Arianism
312	"	Constantine became Emperor of Rome
313	"	Decree of Milan by Constantine
319 - 335	"	Chandragupta I of Gupta dynasty
325	"	General Council of Nicaea and Nicean creed
334	"	Construction of the City of Constantinople (Byzantium renamed after Constantine)
335 - 375	"	Samudra Gupta
337	"	Death of Constantine

Year		Events
345	AD	Immigration of Knanites to India under the leadership of Thomas Cana
375 - 414	"	Chandragupta II (Vikramaditya)
380	"	Emperor Teodosius declared Christianity the official religion of the Empire
381	"	The General Council of Constantinople
428 to 431	"	Nestorius, the patriarch of Constantinople the proponent of Nestorianism
431	"	The General Council of Ephesus
448	"	Eutychus, the proponent of Monophysitism
451	"	The General Council of Chalcedon
455 - 467	"	Skanda Gupta
476	"	Fall of the Roman Empire
476	"	Birth of Aryabhatta, the Great Astronomer
520-525	"	Visit to India by Cosmos Indicopleastus, the author of 'Universal Christian Topography'
606 - 647	"	Harsha Vardhan
636 - 664	"	Six Arab Expeditions in India
711	"	Moors (North African Muslims) conquered and occupied Spain
712	"	Mohammed-bin-Quasim conquered Sind and Multan
787	"	Second General Council of Nicaea
800	"	Charlemagne crowned Roman Emperor by St. Leo III
813	"	The name of the residence of Pope changed from 'Patriarchate' to 'Sacred Palace of Lateran'
825	"	Malayalam Era (Kolla Varsha) begins
849	"	Theresapally Copper Plates granted by the King to Mar Sabariso and Mar Aphroth
852	"	Visit to India by Arab traveller, Sulaiman
997 - 1030	"	Sixteen Expeditions by Mahmud Ghazni
1054	"	Schism in the Eastern Church and birth of Orthodox Churches
1085	"	Death of Pope Gregory VII in self-imposed exile at Salerno
1096	"	First Crusade
1147	"	Second Crusade

Year		Events
1175 - 1206	AD	Muhammad Ghori (The first Muslim King in India)
1189	"	Third Crusade
1201	"	Fourth Crusade
1215	"	The fourth Lateran General Council – 'Auricular Confession' and 'Transubstantiation as dogmas'
1215	"	Magna Carta signed by King John of England
1217	"	Fifth Crusade
1228	"	Sixth Crusade
1231	"	Foundation of Qutb Minar
1248	"	Seventh Crusade
1270	"	Eighth Crusade
1271	"	Marco Polo's visit to India
1290 - 1320	"	Khalji Dynasty in India
1291	"	Visit to India by John Monte Corvino, the papal delegate
1302 - 1303	"	Capture and destruction of Chitor
1305	"	Papal, H.Q. shifted from Rome to Avignon in France
1320 - 1414	"	Tuglaqs or Quaraunah Turks
1321	"	Visit to India by Jordanus de Severac a Dominican missionary
1323	"	Mongol Invasion
1329	"	Erection of 'Kollam' (Columbum) diocese and Jordanus appointed as bishop (both not materialised)
1336	"	Foundation of Vijayanagar Empire
1341	"	Kochi became a harbour – 'Kochazhy'
1348	"	Visit to Kollam by Johannas De Marinjoli
1351	"	Death of Mohammed-bin-Tuglaq
1378	"	Return of papacy from Avignon to Rome
1398	"	Timur's Invasion and massacre
1414	"	The General Council of Constance and Conciliarism
1414 - 1451	"	Sayyid Dynasty
1431	"	The General Council of Basel
1451 - 1526	"	Lodhi Dynasty
1453	"	Turkey conquered Constantinople

Year		Events
1469	AD	Birth of Guru Nanak, the founder of Sikhism
1498	"	Arrival of Vasco de Gama at Kozhikode (India)
1502	"	The Second arrival of Vasco de Gama
1504	"	Babur (Mughul) occupied Kabul
1510	"	Invasion of Goa by Albuquerque, the Portuguese General
1510	"	Portuguese captured Goa
1514	"	Padroado came into effect in India
1521	"	Martin Luther excommunicated by Pope Leo X
1526	"	Battle of Panipat – Babur ascended the throne in India
1530	"	Goa made capital of Portuguese territories in India
1530 - 1556	"	Humayun S/o Babur ascended as Emperor
1533	"	Diocese of Goa erected
1539	"	Religious congregations banned in England
1539	"	Sher Shah defeated Humayun
1546	"	Death of Martin Luther
1547	"	The General Council of Trent
1553	"	Pope Julius III confirmed the jurisdiction of the East Syrian Church over St. Thomas Christians
1556 - 1605	"	Akbar the Great
1556	"	Second Battle of Panipat – Akbar
1558	"	Erection of Cochin diocese as Suffragan to Goa
1565	"	Talikotta War between Deccan Sultans and Vijayanagar
1572	"	Akbar annexed Gujarat
1582	"	Gregorian Calendar published by Pope Gregory XIII
1597	"	Death of Mar Abraham, the Syrian bishop of Angamaly
1599	"	Synod of Diamper (Udayamperoor)
1600	"	Francis Roz appointed Bishop of Angamaly
1604	"	Guru Arjan Dev compiled the Guru Granth Sahib, the scripture of Sikhism
1605	"	Death of Akbar and accession of Jehangir

Year		Events
1612	AD	Establishment of the Congregation of Propaganda Fide
1624	"	Stephen Britto appointed Archbishop of Angamaly
1641	"	Francis Garcia appointed Archbishop of Angamaly
1653	"	The Slant Cross Oath of St. Thomas Christians
1657	"	Apostolic Commission Sebestiani reached Malabar for enquiry
1658	"	Erected Vicariate Apostolic of Malabar with Sebastiani as Vicar Apostolic
1658 - 1707	"	Aurangazeb of the Mughul dynasty
1663	"	Alexander Campo appointed Bishop of Malabar Vicariate
1663	"	The Dutch defeated the Portuguese and occupied their territories in Kerala
1665	"	Jacobite Church established in India
1670	"	Death of Mar Gregoriose and Mar Thoma I
1674	"	Franceis Martin founded Pondicherry
1680	"	Death of Shivaji
1707	"	Death of Aurangzeb
1708	"	Guru Gobind Singh, the tenth Guru of Sikhism passed away
1712	"	Death of Bahadur Shah (Mughul)
1739	"	Nadir Shah occupied Delhi
1751	"	Introduction of Antiochian Liturgy in India
1754	"	Carnatic War – Dupleix vacated
1757	"	Battle of Plassey
1761	"	The third battle of Panipat
1764	"	Battle of Buxar
1769	"	Suppression of Jesuits by Pope
1775 - 1782	"	The first Anglo-Mahratha War
1776	"	American war of Independence
1776	"	Invasion of Kerala by Tippu Sultan
1782	"	Death of Hyder Ali
1784	"	Treaty of Mangalore

Year		Events
1789	AD	HQ of the Jacobite Church shifted from Angamaly to Kottayam
1789	"	French Revolution
1792	"	Ranjit Singh of Punjab succeeded his father
1792	"	Treaty of Sreerangapattnam after third Mysore War
1795	"	England routed Dutch from Cochin
1799	"	The English defeated Tippu Sultan
1802	"	Concordat between Pope and Napoleon
1814	"	Society of Jesus revived
1808 to 1814	"	Pope Pius VII kept in captivity in France by Napoleon
1814	"	Pope Pius VII released from captivity
1814	"	Russia defeated Napoleon
1815	"	Wellington defeated Napoleon at Waterloo
1824 - 1826	"	The first Burmese War
1829	"	Establishment of Brahma Samaj by Raja Ram Mohan Roy
1838	"	Padroado discontinued and the Sees of Cranganore and Cochin suppressed
1839	"	Death of Ranjit Singh of Punjab
1854	"	Pope Pius IX declared the dogma, 'Immaculate Conception of Mary'
1857 - 1858	"	The Great Revolt (the first war of Independence in India)
1858	"	British India under the Crown of England
1863	"	Independent Syrian Church of Malabar (Thozhiyoor/ Anjoor)
1863	"	Swamy Vivekananda founded the Sree Ramakrishan Mission
1864	"	'Syllabus of Errors' published by Pope Pius IX
1864	"	The Bhutan War
1867 - 1870	"	The General Council of Vatican I
1870	"	'Infallibility of Pope' upheld by Vatican I
1876	"	Mulanthurithy Synod in the Jacobite Church
1886	"	Indian Latin Hierarchy established by Pope Leo XIII
1886	"	Annexation of Burma

Year		Events
1887	AD	Two Vicariates for St. Thomas Christians in India (Trichur and Kottayam)
1889	"	Registration of the Marthoma Evangelistic Association by the reform group in the Jacobite Church, which later assumed the name 'The Marthoma Syrian Church'
1893	"	Pope Leo XIII declared the inerrancy of the Bible
1905	"	Partition of Bengal – Lord Curzon
1912	"	Catholicate created for the Bishop's party in the Jacobite Church in India
1914	"	Beginning of World War I
1917	"	Bolshevik Revolution in Russia – Lenin
1922	"	Fascism in Italy. Benito Mussolini
1923	"	Syro Malabar Hierarchy established in India by Pope Pius XI
1929	"	Lateran Concordat by which the church obtained a plot around St. Peter's Basilica
1930	"	The Dandi March by Gandhiji
1930	"	The Civil Disobedience Movement in India
1931	"	Irwin-Gandhi Pact
1932	"	Syro Malankara Hierarchy established in India – Pope Pius XI
1934	"	Constitution promulgated for the Catholicos party in the Jacobite Church
1935	"	The Government of India Act, 1935
1939	"	World War II
1942	"	Pope Pius XI declared Mary 'the queen of the world' and 'assumption of Mary' as infallible dogma.
1942	"	The Quit India Movement
1943	"	Church defined as 'the mystical body of Christ'
1945	"	End of World War II
1946	"	Interim Government in India with Jawaharlal Nehru as Prime Minister
1947	"	Independence of India and Pakistan.
1947	"	Church of South India (CSI) inaugurated at Madras.
1948	"	Gandhiji shot dead (Jan. 30th)

Year		Events
1950	AD	India became a Sovereign Democratic Republic
1950	"	Padroado jurisdiction over Cochin diocese suppressed and brought Cochin under Verapoly
1952	"	First General Election in India
1953	"	Oriental and Eastern Churches recognized the Gregorian Calendar
1953	"	New State of Andhra
1956	"	States reorganization in India
1960	"	Afro-Asian Conference at Delhi
1961	"	Establishment of the St. Thomas Evangelical Church of India
1962	"	The General Council of Vatican II
1962	"	China invaded India
1963	"	Death of Pope John XXIII
1964	"	Pope Paul VI visited India
1975	"	Catholicate for the Patriarchal party in the Jacobite Church
1975	"	The first Hindu World Conference at Nagpur
1975	"	Death of Dr. S. Radhakrishnan, former President of India
1977	"	Bishop Romeiro of El Salvador shot dead during Mass, a side effect of Liberation Theology
1978	"	Pope John Paul II ascended the papal throne
1986	"	Pope John Paul II visited India
1997	"	Final judgment of the Supreme Court of India in the Jacoubite Church suits, urging reconciliation
2000	"	Grand Jubilee 2000 and advent of Third Millennium

ANNEXURE III

Faith of Various Christian Denominations – Compared

Sl. No.	Subject	The Catholic Church	Orthodox Church	Other Churches	Protestant Churches
1	2	3	4	5	6
1. A.	Holy Trinity	Believes in Trinitarian profession, Father the Creator, Son the Saviour, Holy Spirit, the giver of life and sanctifier.	Concurs with the Catholic teaching.	–	Unitarians deny the doctrine of Trinity.
B.	**Jesus Christ.** Who is Jesus Christ ?	Believes in Christological profession, Jesus is the Christ, Jesus is the Lord, Jesus is the Son of God.	as above	Arianism denied the divinity of Christ. Monophysites denied His Humanity.	The Unitarians deny the divinity of Jesus.
C.	What is the Nature of Christ?	Christ is full man and full God. Christ is one person with two Natures, divine and human (*Prosopon*). The early profession of faith results	as above	Nestorians put forth the theory of two persons in Christ ***(Prosopa)*** one	The Unitarians deny the divinity of Jesus. Protestants deny the term 'mother of God'.

(*Contd...*)

1	2	3	4	5	6
		from the merger of two enunciations Christological and Trinitarian.		divine and the other human. Hence Mary is mother of Christ; not 'mother of God'.	
2.	**The Church.** What is Church?	Jesus founded one church to continue His mission till His Second Coming. As Lord Jesus Christ is the founder of the Church, the Church is holy. The Church is the bride of Jesus, the bridegroom. The Church is the mystical body of Christ. The Church is the Sacrament of Salvation. Vatican II defined the Church as 'the people of God'. Church is the Mission of Christ.	Concurs with the Catholic teaching.	No opinion.	The Church is an assembly or Congregation of the faithful. According to Calvin, the Church exists wherever the Word of God is preached and the sacrament administered according to Christ's Institution.
3.	Foundation of the Church. Is the Bible alone the foundation of the Church?	No. The Bible, Tradition and Revelation form the foundation of the Church. The New Testament itself demonstrates the process of living tradition. Tradition transmits the Word of God.	Concurs with the Catholic teaching.	No opinion.	Bible alone is the foundation of the Church. All protestant groups are unanimous in this view, which is a cardinal basis of protestantism. Traditions

(*Contd...*)

1	2	3	4	5	6
		The first generation did not have a New Testament (Pages 23-25. The Catechism of the Catholic Church - Veritas). Christ is the Lord in Whom the entire revelations of the most high God is summed up. There are two kinds of knowledge, natural by reason and supernatural by faith. Through revelations, God confirms the religious truths.			and revelations are unreliable.
4.	**Sacraments.** Word, Faith & Sacraments are linked together.	Seven Sacraments in the Catholic Church: 1. Baptism 2. Confirmation 3. Penance & Reconciliation 4. Holy Eucharist 5. Order (Priesthood) 6. Matrimony 7. Anointing the sick	Orthodox Churches accept the faith and practice of seven sacraments in the Catholic Church.	No disagreement	The Protestants generally accept only two Sacraments; Baptism and Holy Supper (Holy Eucharist). They disagree on certain aspects of the faith of even these two sacraments in the Catholic Church (Details follow).
5.	**Baptism:**	Baptism is a true sacrament institued by Christ. By Baptism, Christians share the	Concurs with the Catholic teaching.	No comments	The word 'baptisma' means bath by immersion. The

(Contd...)

1	2	3	4	5	6
	(a) Whether sprinkling of water or bath by immersion. (b) Child Baptism followed by confirmation or Adult Baptism.	priesthood of Christ. It cannot be repeated. It is Trinitarian formula. True natural water, either cold or warm, is to be used. Any man can baptise validly. Infants can and should be baptized. Confirmation confers a sacramental character. Administration is by anointing oil (Chrism) blessed by the Bishop. Baptism remits both original and personal sins and confers the life of Grace.			Baptist Church and the Pentecostalists insist on adult baptism by immersion in water. Sprinkling of water does not suffice. Many other Protestant Churches also follow this line. In adult baptism, later confirmation is not required as Chrism can be anointed just after the baptism. The Pentecostalism added a new dimension to the Sacrament of Baptism by insisting on Baptism in the Holy Spirit.
6.	**Penance.** Is auricular confession tenable in the light of the Scripture?	Penance is a sacrament instituted by Christ. The Church teaches and insists on confession before a Priest. This is known as auricular confession. The priest is ordained and sacred to	Concurs	Nil	Few Protestant Churches oppose the very concept of priesthood in the Church on the ground that all chosen people of God share the Royal priesthood of Christ (1 Pet. 2 : 9).

(*Contd...*)

1	2	3	4	5	6
		represent the Church, which is empowered by Christ (Mt. : 16:19). In the ancient period, public penance was practised. Now, it is almost extinct.			Absolution or remission of sins can be granted only by God. The mediation of a priest is neither required nor authorised. This practice is against the Scripture - the Bible. A sinner has to confess before God.
7.	Moral Theology	Morality is based on Natural Law, Revelation and teaching of Christ. Divorce, Abortion, Homosexuality, Masturbation, Surrogate motherhood, Contraceptives, Human cloning Invitro-fertilization etc. are sins both theologically and morally, according to the Catholic Church.	Silent	Silent	A few Protestant churches agree with the catholic teachings. A few others are in favour of all or some of them. Some other Churches are either silent or neutral. Here, Christians who believe that life is the gift of God, fail to reconcile and project a unified stand against these vices.
8.	**Holy Eucharist** (a) The doctrine of 'Real Presence of Christ'.	(a) The Catholic Church believes in Transubstantiation: The presence of Christ is realised by complete change of substance of bread and wine	(a) Orthodox Churches agree the Real Presence, but rejects the	Nil	Swingli upheld only a memorial presence of Christ in the Eucharist. Luther asserts the objective

(Contd...)

1	2	3	4	5	6
	(b) Whether the whole Christ is received under one of the species.	into the body and blood of Christ in the Eucharistic sacrifice. This change from one substance to another substance is aptly called Transubstantiation. This is a doctrine of faith. The Eucharist is the Church's greatest treasure. It is at once a sacrifice and a meal. (b) Another doctrine of faith is that the whole Christ is received under one of the species. Communion under both kinds shows forth better the sacramental sign. Both the body and blood of Christ are present under each kind and their particle. Modern theology has coined a word 'Transignification' as a corollary to the word 'Transubstantiation'.	terminology 'transubstantiation'. (b) Communion in both species insisted.		Real presence of Christ's body in the Bread and wine. This is known as Consubstantiation. Calvin accepted the real presence. (b) All Protestant Churches insist on both species, bread and wine, in the communion.

(Contd...)

1	2	3	4	5	6
9.	Anointing the Sick Reconciliation and Anointing the sick, accompanied by prayer to save the Sick.	Prayer for the sick and anointing the sick with oil in the name of the Lord to save the sick is a practice in vogue in the Catholic Church based on St. James 5 : 14. This practice, raised as a sacrament in the medieval period is known as 'Anointing the Sick'.	The Orthodox Church accepts this faith and practises it as in the Catholic Church.	The Jacobite Church and few other heretical Churches also follow this practice.	Protestants accept prayer for the sick, but oppose anointing the sick. They do not recognise it as a sacrament.
10.	Prayer and mass for the dead.	The Sacrifice of Mass is truly propitiatory. The Eucharistic sacrifice is also offered for the faithful departed, who 'have died in Christ but are not yet wholly purified', so that they may be able to enter into the light and peace of Christ. The Mass is offered for those who have died in Christ, but not yet wholly purified.[1]	Accepts the Catholic faith and practice.	Accepts.	The Protestant Churches argue that mass for the dead is of no avail. The Reformers challenged the sacrificial value of the Eucharist which they feared would detract from the uniqueness of Christ's sacrifice. They quote 2 Cor. 5 : 10 to substantiate their argument of futility of mass for the dead.
11.	**Papacy:** Papacy stands for the	Four aspects are involved in the Faith on papacy:	The Schism leading to the	No definite stand on the issue.	The Protestants generally oppose all the

(Contd...)

1	2	3	4	5	6
	instituational leadership of the Catholic Church.	(a) Primacy of Peter among the apostles (Mt: 16 : 18 - 19). (b) Episcopate had its origin in Peter. (c) Pipeline succession of Peter. (d) Infallibility of Pope in Ex-Cathedra Proclamation on faith and morals. In the Catholic Church, the Pope is Bishop of Rome and Vicar of Jesus Christ, Successor of St. Peter, Prince of Apostles, Supreme Pontiff of the Universal Church, Patriarch of the West, Primate of Italy, Archbishop and Metropolitan of the Roman Province and the Sovereign of the State of Vatican City.[2]	birth of orthodox Churches was primarily on the claim of primacy of Popes. They agree with the first and second contentions and disagree on the third and fourth contentions.		contentions. This issue still remains a stumbling block in the unity efforts. Of late, some groups are veering round the necessity of episcopate and a non-monarchical head for the Church.
12.	Original Sin.	Original Sin must be distinguished from actual sin; original sin is without consent, actual sin is with consent. Sin without consent is remitted by	The Catholic faith is followed.	No definite stand.	Jesus, through his death, absolved man from original sin. Justification is by faith alone!

(Contd...)

1	2	3	4	5	6
		baptism, but actual sin (concupiscence) remains. The punishment for original sin is loss of beatific vision while the punishment for actual sin is torture of eternal hell.			
13.	Purgatory: Purgatory is the stage for purification of soul after death. This teaching is especially concerned with what happens between the death of the Christian and the general resurrection. All, who die in God's Grace and friendship,	This teaching is on the basis of 'eschatology' and the 'resurrection of the dead'. The faith in 'purgatory' is interconnected with the 'intercession of Saints' indulgence' and 'justification'. The Church believes in the happiness of the just, who will one day be with Christ. She believes in the eternal punishment of the sinner, who will be deprived of the sight of God. This punishment will have a repercussion on the whole being of the sinner. She believes the possibility of a purification for the elect	The orthodox Churches do not subscribe to this view.	No definite stand.	Martin Luther denied the doctrine of indulgence in 1517. He rejected the doctrine of Purgatory as well. The protestants argue that there is no scriptural basis for this faith.

(*Contd...*)

1	2	3	4	5	6
	but still imperfectly purified are indeed assured of their eternal salvation: but after death by undergoing purification, so as to achieve the holiness necessary to enter the joy of heaven.[3]	before they see God, a purification different from the punishment of the damned. This purification is possible through prayer, intercession of Saints, mass, indulgence, deeds of charity etc. for this intention. This is what the Church means when speaking of hell and purgatory.			
14.	**Indulgence:** The remission of penances and with them of the temporal punishment of sins, either partially or totally, is called indulgence.	Church has the authority to grant Indulgence. It should be clearly distinguished from the forgiveness of sins themselves which must be first obtained in the sacrament of penance. It can be applied to the dead. Abuses must be avoided. The immediate provocation for the reformation movement was the abuse of indulgence.	See column # 6.	See column # 6.	All the non-Catholic churches oppose this doctrine of faith not supported by the scripture - the Bible. The practice of indulgence in the Catholic Church gives vast scope for corruption and abuse and it is also licence to sin, according to Luther.

(*Contd...*)

1	2	3	4	5	6
15.	St. Mary.	The faith of Catholic Church has four ingredients: (1) Virginity of Mary (2) Immaculate conception of Mary (3) Mary is mother of God (*theotokos*) and (4) Assumption of Mary to heaven. Vatican II has emphasised that Mary is first and foremost a member and part of the Church and not above the Church.	The Catholic faith is followed by the orthodox churches.	On the question as to whether Mary is mother of God *(theotokos)* or only mother of Christ (*kristotokos*). Monophysites opted for 'mother of Chirst'. The jacobites accept the term 'mother of God'.	Protestants admit her virginity as she herself declared 'because I know not man' (Mt. 1 : 34). They reject 'immaculate conception' and 'assumption to heaven'. The term 'Mother of God' is also not acceptable to them.
16.	**Church Governemnt:** Three distinct systems exist: (i) Episcopal (ii) Presbyterian and (iii) Congregational	The Catholic Church follows the episcopal system.	Episcopal system is followed.	Nestorians and monophysites like Jacobite. Abyssinian, Coptic etc. also follow the episcopal system.	All the three systems are found among the Protestant Churches.
17.	Canonisation and intercession of saints.	The Practices are in vogue in the Catholic Church. This is based on the authority granted by Jesus (Mt: 16:18 & 19).	The Orthodox Church follows the Catholic	No definite stand.	The Protestants argue that there is no scriptural basis for this practice. It is for

(Contd...)

1	2	3	4	5	6
			faith and practice.		God alone to decide whether one is Saint or sinner. Intercession of saints for the dead is of no avail.
18.	Justification (salvation).	When M. Luther advanced the theory of 'Justification by faith alone', the Catholic Church clarified that 'Justification by faith supported by good works' alone.	Nil.	No definite stand.	Justification by faith in 'Jesus Christ alone' is a cardinal faith and principle of Protestantism. According to M. Luther, good works are to be done and bad works are to be avoided to increase one's faith.
19.	**Images and Relics:** The Church recommends the cult of Saints. It also recommends the cult of relics and sacred images	The Catholic Church has always defended as legitimate the veneration of sacred images; the reason is that their veneration goes to the person whom they represent. As for the veneration of Saints, it arises naturally from the lively awareness of the deep communication which binds	The Orthodox church venerates saints and their sacred images.	Nil.	The protestants outright oppose such veneration of images and relics as they are idols or gravel things or pillars or stone in the sand. To adore it is strictly prohibited by God, they argue (Vide Lev: 19:4 and 26:1).

(*Contd...*)

1	2	3	4	5	6
	and popular piety, provided this is purified of possible distortions.	together in Christ all those redeemed by Him. While venerating the Saints, the Church celebrates in them the triumph of the mystery of Christ: She draws inspiration from their example and pleads for God's favour through their intercession.			

20. There are several other minor or major points of disagreement among the Christian Churches as detailed below:

(a) The Seventh Day Adventists observe Sabat on Saturday, the seventh day of the week. All other churches observe Sabat on Sunday, the day of Resurrection of Jesus Christ.

(b) From ancient days, the Oriental Churches were using leavened bread and the Western Churches were using unleavened bread in the Eucharist. The Catholic Church permits both.

(c) Marriage for priests is a demand from inside and outside the Church. The Catholic Church has not yet positively responded to the proposal.

(d) Woman priesthood is permitted in many Protestant churches inclusive of the Anglican Church. But, the Catholic and the Orthodox churches have not accepted this practice.

(e) Holy spirit in Trinity proceeds from the Father, according to the Nicene Creed followed by the Orthodox Churches. The Catholic Church inserted an amendment in the Nicean Creed stating that the Holy Spirit proceeds from the Father and the Son (*Filioque*). This was one among the bones of contention between the Oriental and Western Churches that ultimately led to the schism and birth of Orthodox Churches.

(f) Catholic Bible has 73 books while Protestants use Bible with 66 books.

(g) Monasticism has become the backbone of the Catholic Church today. The Protestants are still averse to monasticism.

Notes:

(1) All Orthodox Churches are grouped under one head, though there are some localised differences among them.

(2) Anglican Church and Pentecostal Churches are grouped under 'Protestant Churches'.

(3) Other Churches include Nestorianism, Monophysitism and other heretical churches.

Sources:

(1) *The Holy Bible.*

(2) *The Christian Faith* by J. Neuner and J. Dupuis (Revised edition).

FOOTNOTES

1. *Catechism of Catholic Church*; Veritas - item 1371.
2. *C.B.C.I Catholic Directory of India 1994* - Opening page.
3. *Catechism of Catholic Church*; Veritas - item 1030.

ANNEXURE IV
Glossary

A. **Buddhism** (Language: Pali – colloquial Sanskrit polished)

Bodhisattava	-	one who aspires to become a Buddha
Buddha	-	the enlightened
Dhamma	-	equivalent to 'Dharma' in Hinduism; duty, obligation, Justice etc.
Hinayana	-	small vehicle, a system in Buddhism
Madhyamika	-	a middle path philosophy in between Hinayana and Mahayana
Mahayana	-	big vehicle, a system in Buddhism
Nirvana	-	absoluteness, an existence beyond temptations
Shunyata	-	nothingness
Tantrayana	-	Lamaism
Theravada	-	elders school
Tripitaka	-	triple basket, canonical teachings of Buddha
Vihar	-	a Buddhist monastery

B. **Christianity** (Language: Greek and Latin)

Aggiornamento	-	updating the Church with the situations and needs of the world
Baptisma (Greek)	-	bath by immersion
Canon (Greek)	-	law
Congregatio de propaganda fide	-	Congregation for the propagation of the faith
Cujus Regio Ejus Religio	-	religion of the ruler is the religion of the people
Curia	-	Pope's Secretariat
Episcopos (Greek)	-	one who oversees or supervises - Bishop

Filioque	- the Holy Spirit proceeds from the Father and the Son
Glossalia	- speaking in different tongues
Gnosis	- knowledge
Homoousious	- the same one in being
Hypostasis	- not parted or divided into two
Kristotokos (Greek)	- mother of Christ
Latrocinium	- Synod of robbers (Synod of Ephesus in 449 AD)
Magisterium	- teaching office of the Church
Oikoumene (Greek)	- Empire
Papa (Pope)	- Father
Prosopa (plural)	- more than one person
Prosopon (singular)	- a unique figure
Regale	- a traditional royal right of the King to administer the revenue and selecting bishops
Risorgimento	- an Italian movement for liberation and unification of Italy
Theotokos (Greek)	- mother of God

C. Hinduism (Language: Sanskrit)

Abhayam vy Brahma	- Refuge in Brahma (God)
Abhyasa Yoga	- Weaning away the mind ceaselessly from the world
Achadaneeyam	- covered
Acharya	- teacher
Adhikara	- eligibility
Adi	- the beginning or the first
Advaita	- Non-dualism (a branch of Vedanta philosophy)
Agnideva	- the god of fire
Agnipareeksha	- an ordeal of fire
Agnisala	- fire place
Aham Brahmasmi	- I am Brahman
Ahimsa	- Non-violence or non-injury
Ajivaka	- a special way of life

Ajnanavaada	- argument of ignorance, agnosticism, equivocation
Amruth	- a medicine for health and immortality
Amsavatara	- fractional incarnation
Ananda	- bliss, happiness
Anandarupa	- personified bliss
Annam	- food
Anor aniyan	- smaller than the smallest
Antyajas	- other communities
Apana	- exhaling breath
Aparavidya	- knowledge other than Paravidya
Aparigraha	- non-accumulation of material possessions and avoidance of avarice
Apaureshaya	- not man-made
App	- water
Aranyakas	- forest books (Aranya = forests)
Artha	- wealth
Asana	- posture
Ashtanga Yoga	- eight limbs of Yoga
Asphra	- detachment
Asrama	- status or station or stage in life
Asteya	- non-stealing, recognition of right of others to possess wealth
Astra	- archery, bow and arrow
Asumbandha	- absurd talk
Asura	- demon or wicked man
Aswameda	- horse sacrifice
Athithi	- guest
Atmajnana	- spiritual knowledge
Atman	- self, human soul
Atmasabda	- the sound of Atma (O'm)
Avasadana	- ending
Avatara	- incarnation, God's descent to earth
Avesavathara	- momentary incarnations in extraordinary circumstances
Avidya	- absence of knowledge

Ayamatma Brahma	- whatever we find in Brahma, the human soul
Ayurveda	- knowledge of longevity
Bhagavad Gita	- Lord's song
Bhakti	- devotion, love
Bhashasastra	- Science of Linguistics
Bhoomav	- that which has none other to be seen or heard or known
Bhoomi	- earth
Bhoomi Devi	- goddess earth
Bhuta	- elements
Brahma or Brahman	- Supreme God
Brahmacariya	- conduct that puts one in touch with God (not continence alone)
Brahmacharin	- one vowed to chastity
Brahmahatya	- mortal sin
Brahmajnana	- knowledge of Brahma (God)
Brahmakanda	- aimed at self-sanctification or experience of bliss
Brahmananda	- the eternal bliss by realisation of Brahma
Brahmapuram	- human body
Brahmavidya	- knowledge of Brahma
Brihat	- big
Caitanya	- consciousness, thought
Chakra	- wheel
Chandan	- sandalwood
Chandas	- metrics
Charanas	- Vedic schools
Chathushpadom	- four legs (chariots, elephants, cavalry and infantry)
Chavi	- key
Chith	- Intelligence
Chithasudhi	- purification of mind
Dana	- charity, alms
Desam	- ten
Dhanurveda	- the science of ancient warfare

Dhaarana	-	concentration of mind
Dharma (in Hinduism)	-	justice, duty, obligations, virtue etc.
Dharmakanda	-	laudatory verses for adoration
Dharmam chara	-	never deviate from Dharma
Dharmanirapekshata	-	secularism
Dharma Sutras	-	customary laws and practices
Dhyaana	-	meditation
Dravya	-	substances (earth, water, air etc.)
Dvaitha	-	divisible, dualistic (a Vedanta philosophy)
Dvija	-	twice born
Eka Satyam	-	the one and only truth (God)
Gada	-	club or mace
Gandharva	-	celestial musician or artist
Garuda	-	eagle
Grama	-	village
Grihapati	-	the head of a house or family
Grihasthya	-	married householder
Guna	-	quality
Gurukula	-	ancient open air school with one teacher
Hatayoga	-	physical exercises
Himavan	-	personification of Mt. Himalayas
Hindutva	-	aggressive sense of Hindu identity
Hitavacana	-	talk with good intentions
Hridayapundareekom	-	a house in the human body in the form of a lotus flower
Indra	-	the King of gods
Ishtadevata	-	god of one's personal preference
Ithihasa	-	ancient history, legend, story and mythological classic
Iti iti	-	it is that, it is this
Jaagrat	-	waken state of the mind (conscious)
Jagat	-	universe
Jambudweepa	-	the prehistoric name of an island, of which 'Bharat' is a part
Jana	-	block or district
Jata	-	matted hair

Jathavedas	-	god of fire
Jijnasu	-	man seeking knowledge
Jiva	-	life, living being, man
Jnana	-	knowledge or wisdom
Jnanendrias	-	organs sensing knowledge
Jnani	-	man of wisdom
Jyotisha	-	astrology
Kalal	-	infantry
Kaliyuga	-	the Yuga of Kalki incarnation, the last among the four yugas
Kalpa	-	rituals; a cycle of fourteen Manvantharams
Kalpantha	-	the end of each Kalpa
Kama	-	worldly pleasure including sex
Kamyakarma	-	action for specific objects
Karma	-	activity, performance
Karmakand	-	performance of sacrifices
Karmasamsar	-	transmigration of soul
Karmendrias	-	organs of bodily senses
Karuna	-	compassion
Kaumara	-	age between 13 and 19, teens
Kaumodaki	-	a club or mace of Vishnu
Kausthubhom	-	a jewel worn by Vishnu
Kena	-	by whom?
Khadga	-	sword
Khandas	-	sections or chapters
Khilya	-	grazing ground
Koorma	-	tortoise
Kirpan	-	dagger
Kshetra	-	land, field, the body of beings
Kulala	-	potter
Kurukshetra	-	battlefield
Linga	-	the genital organ of the male, penis
Lokayata	-	widespread in the world; naturalism
Mahabashya	-	big commentary
Maharishi	-	a great man of wisdom

Mahato mahiyan	-	greater than the greatest
Mahaprastana	-	the great march
Mahavakyam	-	sentence sublime, cardinal message
Maitri (Buddhism)	-	friendship (spirit of)
Manana	-	thinking, analysing
Manasa, Vacha, Karmana	-	by thought, word or deed
Manava Dharma Sastra	-	science of human behaviour
Mandala	-	circle, cycle, chapter, book
Manu	-	one of the early fourteen Kings of the universe
Manvamtharam	-	the period of Manu
Maryada Purushothama	-	perfect gentleman
Matha	-	mother
Mathaviswav	-	the god of air
Mathra	-	particle
Matsya	-	fish
Maya	-	illusion, not real
Mithya	-	falsehood
Mlechas	-	untouchables
Moksha	-	salvation
Mrityu	-	death
Mukti	-	liberation
Murti	-	idols of divinities
Nadabrahmom	-	O'm
Nagas	-	snakes
Nama	-	name
Nandakom	-	a sword of Vishnu
Narasimha	-	Nara = man, Simha = lion; half man and half beast
Nastikya	-	irreligious
Natyasastra	-	the science of dance
Navya	-	new
Neti neti	-	neither this, nor that, not a third one – *ad infinitum*

Nirguna Brahma	-	Absolute Reality, static, Impersonal God
Nirukti	-	etymology
Nishka	-	necklace
Nishkama karma	-	unselfish activity
Nitya	-	eternal, permanent
Niyamom	-	tied or bound to something (a branch of Yoga)
Niyathi	-	destiny, fate
Nyaya	-	logic
O'm	-	the Pranava, the Logos, the Word, the God
Pada patha	-	the word text
Padala	-	goddess
Padartha	-	substance or material
Panchajanyam	-	a conch used by Vishnu
Panineeyam	-	the grammar book of Panini (Ashtadyayi)
Pankaj	-	lotus
Paradravyabhipsa	-	covetousness
Paradroha	-	ill-will or trouble to others
Paramatma	-	Supreme Soul
Parameswar	-	Supreme God (Siva)
Parasu	-	axe
Parasurama	-	Rama, who has Parasu (axe) as weapon
Paravidya	-	transcendental knowledge
Paricarana	-	service, nursing
Paritrana	-	succour to the distressed
Parusa	-	caustic talk
Pasa	-	rope
Pippaladan	-	one who lives on pippala fruits
Pitha	-	father
Poornavataras	-	full incarnations
Prajapathi	-	the Lord of creations
Prajna	-	consciousness
Prakriti	-	all the created things in the universe, the female principle
Prana	-	life, breathing, soul

Pranayama	-	regularity of breath
Prasna	-	problem, question
Prathyahara	-	free from the world of senses, withdrawal of senses
Pratisargam	-	cosmogony
Pratisidhamaithuna	-	unlawful sexual indulgence
Preyas	-	path to temporary worldly pleasures
Prithvi	-	the earth
Priyavacana	-	gentle talk
Puja	-	worship, ritual
Puranas	-	books on sacred subjects, ancient history, tales, mythological classic
Purohit	-	priest
Purusha	-	the personification of the cosmic principle, male
Purushartha	-	four goals in life; Dharma, Artha, Kama and Moksha
Purushasukta	-	principles of universal man
Purusho vava sukrutam	-	man is a fine creation
Putrakameshtiyaga	-	sacrifice for the birth of sons
Rajan	-	King
Rajas	-	traits like wrath, revenge and vandalism
Rajayoga	-	ethical, physical and psychical exercises
Rashtra	-	nation, state
Ratha	-	chariot
Rickwick	-	priest who performs sacrifices
Rig	-	hymn, ode, laudatory verse
Rishi	-	poet and wise man
Sabha	-	an assembly of elders
Saddarsanas	-	(Sad = six, Darsana = vision); six philosophies
Sadhaka	-	one who accomplishes
Saguna Brahma	-	Conditional Reality, Personal God, Kinetic Brahma
Sama Veda	-	the book of chants

Samadhi	-	union of mind and soul, concentration
Samanya	-	generality
Samana	-	inner breath
Samavaya	-	inference, consensus
Samhara	-	consummation
Samhitas	-	collections
Samjna	-	perception
Samsara	-	world
Samskara	-	sacrament, purification ceremony
Samudra	-	sea, ocean
Sanatan Dharma	-	eternal order and righteousness
Sannyasi	-	an ascetic who renounces the world
Sapta dweepa	-	seven islands
Sapta samudra	-	seven oceans
Sarasayya	-	bed of arrows
Sarvabhuteshu gudha	-	present in hidden manner in all beings
Sarvadharma sadbhava	-	respect and honour for all religions
Sarvadharma samabhava	-	recognising and treating all religions equally
Sarvameva Avisanthi	-	once for all liberated
Sarvasva danam	-	gifting of all wealth to the poor, a religious obligation of a Brahmin
Satchitananda	-	definition of God; Existence + intelligence + bliss (sat + chit + ananda)
Satyam Vada	-	always speak truth (Satyam = truth)
Satyasya Satya	-	Truth of all truths – God, the Ultimate Truth
Sattva	-	luminous, stainless and unobstructive
Senani	-	Commander of the army
Sethu	-	bridge
Shanti	-	peace
Sharngom	-	a bow known as Vishnuchapom
Shilpa	-	architecture
Shuddhi	-	purification, cleaning
Shulam	-	pike, spear, trident
Siksha	-	phonetics, accent, pronunciation
Sivalinga	-	Siva manifested as linga

Skandas	-	parts of a book (Desama skanda = tenth part)
Sloka	-	Stanza
Smriti	-	memory, remembering, tradition
Sraddha	-	faith or devotion
Sraddhatraya	-	three qualities of Sraddha-Sattva, Rajas and Thamas
Sramana	-	strivers of truth (a set of philosophers)
Sravana	-	hearing
Sreevalsom	-	a sign on the chest of Vishnu
Sreyas	-	path to eternal bliss or happiness
Srishti	-	creation
Sruti	-	hearing
Steya	-	theft
Sthithi	-	conservation
Streedhana	-	the wealth granted to a woman by her father
Sucana	-	calumny
Sudharsana chakra	-	a wheel shaped weapon of Sri Krishna; a replica of modern missile
Sukha	-	happiness, comfort
Suktas	-	good words, principles
Surya	-	Sun
Sushupti	-	deep sleeping state of the mind
Sutra	-	sacred thread, guide, clue
Svabhava	-	own being
Svadharma	-	individual dharma according to potentialities
Swadhyaya	-	recitation of scripture
Swapna	-	dreaming state of the mind
Swarga	-	heaven
Swargarohana	-	ascension to heaven
Swarna	-	gold
Tadatmya	-	becoming one with another
Tapas	-	asceticism, penance
Tatvamasi	-	tat + tvam + asi: - that thou art

Thamas	-	lazy, ignorant, darkness, delighted in hurting or teasing others
Thejas	-	halo, glowing, shining, illuminating
Thurian	-	quadrant, one fourth, full consciousness
Trai	-	the three Vedas – Rig, Sama and Yajur
Trisaktam	-	three sixes, three groups of six each
Uccedavaada	-	the theory of annihilation
Udana	-	directing the stream of air upwards in breathing
Udgeeta	-	the loud chanting of O'm
Upanayana	-	wearing of sacred thread
Upanishad	-	sitting near below, philosophical books
Upasana	-	worship
Upavedas	-	subsidiary Vedas, branches of Vedas
Urvara	-	cultivated land
Uthamapurushothama	-	the best man among gentlemen
Uvaca	-	said, told
Valli	-	stem of a creeper
Vamsa	-	chronology
Vamsanucharitam	-	genealogy
Vanaprastha	-	wandering forest life
Vanara	-	monkey
Varaha	-	pig
Varna	-	colour, caste
Varuna	-	god of water
Vedanta	-	the end of Veda (knowledge)
Vedantasarishtam	-	the essence of entire Vedanta
Vedas	-	knowledge
Vidhatri	-	one who ordains
Vidya	-	knowledge
Vijnana	-	knowledge of virtue, morality, ethics, peace, righteousness etc.
Vis	-	group of villages
Visesha	-	particularity
Viseshadisthana	-	foundation making itself visible through an image

Vishada	-	despondency
Visishtadvaita	-	qualified non-dualism
Viswakarman	-	all creating architect
Viswanaran	-	universal man
Viswaroopa	-	transfigured cosmic form
Vyakarna	-	grammar
Vyana	-	intermediate breath between inhaling and exhaling
Yagaswom	-	sacrificial horse
Yajna	-	sacrifice
Yajur	-	prose
Yaksha	-	a ghost
Yamom	-	prohibition or abstention, a branch of Yoga
Yoga	-	path, way

D. Jainism (Language: Sanskrit)

Adharma	-	inactivity
Adharmastikay	-	medium of rest
Ahimsa	-	non-violence or non-injury to all living beings
Ajiva	-	non-living matter
Akasa	-	space
Akshat	-	rice
Arahants	-	supreme human beings; twelve unique qualities
Asrava	-	influx of karmas
Dharanas	-	mental reflections
Dharma	-	activity (Here, Jainism disagrees with Hinduism)
Dharmastikay	-	medium of motion
Dhup	-	incense
Digambara	-	the air clad or naked
Dipak	-	light (candle)
Dravya	-	substance
Fal	-	fruits
Gupti	-	control

Jal	-	water
Jina	-	conqueror of passions
Kala	-	time
Kriya	-	action (possible action)
Mantra	-	incantations
Naivedya	-	sweet food
Nav Tattvas	-	nine fundamentals (Nav = nine)
Nirjara	-	eradication of karmas
Panchpameshti	-	supreme beings
Pap	-	vices or sins, results of bad deeds
Parishaha	-	suffering
Paryaya	-	modification
Pudgala	-	matter
Pudgalastikay	-	medium of matter
Puja	-	worship (rituals)
Punya	-	results of good deeds (virtues)
Pushpa	-	flower
Sadhus	-	sages, 27 unique qualities
Samiti	-	carefulness
Samvar	-	stoppage of karmas
Siddhas	-	pure souls
Swetambara	-	white gowns
Upadhyayas	-	sages who teach
Yatidharma	-	monkhood

E. **Judaism** (Language: Hebrew and Greek)

Ebionites	-	Jewish Christians who accepted Jesus as Messiah, but not his divinity
Exilarch	-	head of the Jews in exile
Gemara		a commentary on Mishna
Haskala	-	enlightenment
Mishna	-	collection of Rabbinic laws
Nagarenes	-	Jewish Christians who accepted Jesus as both Messiah and God
Pax Romana	-	peace imposed by Romans
Pentateuch	-	the first five books of the Old Testament

Talmud	-	a commentary on the law
Tithe	-	an ecclesiastical tax
Torah	-	the Law of Moses
Zionism	-	a political movement concerned with establishing an Independent state of Israel; revival of old religious laws

F. Mohammedanism (Islam) (Language: Arabic)

Ahmadiya	-	a reform group in Islam following Mirza Ghulam Ahmad
Allah	-	God (the term in Arabic)
Caliph	-	designation of Prophet's successors, both civil and religious authority
Hadith	-	writings on the life and work of Prophet Mohammed, Tradition
Hajj	-	pilgrimage to Mecca
Hijrah	-	Mohammed's flight from Mecca (622 AD)
Islam	-	those in the state of grace born out of submission to Allah
Ismaili	-	a sect in Islam following Saint Ismail Ibn Jafar at Sadok
Ka'ba	-	the temple at Mecca
Kalimat Allah	-	the Word of God
Koran (Qur'an)	-	Holy word of God to Prophet Mohammed (the Scripture of Islam)
Moors	-	North African Moslems, whether Arab or Berber
Moslem (Muslim)	-	those who submit to Allah
Nabi	-	Prophet
Razziah	-	Raids
Saracens	-	a name for all non-Christians faced by the Christians in the crusades
Shahada	-	witness
Shias	-	those who do not accept Sunna – a group in Islam
Sunna	-	the traditional teachings of Prophet Mohammed
Sunnites	-	those who accept Sunna

G. Shintoism (Language: Japanese)

Kami - animal and object deities of Spirits

Mikado - Emperor of Japan worshipped by the people

Shintoism - a native religion of Japan (a sort of animism)

H. Sikhism (Language: Gurmukhi - Punjabi based on Devanagari script)

Amrit - Sikh baptism

Anand Karaj - wedding

Ardas - prayer

Darbar Sahib - Golden Temple at Amritsar (pool of nectar)

Granthi - a person who leads the services in the Gurudwara

Guru Granth Sahib - the Holy Scripture of Sikhism

Gurudwara - Sikh temple

Hukumnama - injunction, writs

Kachha - a pair of shorts or underwear

Kanghha - a comb

Kara - a steel bracelet

Kesha - long unshaven hair

Khalsa panth - Sikh commonwealth

Khanda - a double edged sword

Kirpan - a sword, dagger

Kirtans - hymns praising the Lord

Pangat - community kitchen

Ragis - singers

Rehras - evening prayer of a Sikh

Sanghat - congregation

Shabad Kirtan - devotional songs in melodious voice

Sikh - disciple

Sikh rehat maryada - code of conduct of the Sikhs

Sohila - night prayer of a Sikh

Takhats - seats or throne of authority

I. Zoroastrianism (Language: Persian - Iranian)

Ahura Mazda	-	all-wise God
Harstha	-	good actions
Hukata	-	good words
Humata	-	good thoughts
Mazda	-	wisdom
Pairidaeza	-	paradise
Zend Avesta	-	the Scripture of Zoroastrianism

ANNEXURE V

Member Churches in the World Council of Churches

AFRICA

1. African Christian Church – Thika, Kenya
2. African Church of the Holy Spirit – Shinyalu (Kakamega), Kenya
3. African Israel Church – Kisumu, Kenya
4. African Protestant Church – Yaounde, Cameroon
5. Anglican Church of Kenya – Nairobi, Kenya
6. Anglican Church of Tanzania – Dodoma, Tanzania
7. Church of Christ – Light of the Holy Spirit – Democratic Republic of Congo
8. Church of Christ in Congo Anglican Church – Nairobi, Kenya
9. Church of Christ in Congo Baptist – Democratic Republic of Congo
10. Church of Christ in Congo Community – Democratic Republic of Congo
11. Church of Christ in Congo-Episcopal Baptist – Chingola, Zambia
12. Church of Christ in Congo-Evangelical Community – Brazzaville, Congo
13. Church of Christ in Congo-Mennonite, Democratic Republic of Congo
14. Church of Christ in Congo-Presbyterian – Kinshasa, Democratic Republic of Congo
15. Church of Jesus Christ in Madagascar – Madagascar
16. Christ of Jesus Christ on earth, Kinshasa-1

17. Democratic Republic of Congo – Kinbang RDC
18. Church of the Brethren in Nigeria – Nigeria
19. Church of the Lord Worldwide – Ogere Rome, Nigeria
20. Church of the Province of Burundi – Burundi
21. Church of the Province of Central Africa, Gabarone, Botswana
22. Church of the Province of Nigeria, Lagos, Nigeria
23. Church of the Province of Rwanda, Rwanda
24. Church of Province of Southern Africa, Bishopscourt, South Africa
25. Church of the Province of the Indian Ocean, Eveche Anglican, Madagascar
26. Church of the Province of Uganda – Kampala, Uganda
27. Church of the Province of West Africa – Koforidua, Ghana
28. Council of African Instituted Churches – Johanesburg, South Africa
29. Episcopal Church of the Sudan – Juba, Sudan
30. Ethiopian Evangelical Church – Addis Ababa, Ethiopia
31. Ethiopian Orthodox Tewahedo Church – Addis Ababa, Ethiopia
32. Evangelical Church of Cameroon – Douala, Cameroon
33. Evangelical Church of Gabon – Brazzaville, Congo
34. Evangelical Church of Congo – Brazzaville, Congo
35. Evangelical Congregational Church in Angola – Huambo, Angola
36. Evangelical Lutheran Church in Congo – Kitwe, Sambia
37. Evangelical Lutheran Church – Southern Africa, South Africa
38. Evangelical Lutheran Church – Arusha, Tanzania
39. Evangelical Lutheran Church – Namibia
40. Evangelical Lutheran Church – Bulawayo, Zimbabwe

41. Evangelical Pentecostal Mission of Angola – Sul, Angola
42. Evangelical Presbyterian Church in Ghana – Ghana
43. Evangelical Presbyterian Church – South Africa, Bramfomtein
44. Evangelical Presbyterian Church of Togo – Lome, Togo
45. Evangelical Reformed Church of Angola, Luanda Angola
46. Harrist Church – Abidjan Coted'l vore
47. Kenya Evangelical Lutheran Church – Nile
48. Lesotho Evangelical Church – Lesotho
49. Lutheran Church in Liberia – Liberia
50. Malagasy Lutheran Church – Madagascar
51. Methodist Church – Accra, Ghana
52. Methodist Church in Kenya – Nairobi, Kenya
53. Methodist Church in Togo – Lome, Togo
54. Methodist Church in Zimbabwe – Harare, Zimbabwe
55. Methodist Church in Nigeria – Lagos, Nigeria
56. Methodist Church of Southern Africa – Sasol Burg, South Africa
57. Methodist Church Sierra Leone – Sierra Leone
58. Moravian Church of Southern Africa – South Africa
59. Moravian Church in Tanzania – Mbeya, Tanzania
60. Native Baptist Church of Cameroon – Douala, Cameroon
61. Nigerian Baptist Convention – Ibadan, Nigeria
62. Presbyterian Church in Cameroon – SW province, Cameroon
63. Presbyterian Church of Africa – South Africa
64. Presbyterian Church of Cameroon – Yaounde, Cameroon
65. Presbyterian Church of East Africa – Nairobi, Kenya
66. Presbyterian Church of Ghana – Accra, Ghana
67. Presbyterian Church of Mozambique – Maputo, Mozambique
68. Presbyterian Church of Nigeria – Abia State, Nigeria

69. Presbyterian Church of Rwanda – Kigali, Rwanda
70. Presbyterian Church of Southern Africa – Brixton, South Africa
71. Presbyterian Church of Sudan – Khartoum, Sudan
72. Protestant Church of Algeria – Alger, Algeria
73. Protestant Methodist Church – Adidjan Cote d'Ivoire
74. Protestant Methodist Church of Benin – Benin
75. Reformed Church in Zambia – Lusaka, Zambia
76. Reformed Church in Zimbabwe – Masvingo, Zimbabwe
77. Reformed Church of Christ in Nigeria – Taraba State, Nigeria
78. Reformed Presbyterian Church in Southern Africa – Eastern Cape, South Africa
79. Reformed Presbyterian Church – Bata, Equatorial Guinea
80. Union of Baptist Church of Cameroon – Douala, Cameroon
81. United Church of Christ in Zimbabwe – Harare, Zimbabwe
82. United Church of Zambia – Lusaka, Zambia
83. United Congregational Church of Southern Africa – Brixton, South Africa
84. United Evangelical Church – Luanda, Angola
85. Uniting Reformed Church in Southern Africa – Saldanha, South Africa

ASIA, AUSTRALIA

1. Anglican Church in Aotearoa – Hastings, New Zealand
2. Anglican Church of Australia – NSW 1230, Australia
3. Associated Churches of Christ – Wellington, New Zealand
4. Bangladesh Baptist Sangha – Dhaka, Bangladesh
5. Baptist Union of New Zealand – South Auckland, New Zealand
6. Batak Christian Community Church – Jakarta, Indonesia
7. Batak Protestant Christian Church – Tapanuli Utara, Indonesia

8. Bengal-Orissa-Bihar Baptist Convention – Midnapur, West Bengal
9. China Christian Council – Nanjing JS, China
10. Christian Church in East Timor – East Timor, Indonesia
11. Christian Church of Central Sulawesi – Tengah, Indonesia
12. Christian Church of Sumba – Sumba NTT, Indonesia
13. Christian Evangelical Church in Minahasa – Sulawesi Utara, Indonesia
14. Christian Evangelical Church in Sangihe – Sulawesi Utara, Indonesia
15. Christian Protestant Angkola Church – South Tapanuli
16. Christian Protestant Church in Indonesia – Sumatara, Indonesia
17. Church of Bangladesh – Dhaka, Bangladesh
18. Church of Ceylon – Colombo 7, Sri Lanka
19. Church of Christ in Thailand – Bangkok, Thailand
20. Church of North India – CNI Pandit Pant Marg, New Delhi
21. Church of Pakistan – Lahore Cathedral, Pakistan
22. Church of South India – Royapettah, Madras
23. Church of the Province of Myanmar – Yangon, Myanmar
24. Churches of Christ in Australia – Melbourne, Australia
25. East Java Christian Church – Malang, Indonesia
26. Episcopal Church in Philippines – Quezon City, Philippines
27. Evangelical Christian Church in Halmahera – Kemakmuran, Indonesia
28. Evangelical Christian Church in Irian Jaya – Irian Jaya, Indonesia
29. Evangelical Methodist Church – Manila, Philippines
30. Holy Catholic Church in Japan – Tokyo 162, Japan
31. Hong Kong Council of the Church of Christ in China – Hong Kong

32. Indonesian Christian Church – Jakarta, Indonesia
33. Indonesian Christian Church – Indonesia
34. Javanese Christian Churches – Jawa Tengah, Indonesia
35. Kalimantan Evangelical Church – Kalimantam, Indonesia
36. Karo Batak Protestant Church – Sumatra Utara, Indonesia
37. Korean Christian Church in Japan – Shinjuku-ku, Tokyo, Japan
38. Korean Methodist Church – Seoul 110-602, Korea
39. Malankara Orthodox Syrian Church – Kottayam, Kerala, India
40. Mar Thoma Syrian Church of Malabar – Tiruvalla, Kerala, India
41. Methodist Church in India – Mumbai Central, Mumbai
42. Methodist Church in Malaysia – Sclangor, DE Malaysia
43. Methodist Church in Singapore – Mount Sophia, Singapore
44. Methodist Church in New Zealand – Christ Church 1, New Zealand
45. Methodist Church in Sri Lanka – Colombo 3, Sri Lanka
46. Methodist Church – Mandalay, Myanmar
47. Myanmar Baptist Convention – Yangon, Myanmar
48. Nias Protestant Christian Church – Nias Sumut, Indonesia
49. Orthodox Church in Japan – Chiyoda-Ku, Japan
50. Pasundan Christian Church – Bandung, Indonesia
51. Philippine Independent Church – Manila, Philippines
52. Presbyterian Church in Taiwan – Taipei, Taiwan
53. Presbyterian Church in Korea – Seoul 110-470, Korea
54. Presbyterian Church of Aotearoa – Wellington, New Zealand
55. Presbyterian Church of Korea – Seoul 100-611, Korea
56. Presbyterian Church of Pakistan – Lahore 54000, Pakistan
57. Protestant Christian Church in Bali – Bali, Indonesia
58. Protestant Church in Indonesia – Jakarta – Pusat, Indonesia

59. Protestant Church in Sabah – Sabah, Malaysia
60. Protestant Church in South-East Sulawesi – Kendari, Indonesia
61. Protestant Church in Molucas – Ambon, Indonesia
62. Protestant Church in Western Jakarta – Pusat, Indonesia
63. Protestant Evangelical Church in Timor – Kupang, Indonesia
64. Samavesam of Telugu Baptist Churches – Nellore, A.P., India
65. Simalungum Protestant Christian Church – Indonesia
66. Toraja Church – Sulawesi Saletan, Indonesia
67. United Church of Christ in Japan – Shinjuku-ku Tokyo, Japan
68. United Church of Christ in Philippines – Malila Central, Philippines
69. United Evangelical Lutheran Churches in India – Kellys, Chennai, India
70. Uniting Church in Australia – NSW 1235, Australia

CARIBBEAN

1. Church in the Province of the West Indies – St. John's Antigua
2. Jamaica Baptist Union – Jamaica
3. Methodist Church in Cuba – Havana, Cuba
4. Methodist Church in the Caribbean and the Americas – Antigua
5. Moravian Church – Cashew Hill, Antigua
6. Moravian Church in Jamaica – Kingston, Jamaica
7. Moravian Church in Surinam – Surinam
8. Presbyterian Church in Trinidad & Tobago – San Fernando, Trinidad
9. Presbyterian Reformed Church in Cuba – Havana, Cuba
10. United Church in Jamaica & Cayman Islands – Kingston, Jamaica

11. United Protestant Church – Netherlands Antilles

EUROPE

1. Armenian Apostolic Church – AM Etchmyadzin, Armenia
2. Autocephalous Orthodox Church in Polandal – Warsaw, Poland
3. Baptist Union of Denmark – Copenhagen, Denmark
4. Baptist Union of Great Britain – Oxon, UK
5. Baptist Union of Hungary – Budapest, Hungary
6. Catholic Diocese of the Old Catholics in Germany – Bonn, Germany
7. Church in Wales – Cardiff, UK
8. Church of England – London, UK
9. Church of Greece – Athens, Greece
10. Church of Ireland – Dublin – 6, Ireland
11. Church of Norway – Oslo, Norway
12. Church of Scotland – Edinburgh, UK
13. Church of Sweden – Uppsala, Sweden
14. Czechoslovak Hussite Church – Prague, Czech Republic
15. Ecumenial Patriarchate of Constantinople – Istanbul, Turkey
16. Estonian Evangelical Lutheran Church – Tallinn, Estonia
17. European Continental Province of Moravian Church (Netherlands) – Zeist, Netherlands
18. Evangelical Baptist Union of Italy – Rome, Italy
19. Evangelical Church in Germany – Hanover, Germany
20. Evangelical Church of Czech Brethren – Prague Czech Republic
21. Evangelical Church of Augsburg and Helvetic Confession in Austria, Vienna
22. Evangelical Church of Augsburg Confession in Poland – Warsaw, Poland

23. Evangelical Church of Augsburg Confession in Romania – Sibiu, Romania
24. Evangelical Church of Augsburg Confession in the Slovak Republic – Bratislava, Slovak Republic
25. Evangelical Church of Augsburg Confession of Alsace and Lorraine – France
26. Evangelical Lutheran Church in Denmark – Copenhagen, Denmark
27. Evangelical Lutheran Church in Netherlands – Netherlands
28. Evangelical Lutheran Church of Finland – Helsinki, Finland
29. Evangelical Lutheran Church of France – Paris, France
30. Evangelical Lutheran Church of Iceland – Reykjavik, Iceland
31. Evangelical Lutheran Church of Latvia – Riga, Latvia
32. Evangelical Methodist Church of Italy – Rome, Italy
33. Evangelical Presbyterian Church of Portugal – Lisbon, Portugal
34. Evangelical Synodal Presbyterial Church of Augsburg Confession in Romania – Cluj, Romania
35. Greek Evangelical Church – Athens, Greece
36. Latvian Evangelical Lutheran Church – Esslingen, Germany
37. Lusitanian Catholic Apostolic Evangelical Church – Portugal
38. Lutheran Church in Hungary – Budapest, Hungary
39. Mennonite Church in Germany – Heidelberg, Germany
40. Mennonite Church – AW Amsterdam, Netherlands
41. Methodist Church in London – London, UK
42. Methodist Church in Ireland – Belfast, Ireland
43. Mission Covenant Church – Stockhom, Sweden
44. Moravian Church in Great Briton and Ireland – London
45. Netherlands Reformed Church – Netherlands
46. Old Catholic Church of Austria – Vienna, Austria
47. Old Catholic Church of Switzerland – Bern, Switzerland

48. Old Catholic Church of Netherlands – Amersfoort, Netherlands
49. Old Catholic Mariavite Church in Poland – Plock, Poland
50. Orthodox Autocephalous Church of Albania – Tirana, Albania
51. Orthodox Church of Finland – Kuopio, Finland
52. Orthodox Church of the Czech Lands and Slovakia – Prague, Czech Republic
53. Polish Catholic Church in Poland – Warsaw, Poland
54. Presbyterian Church in Wales – Cardiff, UK
55. Reformed Christian Church in Slovakia – Komarno, Slovak Republic
56. Reformed Christian Church in Yugoslavia – Serbia, Yugoslavia
57. Reformed Church in Hungary – Budapest, Hungary
58. Reformed Church in Romania – Cluj, Romania
59. Reformed Church in Romania – Oradea, Romania
60. Reformed Church of Alssce & Lorraine – Strasbourg Cedex, France
61. Reformed Church of France – Paris Cedex-09, France
62. Reformed Church in the Netherlands – AE Leusdan, Netherlands
63. Remonstrant Brotherhood – Utrecht, Netherlands
64. Romanian Orthodox Church – Bucharest-4, Romania
65. Russian Orthodox Church – Moscow, Russia
66. Scottish Congregational Church – Glasgow, UK
67. Scottish Episcopal Church – Edinburgh, UK
68. Serbian Orthodox Church – Belgrade Serbia, Yugoslavia
69. Silesian Evangelical Church of the Augsburg Confession in the Czech Republic – Cesky Tesin, Czech Republic
70. Slovak Evangelical Church of Augsburg Confession in Yugoslavia – Vojvodina, Yugoslavia
71. Spanish Evangelical Church – Madrid, Spain

72. Spanish Reformed Episcopal Church – Madrid, Spain
73. Swiss Protestant Church Federation – Bern 23, Switzerland
74. Union of Welsh Independents – Wales, UK
75. United Free Church of Scotland – Glasgow G3 7PR, Scotland
76. United Protestant Church of Belgium – Brussels, Belgium
77. United Reformed Church – London, UK
78. Waldensian Church – Rome, Italy

LATIN AMERICA

1. Anglican Church of the Southern Cone of America- Salta, Argentina
2. Baptist Association of El Salvador – Sansalvador
3. Baptist Convention of Nicaragua – Managua, Nicaragua
4. Bolivian Evangelical Lutheran Church – Bolivia
5. Christian Biblical Church – Bermudas, Buenos Aires, Argentina
6. Christian Reformed Church of Brazil – Sao Paulo, Brazil
7. Church of God – Buenos Aires, Argentina
8. Church of the Disciples of Christ – Buenos Aires, Argentina
9. Episcopal Anglican Church of Brazil – Porto Alegre-RS, Brazil
10. Evangelical Church of Lutheran Confession in Brazil – Porto Alegre RS, Brazil
11. Evangelical Church of the River Plate – Buenos Aires, Argentina
12. Evangelical Lutheran Church of Chile – Santiago, Chile
13. Evangelical Methodist Church in Bolivia – La Paz, Bolivia
14. Evangelical Methodist Church in Uruguay – Montevideo, Uruguay
15. Evangelical Methodist Church of Argentina – Buenos Aires, Argentina
16. Evangelical Methodist Church of Costa Rica – Costa Rica

17. Free Pentecostal Mission Church of Chile – Santiago, Chile
18. Methodist Church in Brazil – MG, Brazil
19. Methodist Church of Chile – Santiago, Chile
20. Methodist Church in Mexico – Qro, Mexico
21. Methodist Church of Peru – Lima, Peru
22. Moravian Church in Nicaragua – Managua, Nicaragua
23. Pentecostal Church of Chile – Curico, Chile
24. Pentecostal Mission Church – Santiago, Chile
25. Salvadorean Lutheran Synod – San Salvador, El Salvador
26. United Evangelical Lutheran Church – Buenos Aires, Argentina
27. United Presbyterian Church of Brazil – Victoria, ES Brazil

MIDDLE EAST

1. Apostolic Catholic Assyrian Church of the East – Morton Grove, USA
2. Armenian Apostolic Church – Antelias, Lebanon
3. Church of Cyprus – Nicosia, Cyprus
4. Coptic Orthodox Church – Cairo, Egypt
5. Episcopal Church in Jerusalem and the Middle East – Cairo, Egypt
6. Greek Orthodox Patriarchate of Alexandria and All Africa – Alexandria, Egypt
7. Greek Orthodox Patriarchate of Antioch and all the East – Damascus, Syria
8. Greek Orthodox Patriarchate of Jerusalem – Israel
9. National Evangelical Synod of Syria and Lebanon – Beirut, Lebanon
10. Synod of the Evangelical Church of Iran – Tehran, Iran
11. Synod of Nile of the Evangelical Church – Cairo, Egypt
12. Syrian Orthodox Patriarchate of Antioch – Damascus, Syria

13. Union of the Armenian Evangelical Church in the Near East – Beirut, Lebanon

NORTH AMERICA

1. African Methodist Episcopal Church – Jacksonville, USA
2. African Methodist Episcopal Zion Church – Fort Washington, USA
3. American Baptist Churches in the USA – Valli Forge, USA
4. Anglican Church of Canada – Toronto, Canada
5. Canadian Yearly Meeting of the Religious Society of Friends – Ottawa, Canada
6. Christian Church (Disciples of Christ) in Canada – Alberta, Canada
7. Christian Church (Disciples of Christ) in USA – Indianapolis, USA
8. Christian Methodist Episcopal Church – Cincinnati, USA
9. Church of the Brethren – Elgin, USA
10. Episcopal Church – New York, USA
11. Estonian Evangelical Lutheran Church Abroad – Toronto, Canada
12. Evangelical Lutheran Church in America – Chicago, USA
13. Evangelical Lutheran Church in Canada – Winnipeg, Canada
14. Hungarian Reformed Church in America – New York, USA
15. International Council of Community Churches – Frankfort, USA
16. International Evangelical Church – Atlanta, USA
17. Moravian Church in America (Northern Province) – Bethlehem, USA
18. Moravian Church in America (Southern Province) – Winston-Salem, USA
19. National Baptist Convention of America – St. Petersburg, USA

20. Orthodox Church in America – New York, America
21. Polish National Catholic Church of America – Scranton, USA
22. Presbyterian Church in Canada – Ont. M3C 1J7, Canada
23. Presbyterian Church USA – Louisville, USA
24. Progressive National Baptist Convention – Buffalo, New York, USA
25. Reformed Church in America, New York, USA
26. Religious Society of Friends – Philadelphia, USA
27. Religious Society of Friends – Richmond, USA
28. United Church of Canada – Ont. M8X 2Y4, Canada
29. United Church of Christ – Cleveland, USA
30. United Methodist Church – Charleston, USA

PACIFIC

1. Church of the Province of Melanesia – Honiara Solomon Islands
2. Congregational Christian Church in American Samoa – Canana Fou, American Samoa
3. Congregational Christian Church – Western Samoa
4. Cook Islands Christian Church – Cook Islands
5. Evangelical Church – New Caledonia and the Loyalty Isles, New Caledonia
6. Evangelical Church in French Polynesia – French Polynesia
7. Evangelical Lutheran Church of Papua New Guinea – Lae, Papua New Guinea
8. Free Weslyean Church of Tonga – Tonga
9. Kiribati Protestant Church – Republic of Kiribati
10. Methodist Church in Fiji – Suva, Fiji
11. Methodist Church in Samoa – Apia, Western Samoa
12. Presbyterian Church of Vanuatu – Vanuatu
13. Tuvalu Christian Church – Tuvalu

14. United Church in Papua New Guinea – Port Moresby, Papua New Guinea
15. United Church in the Solomon Islands – Solomon Islands
16. United Church of Christ congregational in the Marshal Island – Majuro
17. All Africa Conference of Churches – Nairobi, Kenya
18. Caribbean Conference of Church – West Indies
19. Christian Conferences of Asia – Hong Kong
20. Conference of European Churches – Switzerland
21. Latina American Council of Churches – Ecuador
22. Middle East Council of Churches – Limassol Cyprus
23. Pacific Conference of Churches – Thurston Street

ANNEXURE VI
Chronology of Popes*

Sl. No.	Name as Pope	Country	Period (AD)	Remarks
1.	St. Peter	Bethsaida	84-87	The dates of the first thirteen Popes are not absolutely certain.
2.	St. Linus	Tuscany	67-76	
3.	St. Anacletus	Rome	76-88	
4.	St. Clement	Rome	88-97	
5.	St. Evaristus	Greece	97-105	
6.	St. Alexander I	Rome	105-115	
7.	St. Sixtus I	Rome	115-125	
8.	St. Telesphorus	Greece	125-136	
9.	St. Hyginus	Greece	136-140	
10.	St. Pius I	Aqullela	140-155	
11.	St. Anicetus	Syria	155-166	
12.	St. Soter	Campania	166-175	
13.	St. Eleutherius	Nicopolis	175-189	

* *The Indian Catholic Directory 2001* – Thomas, J. Arukalil V.C., Vincentian Publishing Society, Kottayam.

Sl. No.	Name as Pope	Country	Period (AD)	Remarks
14.	St. Victor I	Africa	189-199	
15.	St. Zephyrinus	Rome	199-217	
16.	St. Callistus I	Rome	217-222	
17.	St. Urban I	Rome	222-230	
18.	St. Pontian	Rome	230-235	
19.	St. Anterus	Greece	235-236	
20.	St. Fabian	Rome	236-250	Heroic Martyrdom
21.	St. Cornelius	Rome	250-253	
22.	St. Lucius I	Rome	253-254	
23.	St. Stephen I	Rome	254-257	
24.	St. Sixtus II	Greece	257-258	
25.	St. Dionysius	Unknown	259-268	
26.	St. Felix I	Rome	269-274	
27.	St. Eutychian	Luni	275-283	
28.	St. Calus	Dalmatia	283-296	
29.	St. Marcellinus	Rome	296-304	
30.	St. Marcellus I	Rome	308-309	
31.	St. Eusebius	Greece	309-310	

Sl. No.	Name as Pope	Country	Period (AD)	Remarks
32.	St. Melchiades	Africa	311-314	Most of the Popes up to Sylvester I were martyrs. General Council of Nicaea (325).
33.	St. Sylvester I	Rome	314-335	
34.	St. Marcus	Rome	336-336	
35.	St. Julius I	Rome	337-352	
36.	Liberius	Rome	352-366	
37.	St. Damasus I	Spain	366-384	General Council of Constantinople (381).
38.	St. Siricius	Rome	384-399	
39.	St. Anastatius I	Rome	399-401	
40.	St. Innocent I	Albano	401-417	
41.	St. Zozimus	Greece	417-418	
42.	St. Boniface I	Rome	418-422	
43.	St. Celestine I	Campania	422-432	General Council Ephesus (431).
44.	St. Sixtus III	Rome	432-440	
45.	St. Leo I (the Great)	Tuscany	440-461	General Council of Chalcedon/Tom of Leo/ Nestorianism (451).
46.	St. Hilary	Sardinia	461-462	
47.	St. Simolicius	Tivoli	468-483	
48.	St. Felix III	Rome	483-492	It is Felix II and not III. The discrepancy is due to the erroneous inclusion of St. Felix of Rome, a martyr.

Sl. No.	Name as Pope	Country	Period (AD)	Remarks
49.	St. Gelasius I	Africa	492-496	
50.	Anastasius II	Rome	496-498	
51.	St. Symmachus	Sardinia	498-514	
52.	St. Hormisdas	Frosinone	514-523	
53.	St. John I – Martyr	Tuscany	523-526	
54.	St. Felix IV	Samnlum	526-530	
55.	Boniface II	Rome	530-532	First Pope to change name.
56.	John II	Rome	533-535	
57.	St. Agapitus I	Rome	535-536	
58.	St. Silverius – Martyr	Campania	536-537	Violently deposed in March 537.
59.	Vigillus	Rome	537-555	General Council Constantinople II (553).
60.	Pelagius I	Rome	556-561	
61.	John III	Rome	561-574	
62.	Benedict I	Rome	575-579	
63.	Pelagius II	Rome	579-590	
64.	St. Gregory I (the Great)	Rome	590-604	Faith in Purgatory / Intercession of saints/ Transubstantiation / Absolution of original sin through Baptism.
65.	Sabinian	Tuscany	604-606	
66.	Boniface III	Rome	607-607	

Sl. No.	Name as Pope	Country	Period (AD)	Remarks
67.	St. Boniface IV	Abruzzi	608-615	
68.	St. Deusdedit	Rome	615-618	
69.	Boniface V	Naples	619-625	
70.	Honorius I	Campania	625-638	Censured by the third Council of Constantinople (680).
71.	Severinus	Rome	640-May-Aug.	
72.	John IV	Dalmatia	640-642	
73.	Theodore I	Greece	642-649	
74.	St. Martin I	Todi	649-653	In exile from June 653.
75.	St. Eugene I	Rome	654-657	Elected during the exile of St. Martin I who endorsed it.
76.	St. Vitalian	Segni	657-672	
77.	Adeodatus II	Rome	672-676	
78.	Donus	Rome	676-678	
79.	St. Agatho	Sicily	678-681	General Council of Constantinople III (680-681).
80.	St. Leo II	Sicily	682-683	
81.	St. Benedict II	Rome	684-685	
82.	John V	Syria	685-686	
83.	Conon	(Not known)	686-687	
84.	St. Sergius I	Syria	687-701	

Sl. No.	Name as Pope	Country	Period (AD)	Remarks
85.	John VI	Greece	701-705	
86.	John VII	Greece	705-707	
87.	Sisinnius	Syria	708 Jan.-Feb.	
88.	Constantine	Syria	708-715	
89.	St. Gregory II	Rome	715-731	
90.	St. Gregory III	Syria	731-741	
91.	St. Zachary	Greece	741-752	
92.	Stephen II	Rome	752-757	One Roman priest named Stephen was elected on the death of St. Zachary but died four days after election, before consecration.
93.	St. Paul I	Rome	757-767	
94.	Stephen III (IV)	Sicily	768-772	
95.	Adrian I	Rome	772-795	General Council of Nicaca II (787)
96.	St. Leo III	Rome	795-816	Crowned Charlemagne as Emperor which exalted the position of Pope to a level of the temporal rulers of Europe.
97.	Stephen IV (V)	Rome	816-817	
98.	St. Paschal I	Rome	817-824	
99.	Eugene II	Rome	824-827	
100.	Valentine	Rome	827 Aug.-Sept.	

Sl. No.	Name as Pope	Country	Period (AD)	Remarks
101.	Gregory IV	Rome	827-844	
102.	Sergius II	Rome	844-847	
103.	St. Leo IV	Rome	847-855	
104.	Benedict III	Rome	855-858	
105.	St. Nicholas (the Great)	Rome	858-867	
106.	Adrian II	Rome	867-872	G.C. of Constantinople IV (869-870).
107.	John VIII	Rome	872-882	
108.	Marinus I	Gallese	882-884	
109.	St. Adrian III	Rome	884-885	
110.	Stephen V (VI)	Rome	885-891	
111.	Formosus		891-896	
112.	Boniface VI	Rome	896 (April)	
113.	Stephen VI	Rome	896-897	
114.	Romanus	Gallese	897 (Aug.-Nov.)	
115.	Theodore II	Rome	897 (Dec.)	
116.	John IX	Tivoli	898-900	
117.	Benedict IV	Rome	900-903	
118.	Leo V	Ardea	903 (July-Sept.)	
119.	Sergius III	Rome	904-911	

Sl. No.	Name as Pope	Country	Period (AD)	Remarks
120.	Anastasius III	Rome	911-913	
121.	Landus	Sabina	913-914	
122.	John X	Tossignano (Imola)	914-928	
123.	Leo VI	Rome	928 (May-Dec.)	
124.	Stephen VII (VIII)	Rome	928-931	
125.	John XI	Rome	931-935	
126.	Leo VII	Rome	936-939	
127.	Stephen VIII (IX)	Rome	939-942	
128.	Marinus II	Rome	942-946	
129.	Agapitus II	Rome	946-955	
130.	John XII	Tusculum	955-964	Ascended at the age of 18, style of life of Nero. Emperor Otto deposed him in 963.
131.	Leo VIII	Rome	963-965	If the deposition of John XII is invalid, Leo is anti-pope.
132.	Benedict V	Rome	964-966	If Leo is legitimate, Benedict is anti-pope.
133.	John XIII	Rome	965-972	
134.	Benedict VI	Rome	973-974	
135.	Benedict VII	Rome	974-983	
136.	John XIV	Pavia	983-984	
137.	John XV	Rome	985-996	

Sl. No.	Name as Pope	Country	Period (AD)	Remarks
138.	Gregory V	Saxony	996-999	
139.	Sylvester II	Auvergne	999-1003	
140.	John XVII (?)	Rome	1003-Jun.-Dec.	
141.	John XVIII	Rome	1004-1009	
142.	Sergius IV	Rome	1009-1012	Name change commences.
143.	Benedict VIII	Tusculum	1012-1024	
144.	John XIX	Tusculum	1024-1032	
145.	Benedict IX	Tusculum	1032-1044	Chased out by an anti-pope.
146.	Sylvester III	Rome	1045-1045	Anti-pope, if the removal of Benedict IX is invalid.
147.	Benedict IX (2nd time)		1045 April-May	
148.	Gregory VI	Rome	1045-1046	
149.	Clement II	Saxony	1046-1047	Installed by King Henry III of Germany.
150.	Benedict IX (3rd time)		1047-1048	
151.	Domasus II	Bavaria	1048 July-Aug.	
152.	St. Leo IX	Alsace	1049-1054	Installed by King Henry III.
153.	Victor II	Swabia	1055-1057	Installed by King Henry III.
154.	Stephen IX	Lorraine	1057-1058	
155.	Nicholas II	Burgundy	1059-1061	Decreed in 1959 that only Cardinals to elect Pope.

Sl. No.	Name as Pope	Country	Period (AD)	Remarks
156.	Alexander II	Milan	1061-1073	
157.	St. Gregory VII	Tuscany	1073-1085	Sought refuge in Salerno and breathed his last on May 25, 1085.
158.	Bl. Victor III	Benevento	1086-1087	Nominee of German Emperor Henry IV.
159.	Bl. Urban II	France	1088-1099	Crusade I – 1095 – 1099. Took over Jerusalem from the Turks.
160.	Paschal II	Ravenna	1099-1118	
161.	Gelasius II	Gaeta	1118-1119	
162.	Callistus II	Burgundy	1119-1124	General Council of Lateran I – 1123.
163.	Honorius II	Flagnano (Imola)	1124-1130	
164.	Innocent II	Rome	1130-1143	General Council of Lateran II – 1139.
165.	Celestine II	Citta di castello	1143-1144	
166.	Lucius II	Bologna	1144-1145	
167.	Bl. Eugene III	Pisso	1145-1153	IInd Crusade 1147 – Failed to Defeat the Muslims.
168.	Anastasius IV	Rome	1153-1154	
169.	Adrian IV	England	1151-1159	
170.	Alexander III	Siena	1159-1181	General Council of Lateran III – 1179.
171.	Lucius III	Lucca	1181-1185	
172.	Urban III	Milan	1185-1187	
173.	Gregory VIII	Benevento	1187 Oct.-Dec.	

Sl. No.	Name as Pope	Country	Period (AD)	Remarks
174.	Clement III	Rome	1187-1191	IIIrd Crusade 1189.
175.	Celestine III	Rome	1191-1198	
176.	Innocent III	Anagni	1198-1216	Dogma Transubstantiation approved / introduced Auricular confession, made annual confession and reception of Holy Eucharist obligatory / reformed the Curia. / First Pope to take the title 'Vicar of Christ'/ Guidelines for selection of bishops and clergy/ Introduced inquisition/ General Council of Lateran IV 1215.
177.	Honorius III	Rome	1216-1227	
178.	Gregory IX	Anagni	1227-1241	
179.	Celestine IV	Milan	1241 (Oct.-Nov.)	
180.	Innocent IV	Genoa	1243-1254	General Council of Lyons I – 1245.
181.	Alexander IV	Rome	1254-1261	
182.	Urban IV	Troyes	1261-1264	
183.	Clement IV	France	1265-1268	
184.	Bl. Gregory X	Piacenza	1272-1276	General Council of Lyons II – 1274.
185.	Bl. Innocent V	Savoy	1276 Jan.-June	
186.	Adrian V	Genoa	1276 July-Aug.	
187.	John XXI	Portugal	1276-1277	Confusion of numerical designation from John XV.
188.	Nicholas III	Rome	1277-1280	

Sl. No.	Name as Pope	Country	Period (AD)	Remarks
189.	Martin IV	France	1281-1285	Confusion in number due to inclusion of Marinus I & II.
190.	Honorius IV	Rome	1285-1287	
191.	Nicholas IV	Ascoli	1288-1292	
192.	St. Celestine V	Isernia	1294 (Aug.-Dec.)	
193.	Boniface VIII	Anagni	1294-1303	First Papal Jubilee proclaimed in 1303 'Unam Sanctum' the papal Bull emphasising the powers of the Pope. King Phillip of France imprisoned him but passed away before being taken to France.
194.	Bl. Benedict XI	Treviso	1303-1304	
195.	Clement V	France	1305-1314	The GC of Vienna 1311 – 1312 / The Papal H.Q. shifted from Rome to Avignon in France beginning the line of Avignon Popes.
196.	John XXII	Cahors	1316-1334	
197.	Benedict XII	France	1334-1342	
198.	Clement VI	France	1342-1352	
199.	Innocent VI	France	1352-1362	
200.	Bl. Urban V	France	1362-1370	Came back to Rome but returned.
201.	Gregory XI	France	1370-1378	Papacy returned to Rome in 1378. But the Pope passed away.

Sl. No.	Name as Pope	Country	Period (AD)	Remarks
202.	Urban VI	Naples	1378-1389	Another Pope in Avignon. The Cardinals who elected him invalidated his election and elected another Pope Clement VI leading to the Great Schism.
203.	Boniface IX	Naples	1389-1404	
204.	Innocent VII	Sulmania	1404-1406	
205.	Gregory XII	Venice	1406-1415	Officially convoked the Council of Constance after ending the Papal Schism.
206.	Martin V	Rome	1417-1431	Pope elected by the Council of Constance (1414-1418) after ending the Papal Schism.
207.	Eugene IV	Venice	1431-1447	General Council of Florence (1431-1443).
208.	Nicholas V	Sarzana	1447-1455	
209.	Callistus III	Jativa	1455-1458	
210.	Pius II	Siena	1458-1464	
211.	Paul II	Venice	1464-1471	
212.	Sixtus IV	Savona	1471-1484	
213.	Innocent VIII	Genoa	1481-1492	
214.	Alexander VI	Jativa	1492-1503	
215.	Pius III	Siena	1503 Sept.-Oct.	
216.	Julius II	Savona	1503-1513	General Council of Lateran V (1512-1517).

Sl. No.	Name as Pope	Country	Period (AD)	Remarks
217.	Leo X	Florence	1513-1521	General Council of Lateran V continued. Failed to act in time on Luther's propositions resulting in a vertical split in Christendom / Establishment of Padroado.
218.	Adrian VI	Ulrecht	1522-1523	
219.	Clement VII	Florence	1523-1534	
220.	Paul III	Rome	1534-1549	Convoked the General Council of Trent (1545-1563).
221.	Julius III	Rome	1550-1555	
222.	Marcellus II	Montepulciano	1555 Apr.-Aug.	
223.	Paul IV	Naples	1555-1559	
224.	Pius IV	Milan	1559-1565	Convened the third session of the General Council of Trent.
225.	Pius V	Alexandria	1566-1572	
226.	Gregory XIII	Bologna	1572-1585	The author of Gregorian Calendar.
227.	Sixtus V	Grottammare	1585-1590	He erected the towering obelisk in the St. Peter's square in Vatican / Reogranisation of the Curia.
228.	Urban VII	Rome	1590(Sept.)	
229.	Gregory XIV	Cremona	1590-1591	
230.	Innocent IX	Bologna	1591 (Oct.-Dec.)	
231.	Clement VIII	Florence	1592-1605	

Sl. No.	Name as Pope	Country	Period (AD)	Remarks
232.	Leo XI	Florence	1605 -(April)	
233.	Paul V	Rome	1605-1621	
234.	Gregory XV	Bologna	1621-1623	Establishment of the congregation for propagation of faith.
235.	Urban VIII	Fiorence	1623-1644	
236.	Innocent X	Rome	1644-1655	
237.	Alexander VII	Siena	1655-1667	
238.	Clement IX	Pistoia	1667-1669	
239.	Clement X	Rome	1670-1676	
240.	Bl. Innocent	Como	1676-1689	Victory over Gallicanism.
241.	Alexander VIII	Venice	1689-1691	
242.	Innocent XII	Venosa	1691-1700	
243.	Clement XI	Urbino	1700-1721	
244.	Innocent XIII	Rome	1721-1724	
245.	Benedict XIII	Gravina	1724-1730	
246.	Clement XII	Florence	1730-1740	
247.	Benedict XIV	Bologna	1740-1758	
248.	Clement XIII	Venice	1758-1769	
249.	Clement XIV	Rimini	1769-1774	Suppression of the Jesuits 1769.

Sl. No.	Name as Pope	Country	Period (AD)	Remarks
250.	Pius VI	Cesena	1775-1799	Taken prisoner by Napoleon – passed away on way to France.
251.	Pius VII	Cesena	1800-1823	Revival of Jesuit order – 1814. Spent six years in captivity in France. Refuse to co-operate with the coronation of Napoleon as Emperor.
252.	Leo XII	Genga	1823-1829	
253.	Pius VIII	Cingoli	1829-1830	
254.	Gregory XVI	Belluno	1831-1846	1832-Condemned Liberalism-*Mirari Vos.*
255.	Pius IX	Sonigallia	1846-1878	General Council of Vatican I 1869-1870. Immaculate Conception of Virgin Mary 1854. Infallibility of Pope. *Syllabus of Errors* (1864) listed to 80 errors.
256.	Leo XIII	Carpineto Anagni	1878-1903	Indian Hierarchy in 1886. Vicariates of Trichur and Kottayam for Syro Malabar rite 1887. Encyclical *Rerun Novarum.*
257.	St. Pius X	Riese (Treviso)	1903-1914	The first Pope canonised after 16th century.
258.	Benedict XV	Genoa	1914-1922	World war I and Bolshevik Revolution in Russia and birth of USSR.
259.	Pius XI	Milan	1922-1939	Encyclical *Divino Redemptoris* condemning atheistic communism.

Sl. No.	Name as Pope	Country	Period (AD)	Remarks
260.	Pius XII	Rome	1939-1958	Defined church as Mystical Body of Christ. Thousands of Jews saved from the atrocities of Nazis.
261.	John XXIII	Sotto	1958-1963	General Council of Vatican II – 1959 (See notes elsewhere).
262.	Paul VI	Concessio	1963-1978	General Council of Vatican II continued (See notes elsewhere).
263.	John Paul I	Belluno	1979 (Aug.-Sept.)	
264.	John Paul II	Wadowice, Poland	Oct. 1978 to 2005	
265.	Benedict XVI	Germany	2005-	

ANNEXURE VII
Roman Curia*

In the exercise of his responsibilities for the Universal Church, various bodies that constitute the Roman Curia assist the Pope. There are at present, besides the Secretariat of State that is the central coordinating organ, 9 Congregations, 3 Tribunals, 12 Pontifical Councils, 3 Offices and various Commissions and Committees. The most important among them are mentioned below:

I. Secretariat of State

By the Apostolic Constitution "Pastor Bonus" on 26 June 1988, Pope John Paul II reformed the Secretariat of State dividing it into two sections; the section for General Affairs and the section for the Relations with the States.

The first section is meant to assist the Pope in the daily government of the Universal Church and his relations with the Dicasteries of the Roman Curia, as well as in drafting papal documents. It has a Press Office and an office for statistics.

The second section handles the relations of the Holy See with the countries of the World and with the international organisations.

The Secretary of State is the head of this Secretariat.

II. Congregations

1. Congregation for the Doctrine of the Faith

This congregation deals with all matters pertaining to Faith and Morals. The Congregation also acts as a Tribunal when dealing with matters that by law require judicial proceedings.

* Alan Schreck, *The Compact History of the Catholic Church*, p. 151.

2. Congregation of the Oriental Churches

It has jurisdiction over matters regarding the Catholic Oriental Churches except those belonging to the Congregation for the Doctrine of the faith.

The Oriental Rites of the Church are the following:

Alexandrian Rite (Coptic and Ethiopian Churches).

Rite of Antioch or West-Syrian Rite (Syro-Malankara, Maronite, Syrian Churches).

Byzantine rite (Albanian, Belorussian, Bulgarian, Greek, Melkite, Italo-Albanian, Romanian, Russian, Ruthenian, Slovak, Ukranian, Hungarian Churches), Chaldean or East-Syrian Rite (Chaldean, Syro-Malabar Churches).

Armenian Rite.

3. Congregation for Divine Worship and Discipline of the Sacraments

All matters regardings Divine Worship, the revision and preparation of liturgical texts and rites, the approval of liturgical calendars and interpretation of norms and rubrics of liturgical books come under this Congregation. The Congregation has Commissions for cases of nullity of the sacred ordination, for the dispensation from the obligations of the diaconate and the priesthood and for the dispensation of "ratum non consummatum" marriages.

4. Congregation for the Causes of Saints

It deals with everything connected with the beatification and Canonization of Saints.

5. Congregation for Bishops

In countries not under the Congregations for the Oriental Churches or the Evangelization of Peoples, this Dicastery deals with the erection of Dioceses and the appointment of Bishops, also with all matters that concern the person of the Bishop and the state of the Diocese as well as with provincial Councils and Episcopal Conferences.

The Congregation has special Officers for the Military ordinaries and for the Coordination of the "Ad Limina" visits of the Bishops.

Attached to the Congregation is the Pontifical Commission for Latin-America instituted by the Pope Pius XII in 1958. It has the task to study the pastoral problems of Latin-America. It facilitates the contacts between the Episcopal Councils of Latin-America, the various aid agencies for Latin-America and the Roman Curia.

6. Congregation for the Evangelization of Peoples

The congregation has exclusive and full jurisdiction over the ecclesiastical territories that fall under No. 6 of the Decree "Ad Gentes" except in matters belonging to the Congregations for the Doctrine of the Faith, for the Causes of the Saints, for the Oriental Churches, for Catholic Education concerning the Catholic Universities, and for Diving Worship and the sacraments regarding the matrimonial cases "super rato et non consummato" and liturgical questions. The religious come under this Congregation as far as they are missionaries. The central offices of the Pontifical Mission Aid Societies are parts of this Congregation.

7. Congregation for the Clergy

Its functions relate to the clergy. It deals with all matters concerning the apostolate and all its aspects. It approves Catechetical and Pastoral Directories and issues norms for the instruction of the faithful. The "congrua sustentatio" of the Clergy comes under the responsibility of this Congregation.

8. Congregation for the Institutes of Consecrated Life and Societies of Apostolic Life

This Congregation handles all matters concerning religious and similar institutes.

The Congregation has no territorial limits. It refers certain matters to other Congregations.

9. Congregation for Catholic Education (for Seminaries and Educational Institutions)

The competence of this Congregation relates to the erection and running of the Seminaries, the formation houses of Religious and Secular Institutes, the Catholic Universities and institutes of higher education: it grants the faculty to confer academic degrees. Also all Catholic schools up to the pre-university grade, except those existing in the territories of the Congregation of Evangelization, come under its jurisdiction.

Attached to this Congregation is the Pontifical Work for Priestly Vocation.

III. Tribunals

1. Apostolic Penitentiary

This Tribunal has jurisdiction over cases of conscience sacramental and internal non-sacramental forum. It decides matters relating to indulgences.

2. Supreme Tribunal of the Apostolic Signature

This Supreme Tribunal of the Roman Curia hears pleas of nullity against sentences of the Rota and for a new trial. It watches over the administration of justice in the diocesan courts.

3. Tribunal of the Roman Rota

The Rota is mainly a Court of Appeal (Can. 1444). It handles cases defined by the tribunal of the Bishop and deferred to the Holy See by a legitimate appeal; also cases already treated in appeal by the same Rota or by another Ecclesiastical Court of Appeal in third and ultimate instances.

In the cases determined by Can. 1405 and 3, it acts also in the first instance.

Whenever the Roman Pontiff reserves a case to himself whether out of his own free will or at the instance of the parties, he entrusts it to the Rota, in conformity with Can. 1444 and 3.

IV. Pontifical Councils

1. Pontifical Council for the Laity

The Dicastery is competent for the Apostolate of the Laity that is for the participation in the mission of the Church, as members of associations and as individual faithful.

2. Pontifical Council for Promoting Christian Unity

It is entrusted with the fostering of Christian unity.

3. *Pontifical Council for the Family*

Established by Pope Paul VI with the purpose of promoting the spiritual, moral and social values of the family.

4. *Pontifical Council for Justice and Peace*

The Council is entrusted with the fostering of justice and peace in conformity with the Gospel and Social Doctrine of the Church.

5. *Pontifical Council "Cor Unum"*

Its aim is to promote and coordinate Christian Charity and development efforts.

6. *Pontifical Council for the Pastoral Care of Migrants and Itinerant People*

It renders pastoral assistance to migrants and tourists (apostolate of the sea, or nomads, tourists and refugees).

7. *Pontifical Council for Pastoral Assistance to Health Care Workers*

Established by John Paul II by the Motu Proprio "Dolentium Hominum" of 11 Feb. 1985, it is meant to promote the work of various Catholic Organisations operating in the medical field: to propagate and implement the teachings of the Church for these areas.

8. *Pontifical Council for the Interpretation of Legislative Texts*

Founded by John Paul II in 1984, its role is to interpret the canons of the Codes of Canon Law and other legal texts.

9. *Pontifical Council for Inter-religious Dialogue*

It promotes the relations of the Church with the non-Christian religions.

10. *Pontifical Council for Culture*

With his Motu Propio "Inde a Pontificatus", dated 25 March 1993, published on 4 May 1993, the Pope united the Pontifical Council for Culture, which assumes the tasks of the two previous Councils with two sections:

- Faith and Culture
  Dialogue with Culture

The section for Faith and Culture continue the activity until now performed by the Pontifical Council for Culture.

The section for Dialogue with Cultures devotes itself to the activity which till now belonged to the Pontifical Council for Dialogue with Non-Believers.

11. Pontifical Commission of the Cultural Heritage of the Church

With his Motu proprio "Inde a Pontificatus", dated 25 March 1993, the Pope has transformed the Pontifical Commission for the conservation of the Cultural Heritage of the Church into an autonomous organism within the Curia. The tasks of the "Pontifical Commission for the Cultural Heritage of the Church" are the protection of the artistic and historic heritage of the Church; the promotion of its artistic and restoration of its monuments and training of those responsible for the maintenance or the Church's cultural heritage.

12. Pontifical Council for Social Communications

It deals with all the activities of the Church in the field of cinema, radio television and the press.

It has attached to it the Vatican Film-Archives (Filmoteca).

Pope John XXIII on 16 Nov. 1959 founded the Filmoteca. It collects and preserves registrations that refer to the Life of the Church.

V. Offices

1. Apostolic Camera

The Office has the duty to look after the administration of the temporal goods and rights of the Holy See, 'sede vacante'.

2. Administration of the Patrimony of the Apostolic See

The office administers properties, which furnish funds for the realisation of the activities of the Holy See.

3. Prefecture for the Economic Affairs of the Holy See

The prefecture controls the administrations which are either dependent on the Holy See or have to give account to it, whatever autonomy they may otherwise enjoy.

VI. Other Organs of the Roman Curia

1. Prefecture of the Papal Household

The perfect of the Pontifical Household assists the Supreme Pontiff, in the Pontifical Palace. It is his task to make the arrangements for the Papal audience: private, public and solemn ones, e.g. for visiting Heads of State. The Prefecture is also competent for the pontifical ceremonies which are not liturgical.

2. Office for the Liturgical Celebrations of the Supreme Pontiff

This office prepares everything which is necessary for the liturgical celebrations over which the Pontiff either presides, or which he attends, or which are celebrated in his name.

The Office is also competent for the celebration of the Consistories and of the liturgical celebrations of the College of Cardinals "Sede vacante".

VII. Commissions and Committees

1. Press-Office of the Holy See

The Office has the task to inform about the activities of the Pontiff and of the Holy See in general.

2. Central Office of Statistics of the Church

It gathers systematically data regarding the conditions of the Church and publishes the "Annuario Pontificio".

3. Pontifical Biblical Commission

It promotes biblical studies and deals with matters that concern the interpretation of the Bible. Pope Paul VI has restructured this commission placing it now under the Congregation for the Doctrine of the Faith.

4. International Theological Commission

It assists the Congregation for the Doctrine of the Faith in doctrinal questions of major importance.

5. The Pontifical Commission for the Revision and Emendation of the Vulgate

Founded on 27 November 1907 by Pope Pius X, this commission continues the work of the revision of the Old Testament.

6. The Pontifical Committee for the International Eucharistic Congress

This Committee, which was founded by Pope Leo XIII on 27 April 1879 aims at a "more profound knowledge, deeper love and greater service to Our Lord Jesus Christ present in the Mystery of the Eucharist, the centre of life of the Church and of its mission for the salvation of the world" (Statutes, Art. 21).

7. The Pontifical Commission for Sacred Archeology

It was founded by Pius IX, "safeguard the sacred ancient cemeteries and to take care of their preservation, further exploration, and to study; and protect the ancient memories of the early Christian centuries, the illustrious monuments and venerated Basilicas in Rome, in the Roman suburbs and also in other Dioceses, in agreement with their Ordinaries".

8. Pontifical Committee of Historical Sciences

It represents the Holy See at the "Comite International Des Sciences Historiques" and collaborates for the advancement of the Historical Sciences through international cooperation.

9. The Pontifical Commission "Ecclesia Dei"

It has the task to cooperate with Bishops, the Dicasteries of the Roman Curia and others, with the aim to help priests, seminarians, religious communities or individual religious who belonged to the Fraternity founded by Monsignor Marcel Lefebvre who want to be united with the Successor of Peter in the Catholic Church.

(Archives of the Second Vatican Council)

VIII. Institutions Connected with the Holy See

Vatican Secret Archives

Vatican School for Paleography, Diplomatics and Archivists

L 'Osservatore Romano' – Daily Newspaper

Vatican Publishing House

Vatican Radio

Vatican Television Centre

And

The Office of Papal Charities

Source: *The Catholic Directory of India 1998* (Pages 9 to 18) - CBCI.

Index